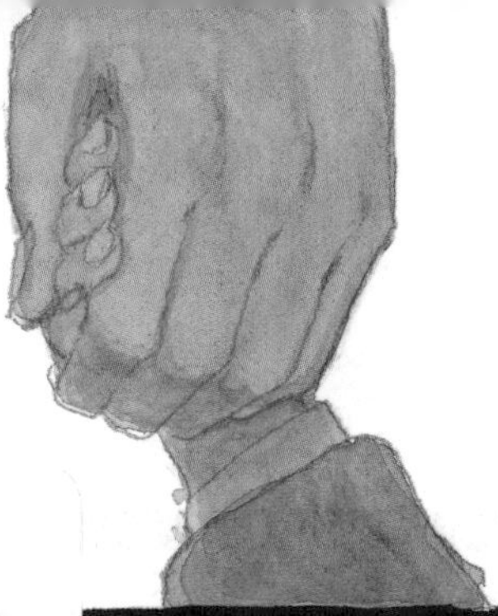

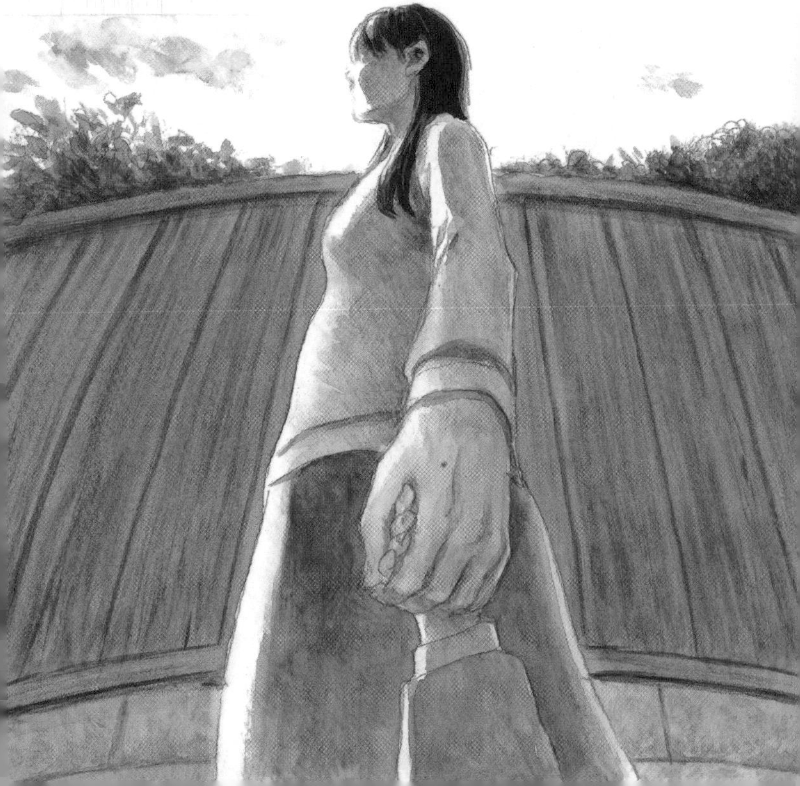

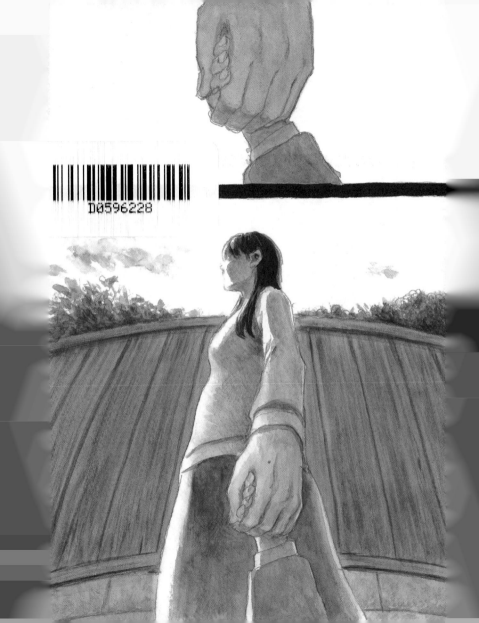

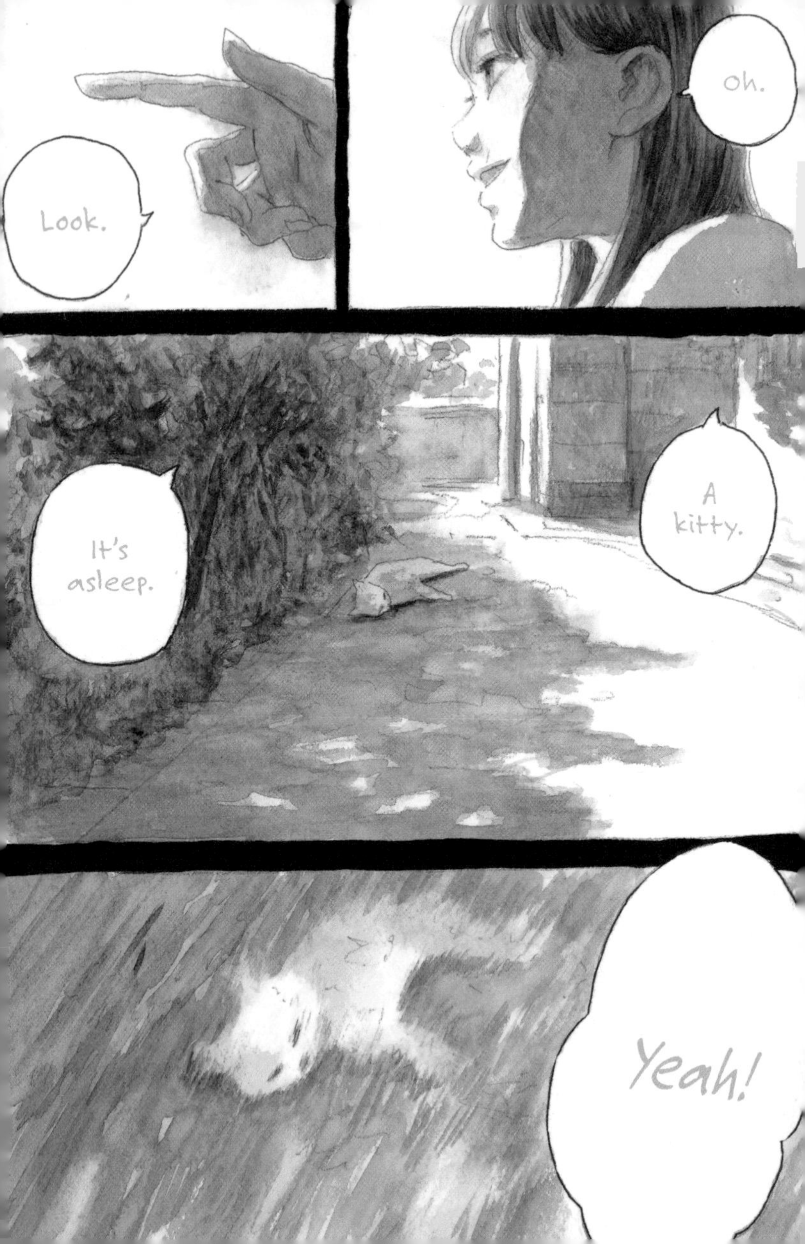
Oh.
Look.
A kitty.
It's asleep.
Yeah!

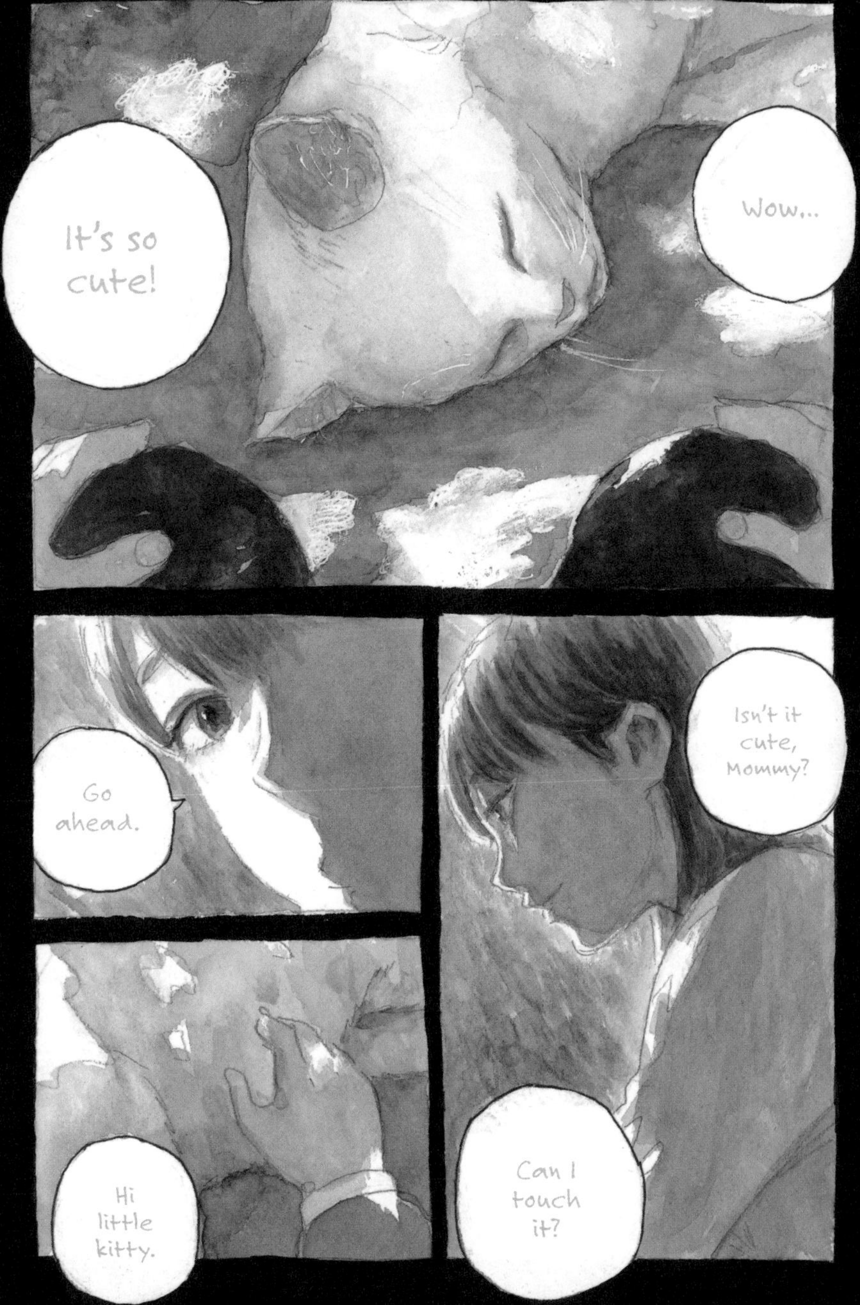
Wow...
It's so cute!
Isn't it cute, Mommy?
Can I touch it?
Go ahead.
Hi little kitty.

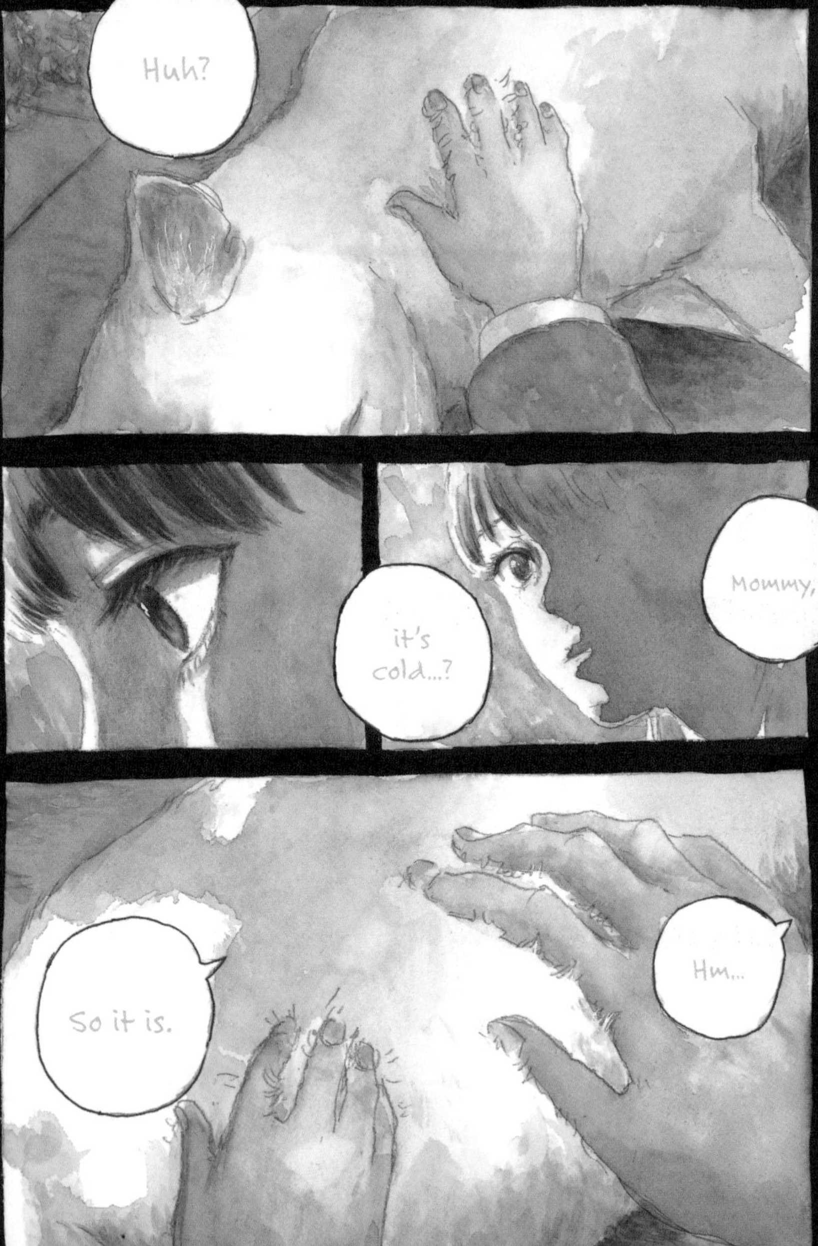
Huh?
Mommy,
it's cold...?
Hm...
So it is.

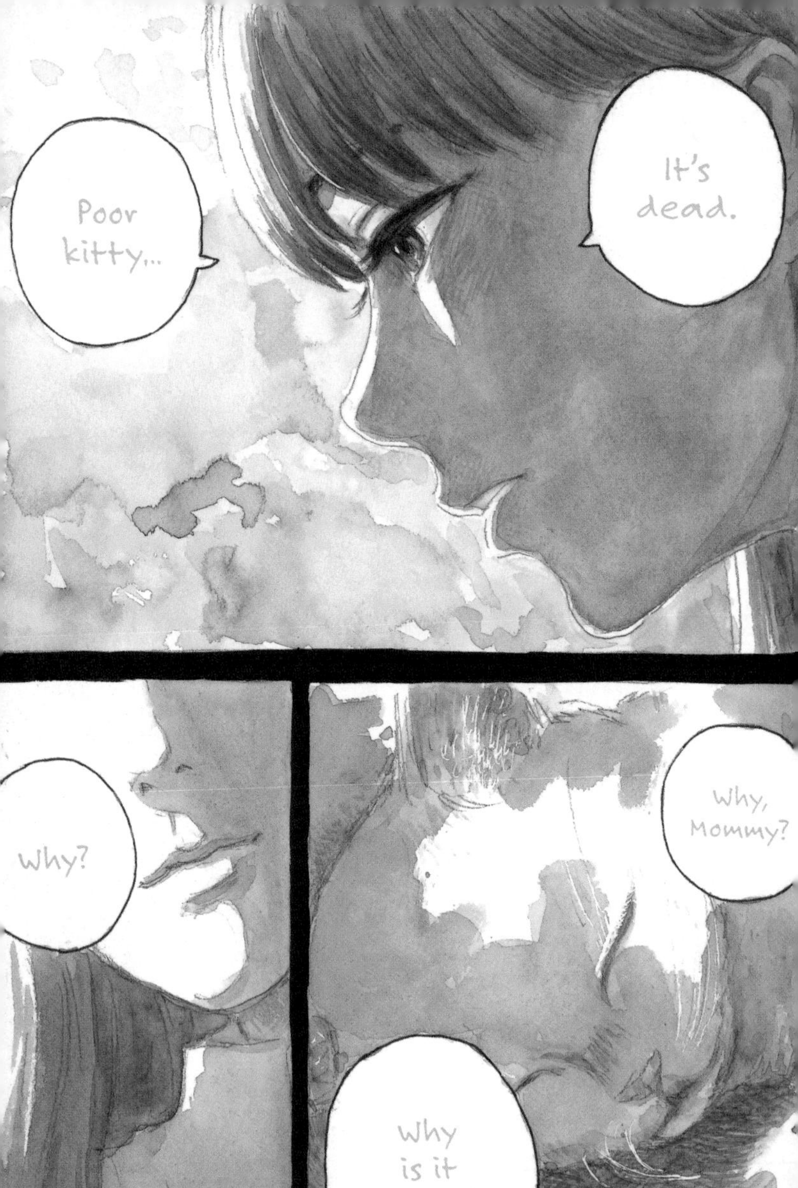
It's dead.
Poor kitty...
Why, Mommy?
Why is it dead?
Why?

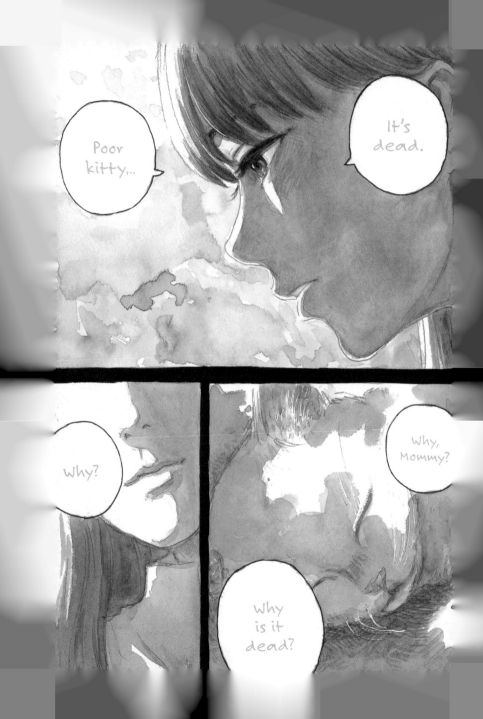

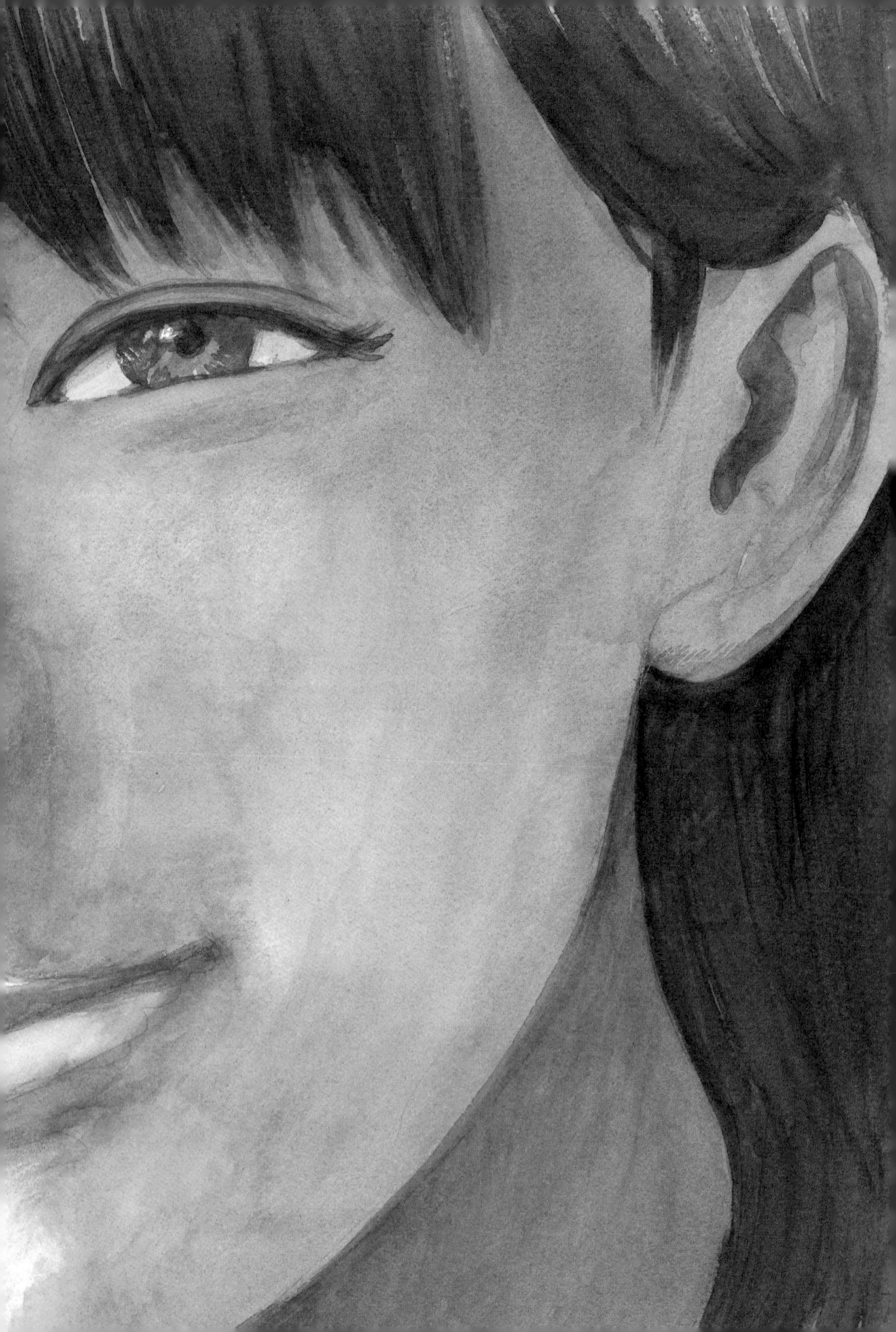

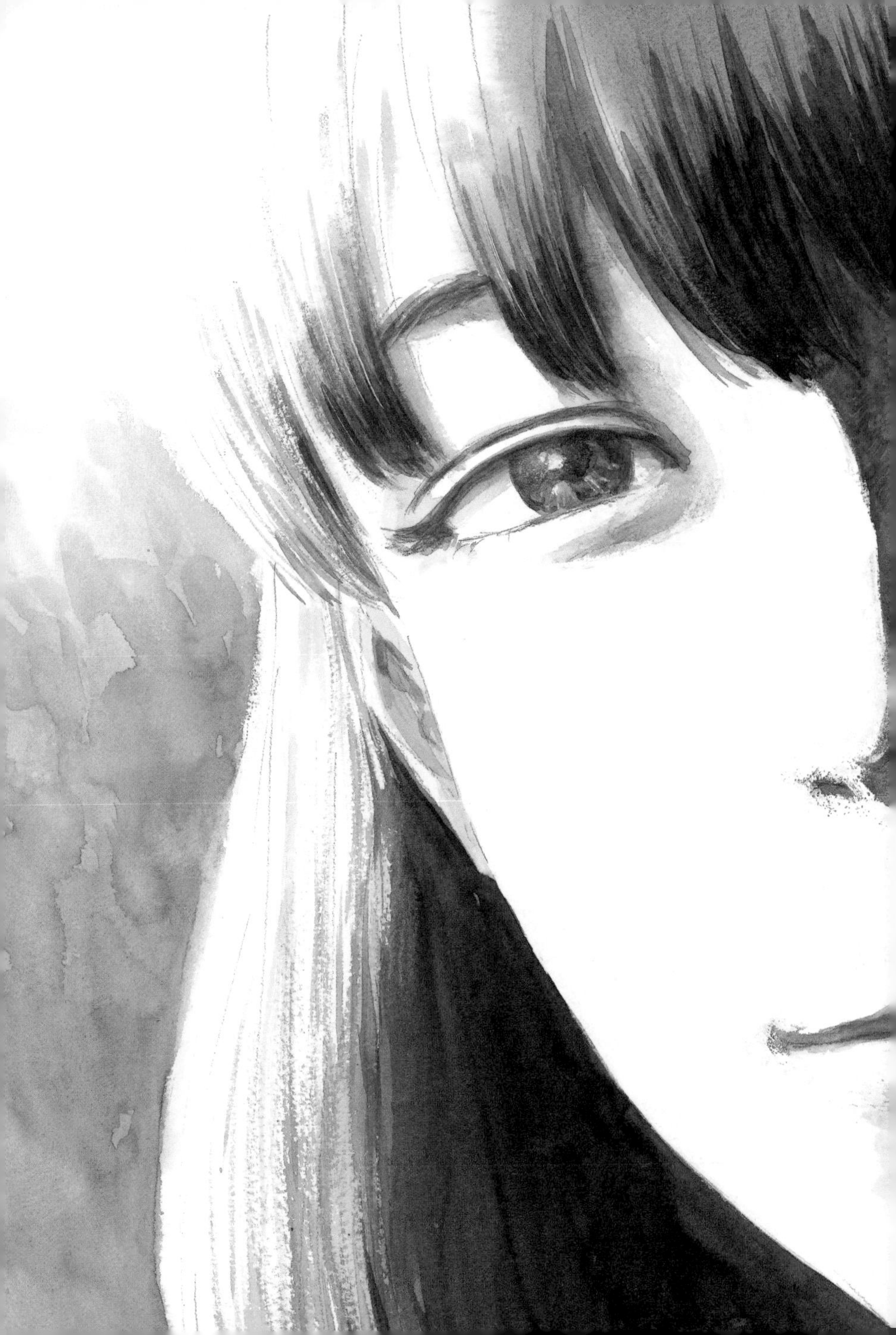

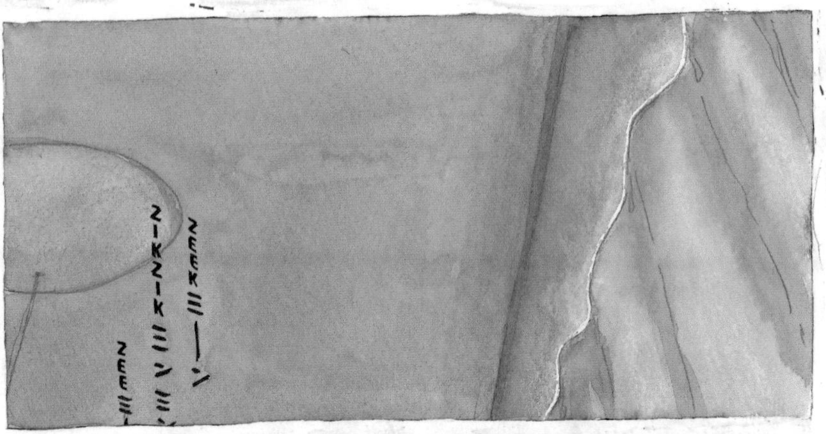
ZEEKミーン
ZIKZIKミンミ
ZEEミ
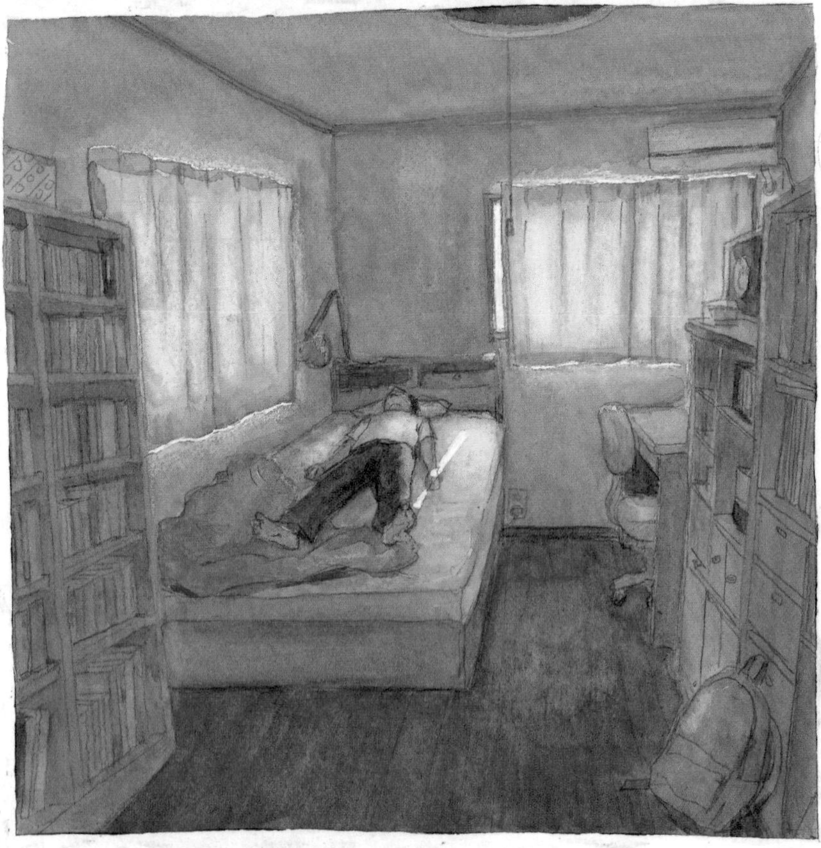

Blood on the Tracks

volume 1

on the Tracks

Shuzo Oshimi

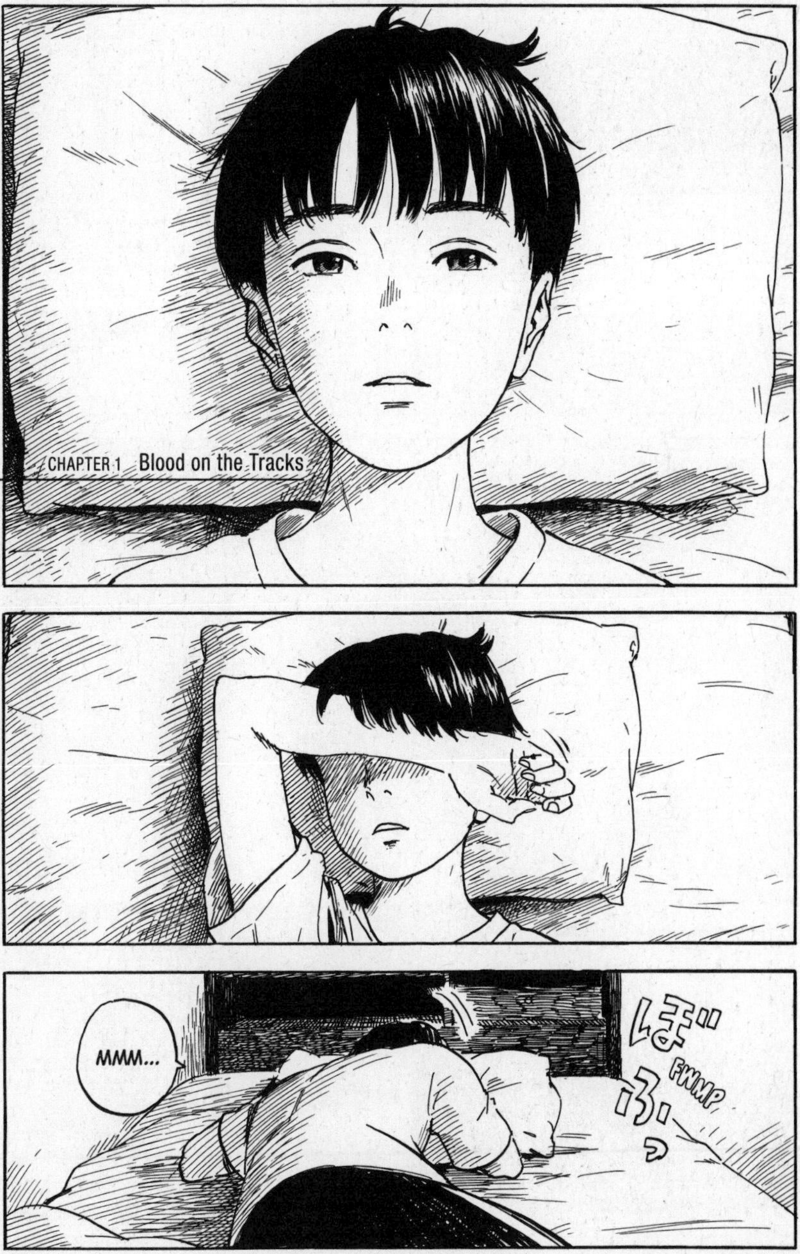
CHAPTER 1 Blood on the Tracks
MMM...
ぼふっ
FWMP

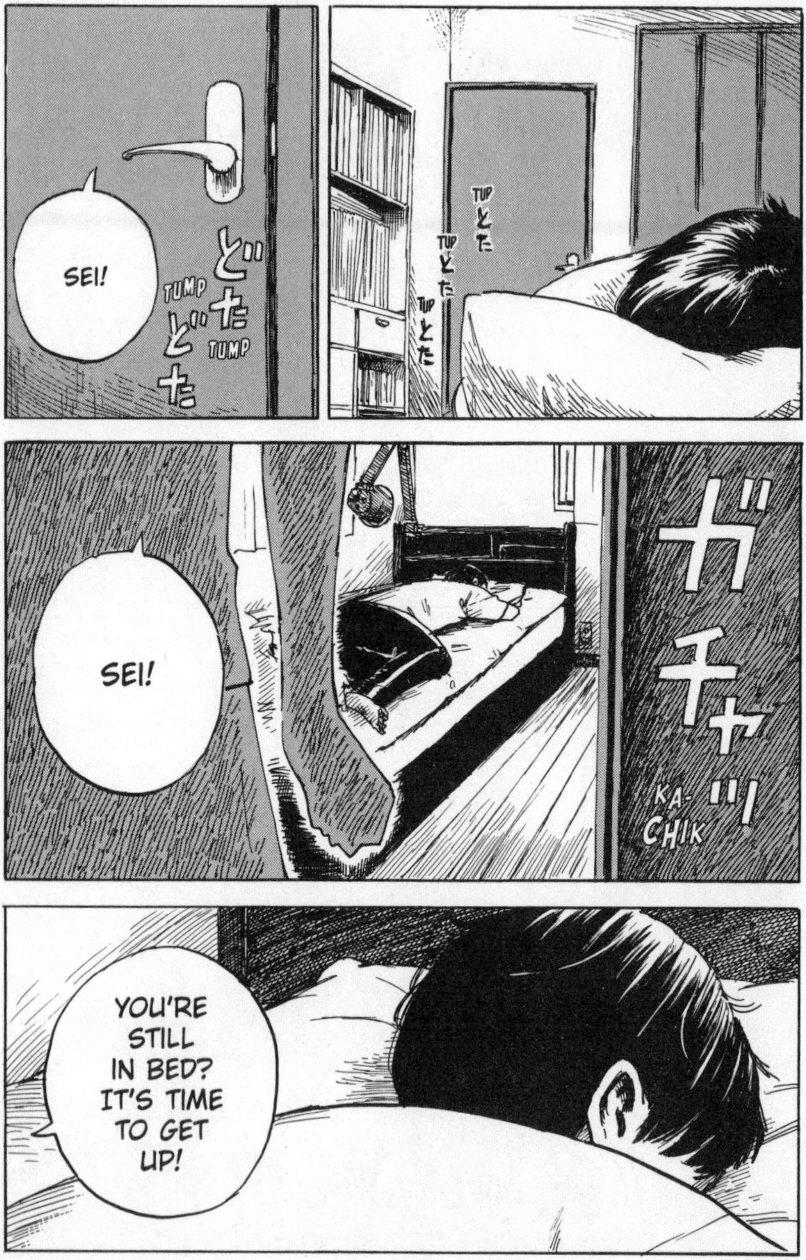
TUP とた
TUP とた
TUP とた
SEI!
どたどた
TUMP TUMP
SEI!
ガチャッ
KA-CHIK
YOU'RE STILL IN BED? IT'S TIME TO GET UP!

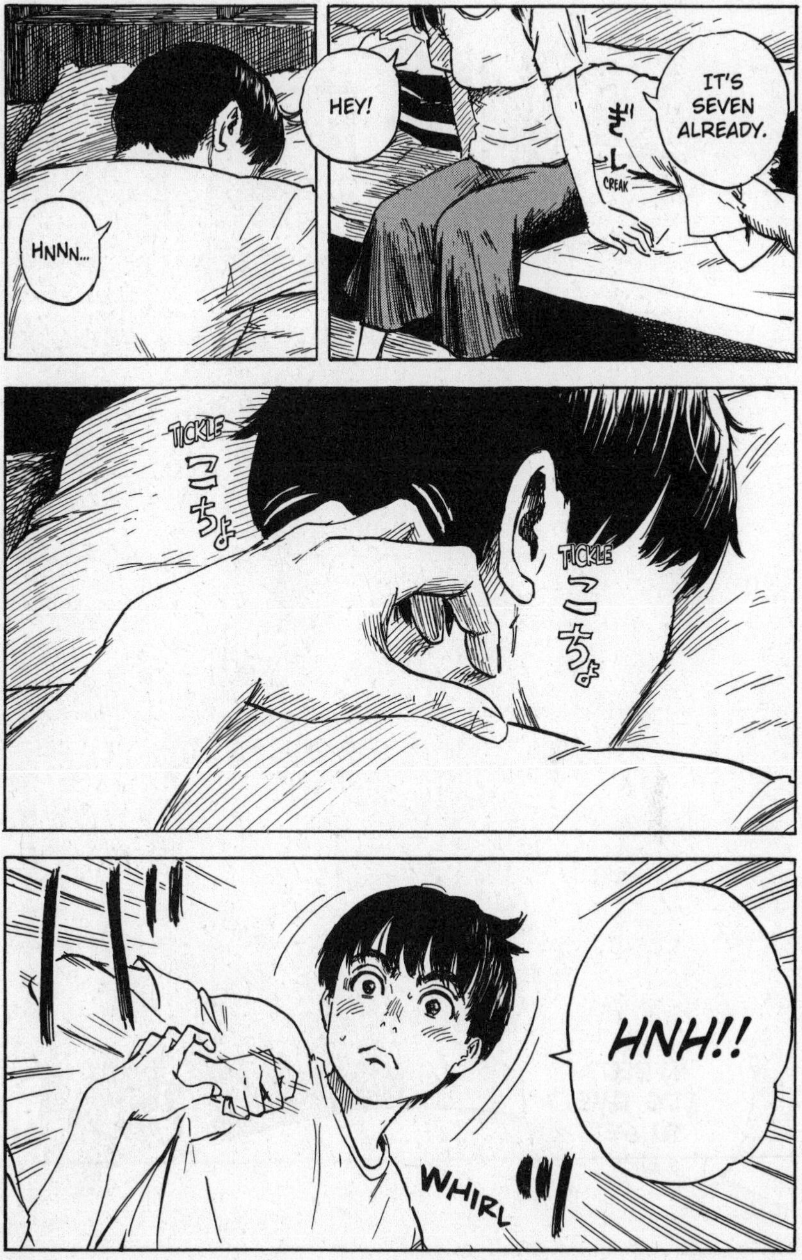
IT'S SEVEN ALREADY.
ぎし
CREAK
HEY!
HNNN...
TICKLE
こちょ
TICKLE
こちょ
HNH!!
WHIRL

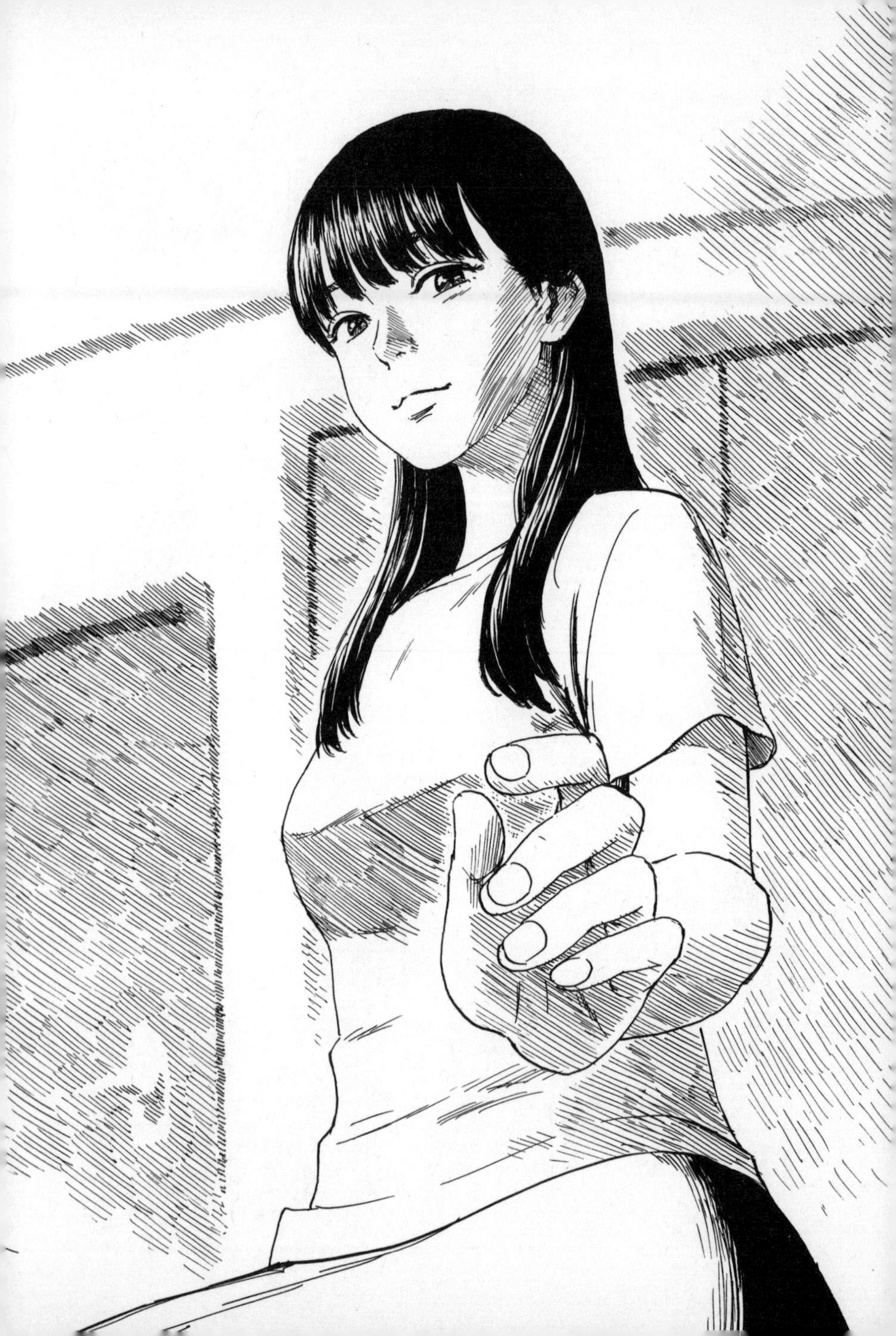

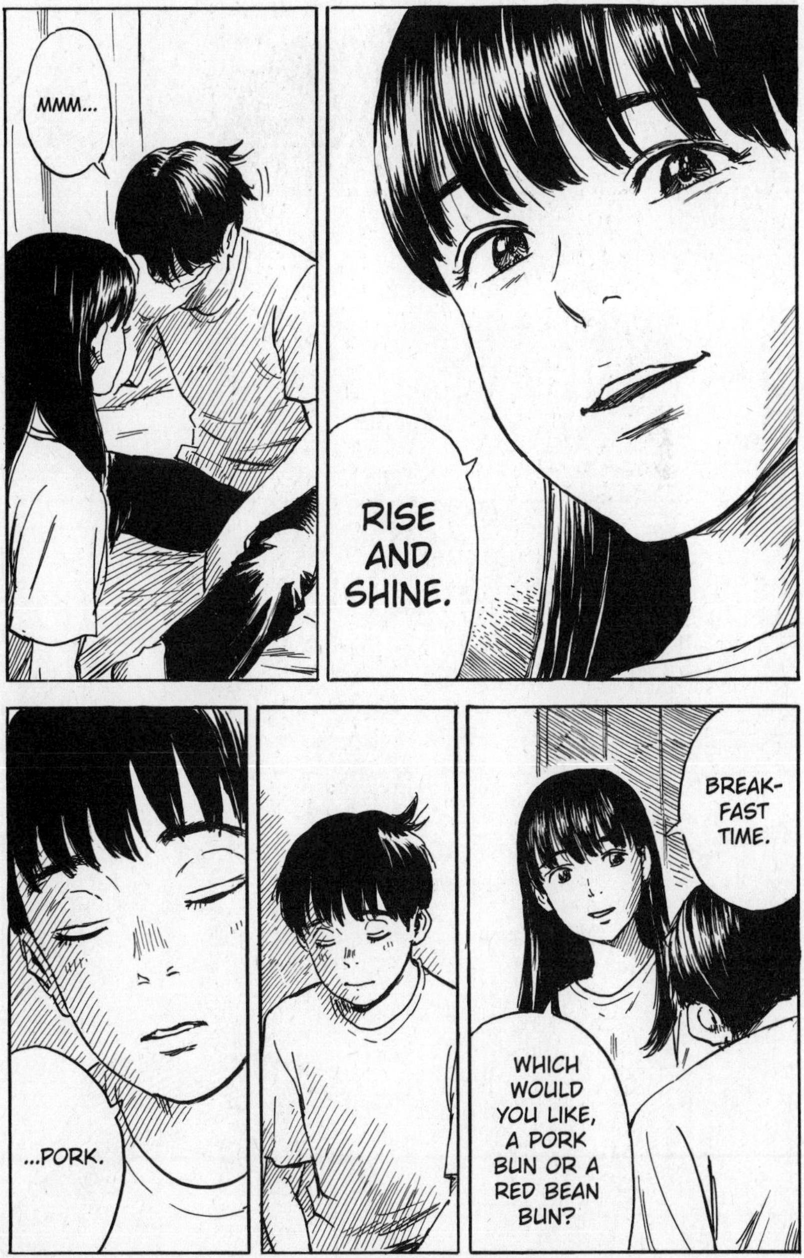
RISE AND SHINE.
MMM...
BREAK-FAST TIME.
WHICH WOULD YOU LIKE, A PORK BUN OR A RED BEAN BUN?
...PORK.

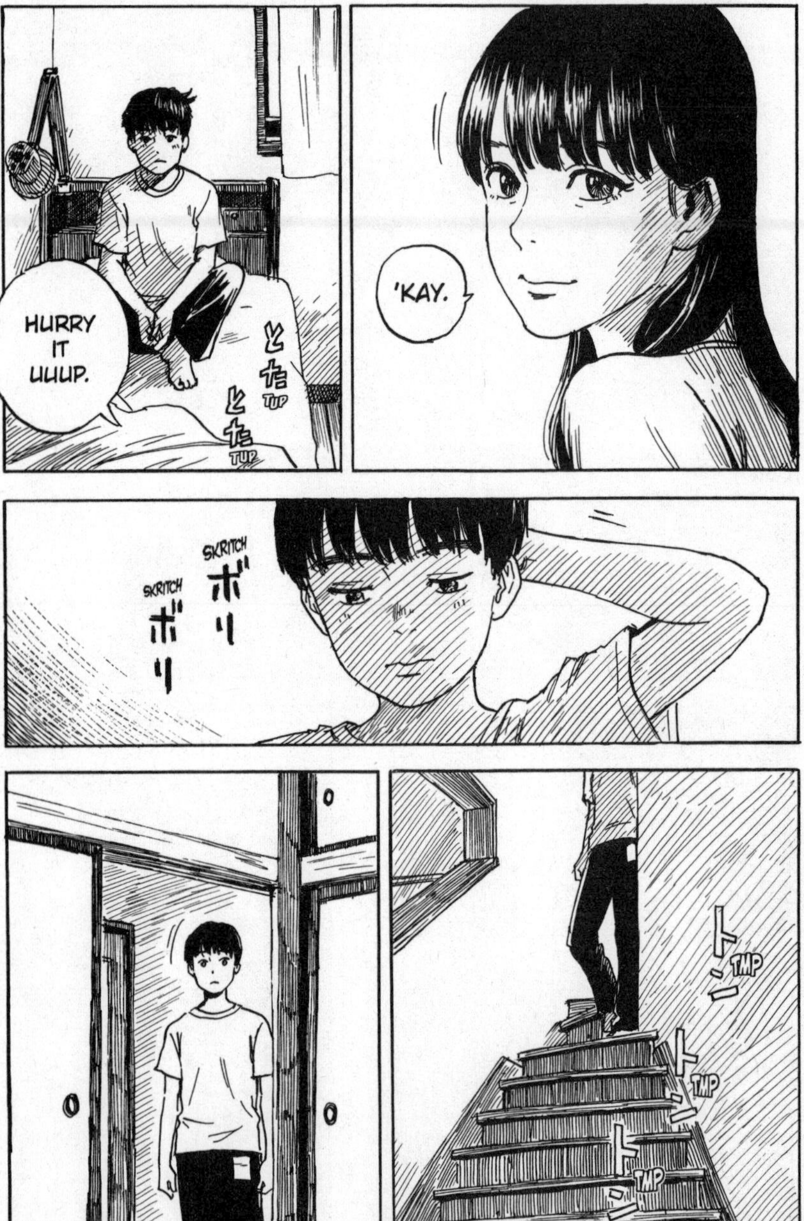
'KAY.
HURRY IT UUUP.
とた TUP
とた TUP
SKRITCH ボリ
SKRITCH ボリ
ト TMP
ト TMP
ト TMP

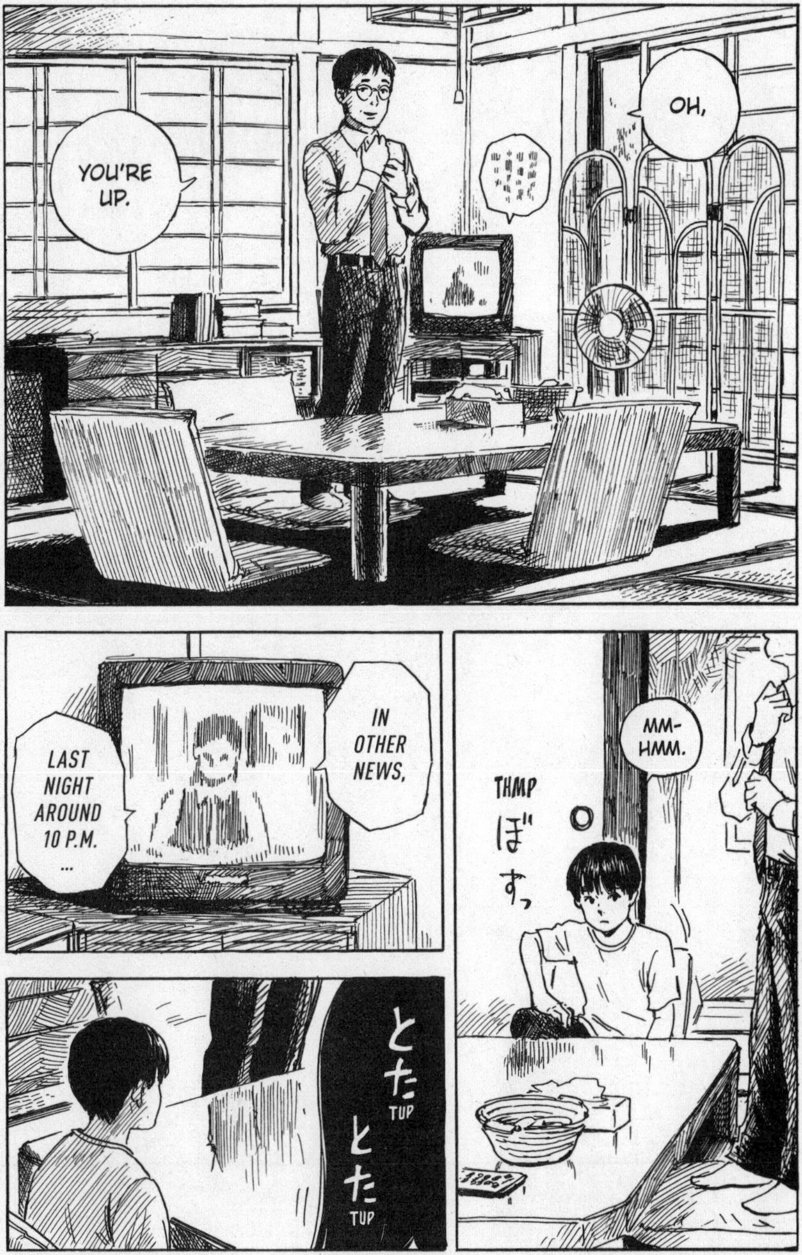
OH,
YOU'RE UP.
MM-HMM.
THMP
ぼすっ
IN OTHER NEWS,
LAST NIGHT AROUND 10 P.M. ...
とた
TUP
とた
TUP

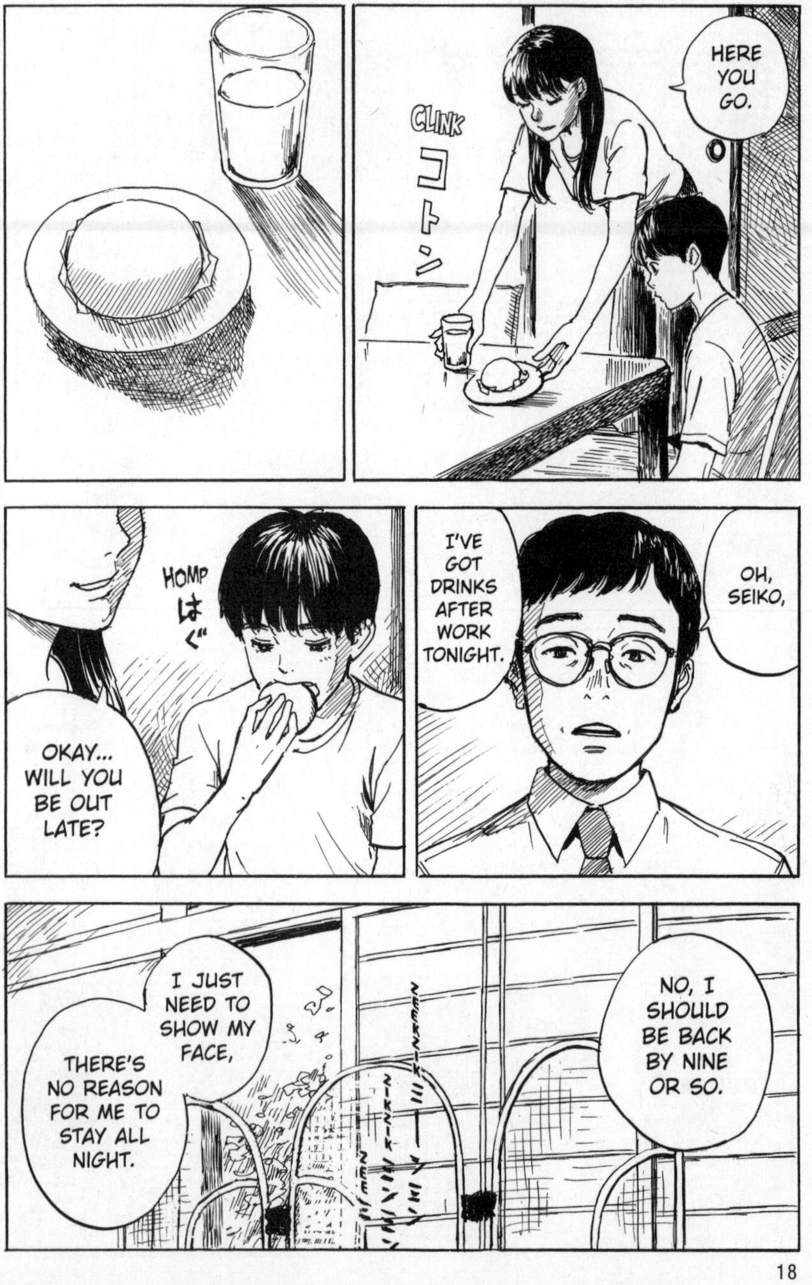

HERE YOU GO.
CLINK
コトン
OH, SEIKO,
I'VE GOT DRINKS AFTER WORK TONIGHT.
HOMP
はぐ
OKAY... WILL YOU BE OUT LATE?
NO, I SHOULD BE BACK BY NINE OR SO.
I JUST NEED TO SHOW MY FACE,
THERE'S NO REASON FOR ME TO STAY ALL NIGHT.

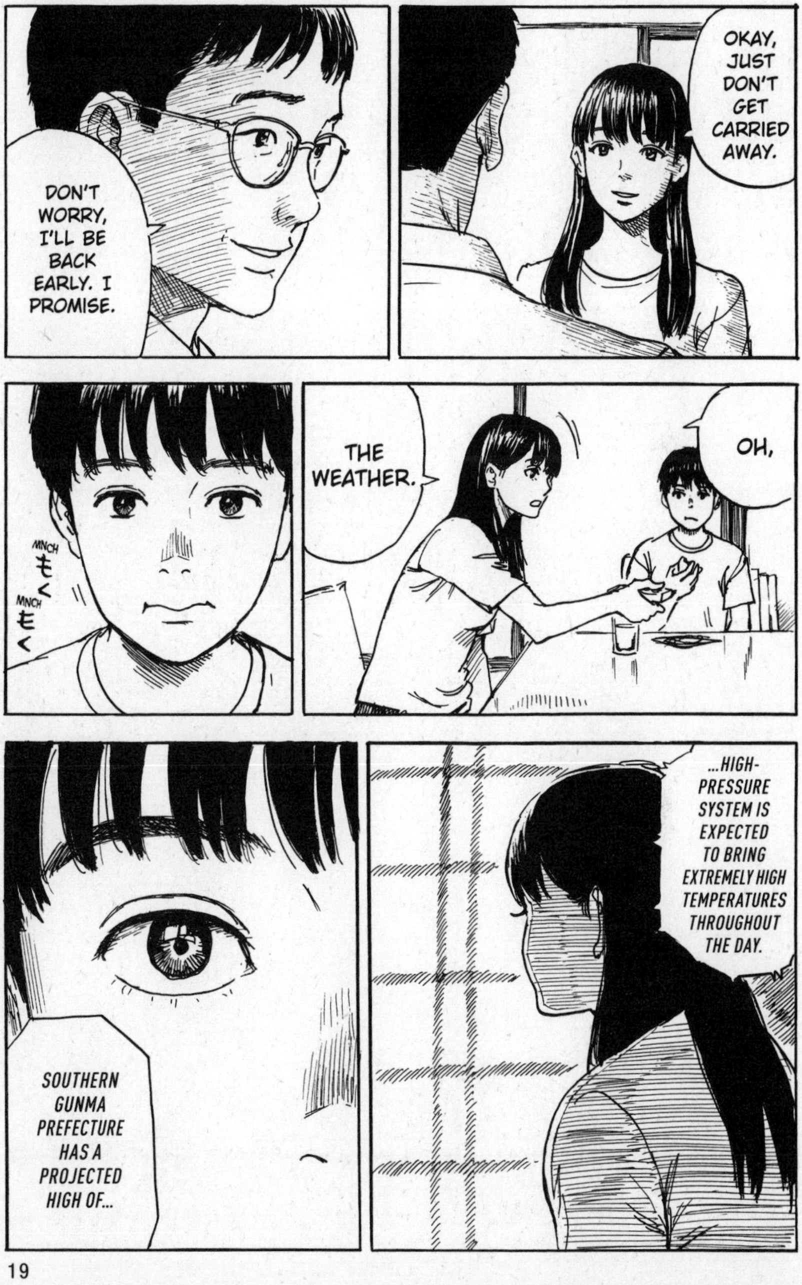
OKAY, JUST DON'T GET CARRIED AWAY.
DON'T WORRY, I'LL BE BACK EARLY. I PROMISE.
OH,
THE WEATHER.
MNCH もく
MNCH もく
...HIGH-PRESSURE SYSTEM IS EXPECTED TO BRING EXTREMELY HIGH TEMPERATURES THROUGHOUT THE DAY.
SOUTHERN GUNMA PREFECTURE HAS A PROJECTED HIGH OF...

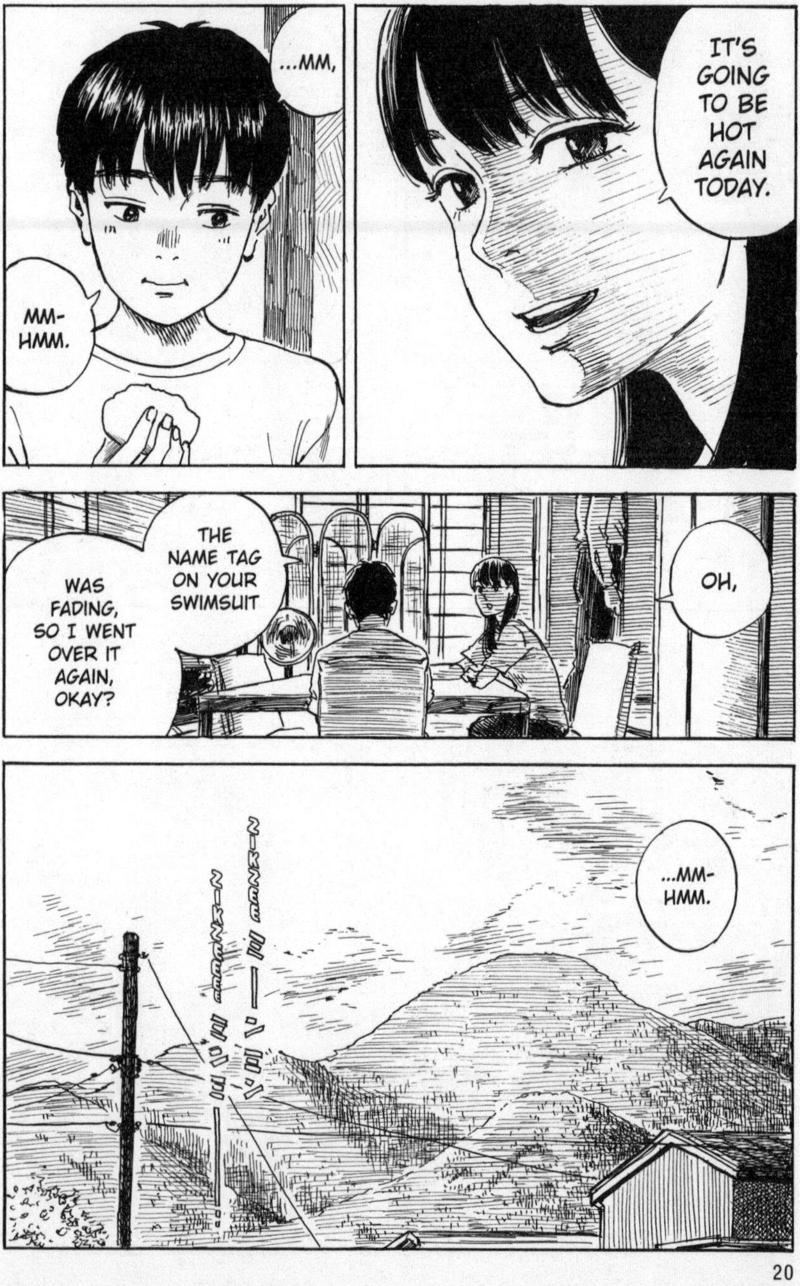
IT'S GOING TO BE HOT AGAIN TODAY.
...MM,
MM-HMM.
OH,
THE NAME TAG ON YOUR SWIMSUIT
WAS FADING, SO I WENT OVER IT AGAIN, OKAY?
...MM-HMM.

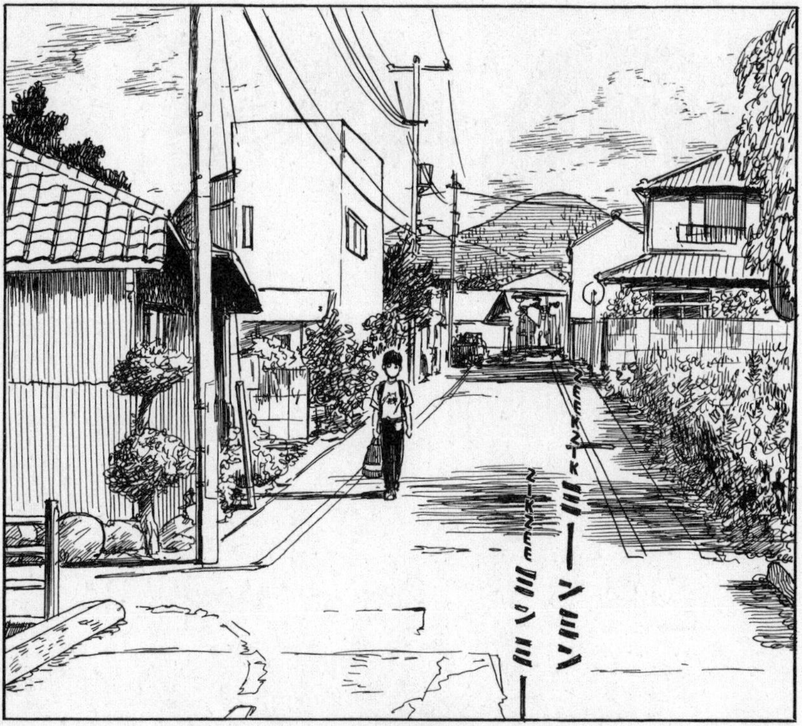
ミーンミン
ZEEKZIK
ミンミンミー
ZIKZEE

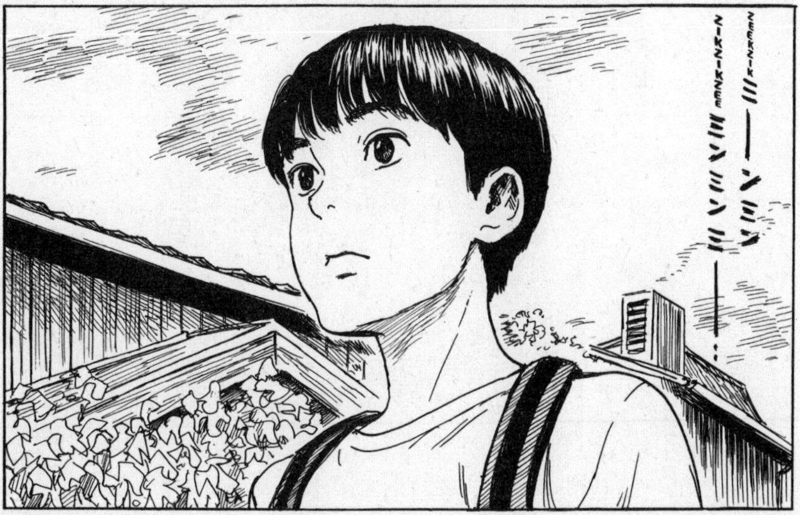
ミーンミン
ZEEKZIK
ミンミンミー…
ZIKZIKZEE

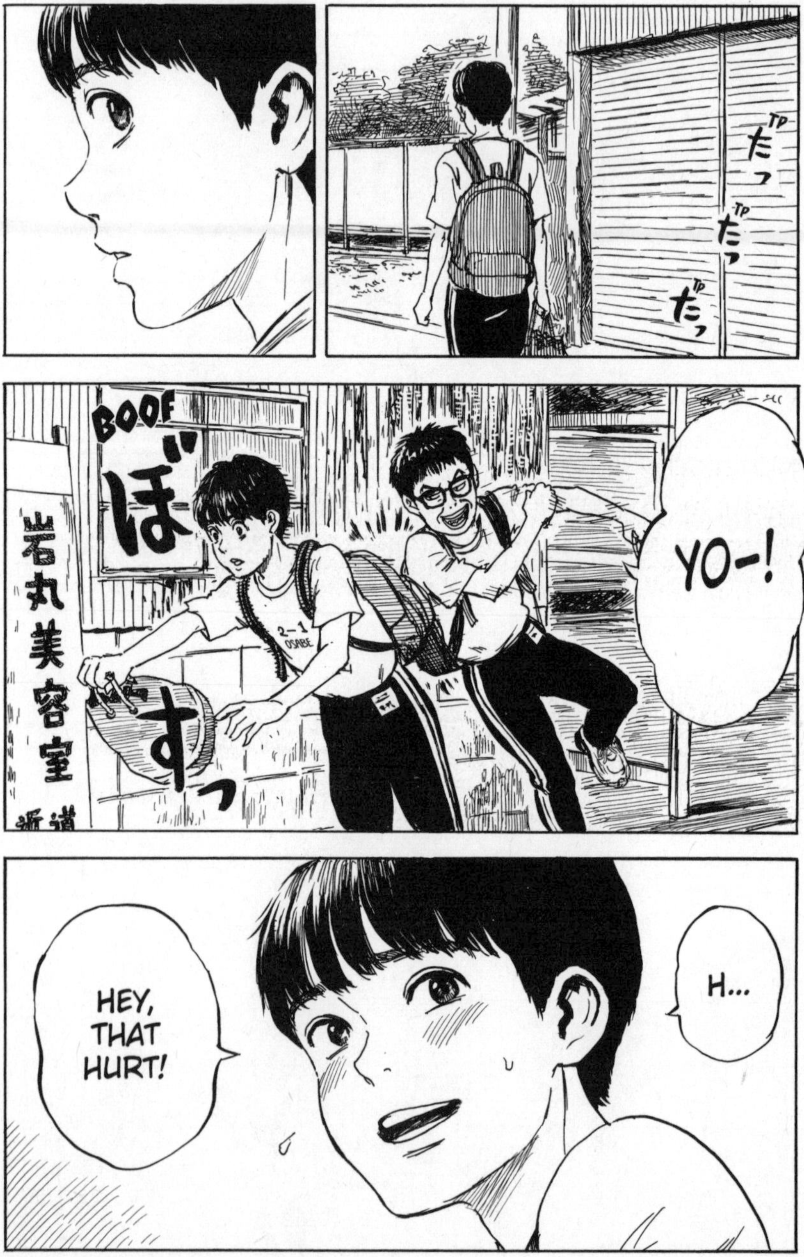
TP
たっ
TP
たっ
TP
たっ
YO–!
BOOF
ぼ
岩丸美容室
ずっ
H...
HEY, THAT HURT!

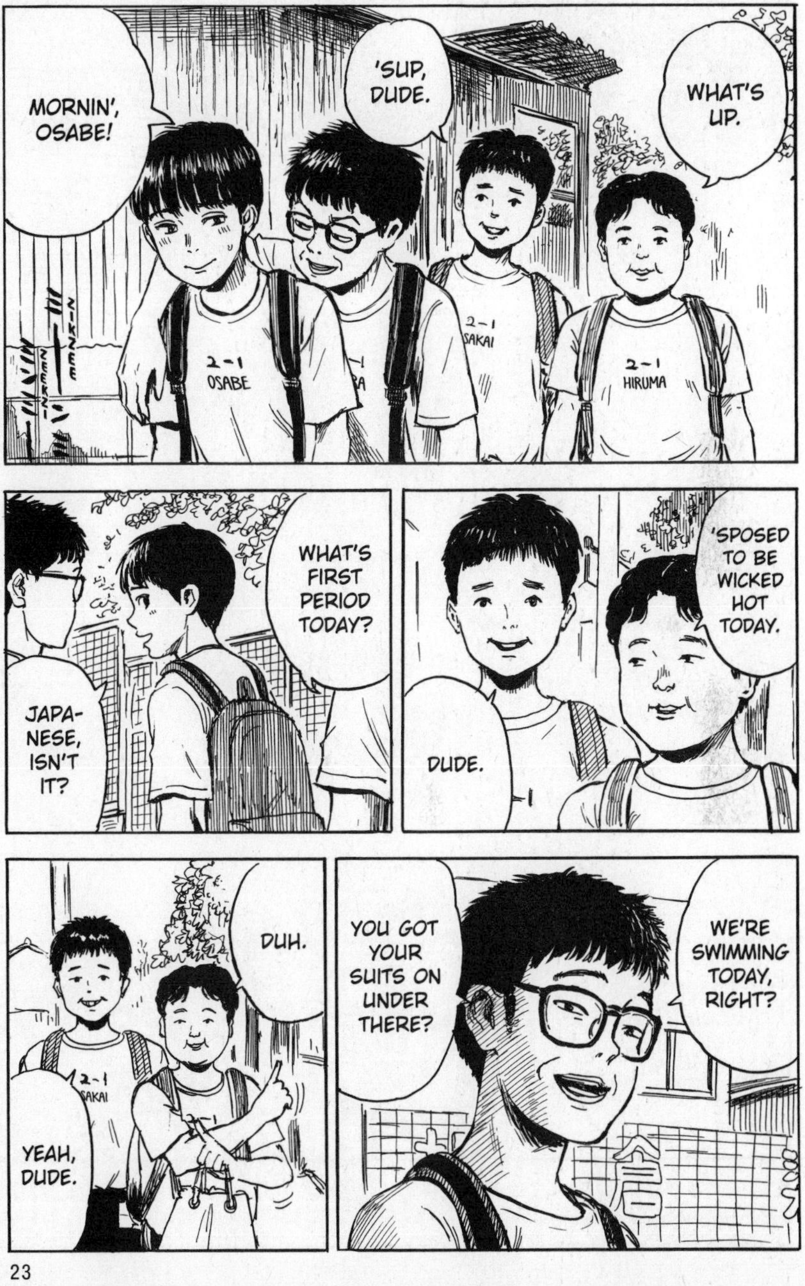
WHAT'S UP.
'SUP, DUDE.
MORNIN', OSABE!
ZIKZEE
ZEERZ
2-1 OSABE
2-1 SAKAI
2-1 HIRUMA
'SPOSED TO BE WICKED HOT TODAY.
DUDE.
WHAT'S FIRST PERIOD TODAY?
JAPA-NESE, ISN'T IT?
WE'RE SWIMMING TODAY, RIGHT?
YOU GOT YOUR SUITS ON UNDER THERE?
DUH.
YEAH, DUDE.
2-1 SAKAI

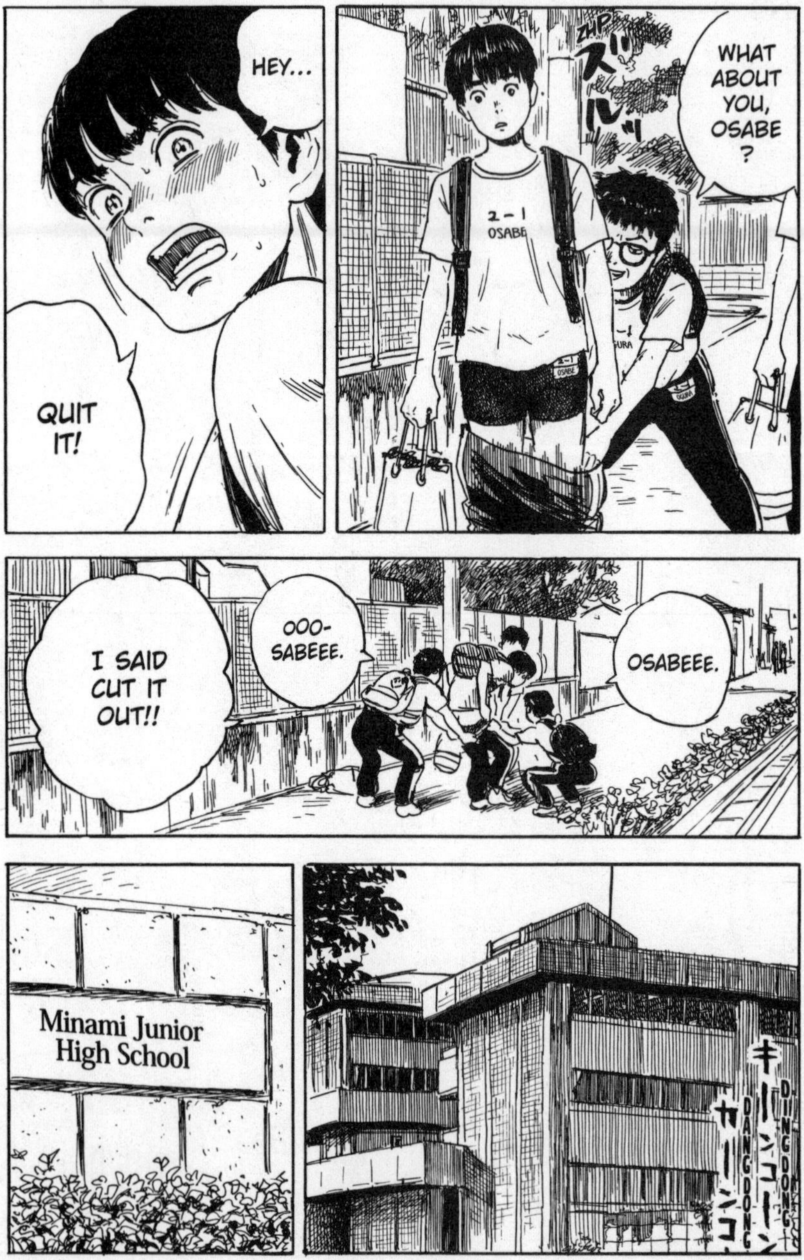
WHAT ABOUT YOU, OSABE?
ZHP
スルッ
2-1 OSABE
HEY...
QUIT IT!
OSABEEE.
OOO-SABEEE.
I SAID CUT IT OUT!!
DING DONG
DANG DONG
Minami Junior High School

ザワ MURMUR
ザワ MURMUR
ザワ MURMUR
ザワ MURMUR
WHOA!
BWA HA HA HA HA!
2-1
YO, MAN.
ザワ MURMUR
MURMUR ザワ
2-1 OSABE
WASSUP.
2-1 FUKISHI

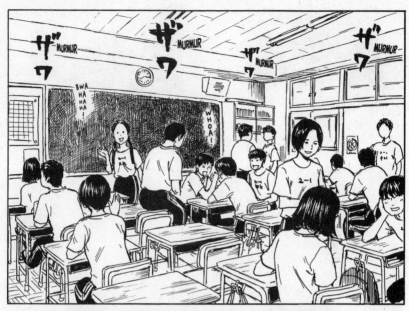

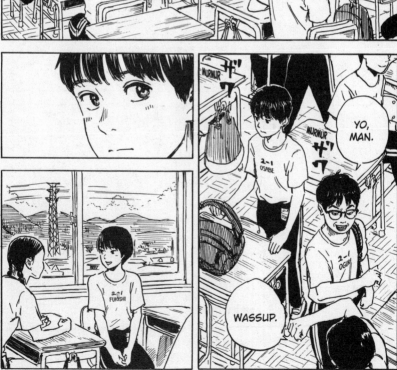

2 - 1
FUKIISHI

キーンコーン
カーンコー

DING DONG
DANG DONG

チラ
GLANCE

2-1
OSABE

26

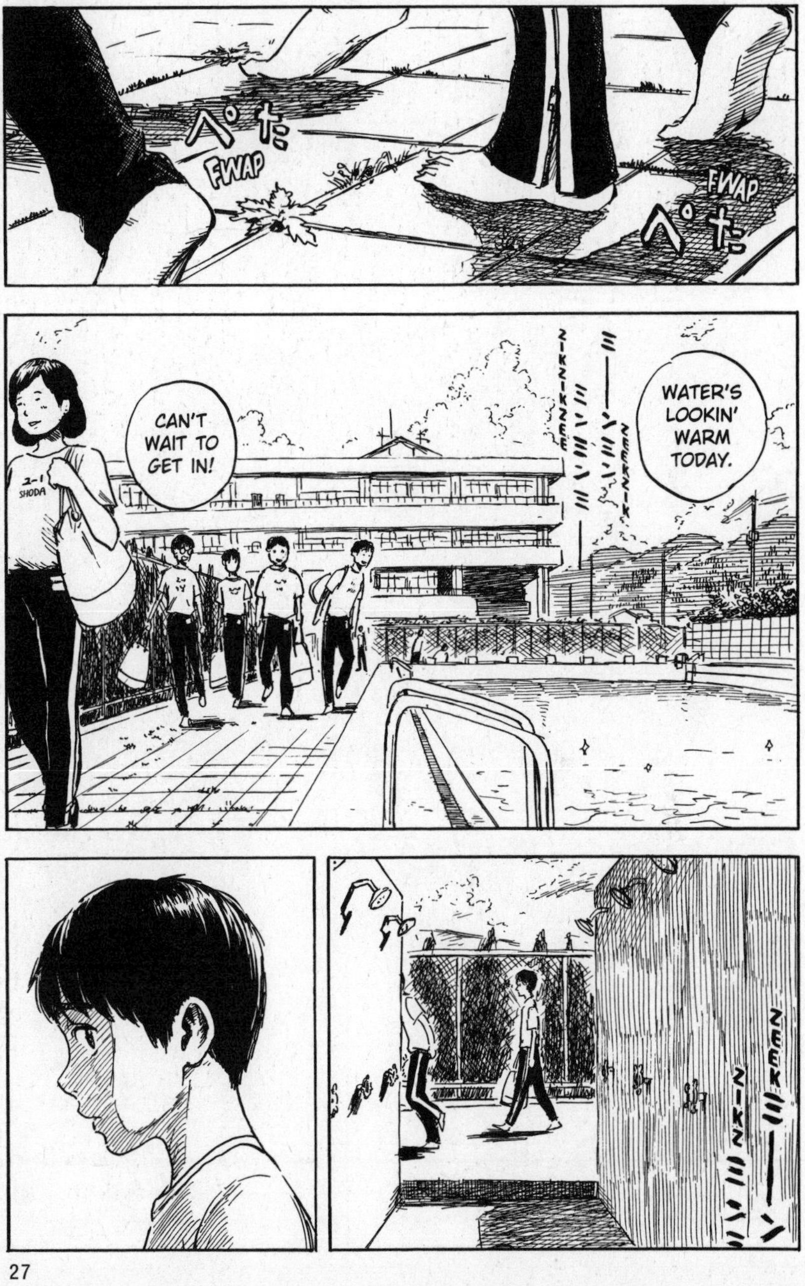
FWAP
ぺた
ぺた
FWAP
WATER'S LOOKIN' WARM TODAY.
ミーンミンミン
ZEEKZIK
ミンミンミ
ZIKZIKZEE
CAN'T WAIT TO GET IN!
2-1 SHODA
ZEEK ミーン
ZIKZ ミンミ

ンミンミー
ZIKZIKZEEE

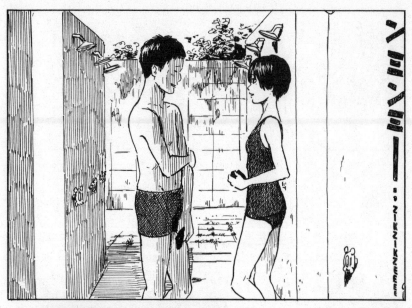

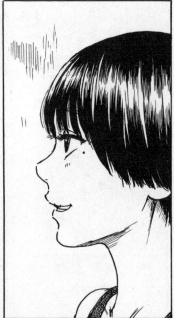

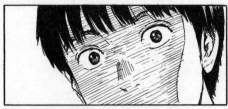

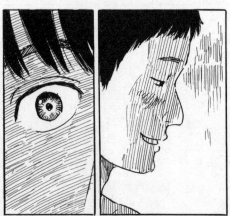

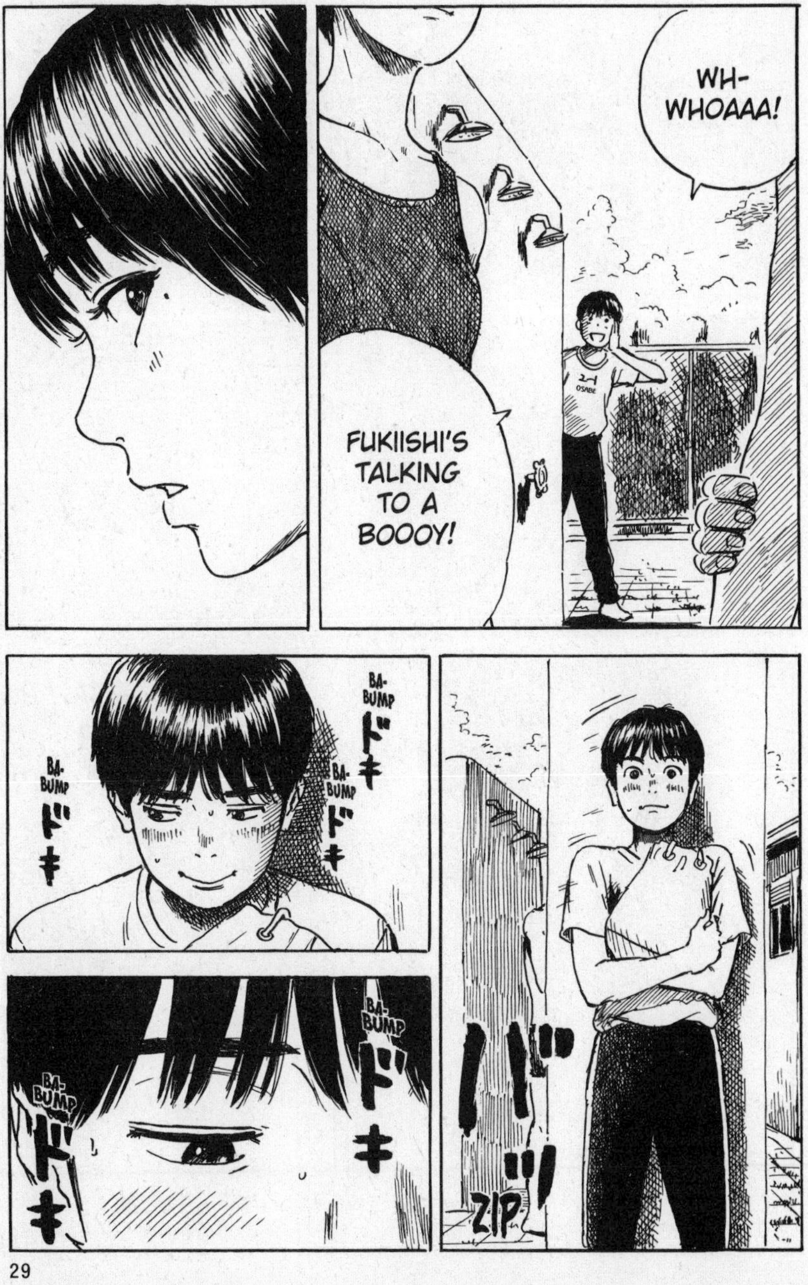
WH- WHOAAA!
FUKIISHI'S TALKING TO A BOOOY!
ZIP
BA- BUMP ドキ
BA- BUMP ドキ
BA- BUMP ドキ
BA- BUMP ドキ
BA- BUMP ドキ

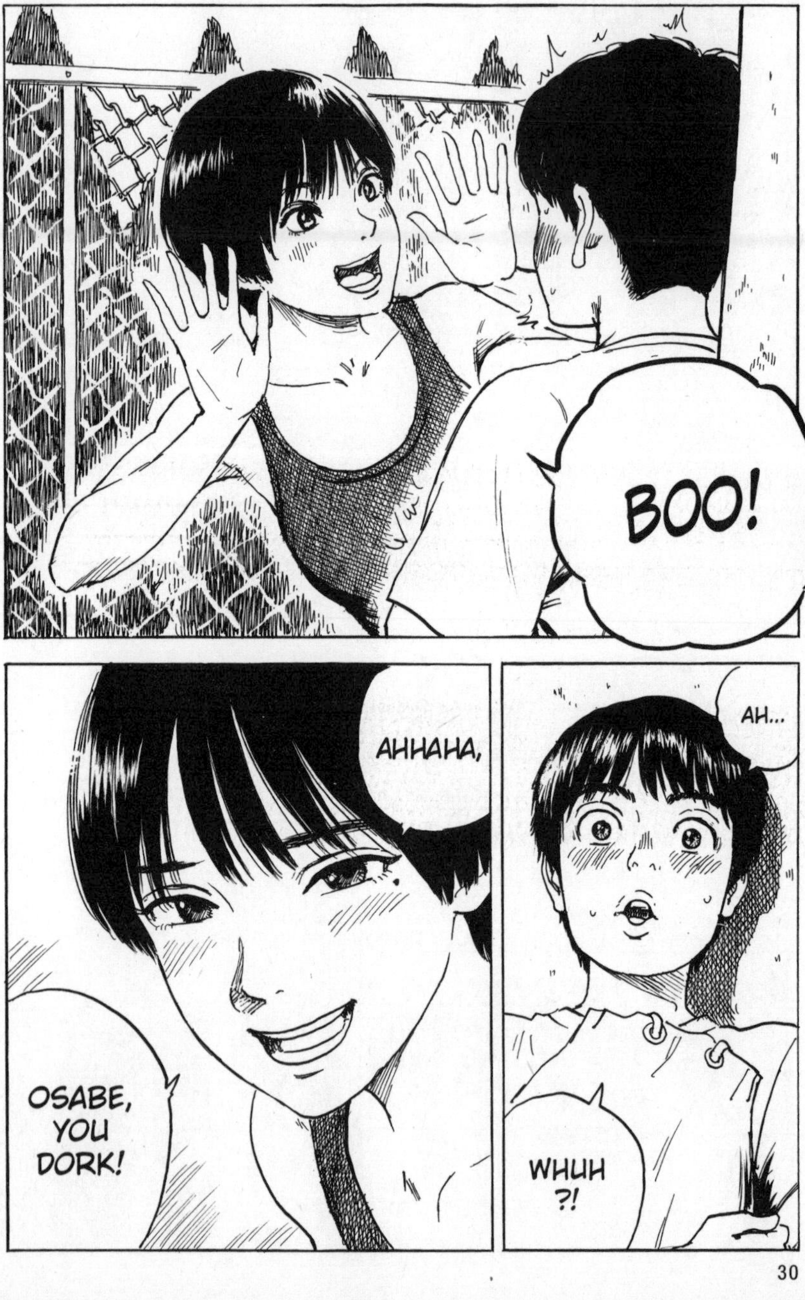
BOO!
AH...
WHUH ?!
AHHAHA,
OSABE, YOU DORK!

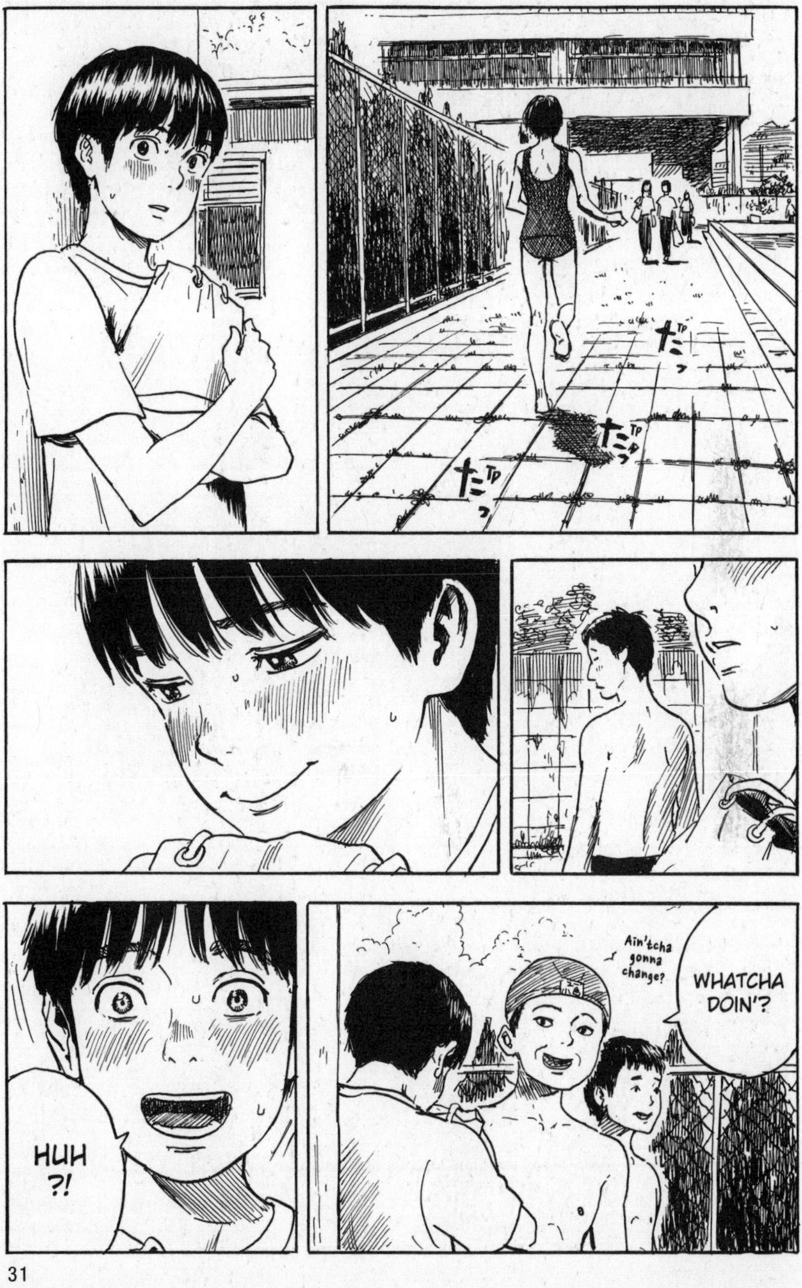
たっ TP
たっ TP
たっ TP
WHATCHA DOIN'?
Ain'tcha gonna change?
HUH ?!

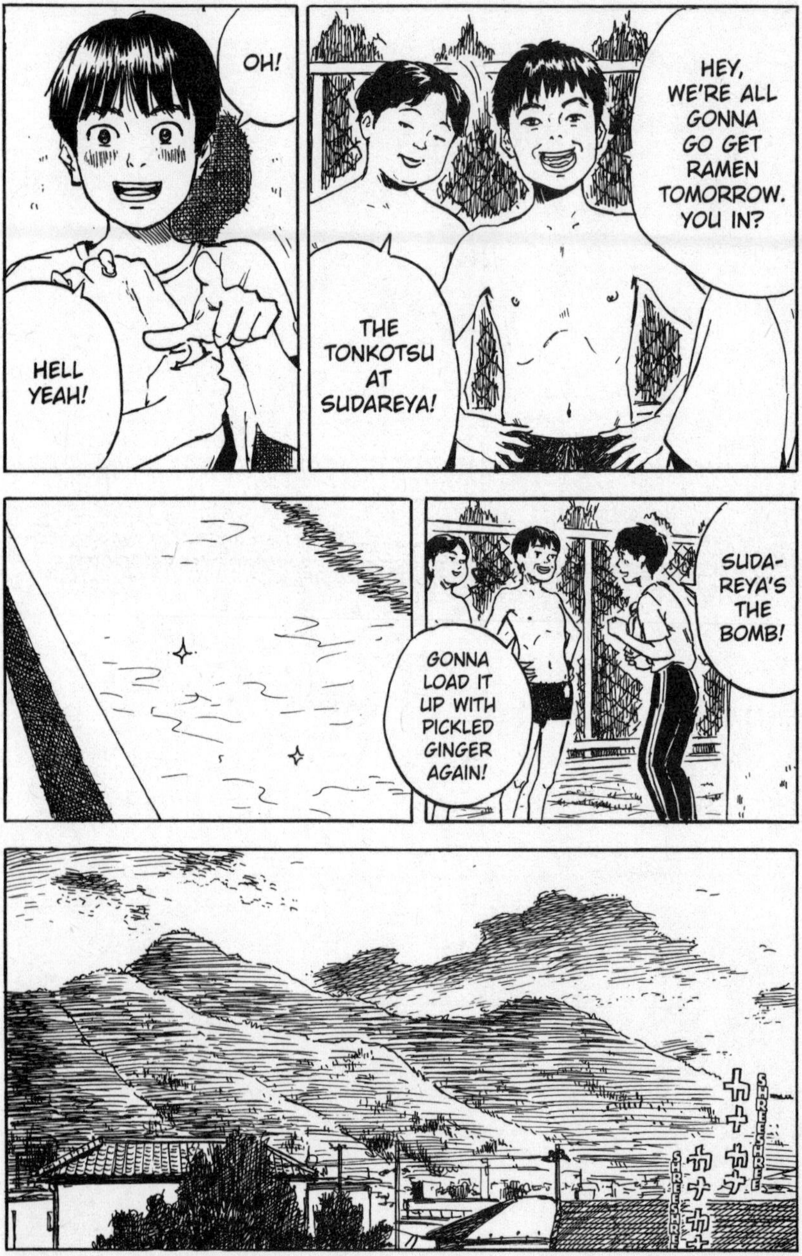
HEY, WE'RE ALL GONNA GO GET RAMEN TOMORROW. YOU IN?
THE TONKOTSU AT SUDAREYA!
OH!
HELL YEAH!
SUDA-REYA'S THE BOMB!
GONNA LOAD IT UP WITH PICKLED GINGER AGAIN!
SHREESHREE
SHREESHREE

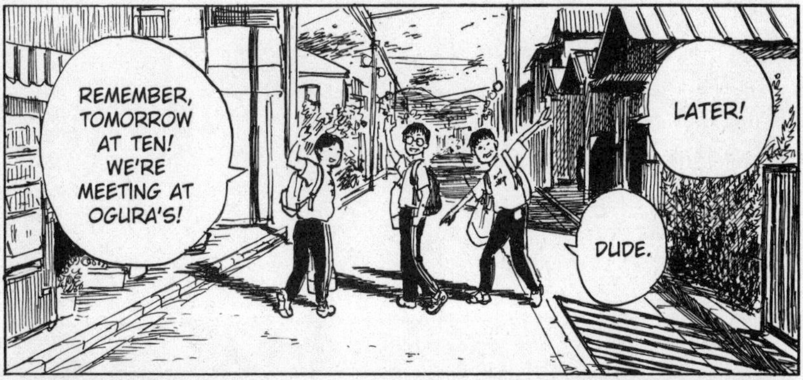
LATER!
REMEMBER, TOMORROW AT TEN! WE'RE MEETING AT OGURA'S!
DUDE.

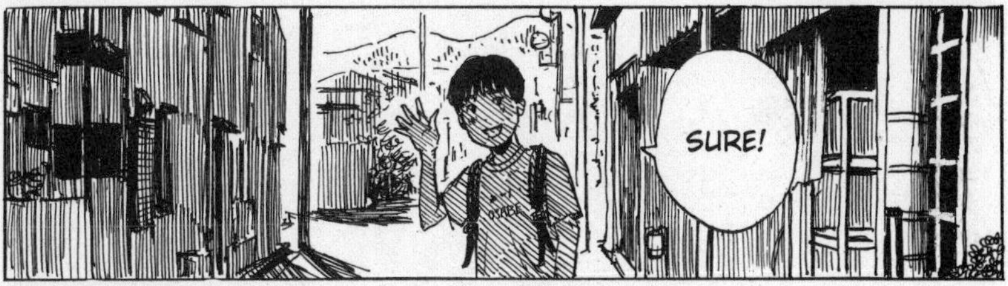
SURE!

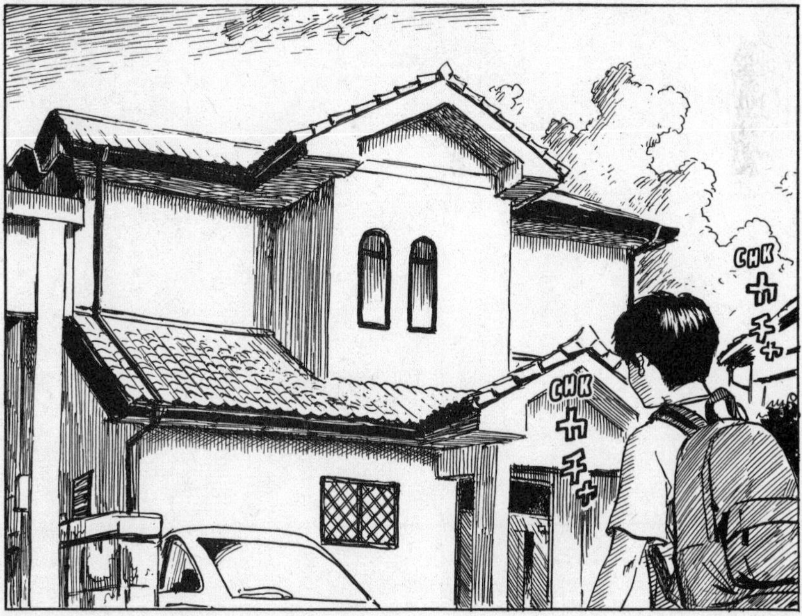
CHK
カチャ
CHK
カチャ

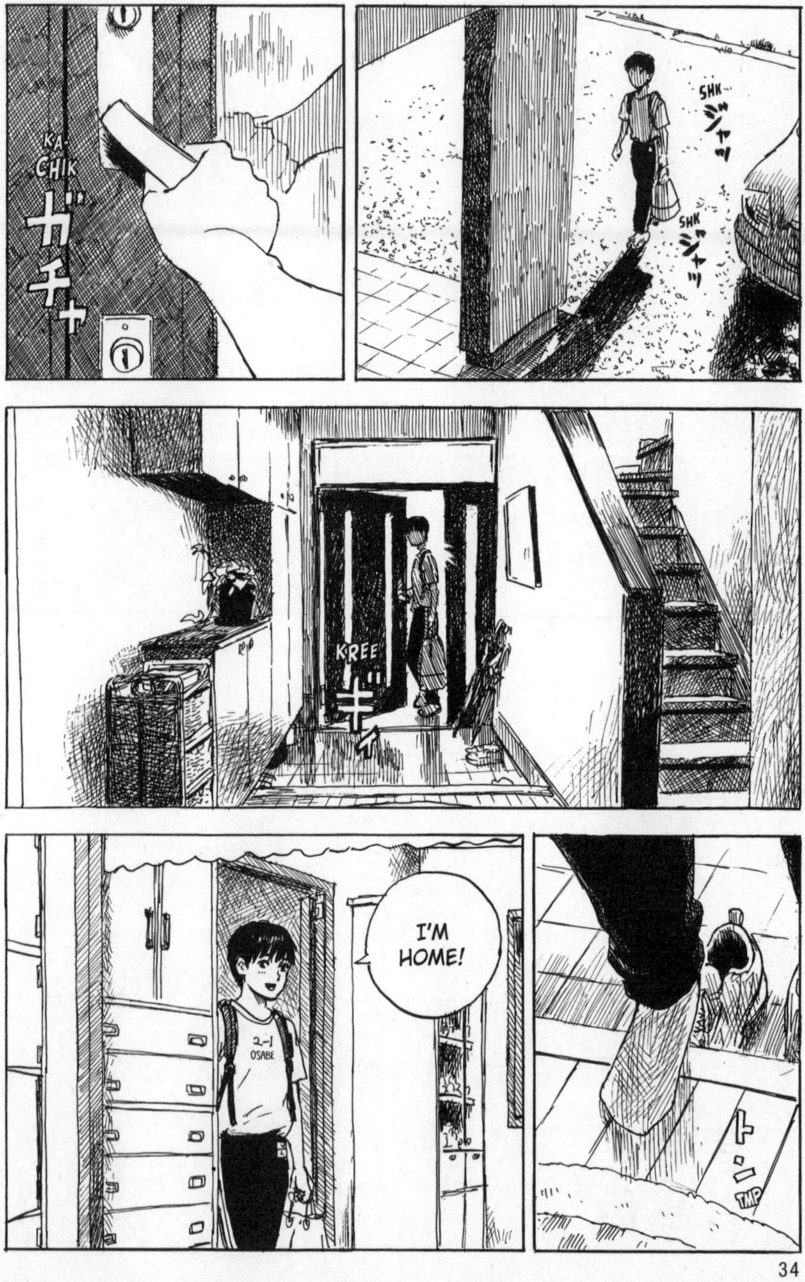
SHK
ジャッ
SHK
ジャッ
KA-CHIK
ガチャ
KREE
キィ
トン
TMP
I'M HOME!
2-1
OSABE

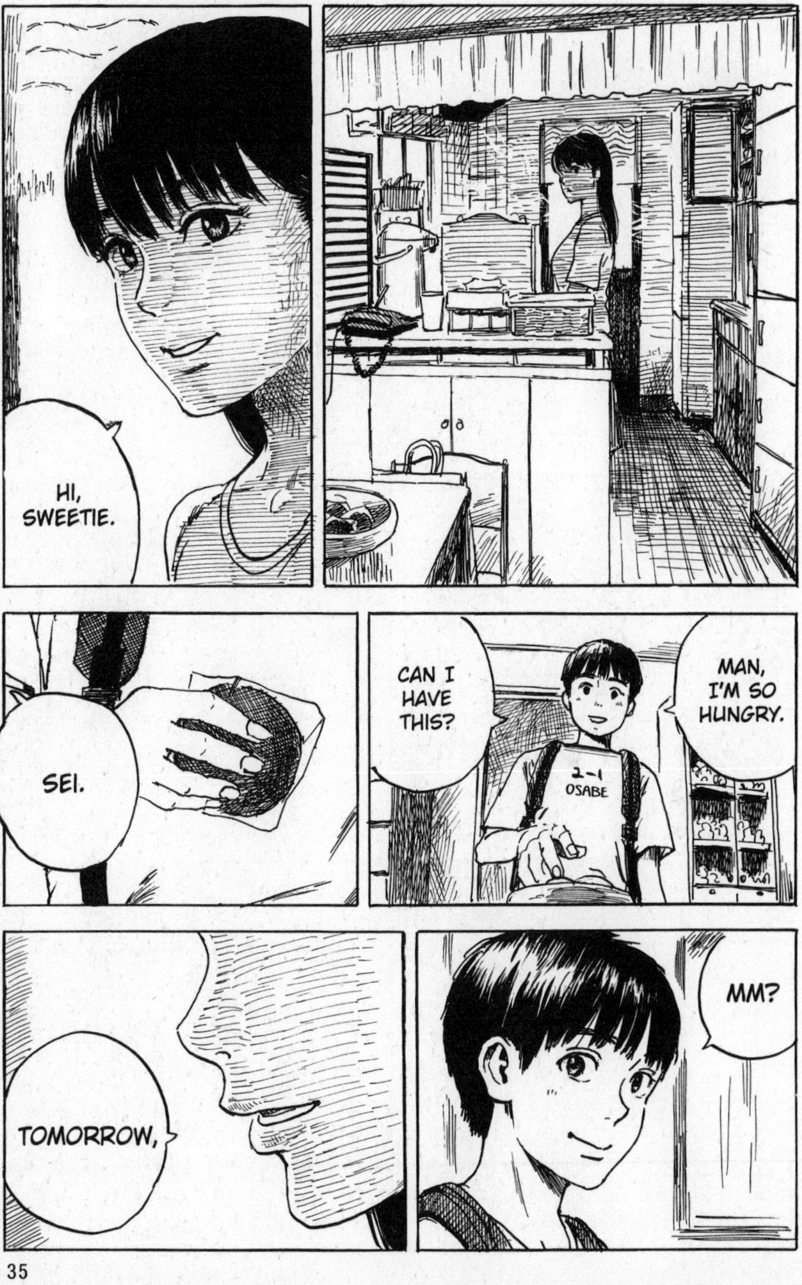
HI, SWEETIE.
MAN, I'M SO HUNGRY.
CAN I HAVE THIS?
2-1 OSABE
SEI.
MM?
TOMORROW,

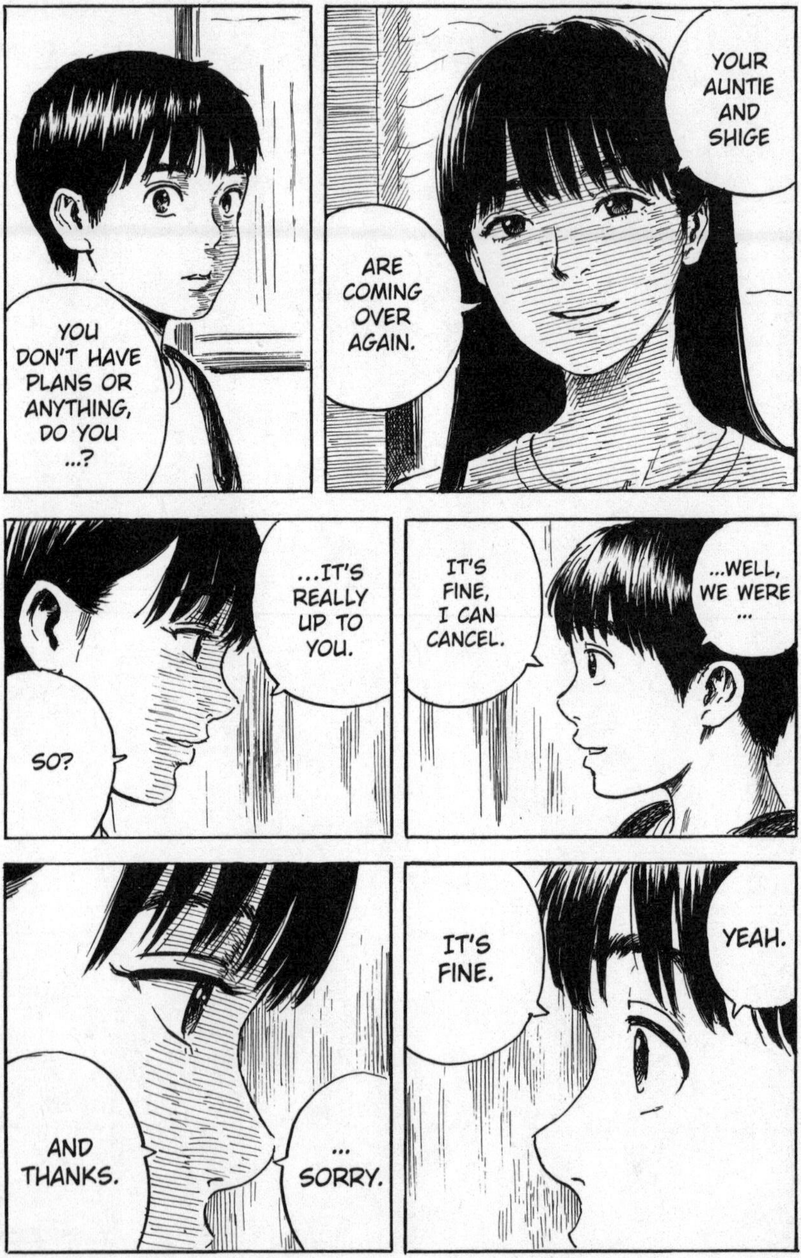
YOUR AUNTIE AND SHIGE
ARE COMING OVER AGAIN.
YOU DON'T HAVE PLANS OR ANYTHING, DO YOU ...?
...WELL, WE WERE ...
IT'S FINE, I CAN CANCEL.
...IT'S REALLY UP TO YOU.
SO?
YEAH.
IT'S FINE.
... SORRY.
AND THANKS.

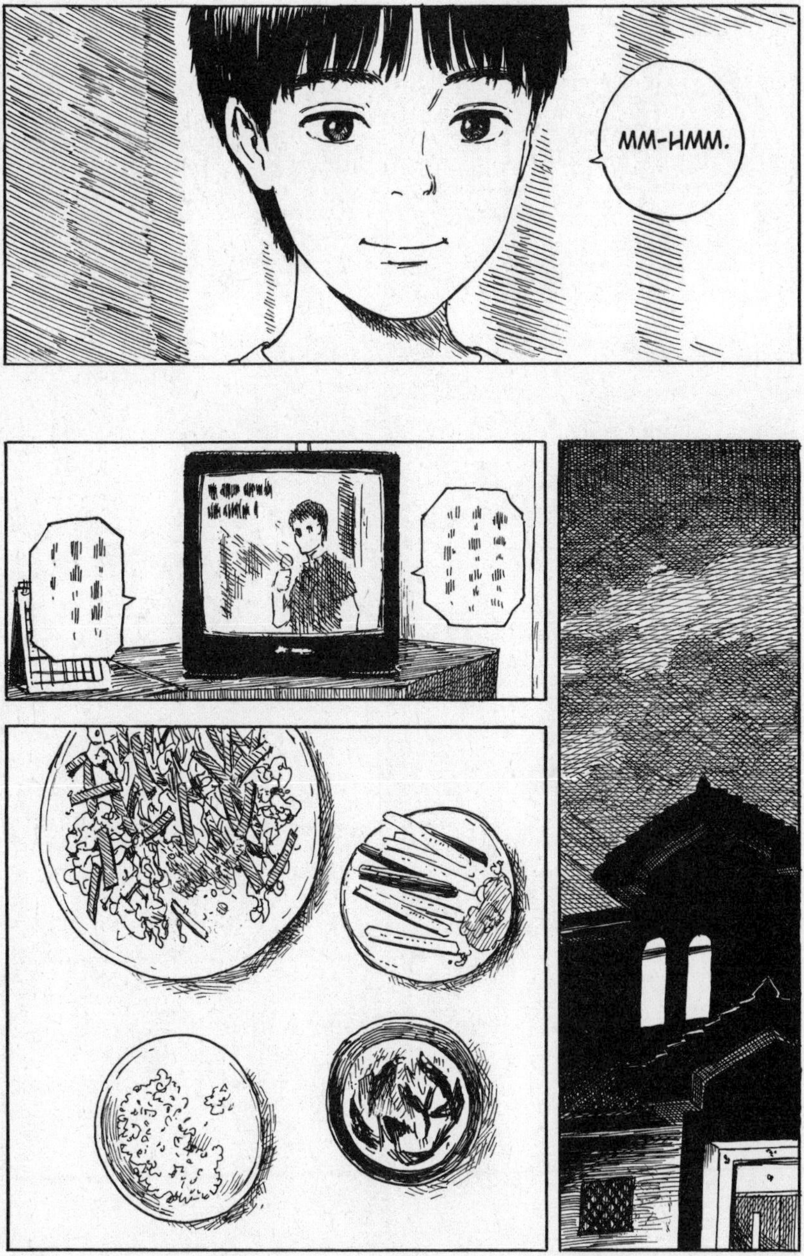
MM-HMM.

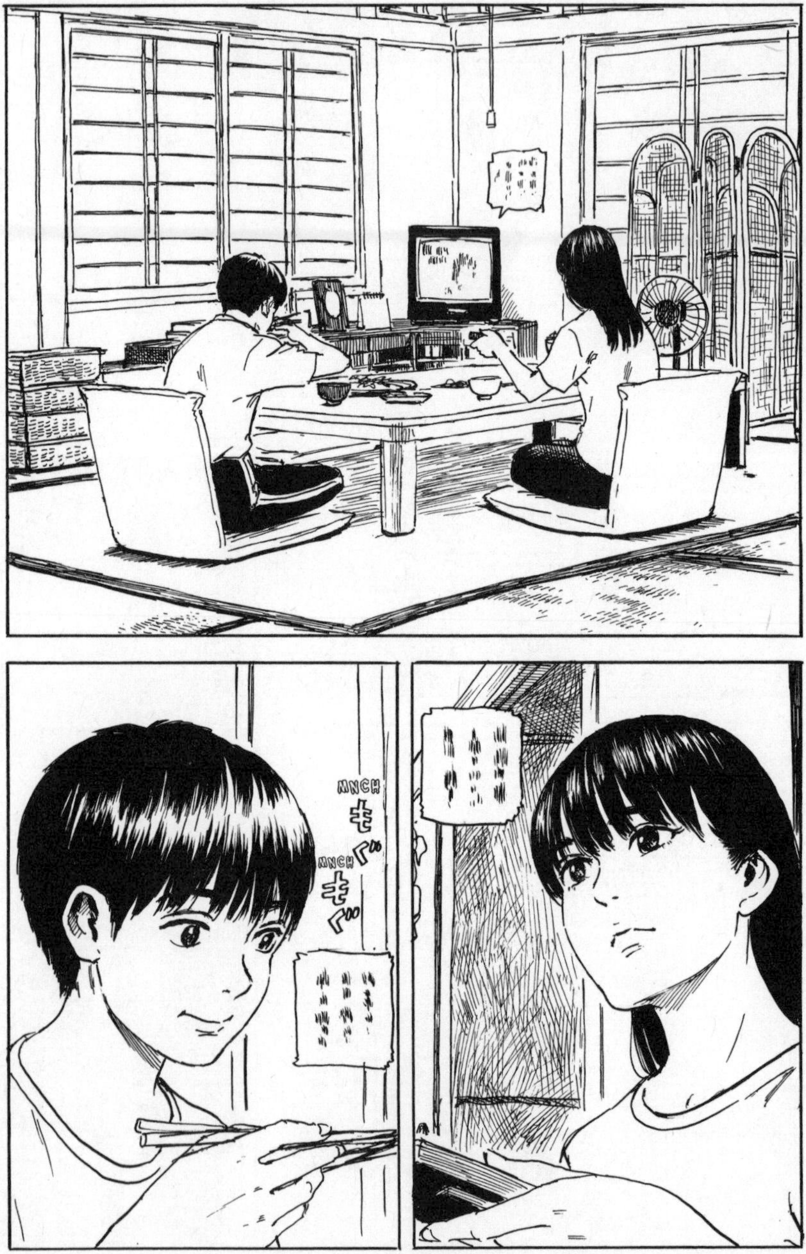
MNCH
もぐ
MNCH
もぐ

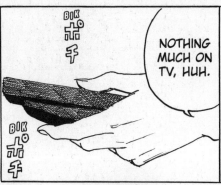

NOTHING MUCH ON TV, HUH.

THAT REMINDS ME...

OH,

ABOUT WHAT?

LAST NIGHT,

I HAD THIS DREAM.

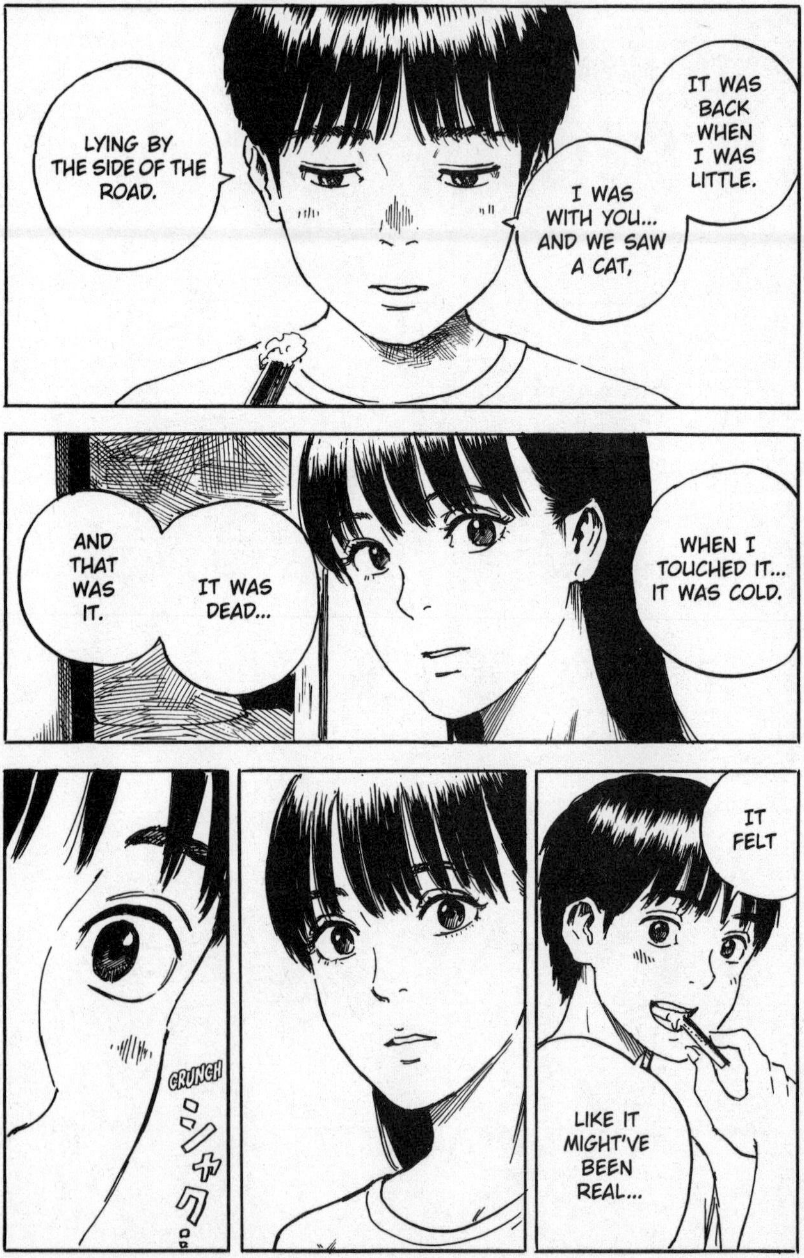
IT WAS BACK WHEN I WAS LITTLE.
I WAS WITH YOU... AND WE SAW A CAT,
LYING BY THE SIDE OF THE ROAD.
WHEN I TOUCHED IT... IT WAS COLD.
IT WAS DEAD...
AND THAT WAS IT.
IT FELT
LIKE IT MIGHT'VE BEEN REAL...
CRUNCH
シャク。。

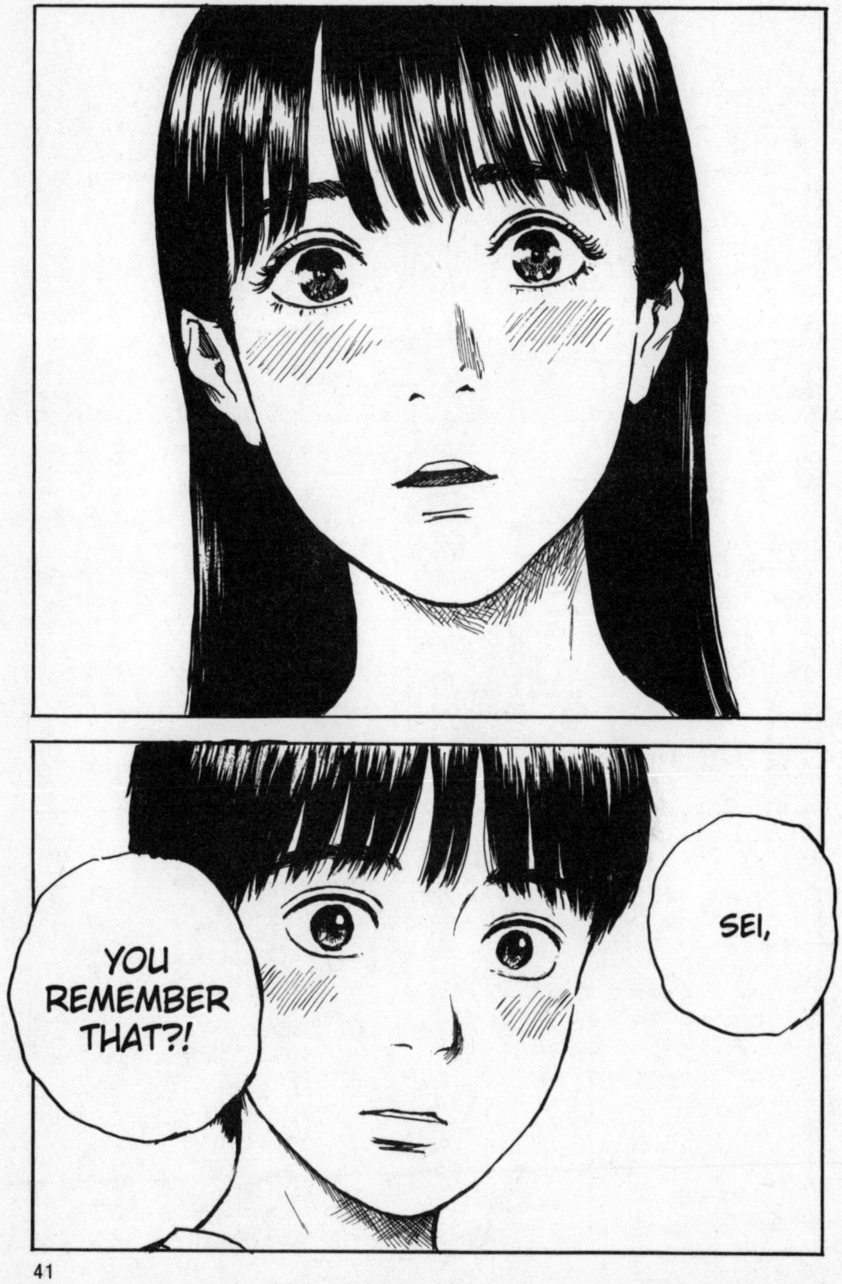
SEI,
YOU REMEMBER THAT?!

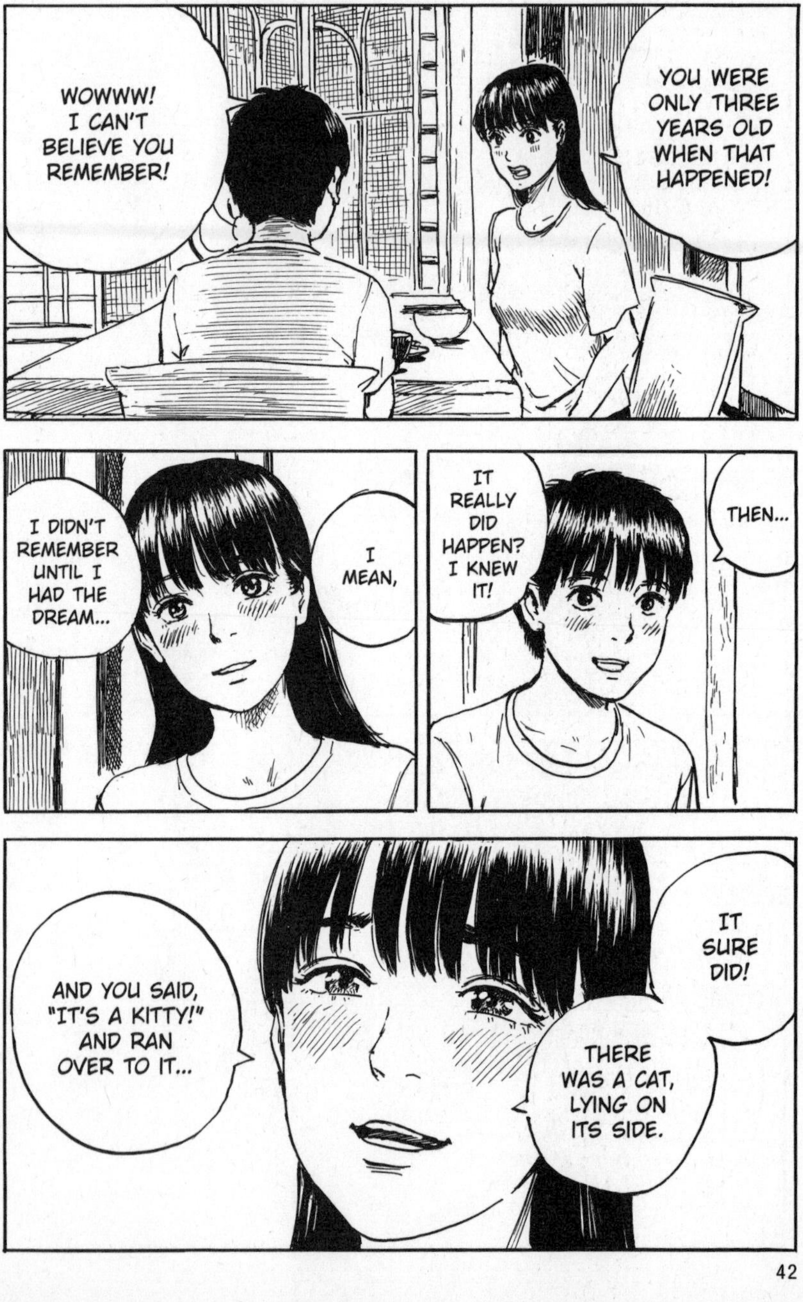
YOU WERE ONLY THREE YEARS OLD WHEN THAT HAPPENED!
WOWWW! I CAN'T BELIEVE YOU REMEMBER!
THEN...
IT REALLY DID HAPPEN? I KNEW IT!
I MEAN,
I DIDN'T REMEMBER UNTIL I HAD THE DREAM...
IT SURE DID!
THERE WAS A CAT, LYING ON ITS SIDE.
AND YOU SAID, "IT'S A KITTY!" AND RAN OVER TO IT...

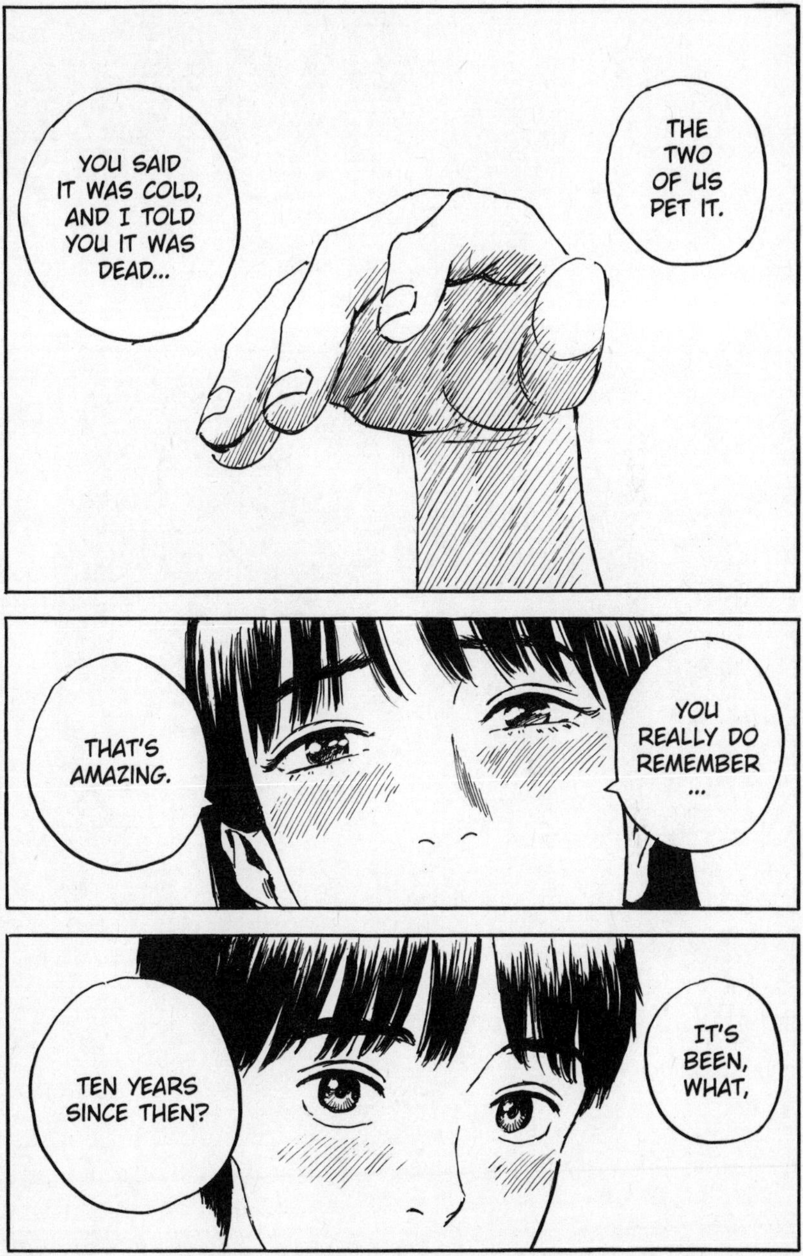
THE TWO OF US PET IT.
YOU SAID IT WAS COLD, AND I TOLD YOU IT WAS DEAD...
YOU REALLY DO REMEMBER ...
THAT'S AMAZING.
IT'S BEEN, WHAT,
TEN YEARS SINCE THEN?

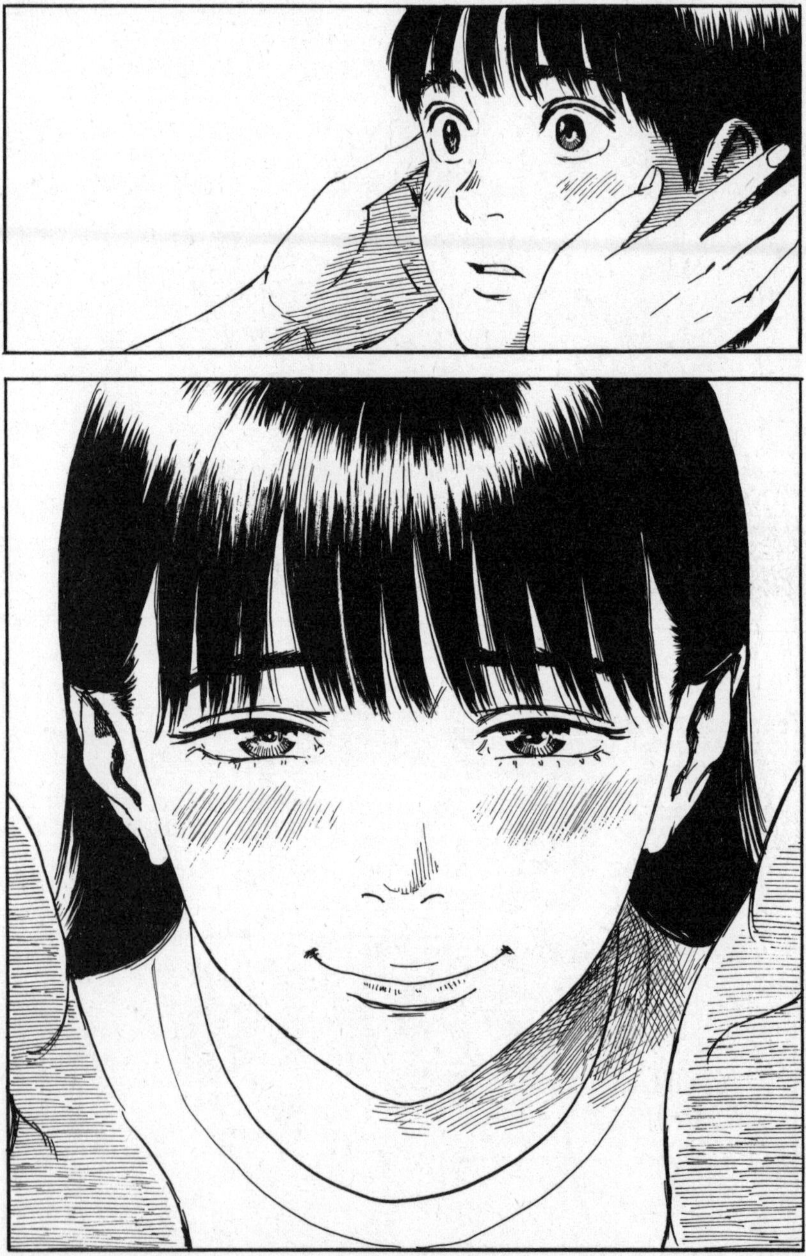

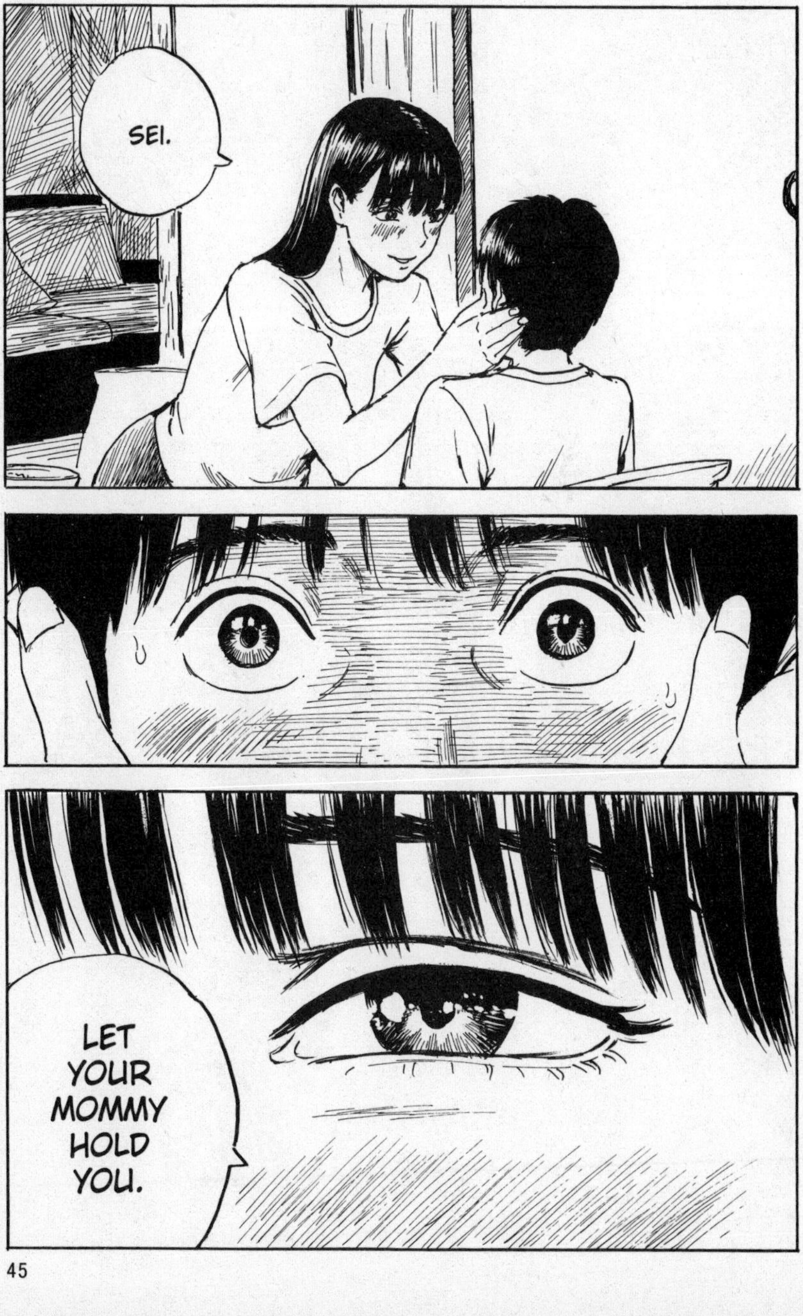
SEI.
LET YOUR MOMMY HOLD YOU.

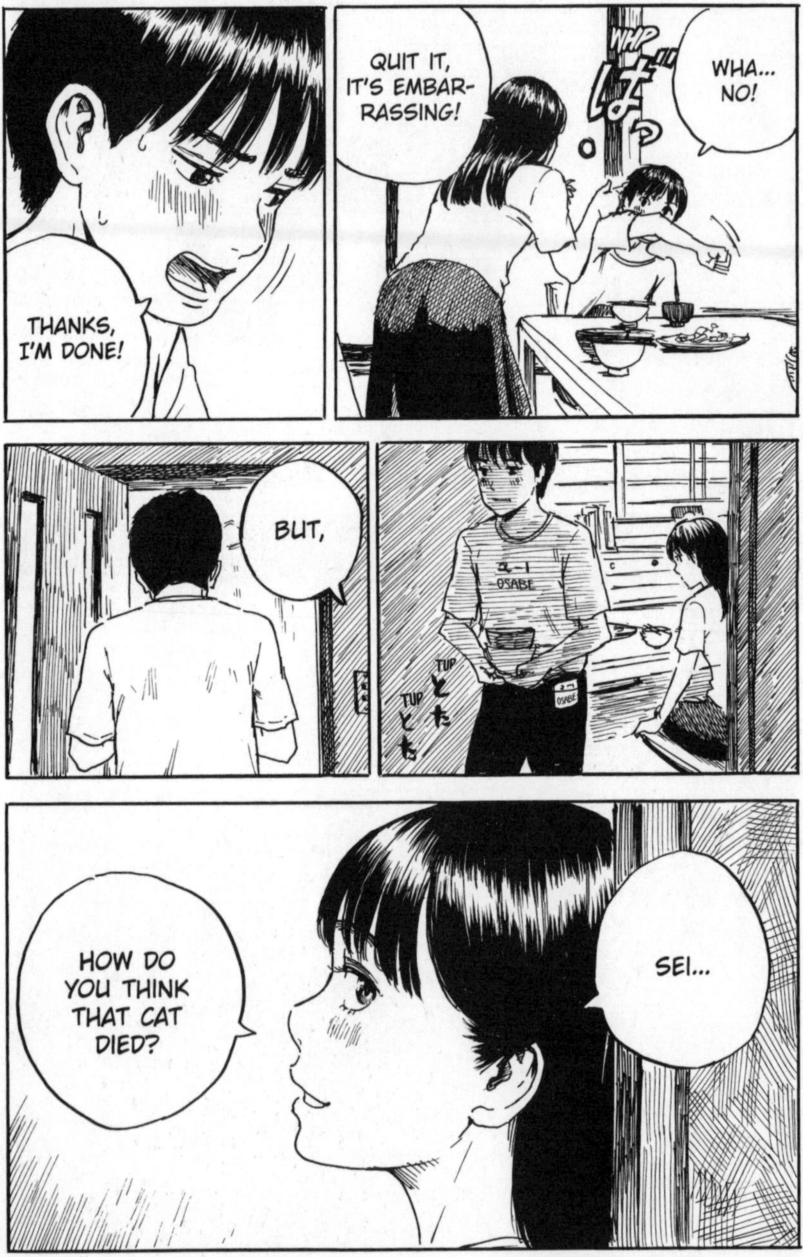
WHA... NO!
WHP
ぱっ
QUIT IT, IT'S EMBARRASSING!
THANKS, I'M DONE!
TUP
とた
TUP
とた
BUT,
SEI...
HOW DO YOU THINK THAT CAT DIED?

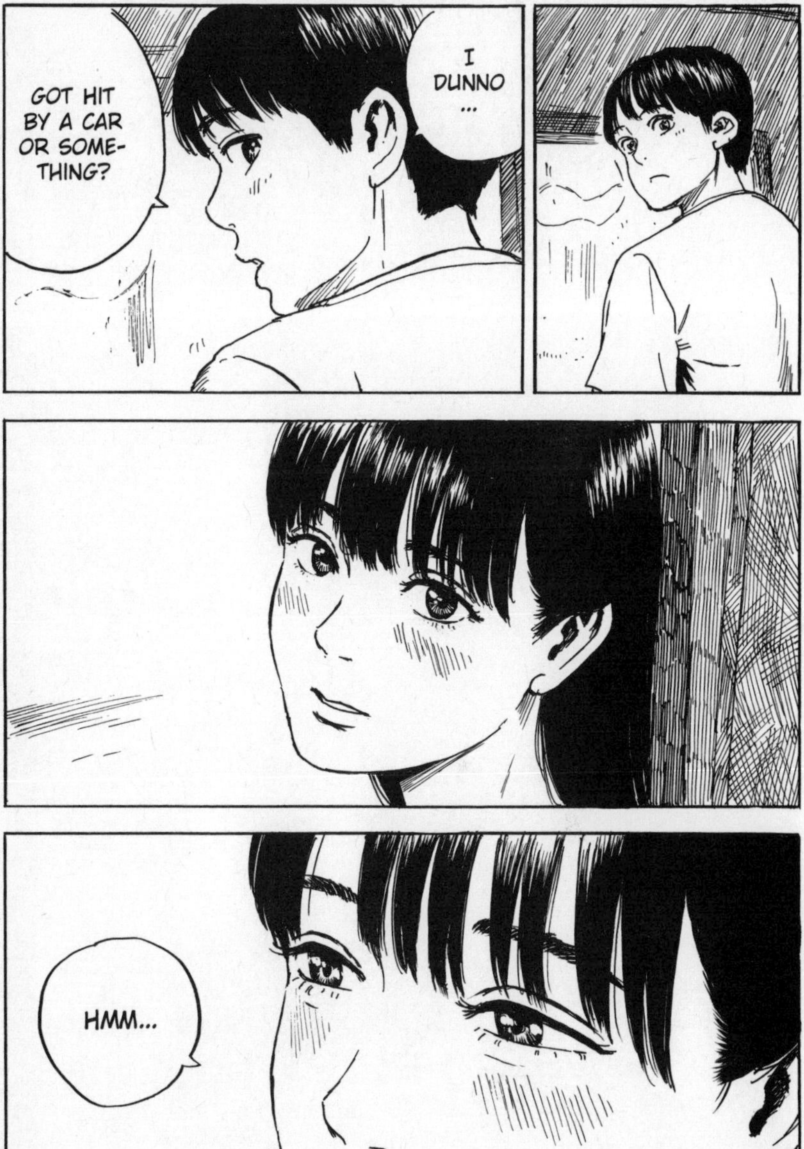
I DUNNO ...
GOT HIT BY A CAR OR SOME-THING?
HMM...

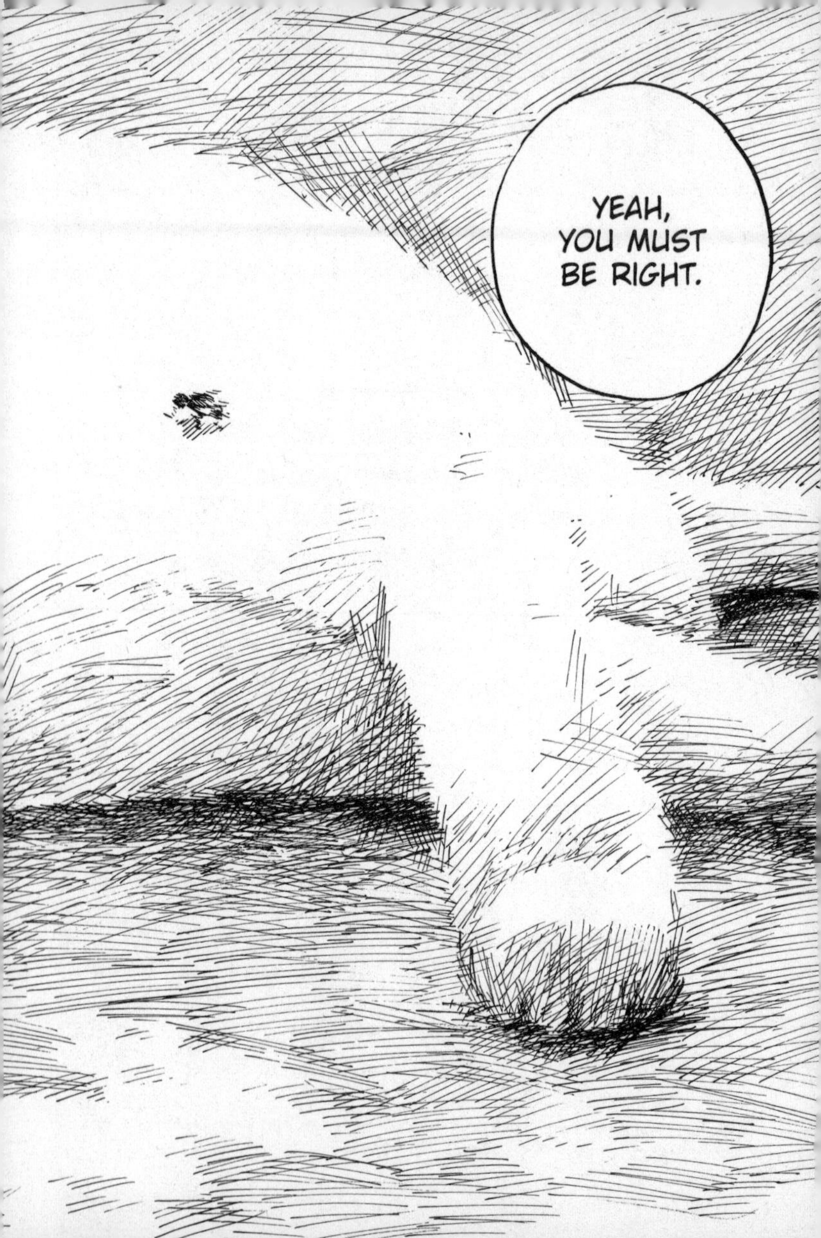
YEAH, YOU MUST BE RIGHT.

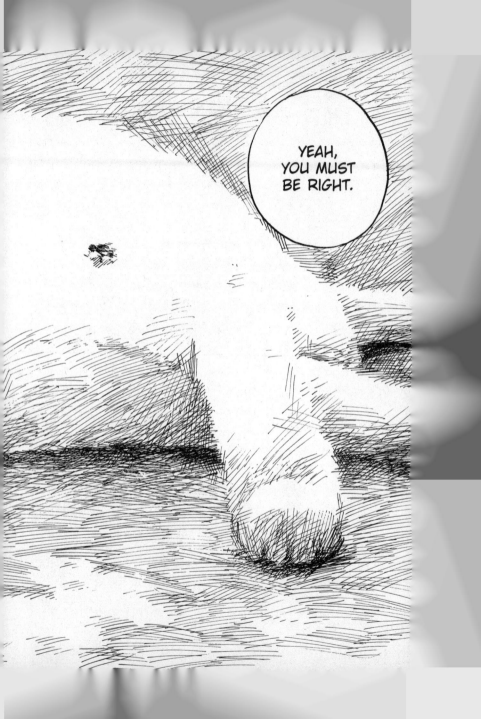

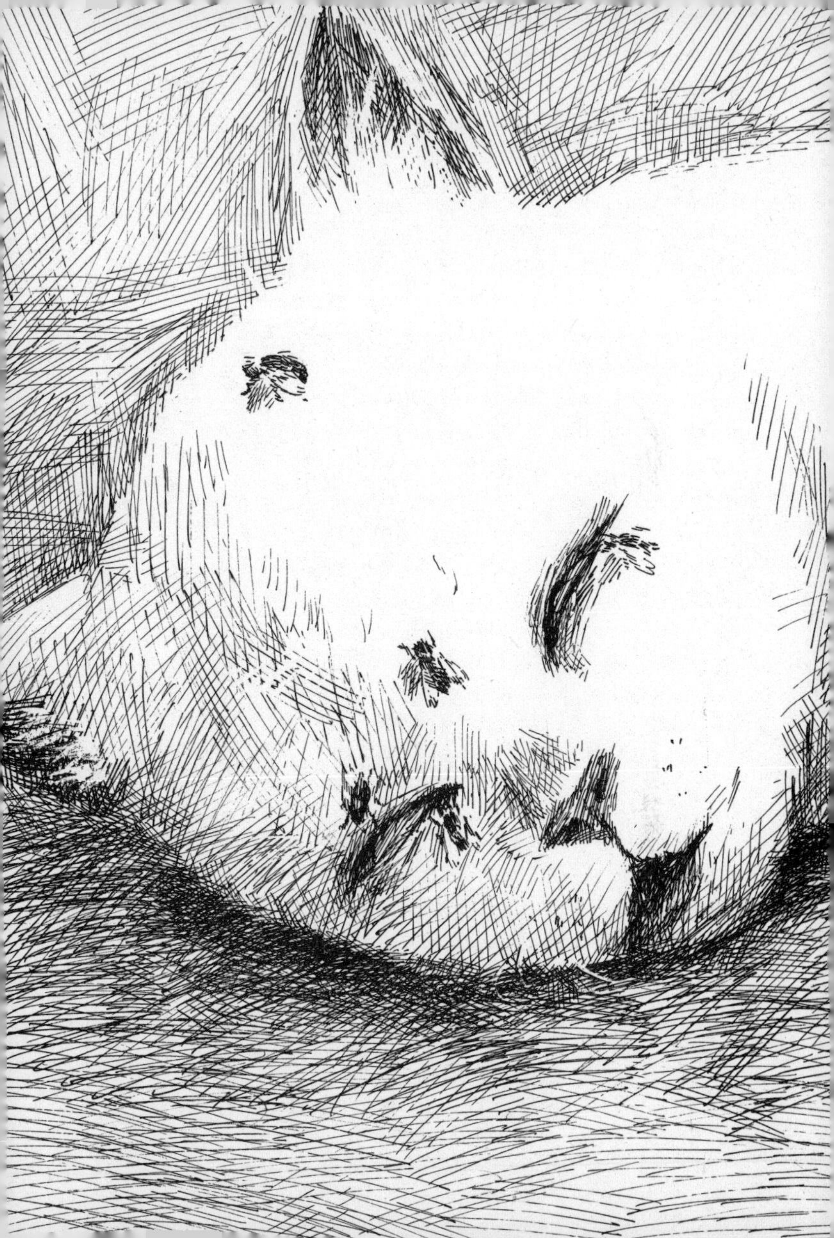

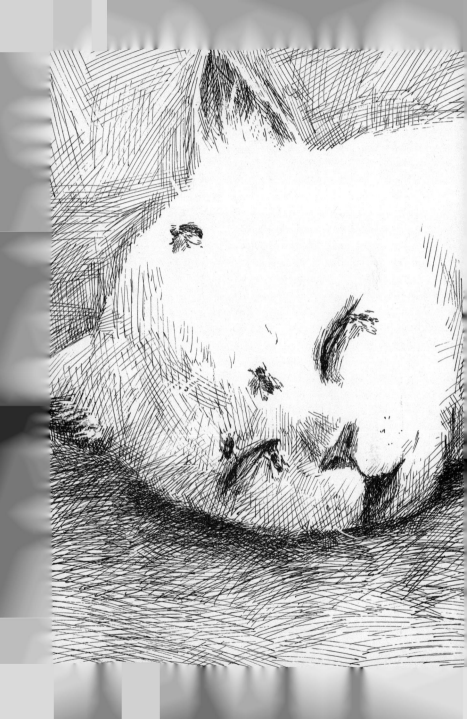

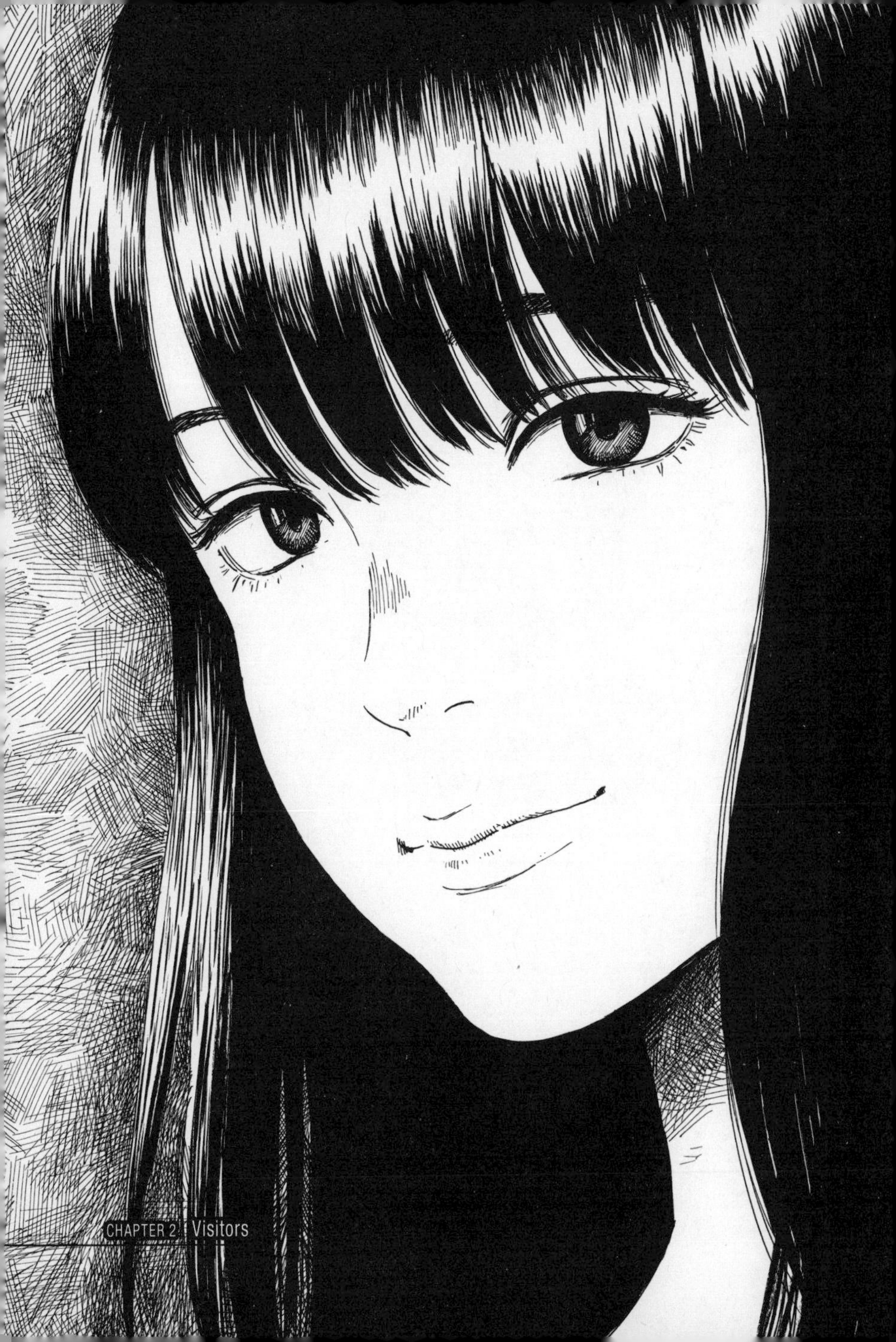
CHAPTER 2 Visitors

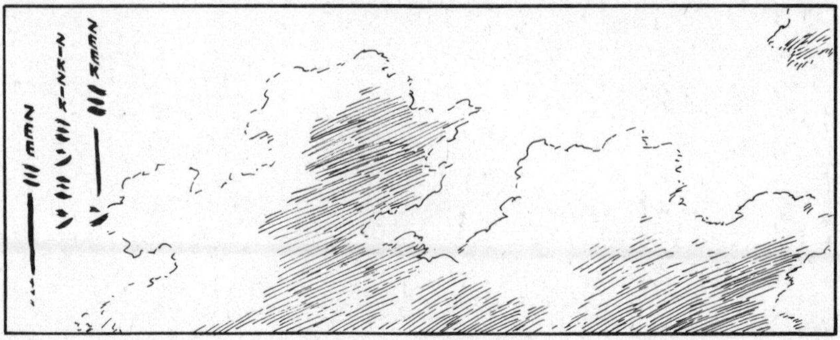
ZEEK ミーーン
ZIKZIK ミンミン
ZEE ミーー…

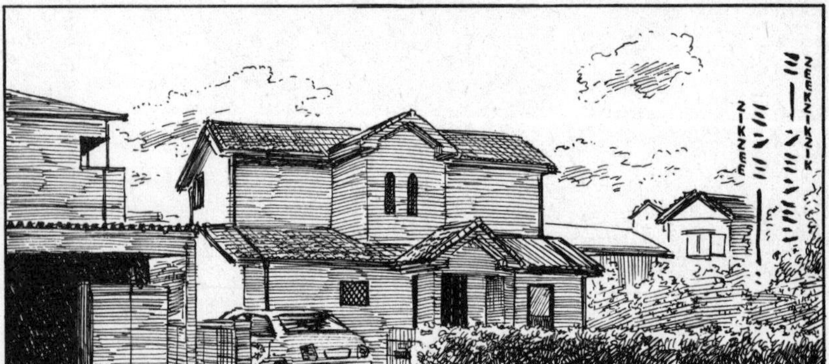
ZEEKZIKZIK ミーンミンミ
ZIKZEE ミンミーー…

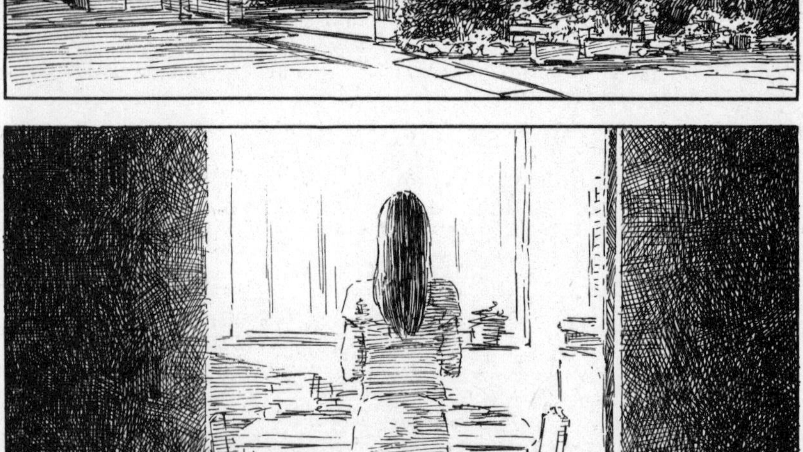

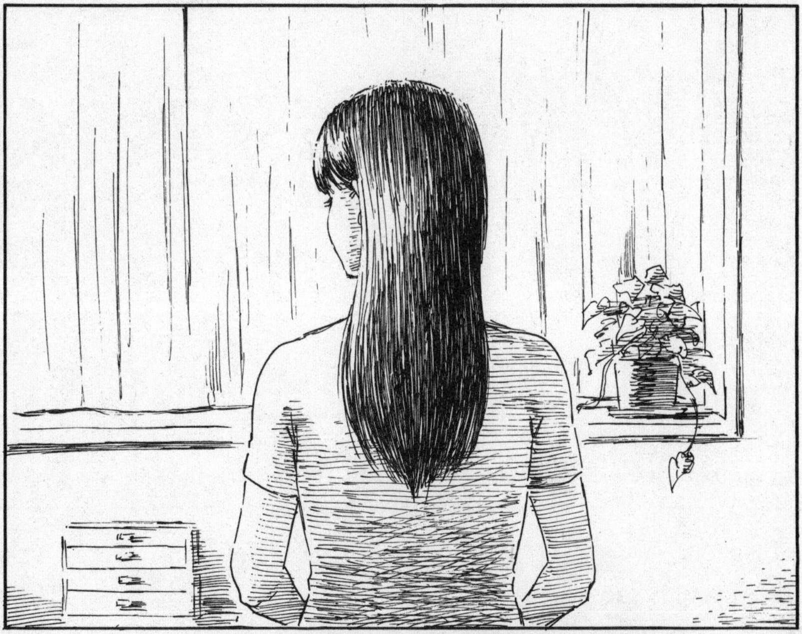

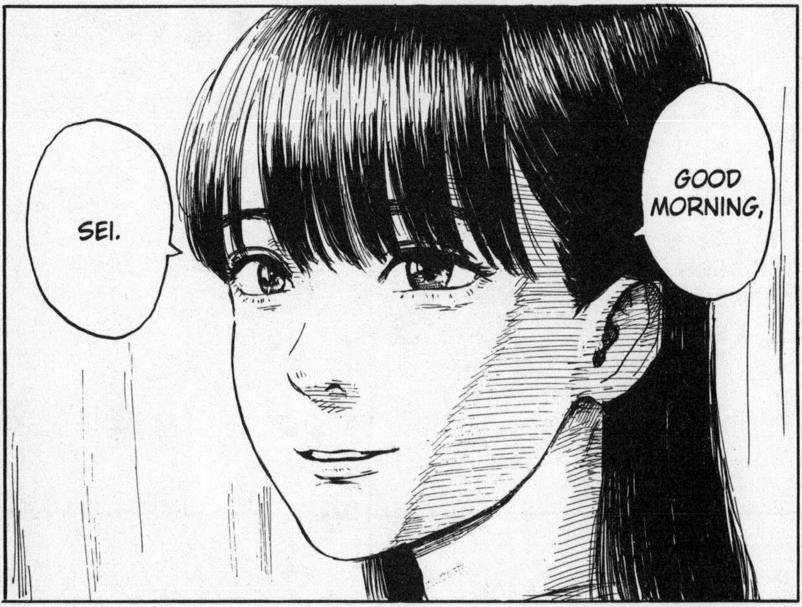
GOOD MORNING,
SEI.

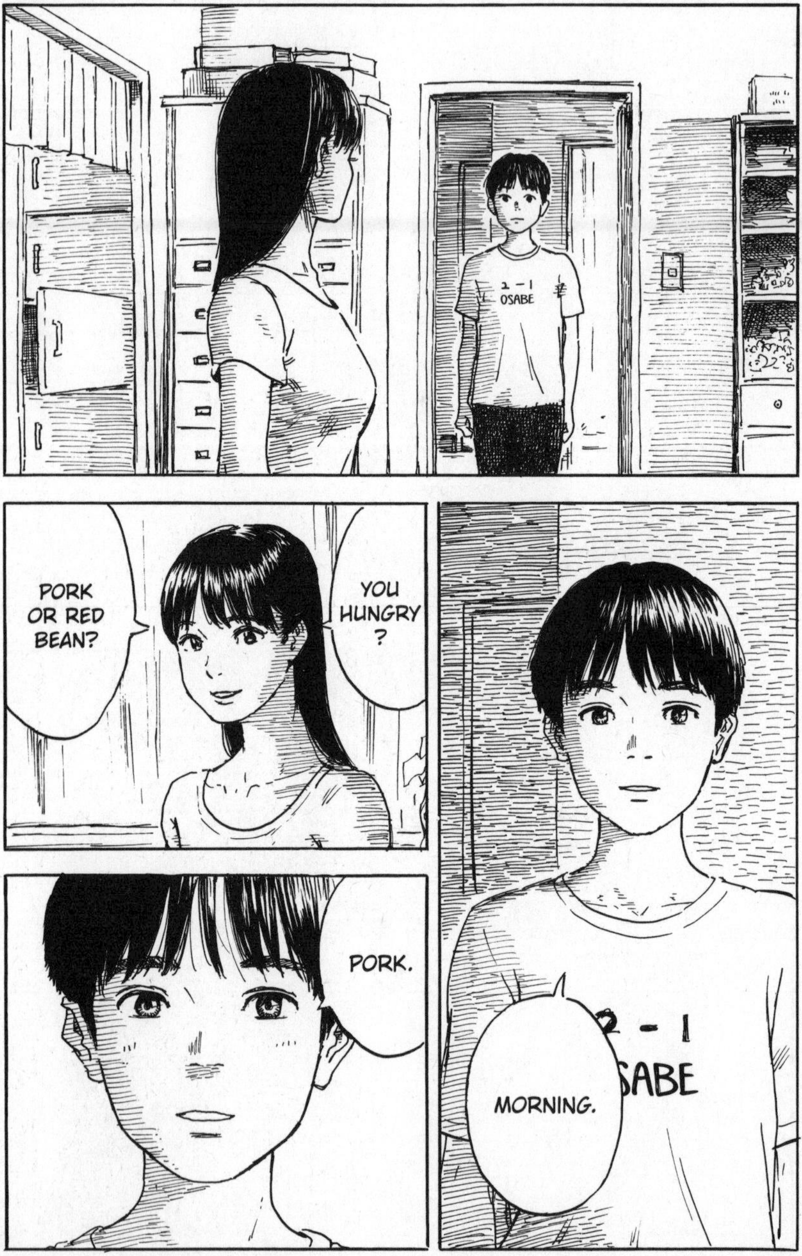
2 - 1
OSABE
MORNING.
2 - 1
SABE
YOU HUNGRY?
PORK OR RED BEAN?
PORK.

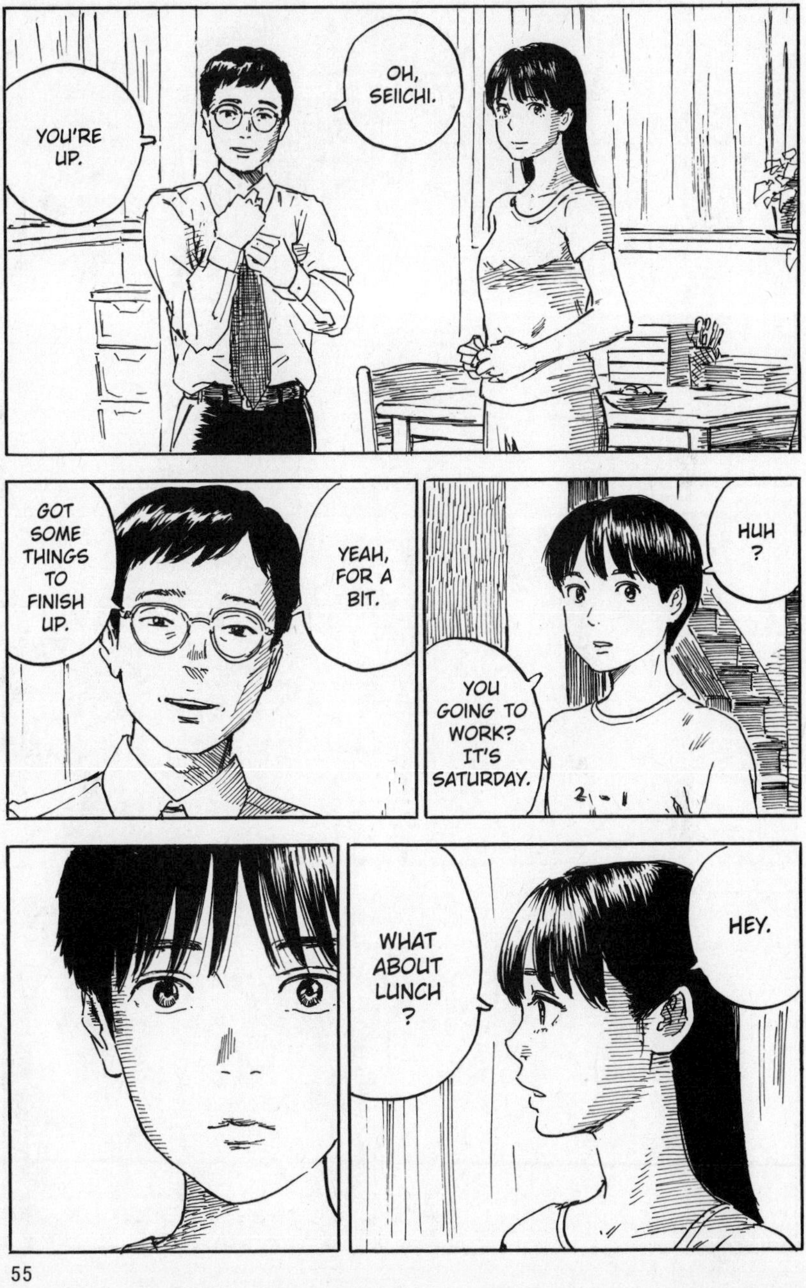
OH, SEIICHI.
YOU'RE UP.
HUH?
YOU GOING TO WORK? IT'S SATURDAY.
YEAH, FOR A BIT.
GOT SOME THINGS TO FINISH UP.
HEY.
WHAT ABOUT LUNCH?

YOUR SISTER AND SHIGE ARE COMING OVER.
AREN'T YOU GOING TO EAT WITH US?
OH RIGHT... WHY DON'T YOU JUST ORDER UDON?
2-1
OSABE
DON'T WORRY, I'LL BE HERE.
OKAY... SURE.
I'LL TAKE CARE OF IT.

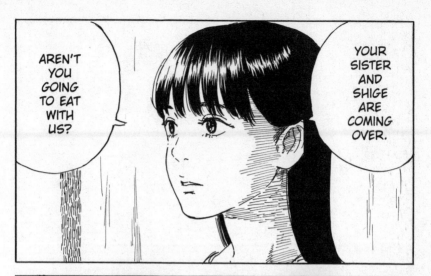

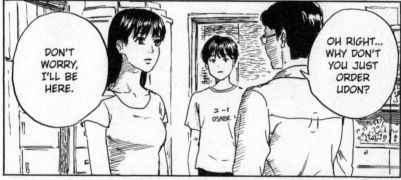

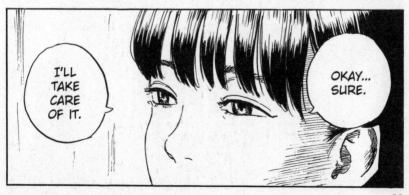

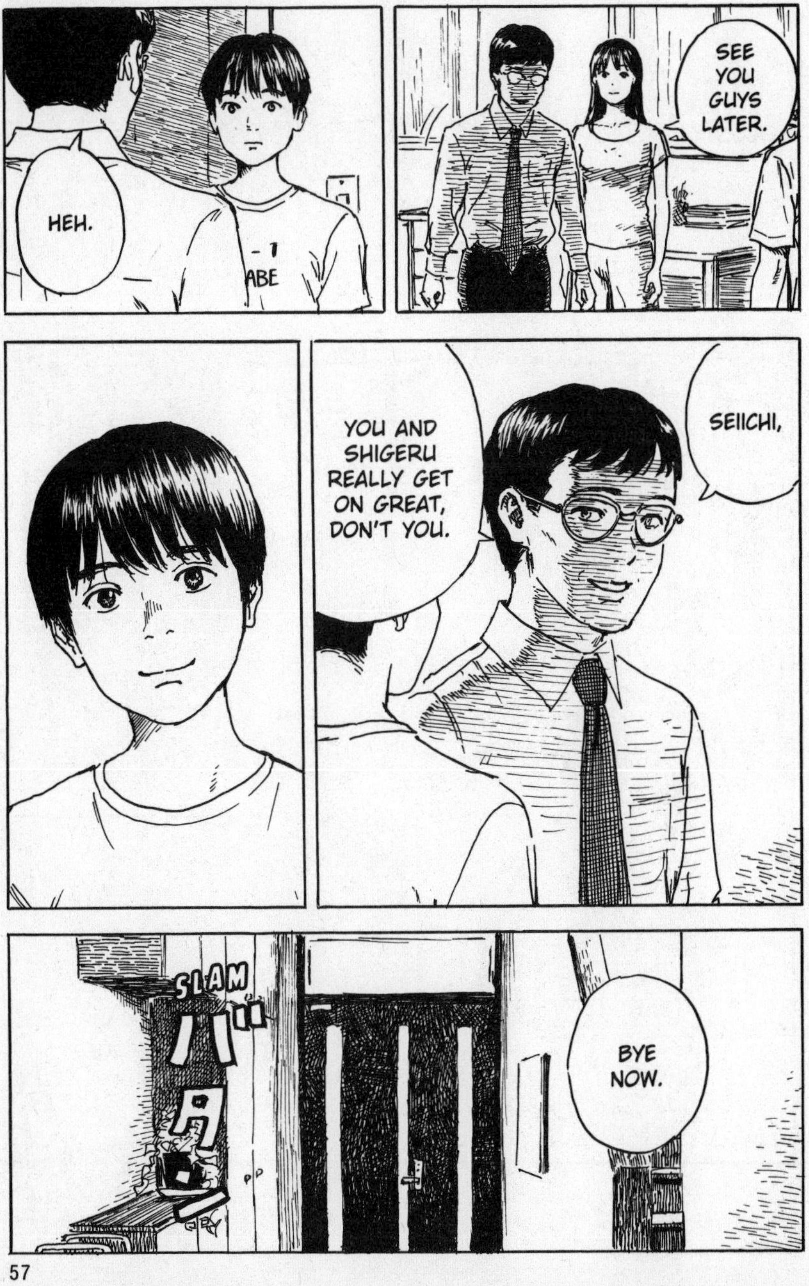
SEE YOU GUYS LATER.
HEH.
ABE
SEIICHI,
YOU AND SHIGERU REALLY GET ON GREAT, DON'T YOU.
BYE NOW.
SLAM

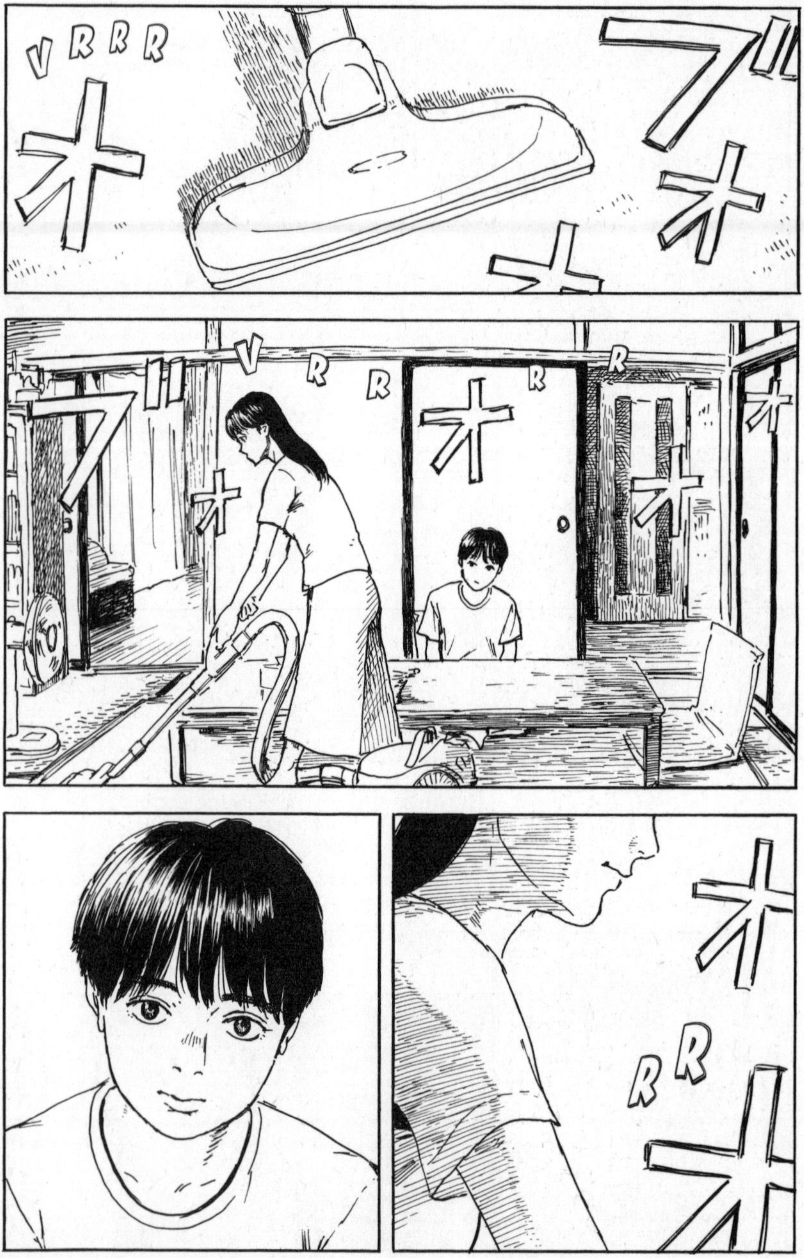
ブオオオ
VRRR
VRRRR
ブオオオオ
オオ
RR

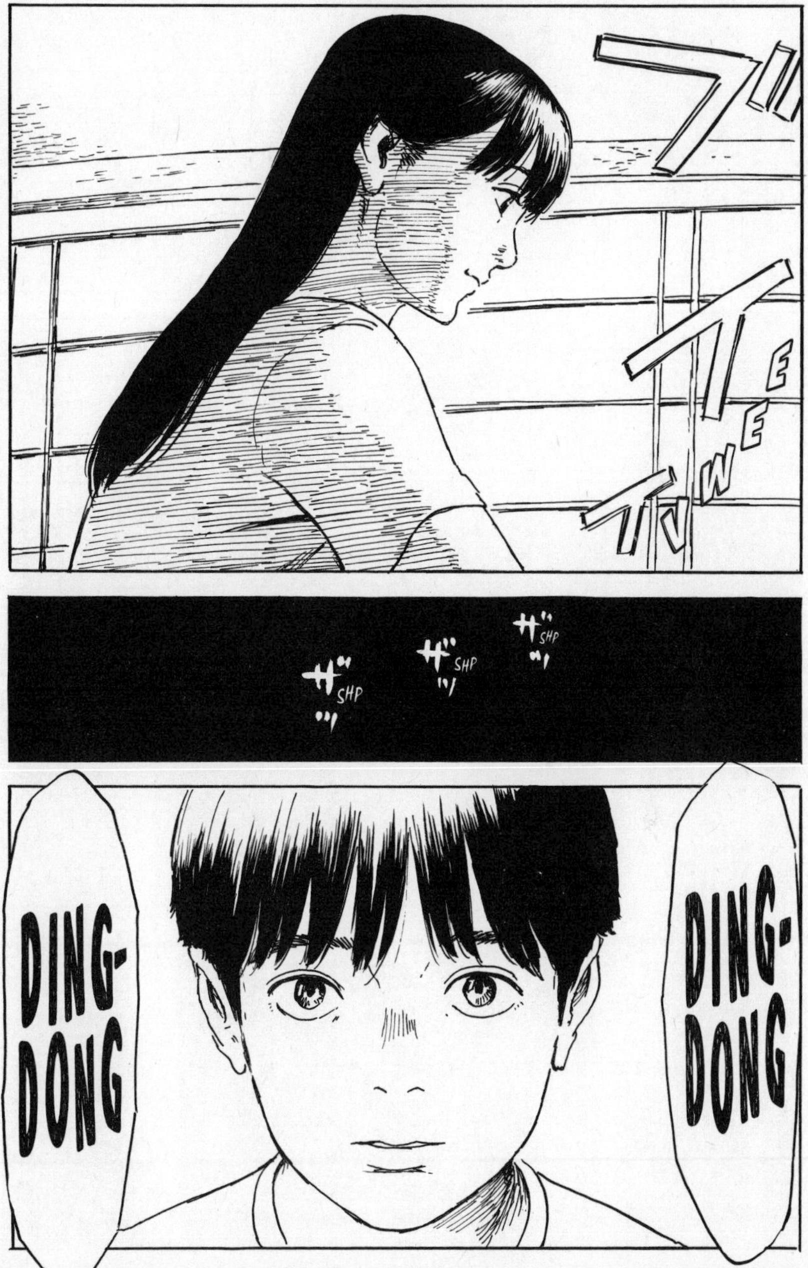
ブイイ
TWEE
ザッ SHP
ザッ SHP
ザッ SHP
DING-DONG
DING-DONG

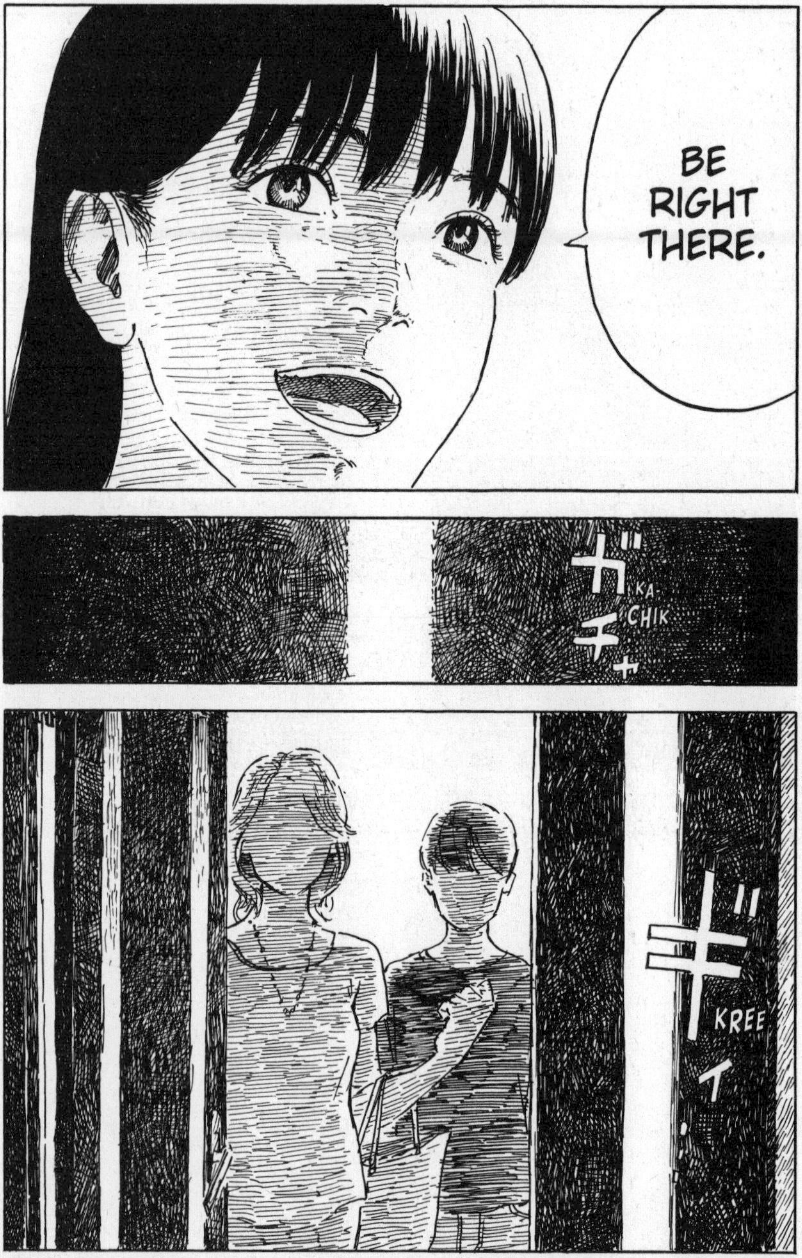
BE RIGHT THERE.
ガチャ
KA CHIK
ギィ
KREE

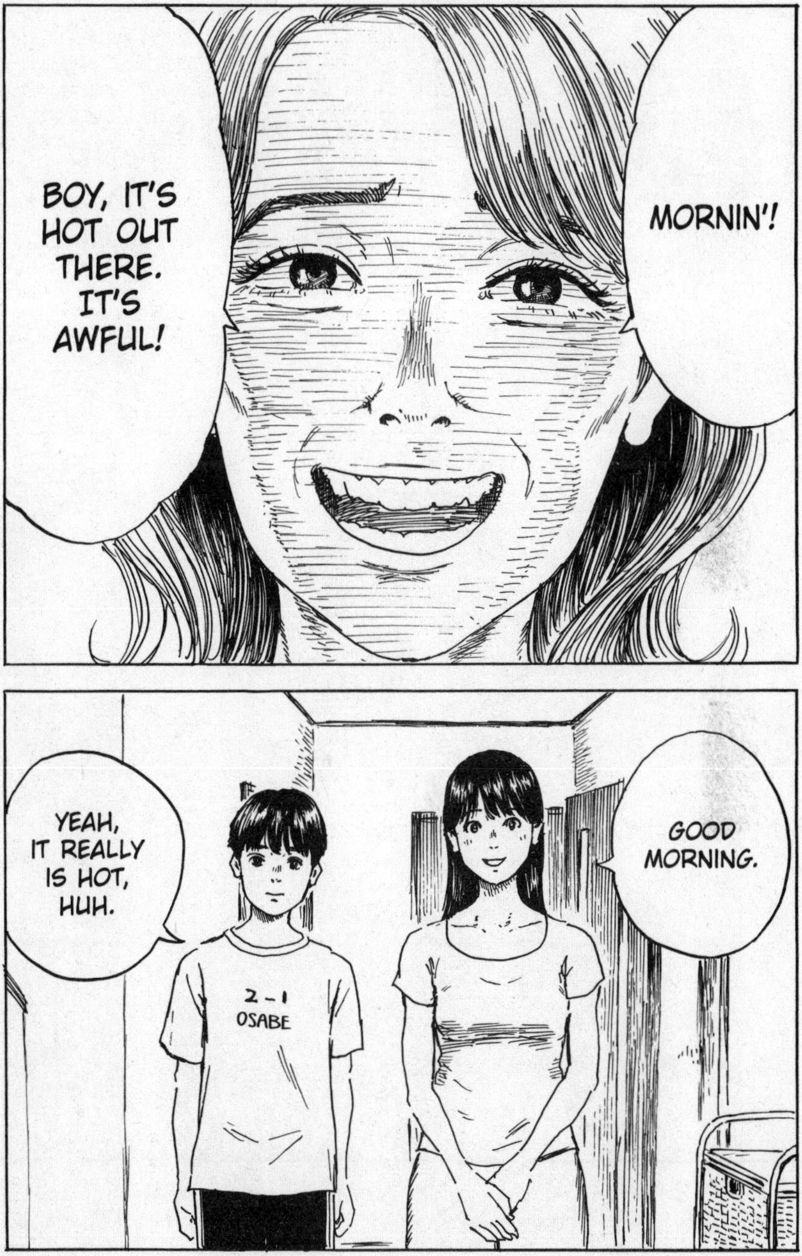
MORNIN'!
BOY, IT'S HOT OUT THERE. IT'S AWFUL!
GOOD MORNING.
2-1 OSABE
YEAH, IT REALLY IS HOT, HUH.

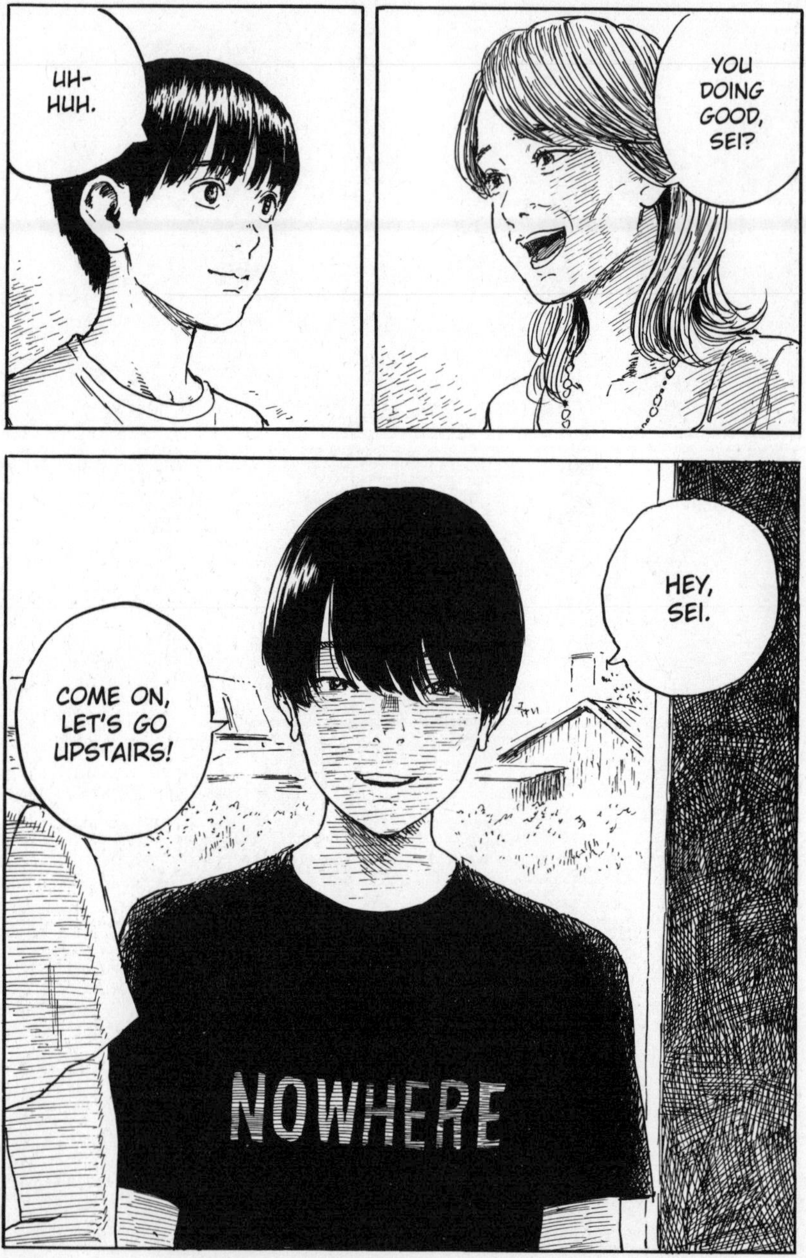
YOU DOING GOOD, SEI?
UH-HUH.
HEY, SEI.
COME ON, LET'S GO UPSTAIRS!
NOWHERE

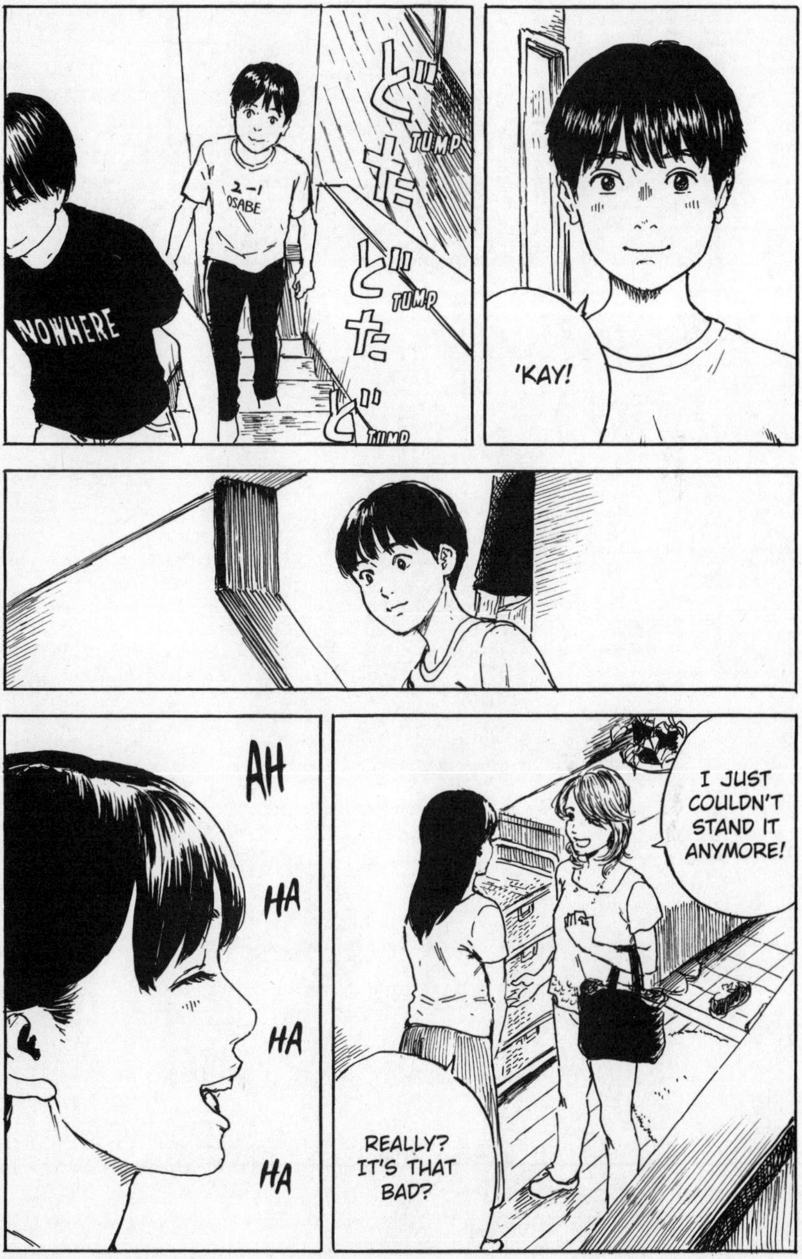
'KAY!
ど TUMP
だ
ど TUMP
だ
ど TUMP
2-1
OSABE
NOWHERE
I JUST COULDN'T STAND IT ANYMORE!
REALLY? IT'S THAT BAD?
AH
HA
HA
HA

ズン♪
ズン♪
ズン♪
ズン♪
ズン♪
ズン♪

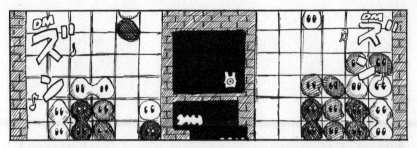

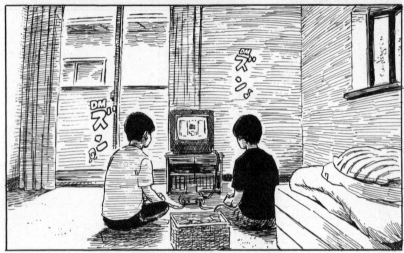

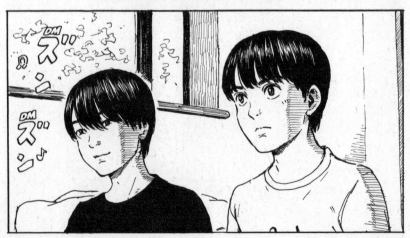

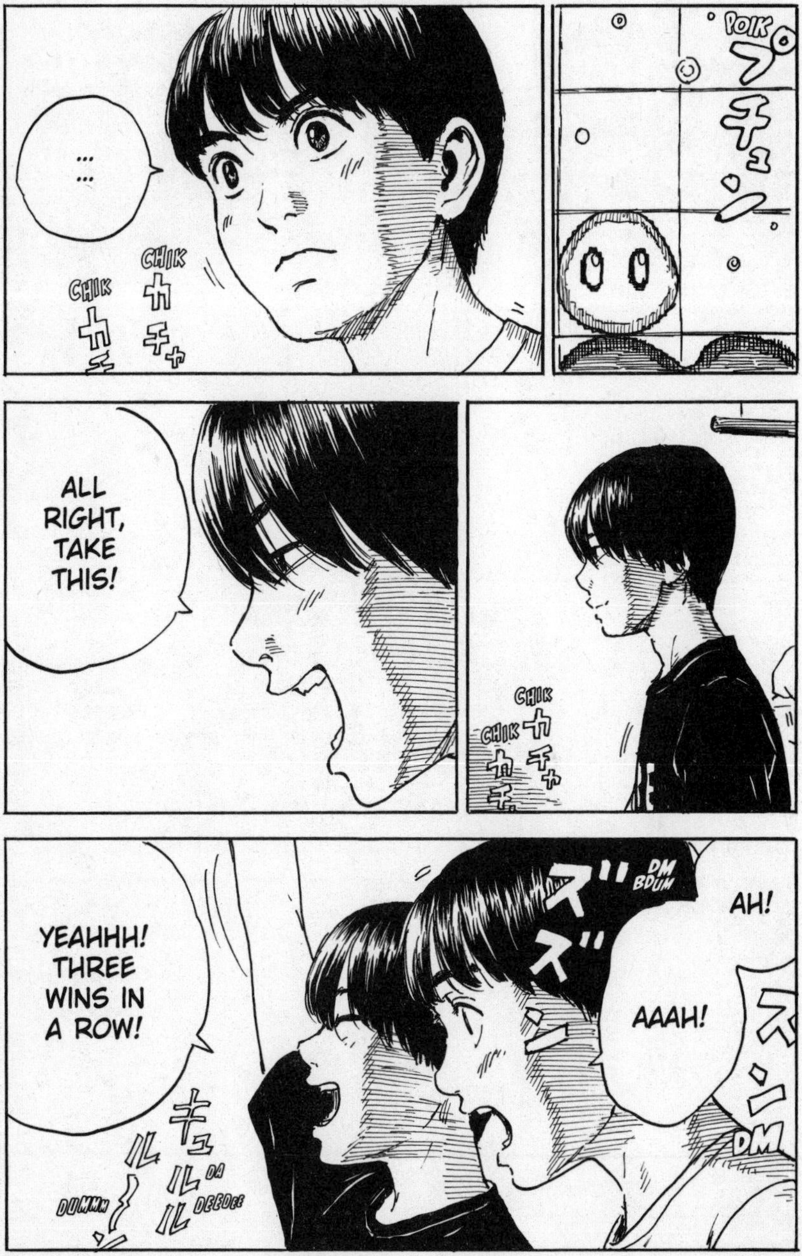
POIK
プチュン
……
……
CHIK
カチャ
CHIK
カチャ
CHIK
カチャ
CHIK
カチャ
ALL RIGHT, TAKE THIS!
AH!
AAAH!
スン
DM
DM BDUM
ズズ
YEAHHH! THREE WINS IN A ROW!
キュルルル
DA DEEDEE
DUMMM

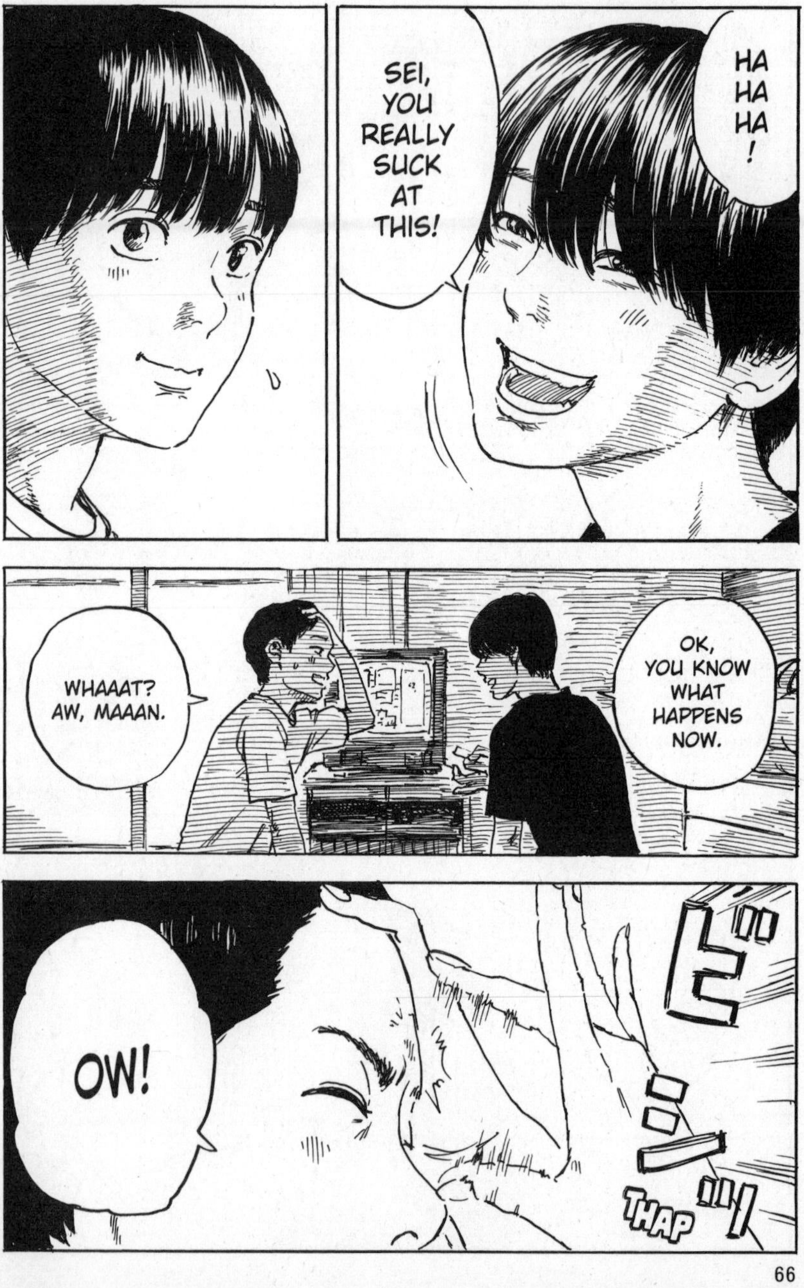
HA HA HA!
SEI, YOU REALLY SUCK AT THIS!
OK, YOU KNOW WHAT HAPPENS NOW.
WHAAAT? AW, MAAAN.
THAP
OW!

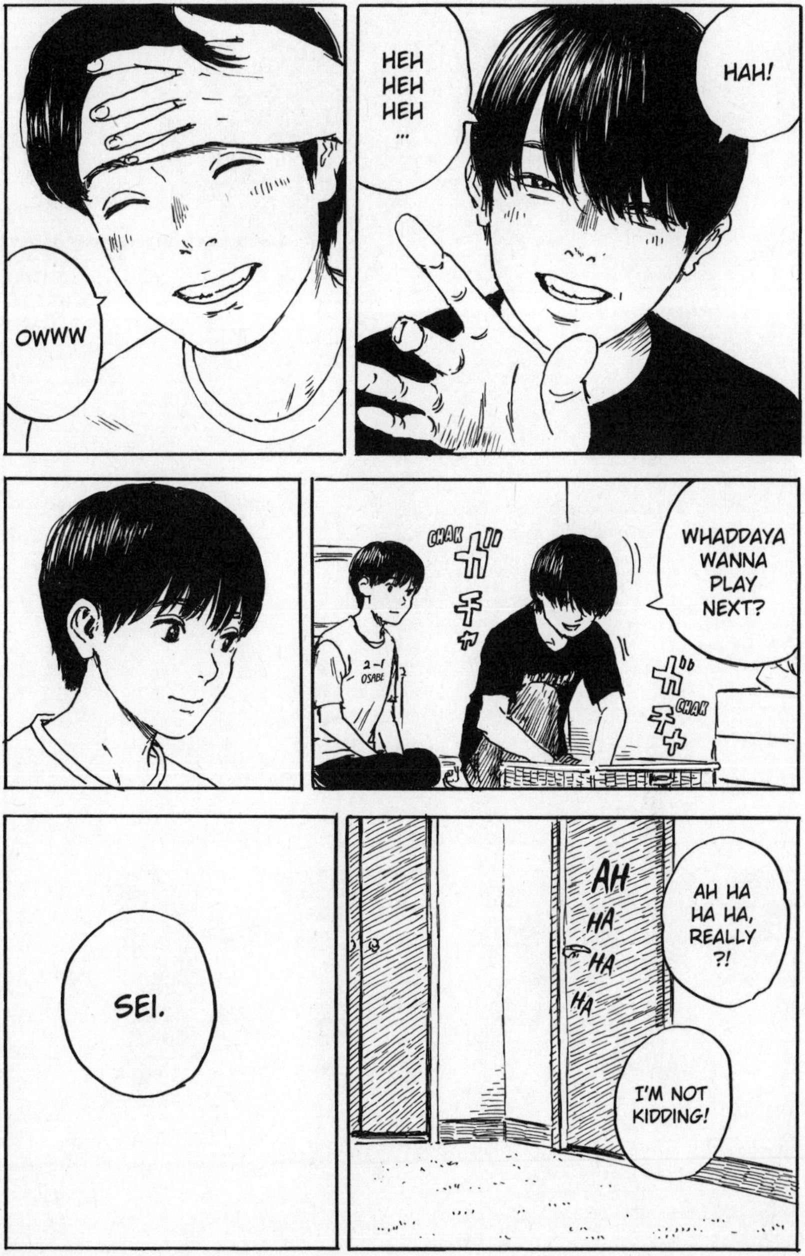
HAH!
HEH HEH HEH ...
OWWW
WHADDAYA WANNA PLAY NEXT?
CHAK ガチャ
CHAK ガチャ
2-1 OSABE
AH HA HA HA, REALLY ?!
AH HA HA HA
I'M NOT KIDDING!
SEI.

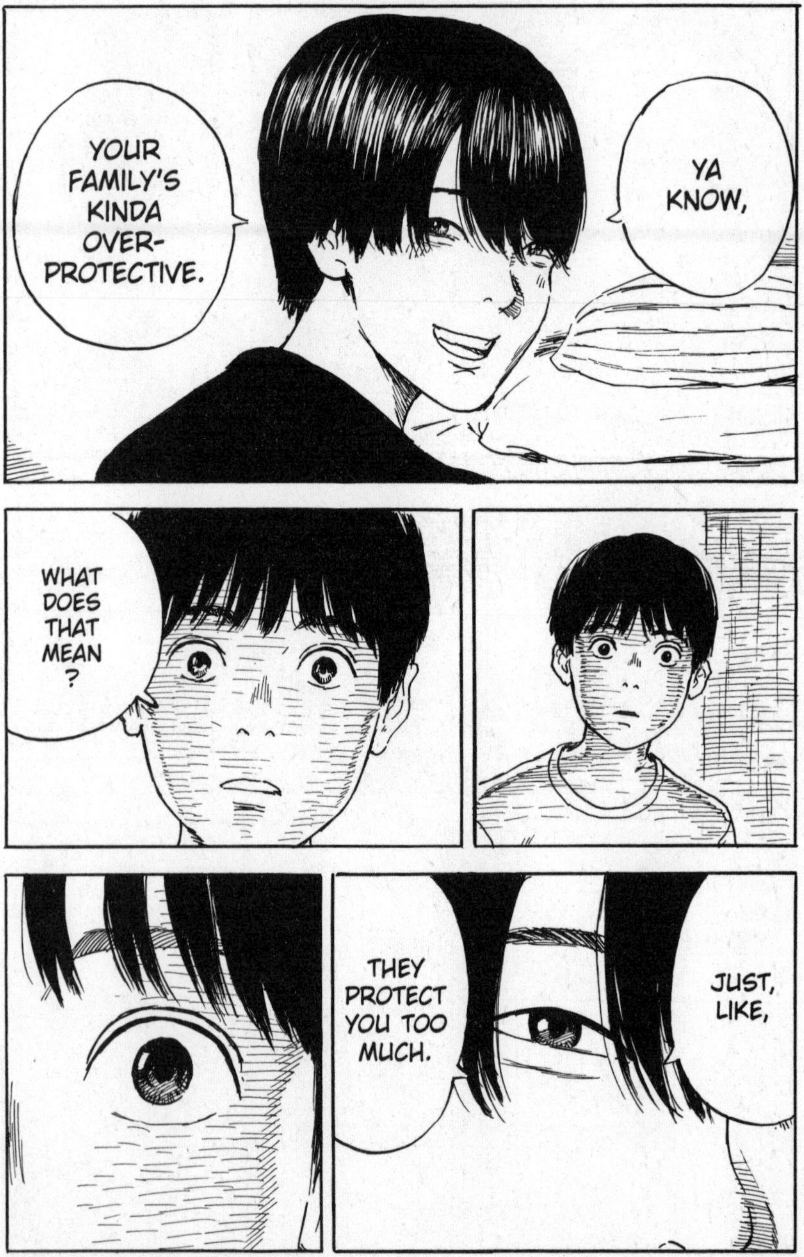
YA KNOW,
YOUR FAMILY'S KINDA OVER-PROTECTIVE.
WHAT DOES THAT MEAN ?
JUST, LIKE,
THEY PROTECT YOU TOO MUCH.

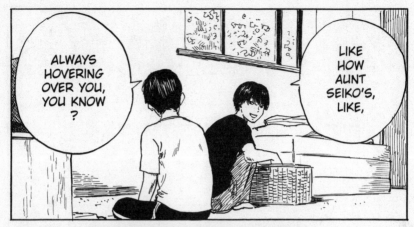

LIKE HOW AUNT SEIKO'S, LIKE,
ALWAYS HOVERING OVER YOU, YOU KNOW ?
SEI.
Y-
YOU THINK SO?
YUP.
I MEAN,

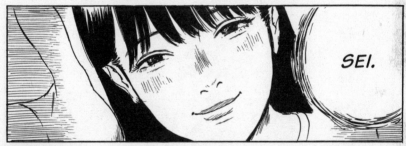

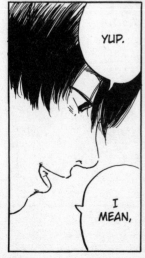

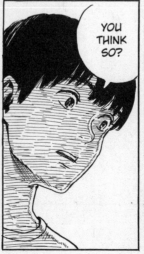

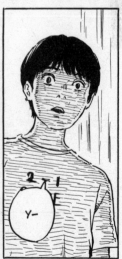

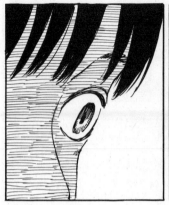

REMEMBER IN KINDERGARTEN?

HOW AUNT SEIKO STOOD THERE IN THE BACK OF THE ROOM EVERY DAY?

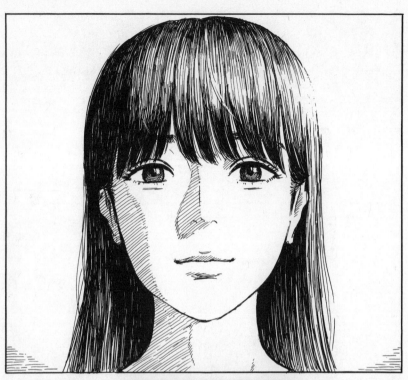

WELL, SHE WAS WORRIED ABOUT ME...

I WAS ALWAYS CRYING AND SAYING I DIDN'T WANT TO GO...

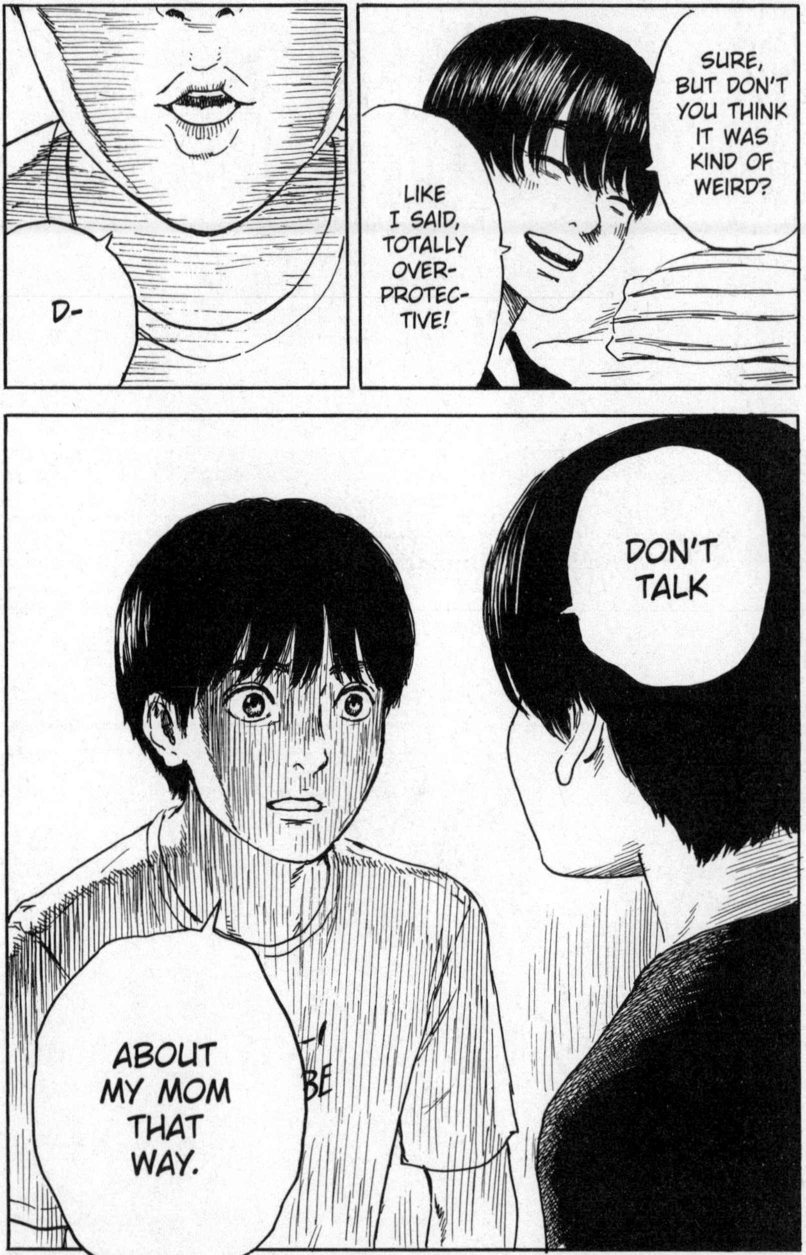
SURE, BUT DON'T YOU THINK IT WAS KIND OF WEIRD?
LIKE I SAID, TOTALLY OVER-PROTECTIVE!
D-
DON'T TALK
ABOUT MY MOM THAT WAY.

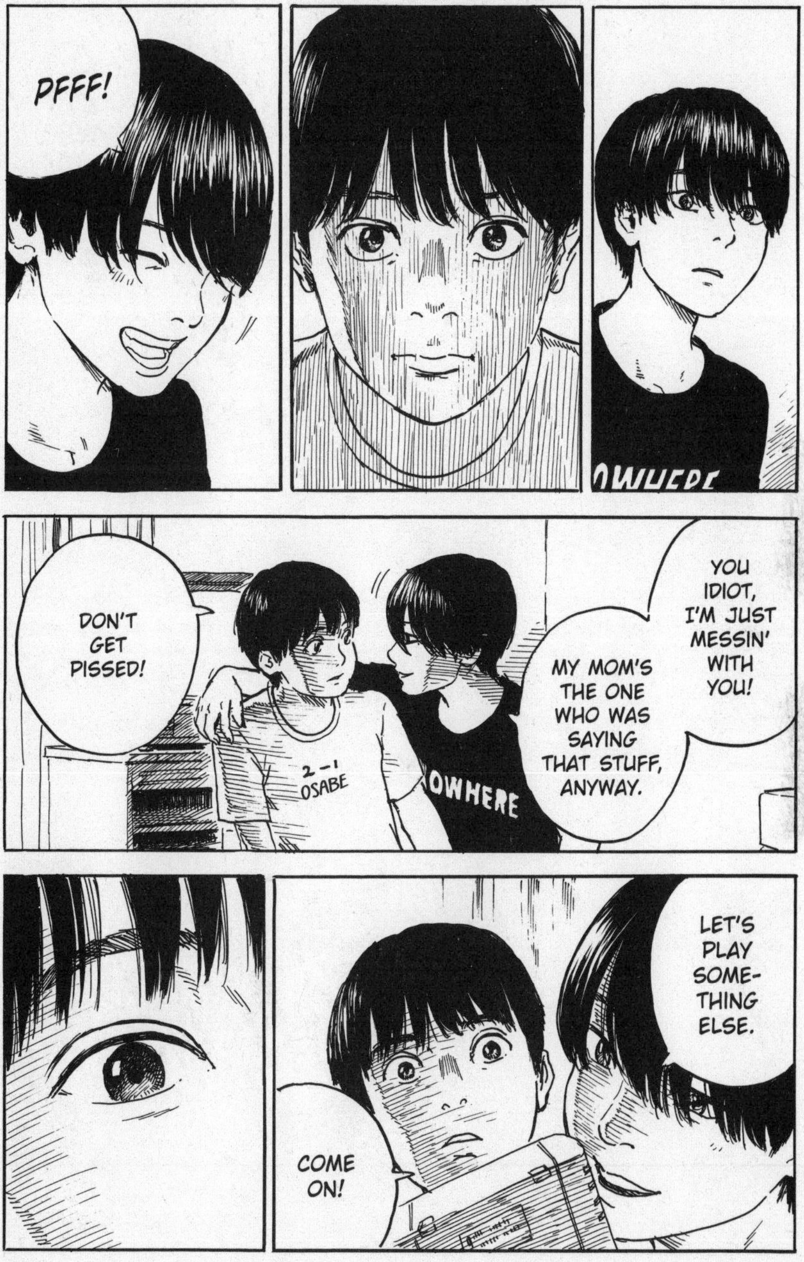
PFFF!
YOU IDIOT, I'M JUST MESSIN' WITH YOU!
MY MOM'S THE ONE WHO WAS SAYING THAT STUFF, ANYWAY.
OWHERE
2-1 OSABE
DON'T GET PISSED!
LET'S PLAY SOME-THING ELSE.
COME ON!

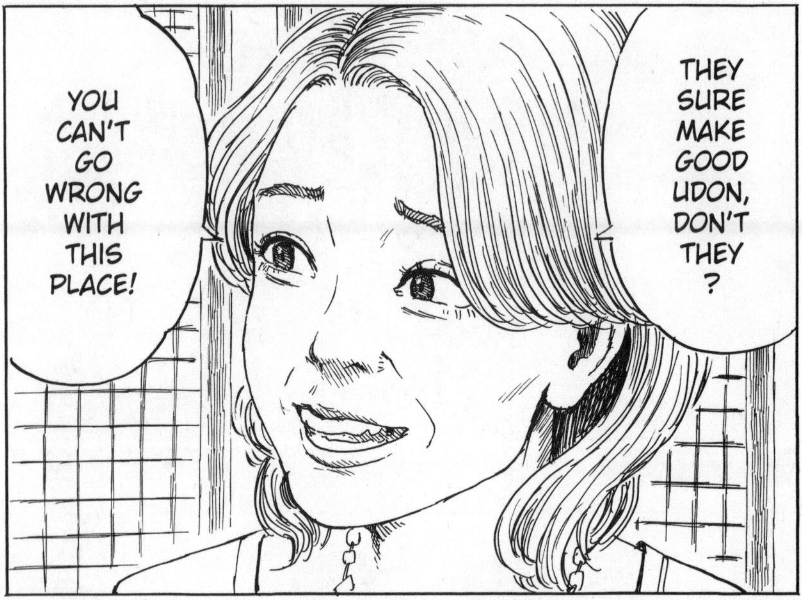
THEY SURE MAKE GOOD UDON, DON'T THEY?
YOU CAN'T GO WRONG WITH THIS PLACE!

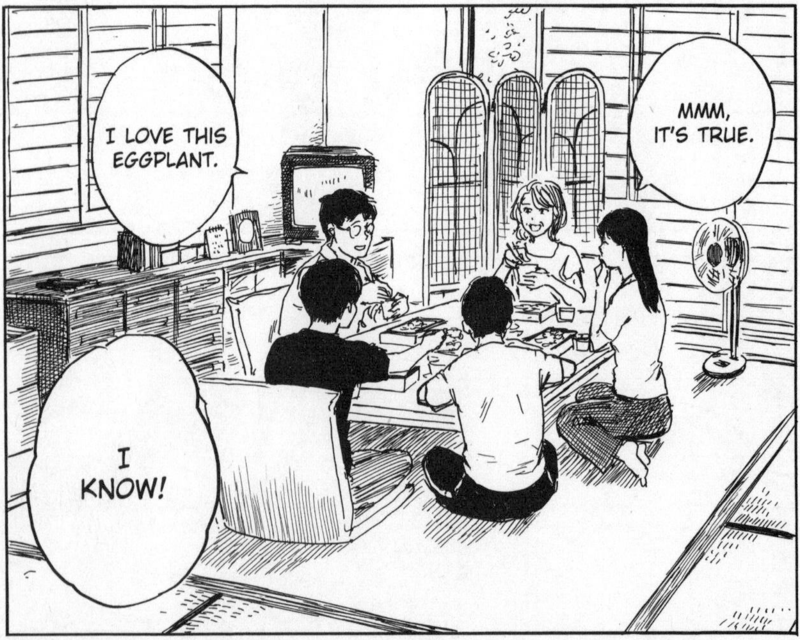
MMM, IT'S TRUE.
I LOVE THIS EGGPLANT.
I KNOW!

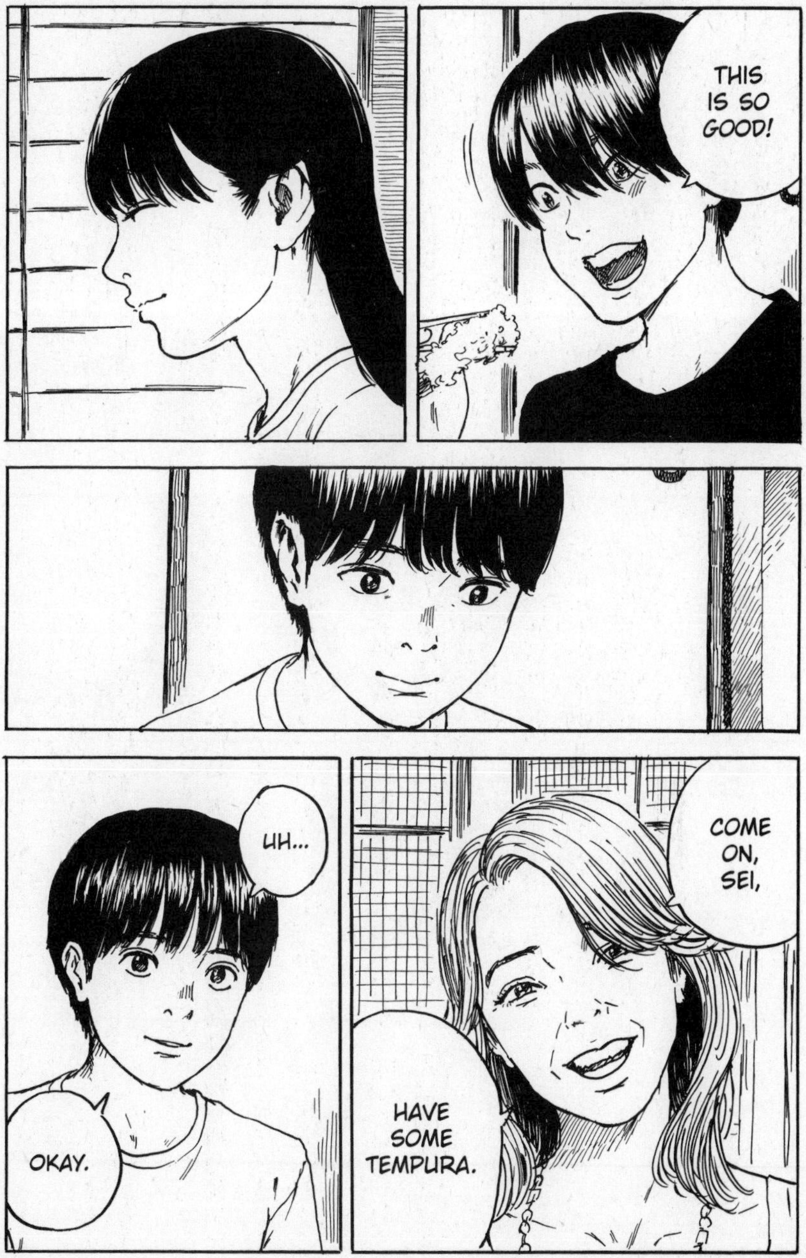
THIS IS SO GOOD!
COME ON, SEI,
HAVE SOME TEMPURA.
UH...
OKAY.

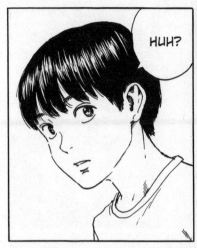

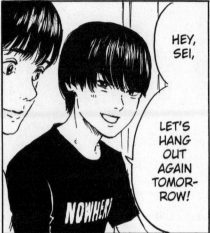

HEY, SEI,
LET'S HANG OUT AGAIN TOMORROW!
HUH?
IT'S OKAY, RIGHT, MOM?
BUT YOU'VE BEEN HERE EVERY WEEK THIS MONTH!
SEI WAS THE ONE WHO SAID HE WANTED TO HANG OUT!
...OH,
IT'S TOTALLY FINE.

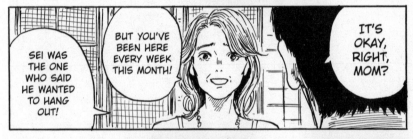

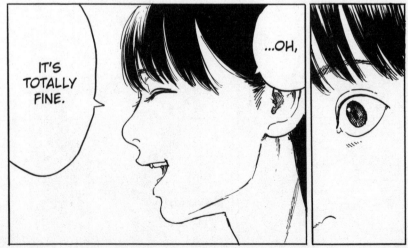

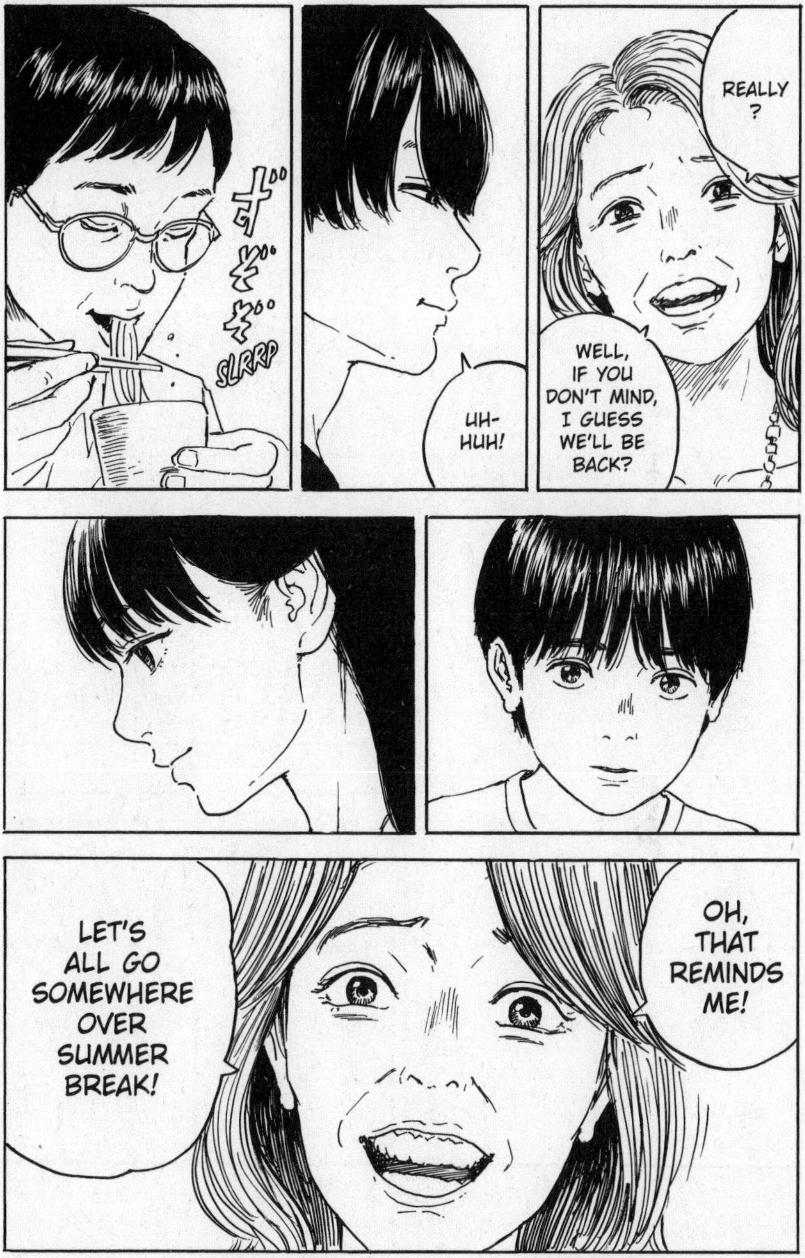
REALLY?
WELL, IF YOU DON'T MIND, I GUESS WE'LL BE BACK?
UH-HUH!
SLRRP
OH, THAT REMINDS ME!
LET'S ALL GO SOMEWHERE OVER SUMMER BREAK!

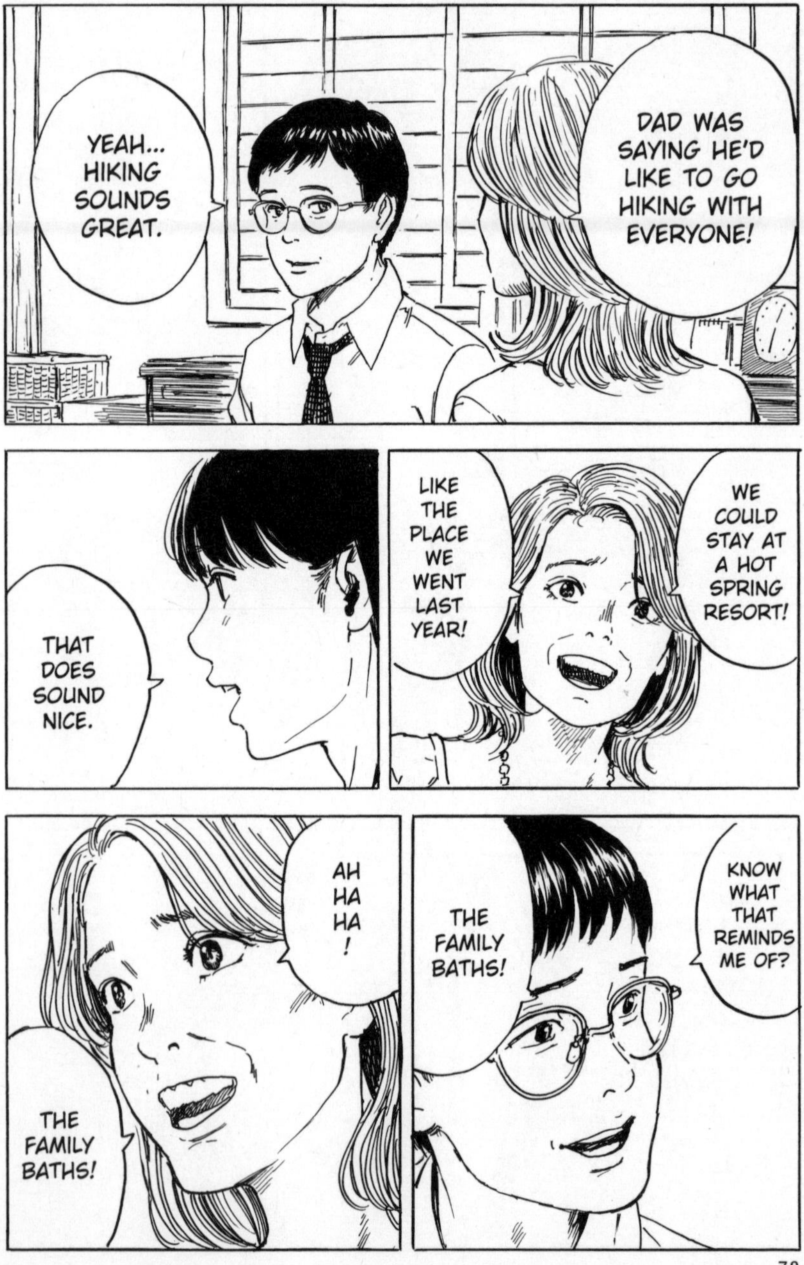
DAD WAS SAYING HE'D LIKE TO GO HIKING WITH EVERYONE!
YEAH... HIKING SOUNDS GREAT.
WE COULD STAY AT A HOT SPRING RESORT!
LIKE THE PLACE WE WENT LAST YEAR!
THAT DOES SOUND NICE.
KNOW WHAT THAT REMINDS ME OF?
THE FAMILY BATHS!
AH HA HA!
THE FAMILY BATHS!

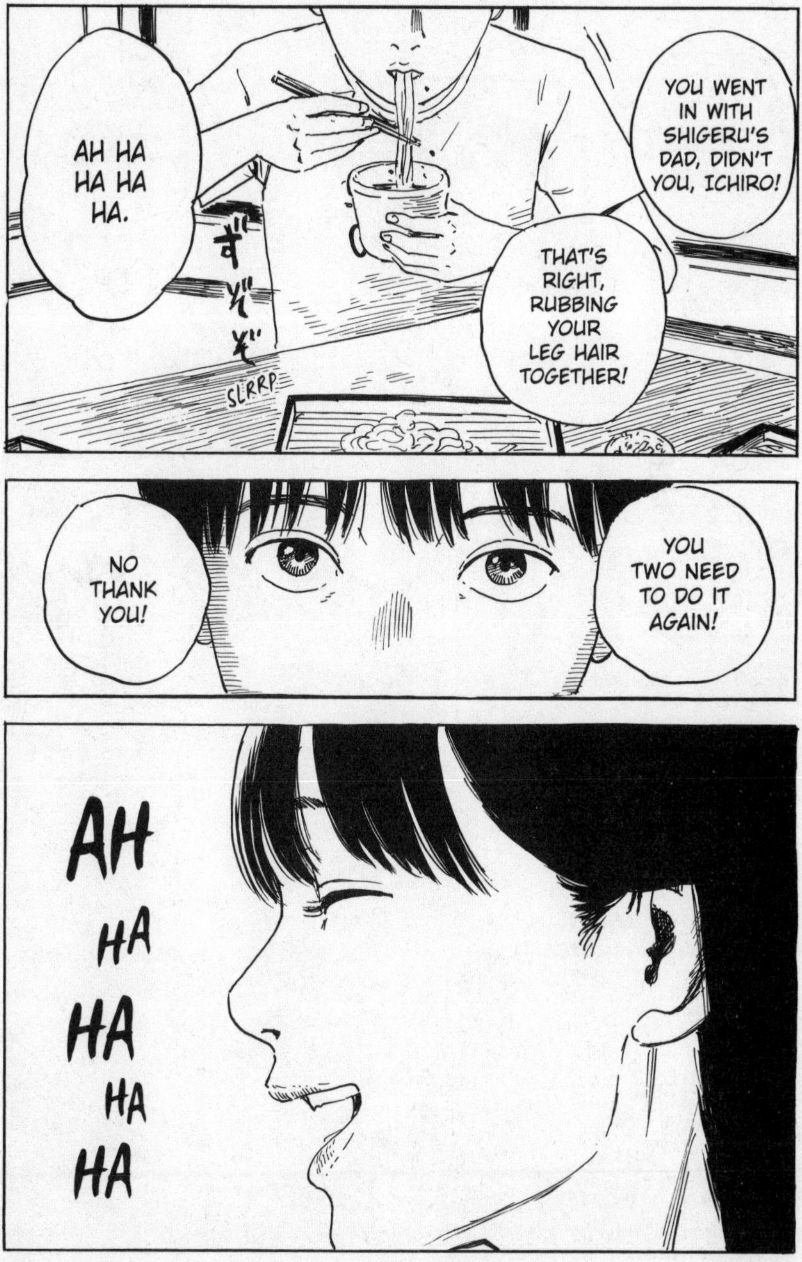
YOU WENT IN WITH SHIGERU'S DAD, DIDN'T YOU, ICHIRO!
THAT'S RIGHT, RUBBING YOUR LEG HAIR TOGETHER!
AH HA HA HA HA.
ずぞぞ
SLRRP
YOU TWO NEED TO DO IT AGAIN!
NO THANK YOU!
AH HA HA HA HA

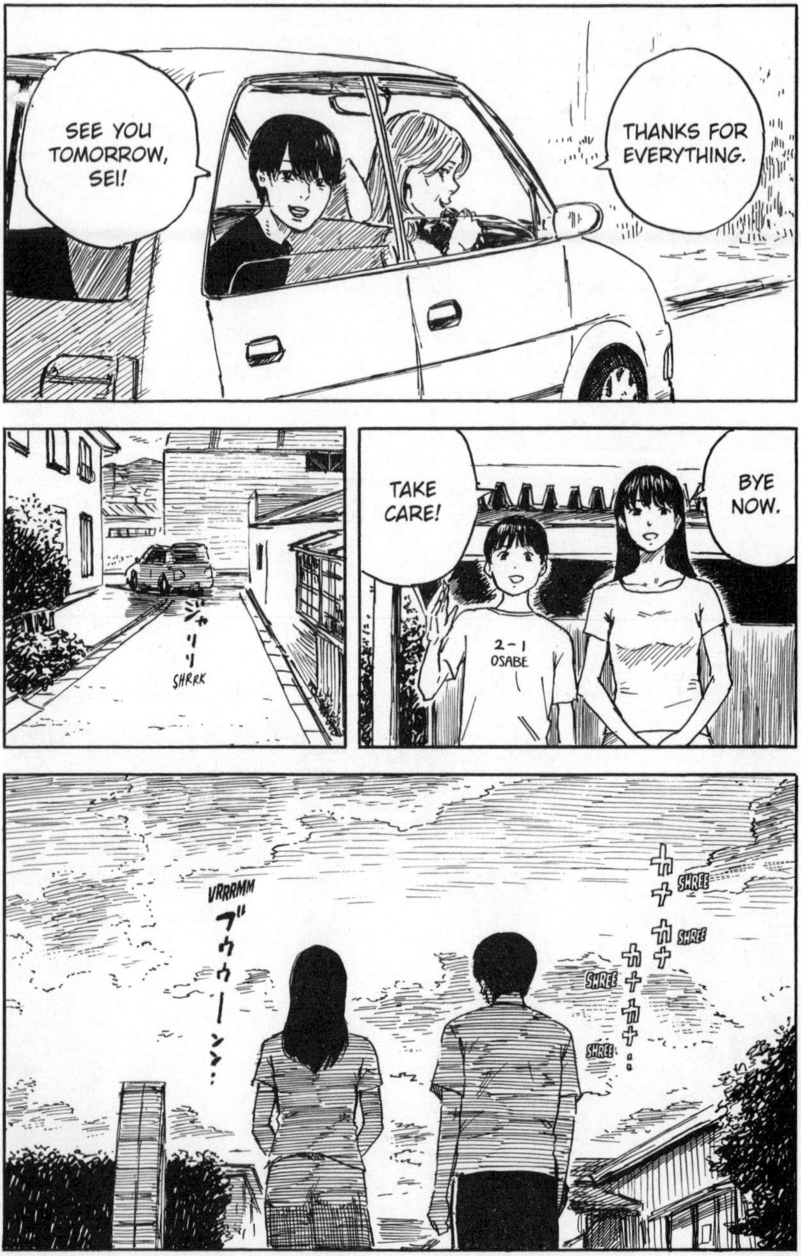
THANKS FOR EVERYTHING.
SEE YOU TOMORROW, SEI!
BYE NOW.
TAKE CARE!
2-1 OSABE
ジャリリ
SHRRK
カナ
SHREE
カナ
SHREE
カナカナカナ…
SHREE
SHREE
VRRRMM
ブウーーン…

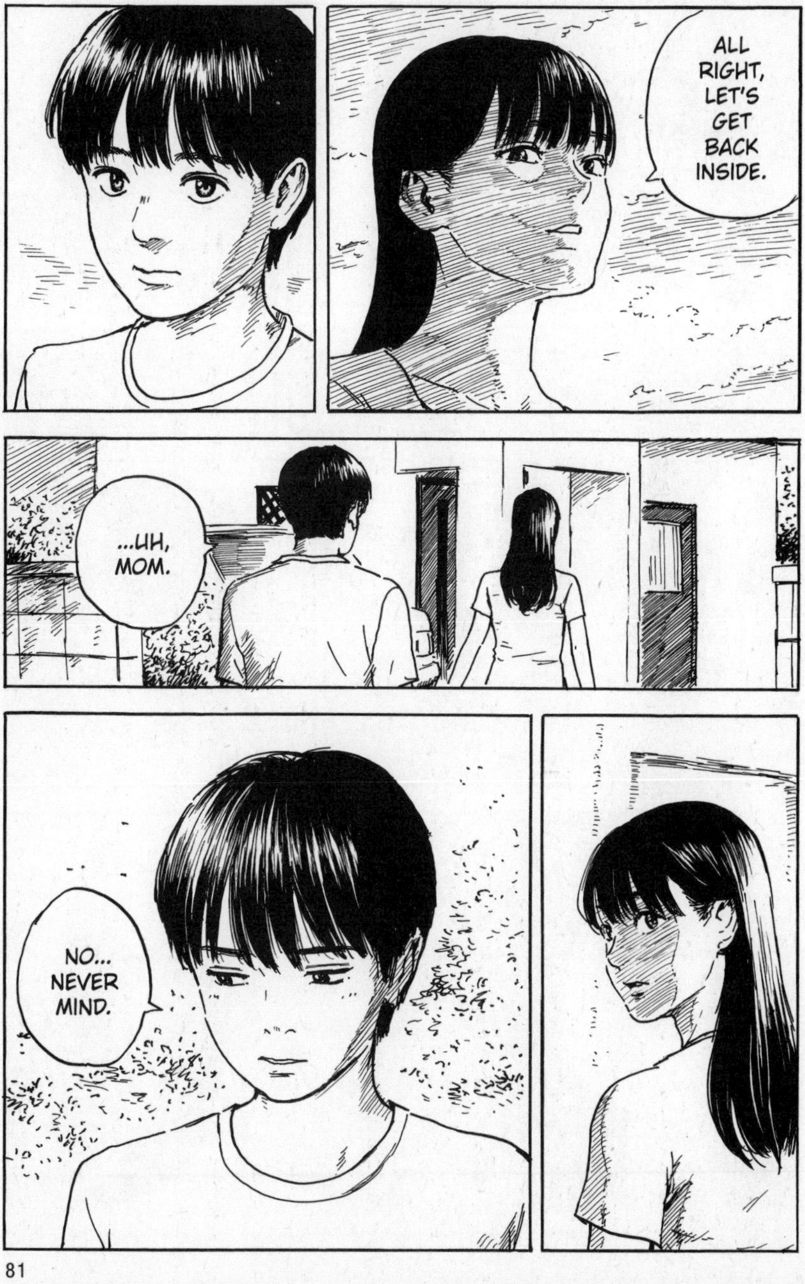
ALL RIGHT, LET'S GET BACK INSIDE.
...UH, MOM.
NO... NEVER MIND.

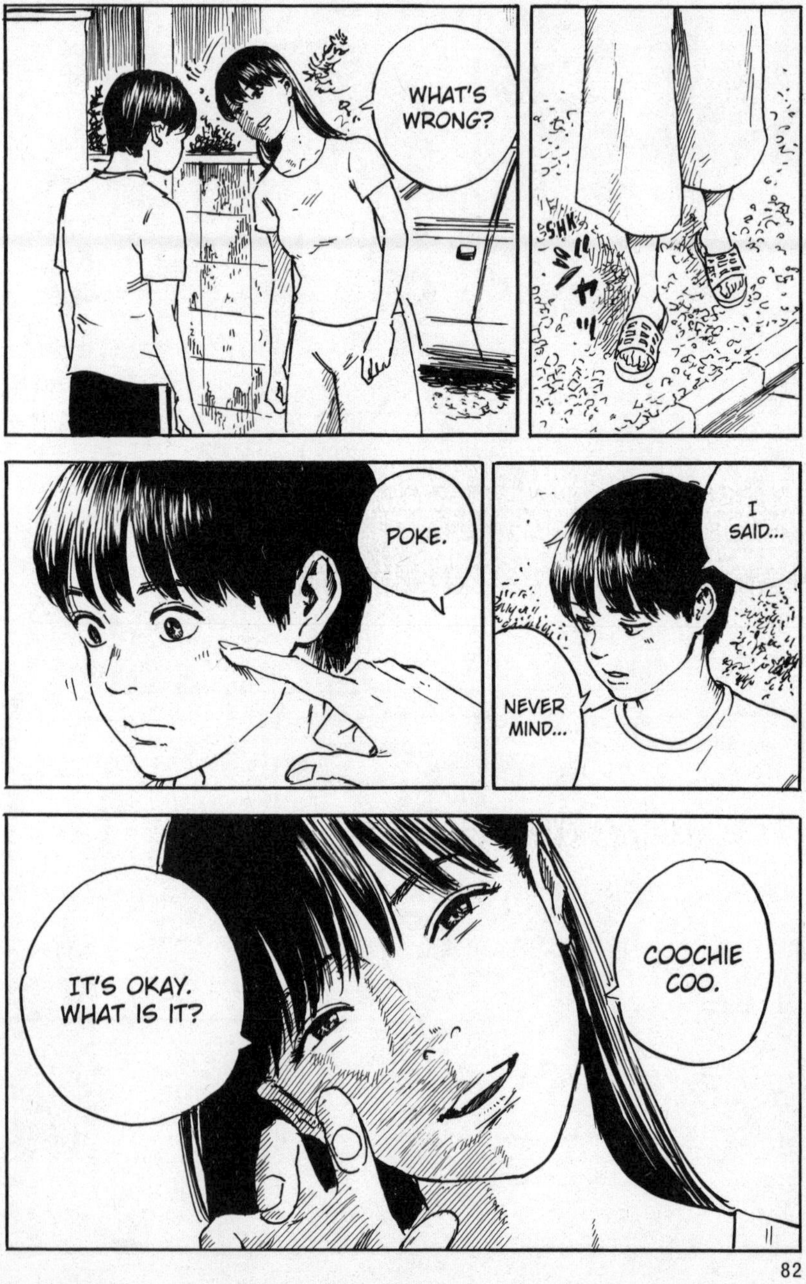
SHK
WHAT'S WRONG?
I SAID...
NEVER MIND...
POKE.
COOCHIE COO.
IT'S OKAY. WHAT IS IT?

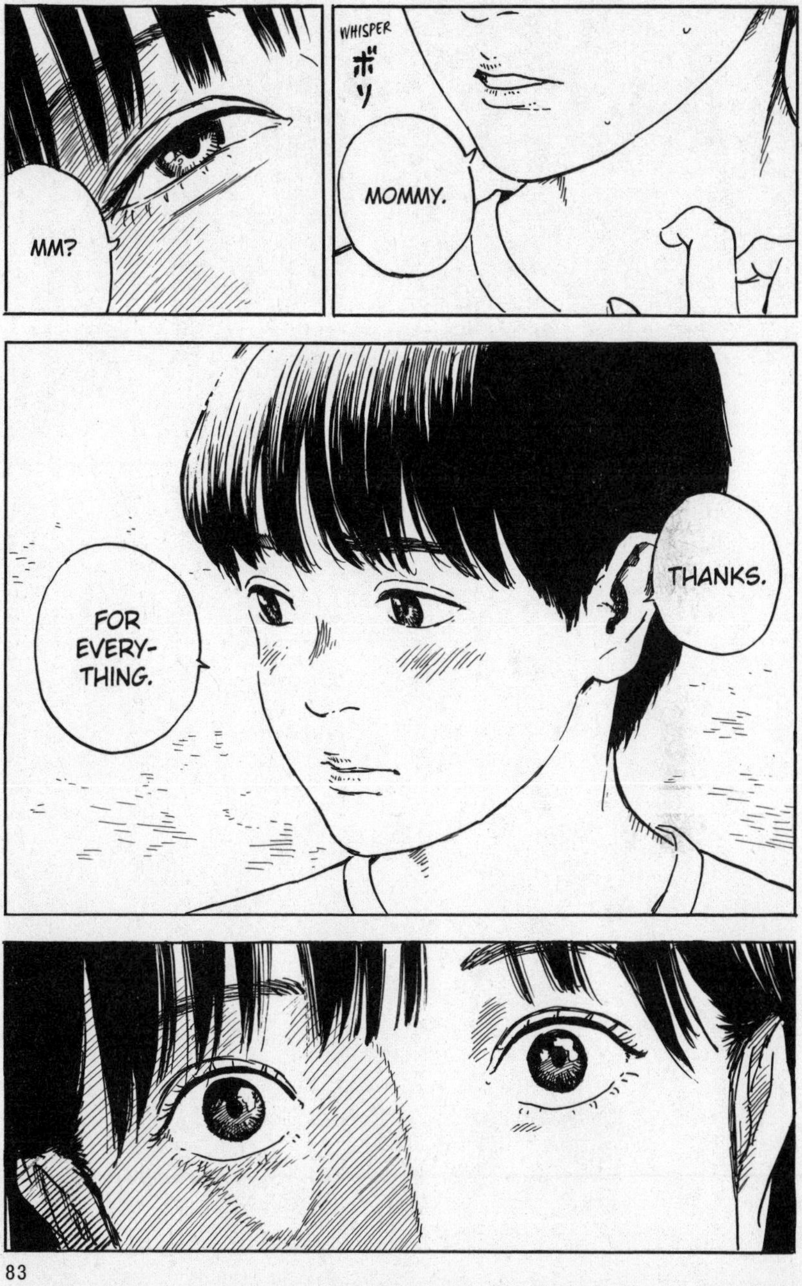
WHISPER
ボソ
MOMMY.
MM?
THANKS.
FOR EVERY-THING.

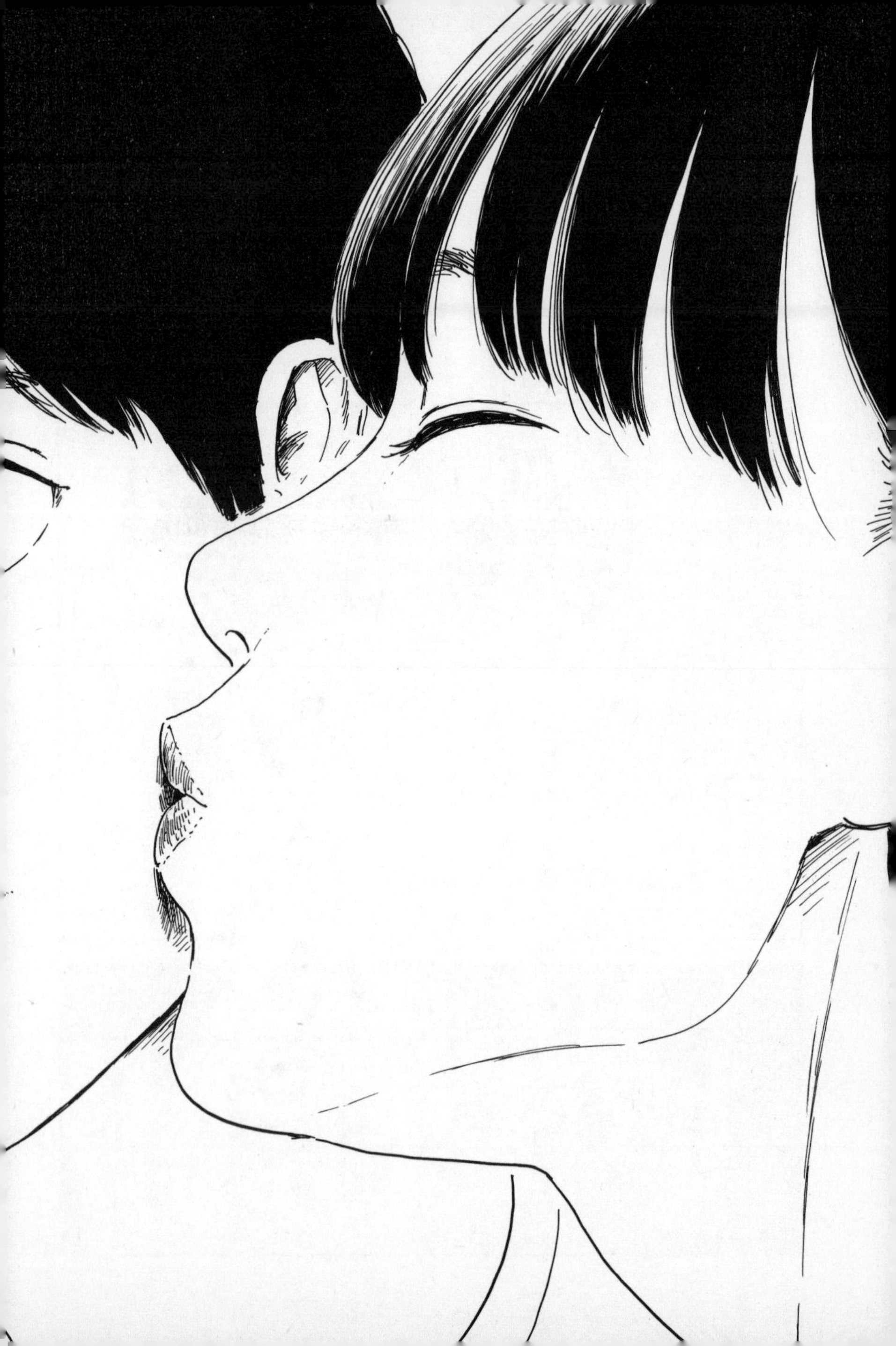

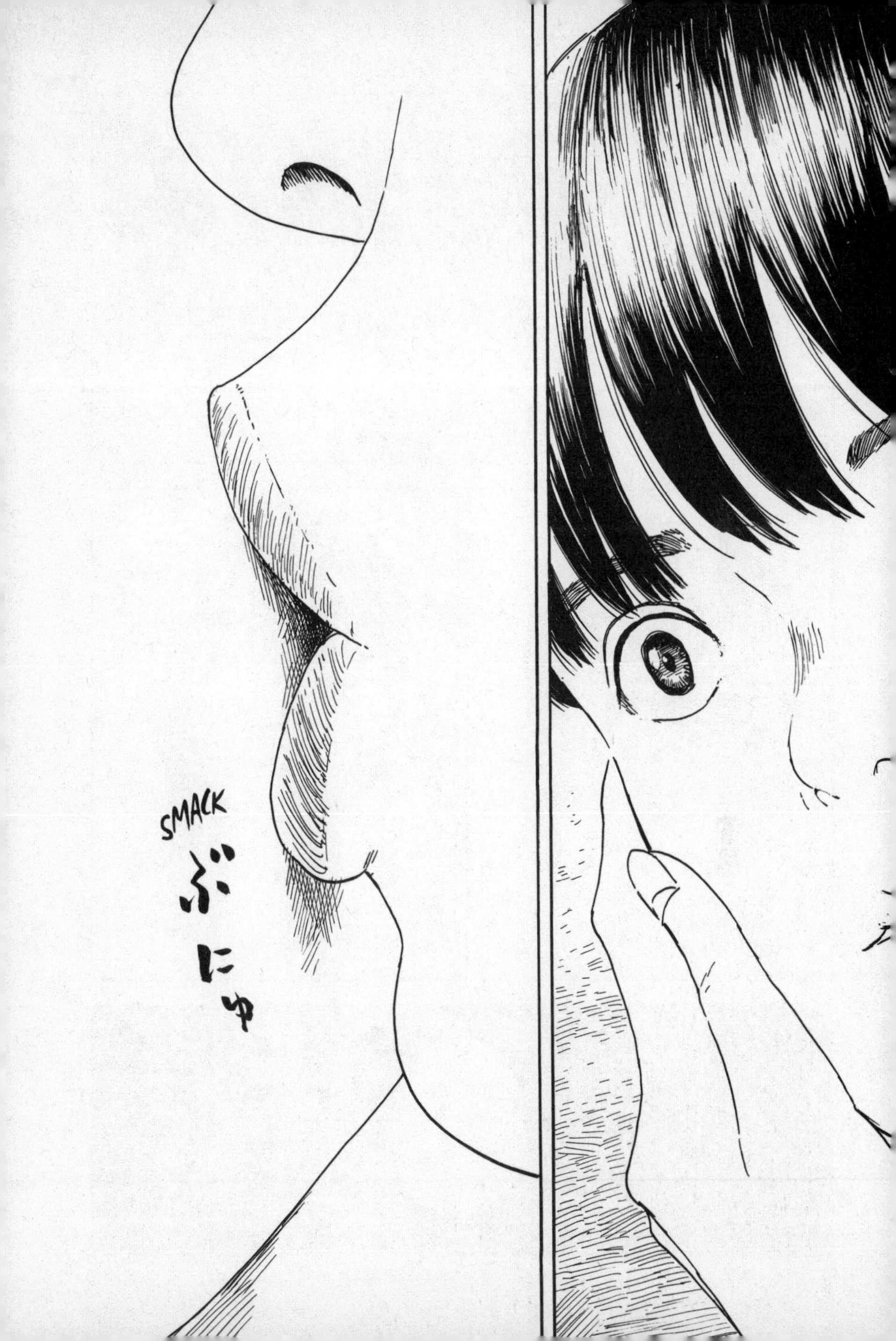
SMACK
ぶにゅ

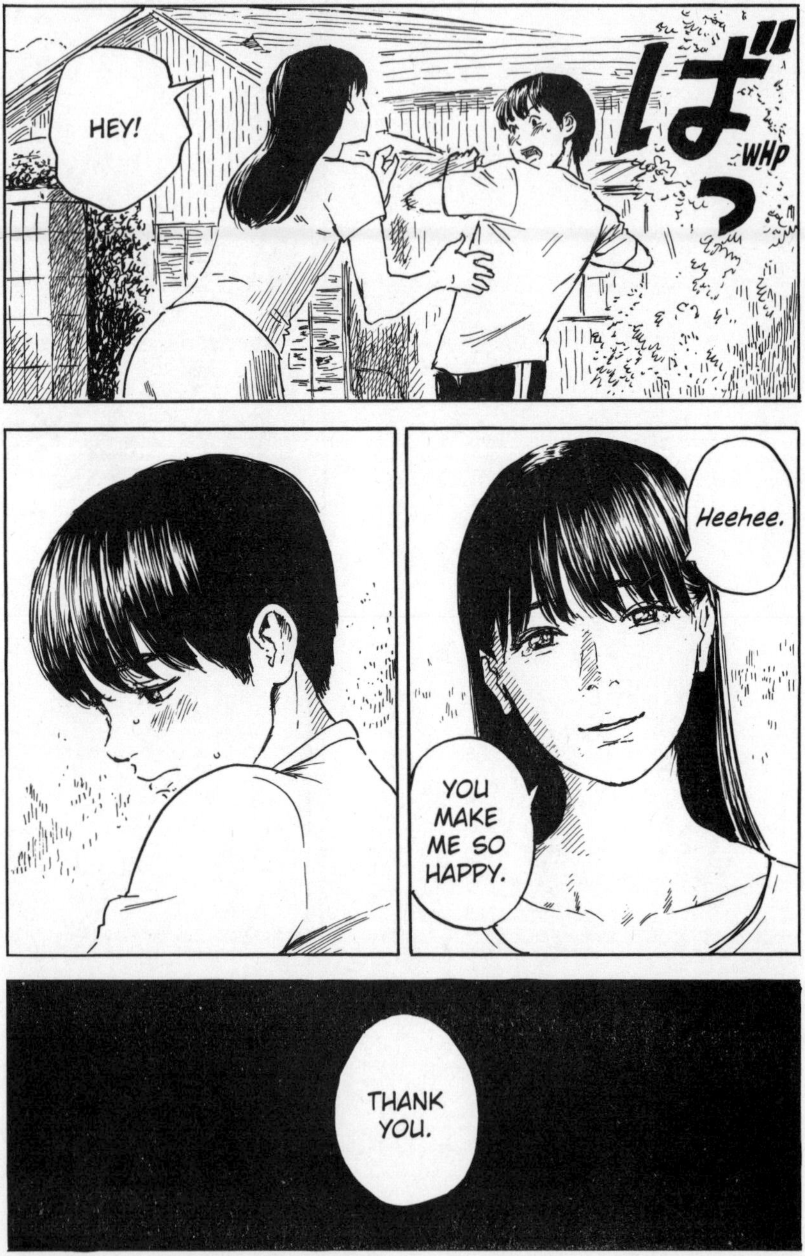
ばっ
WHP
HEY!
Heehee.
YOU MAKE ME SO HAPPY.
THANK YOU.

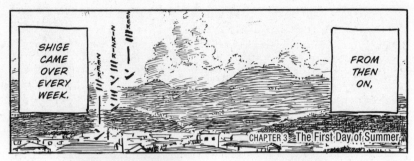

FROM THEN ON,
SHIGE CAME OVER EVERY WEEK.
CHAPTER 3 The First Day of Summer
SATUR-DAY AND SUNDAY,
OSABE
LIKE CLOCK-WORK.
MOMMY
ALWAYS LOOKED HAPPY.
ザァァァ
FSHHHHH

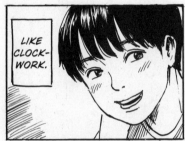

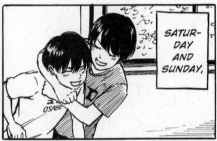

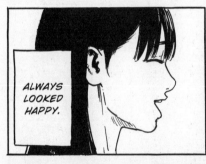

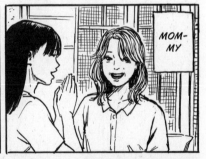

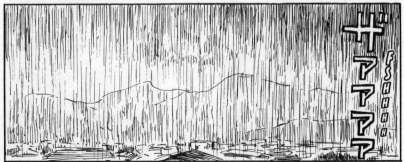

CHAPTER 3 The First Day of Summer

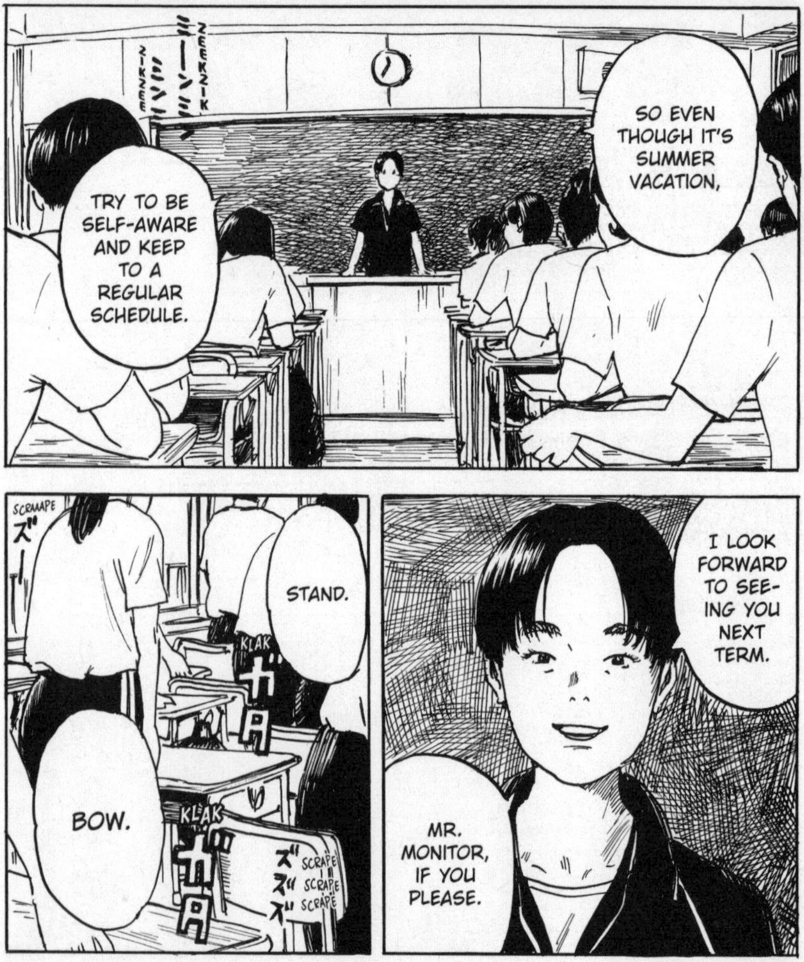
ZEEKZIK
ZIKZEE
SO EVEN THOUGH IT'S SUMMER VACATION,
TRY TO BE SELF-AWARE AND KEEP TO A REGULAR SCHEDULE.
I LOOK FORWARD TO SEE-ING YOU NEXT TERM.
MR. MONITOR, IF YOU PLEASE.
SCRAAAPE
STAND.
KLAK
BOW.
KLAK
SCRAPE SCRAPE SCRAPE

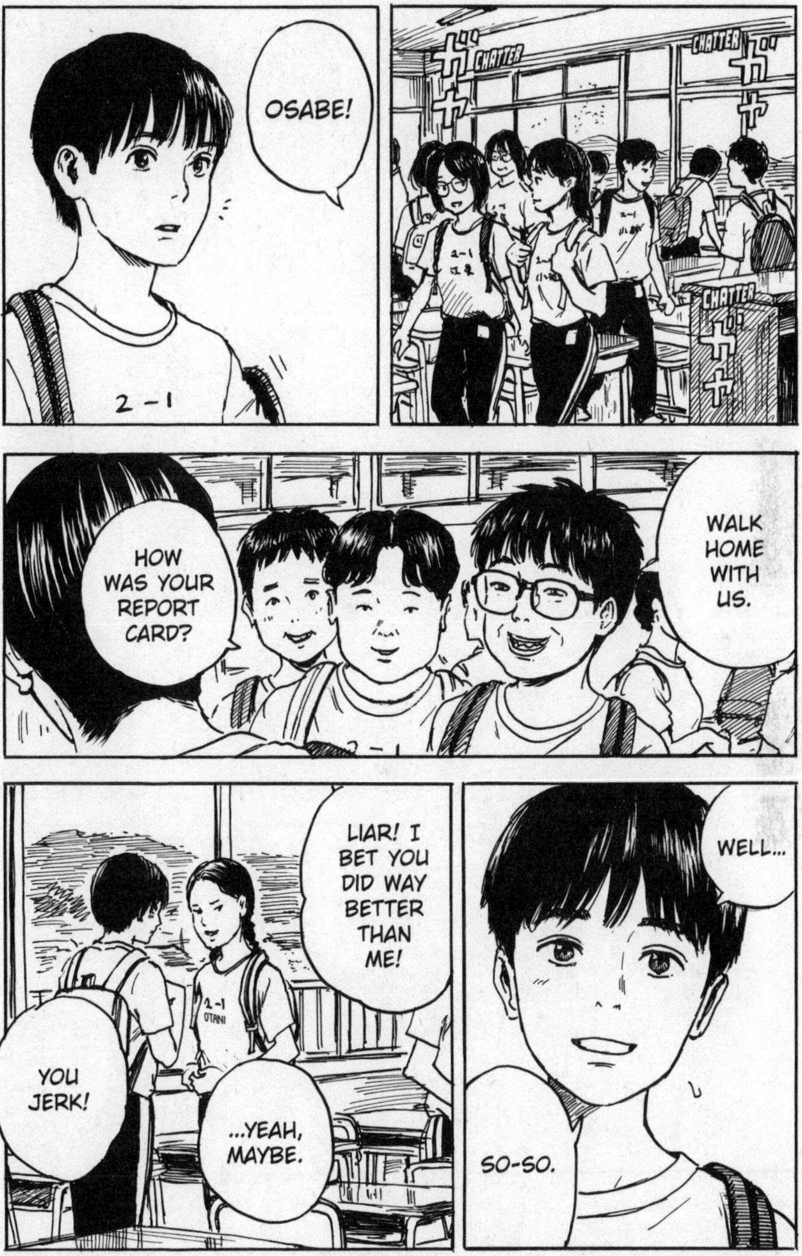
CHATTER
ガヤ
CHATTER
ガヤ
ガヤ
CHATTER
OSABE!
WALK HOME WITH US.
HOW WAS YOUR REPORT CARD?
WELL...
SO-SO.
LIAR! I BET YOU DID WAY BETTER THAN ME!
...YEAH, MAYBE.
YOU JERK!

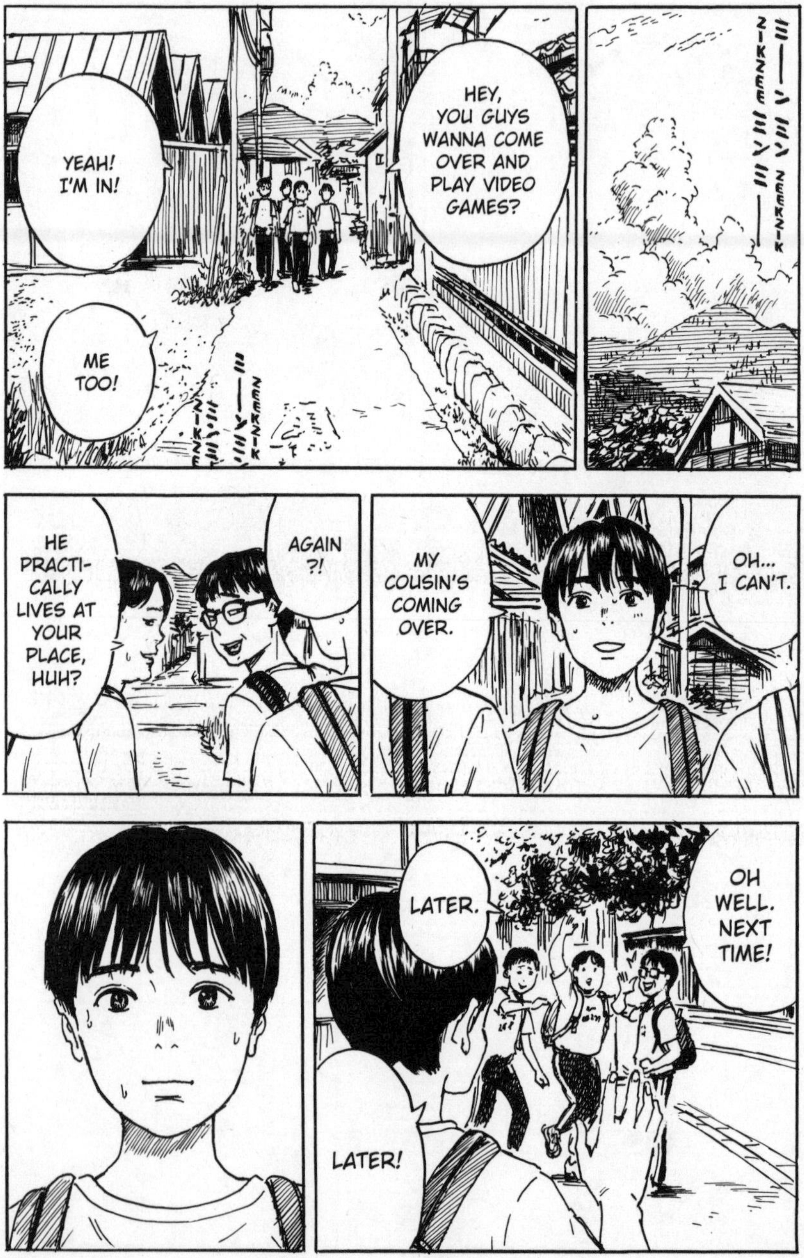
ZIKZEE
ZEEKZIK
HEY, YOU GUYS WANNA COME OVER AND PLAY VIDEO GAMES?
YEAH! I'M IN!
ME TOO!
ZEEKZIK
ZIKZEE
OH... I CAN'T.
MY COUSIN'S COMING OVER.
AGAIN?!
HE PRACTI-CALLY LIVES AT YOUR PLACE, HUH?
OH WELL. NEXT TIME!
LATER.
LATER!

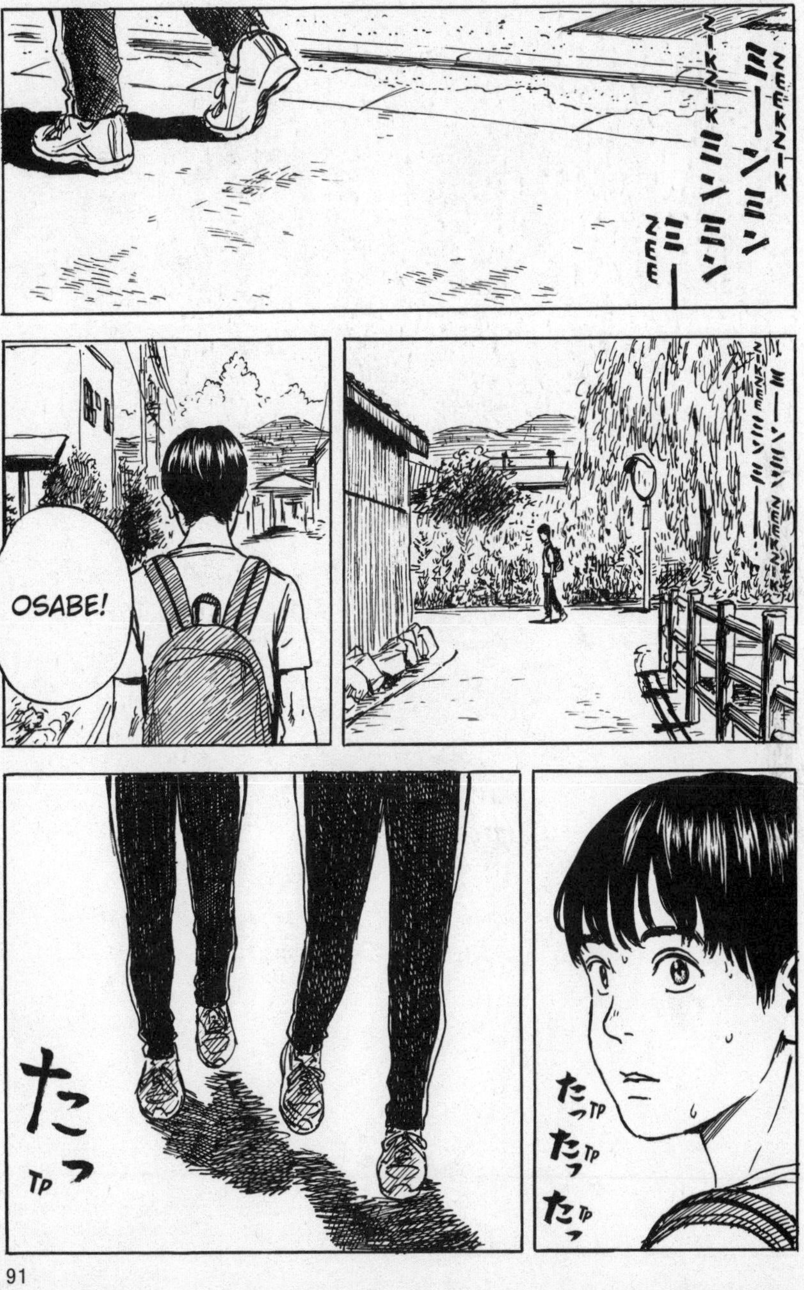
ミーンミン ミンミン ミー
ZEEKZIK ZIKZIK ZEE
ミーンミン ミンミー
ZEEKZIK ZIKZEE
OSABE!
たっ TP
たっ TP
たっ TP
たっ TP

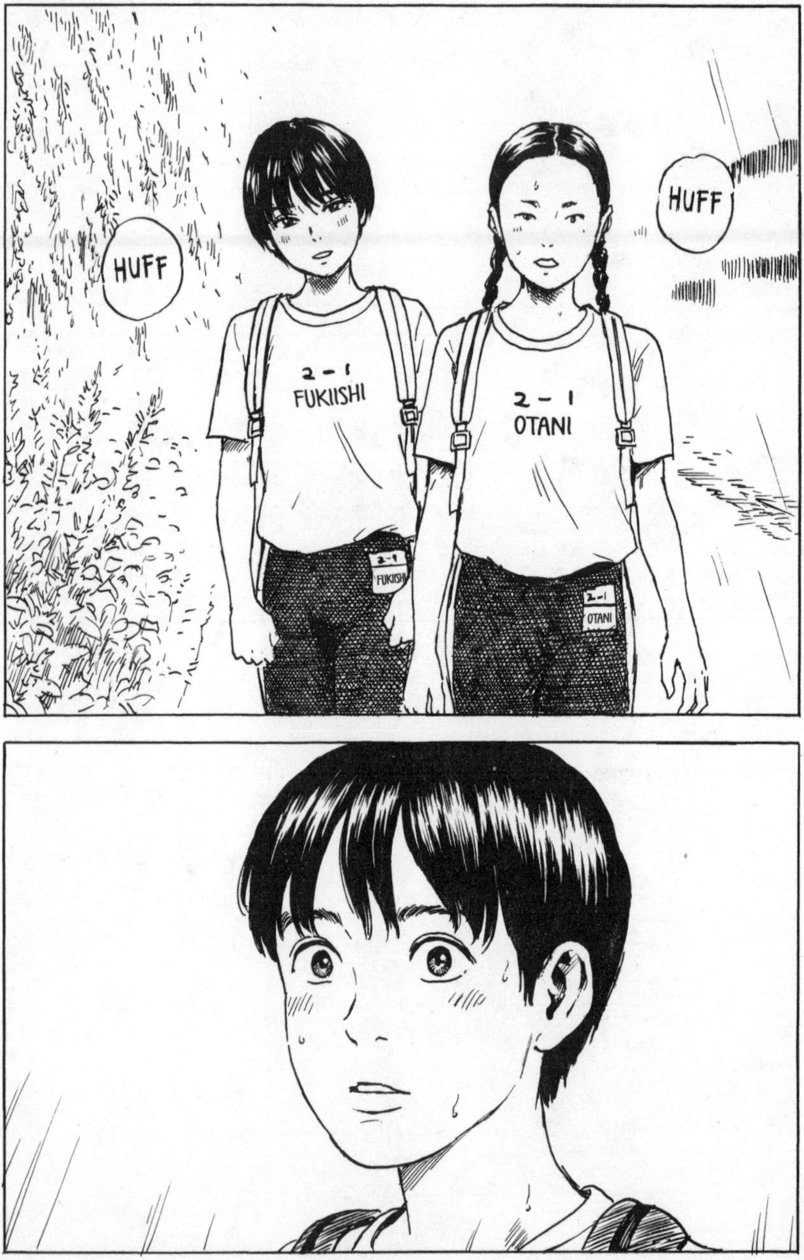
HUFF
2 - 1
OTANI
2-1
OTANI
2 - 1
FUKIISHI
2-1
FUKIISHI
HUFF

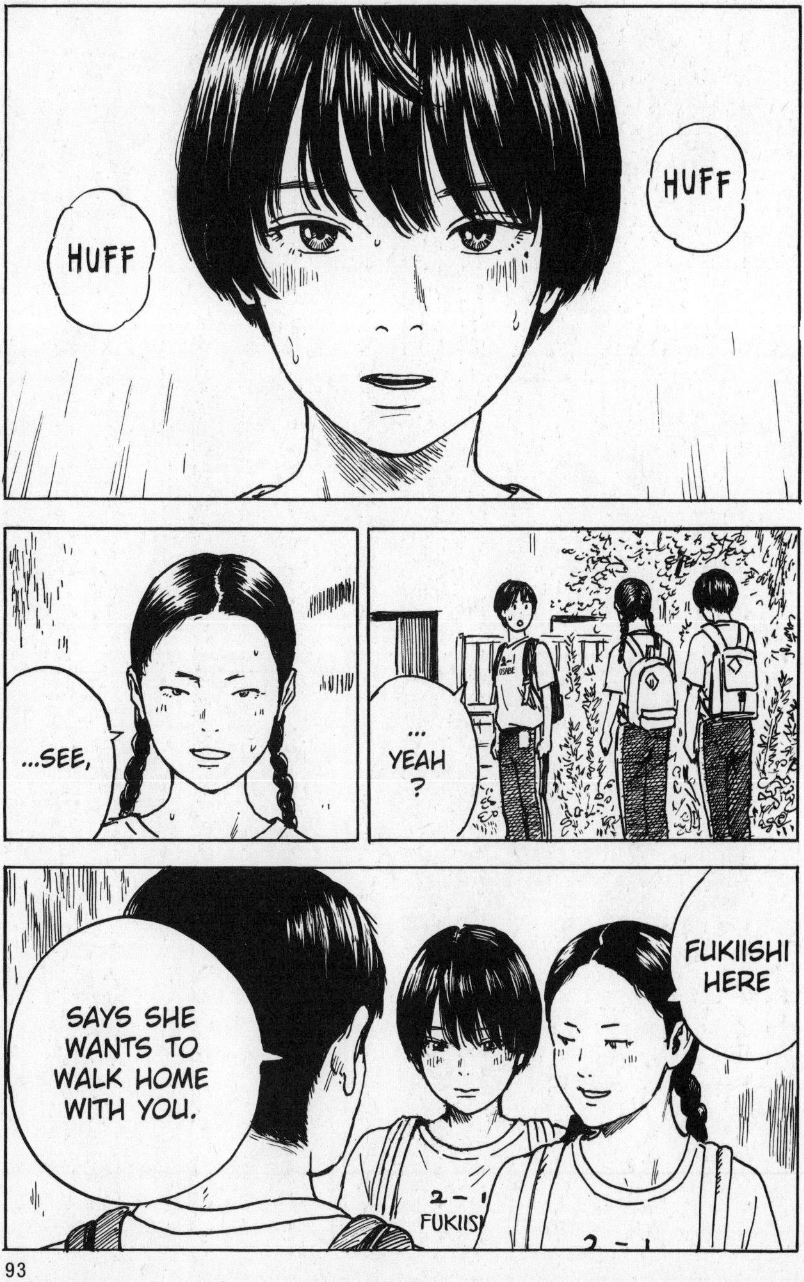
HUFF
HUFF
... YEAH ?
...SEE,
FUKIISHI HERE
SAYS SHE WANTS TO WALK HOME WITH YOU.

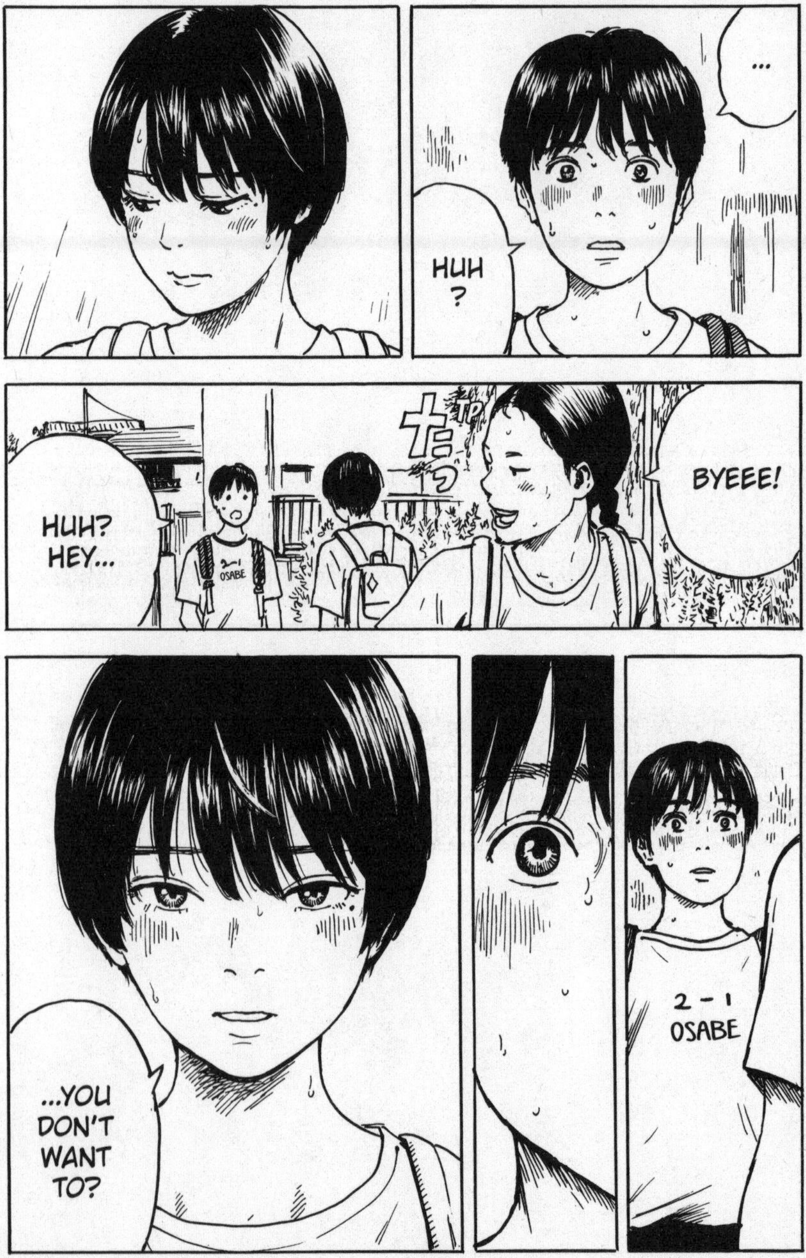
...
HUH ?
BYEEE!
TP
2-1 OSABE
HUH? HEY...
2 - 1 OSABE
...YOU DON'T WANT TO?

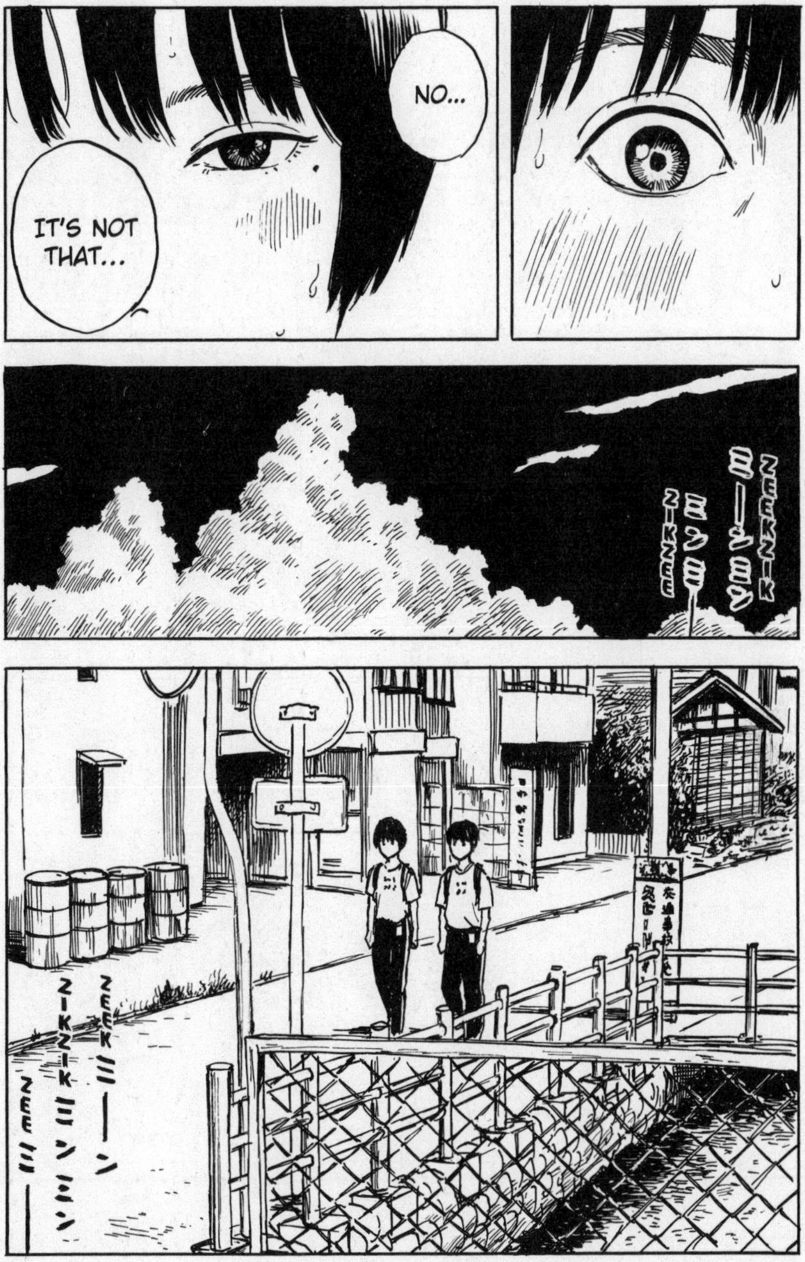
NO...
IT'S NOT THAT...
ZEEKZIK ミーンミン
ZIKZEE ミンミー
ZEEK ミーン
ZIKZIK ミンミン
ZEE ミー

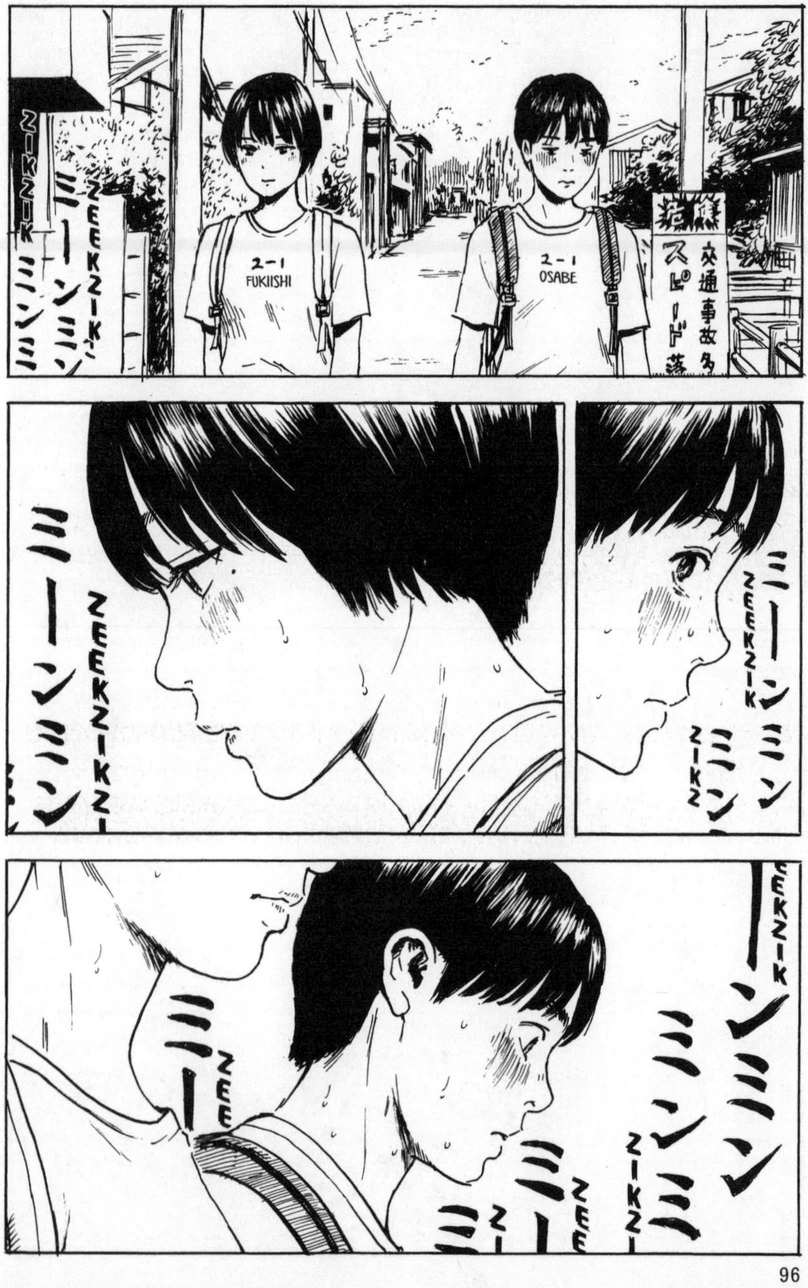
危険
交通事故多
スピード落
2-1
OSABE
2-1
FUKIISHI
ZEEKZIK
ミーンミン
ZIKZIK
ミンミンミ
ミーンミン
ZEEKZIK
ミンミン
ZIKZ
ミーンミン
ZEEKZIKZI
ZEEKZIK
ーンミン
ミンミ
ZIKZI
ミー
ZEE
ミー
ZEE

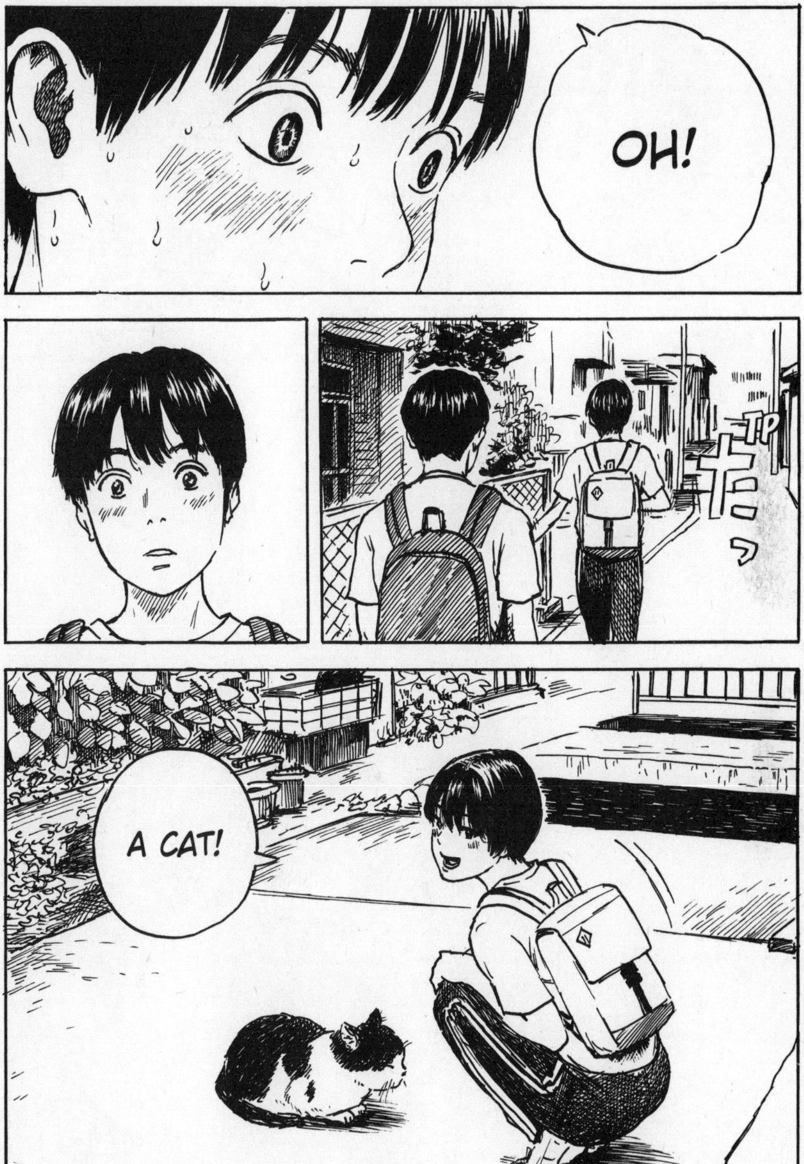
OH!
TP
たたっ
A CAT!

GOOD KITTY.
MEOWWW.
PURR
PURR
YOU LIKE THAT?

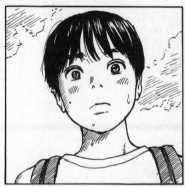

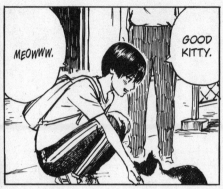

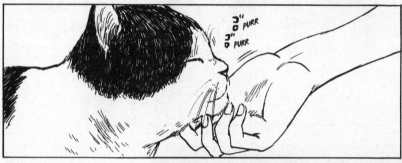

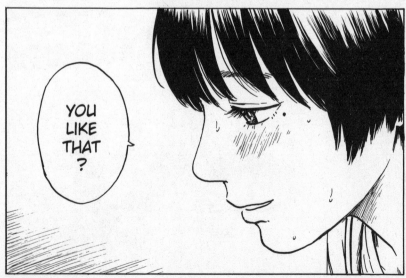

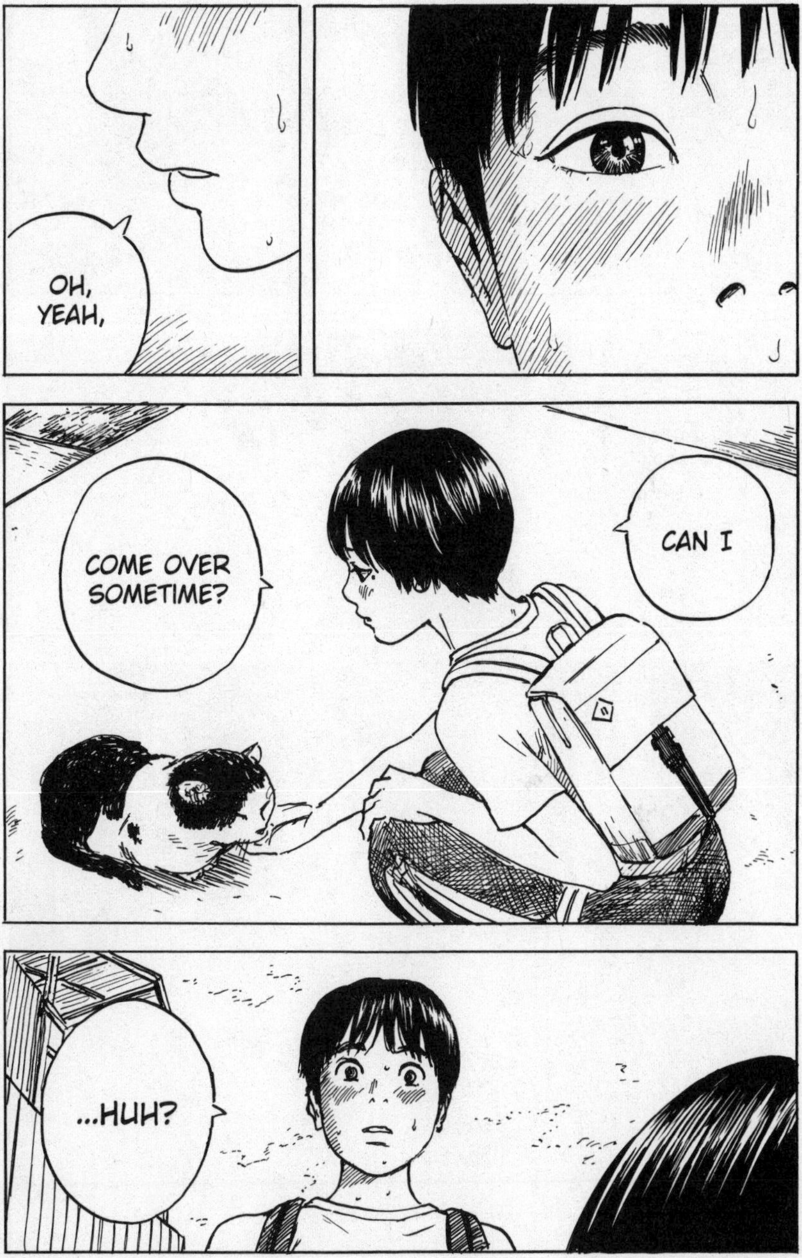
OH, YEAH,
CAN I
COME OVER SOMETIME?
...HUH?

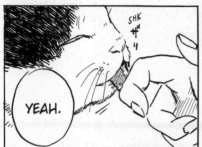

SHK

YEAH.

TO MY HOUSE?

COME OVER...

FOR WHAT...?

...F—

HE-Y

DON'T GET ANY FUNNY IDEAS!

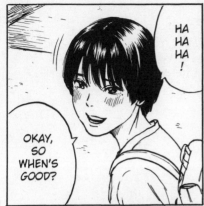

I... I WASN'T!
2-1 OSABE
DON'T BE STUPID!
HA HA HA!
OKAY, SO WHEN'S GOOD?
...YOU'RE SERIOUS?
YOU DON'T WANT ME TO?
OSABE
ZEEKZIK
ZIKZIKZI
...THE THING IS,

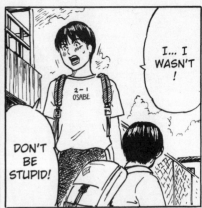

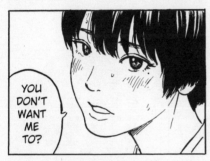

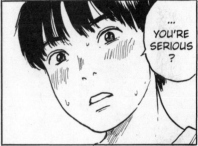

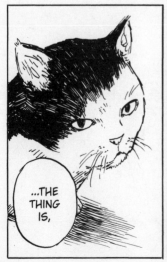

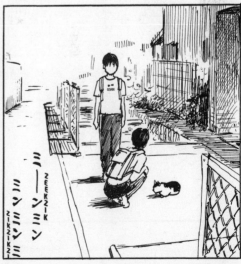

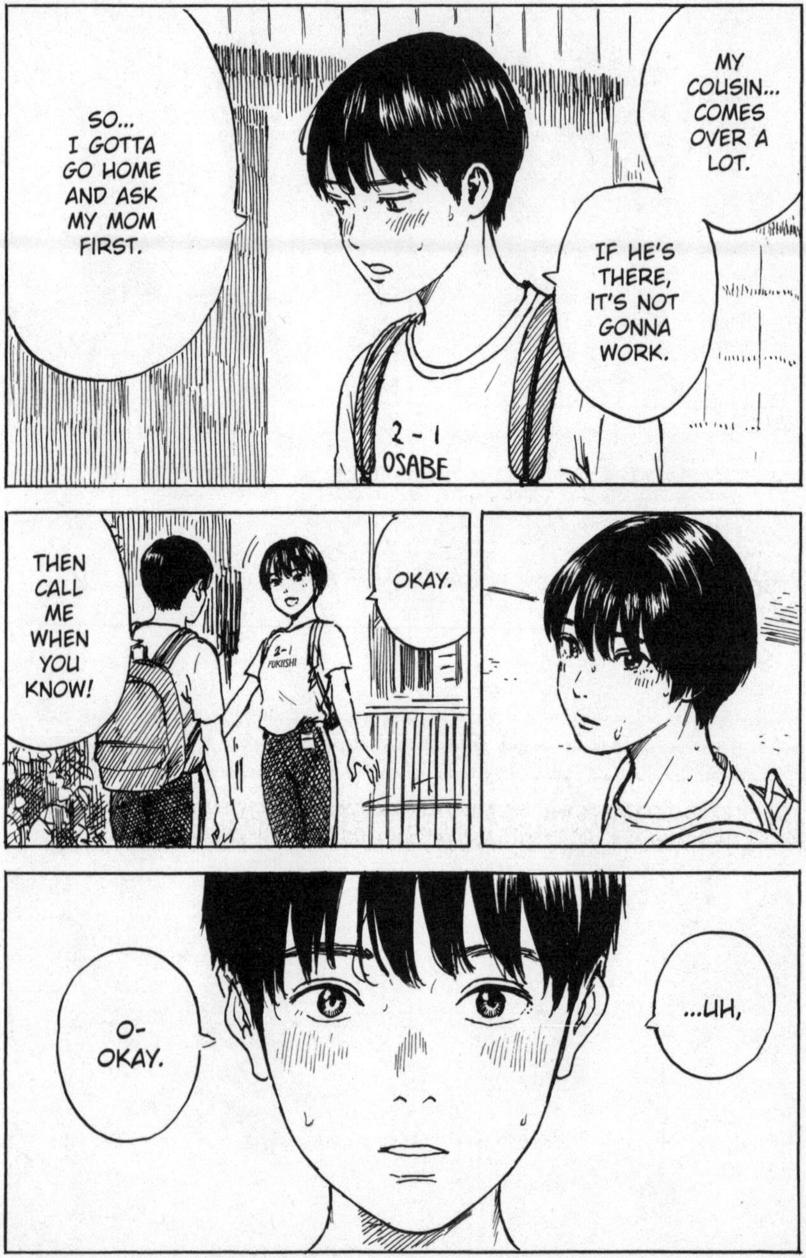
MY COUSIN... COMES OVER A LOT.
IF HE'S THERE, IT'S NOT GONNA WORK.
SO... I GOTTA GO HOME AND ASK MY MOM FIRST.
2 - 1 OSABE
OKAY.
THEN CALL ME WHEN YOU KNOW!
2-1 FUKIISHI
...UH,
O- OKAY.

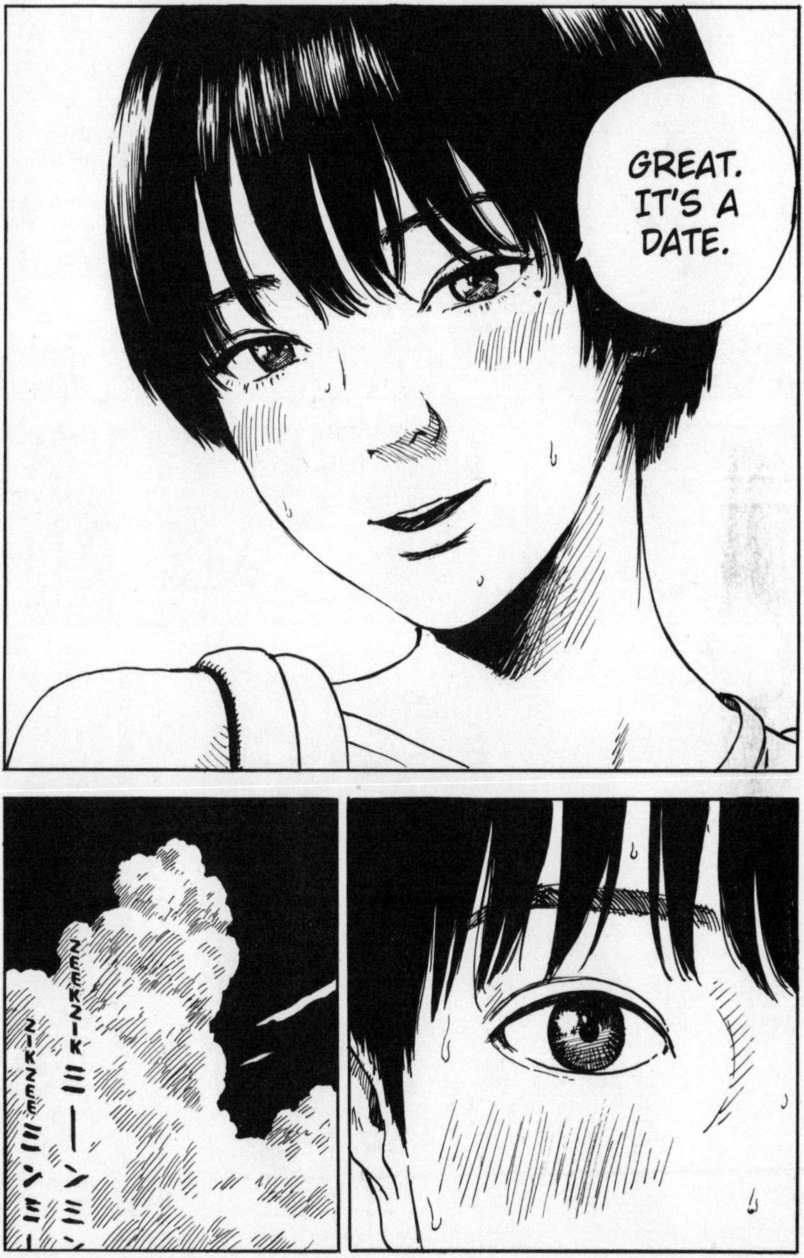
GREAT. IT'S A DATE.
ZEEKZIK ミーンミン
ZIKZEE ミンミー

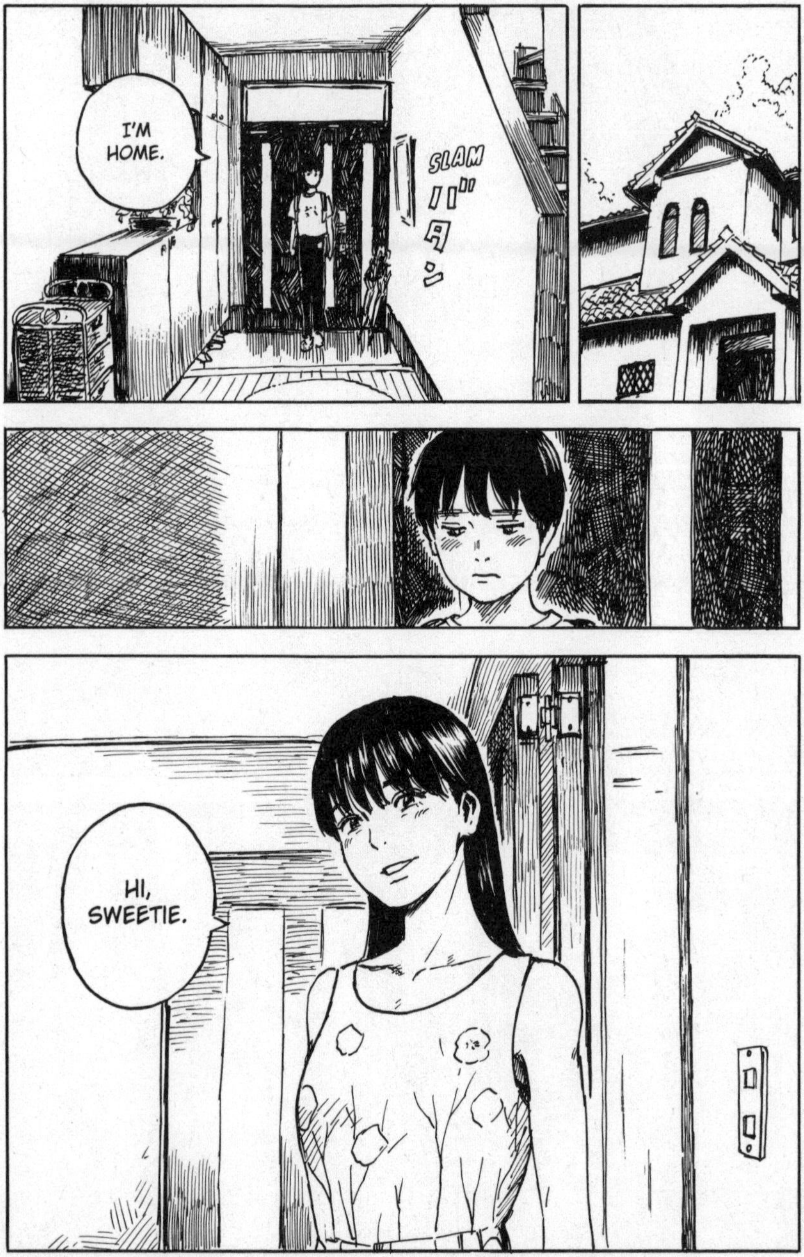
SLAM
バタン
I'M HOME.
HI, SWEETIE.

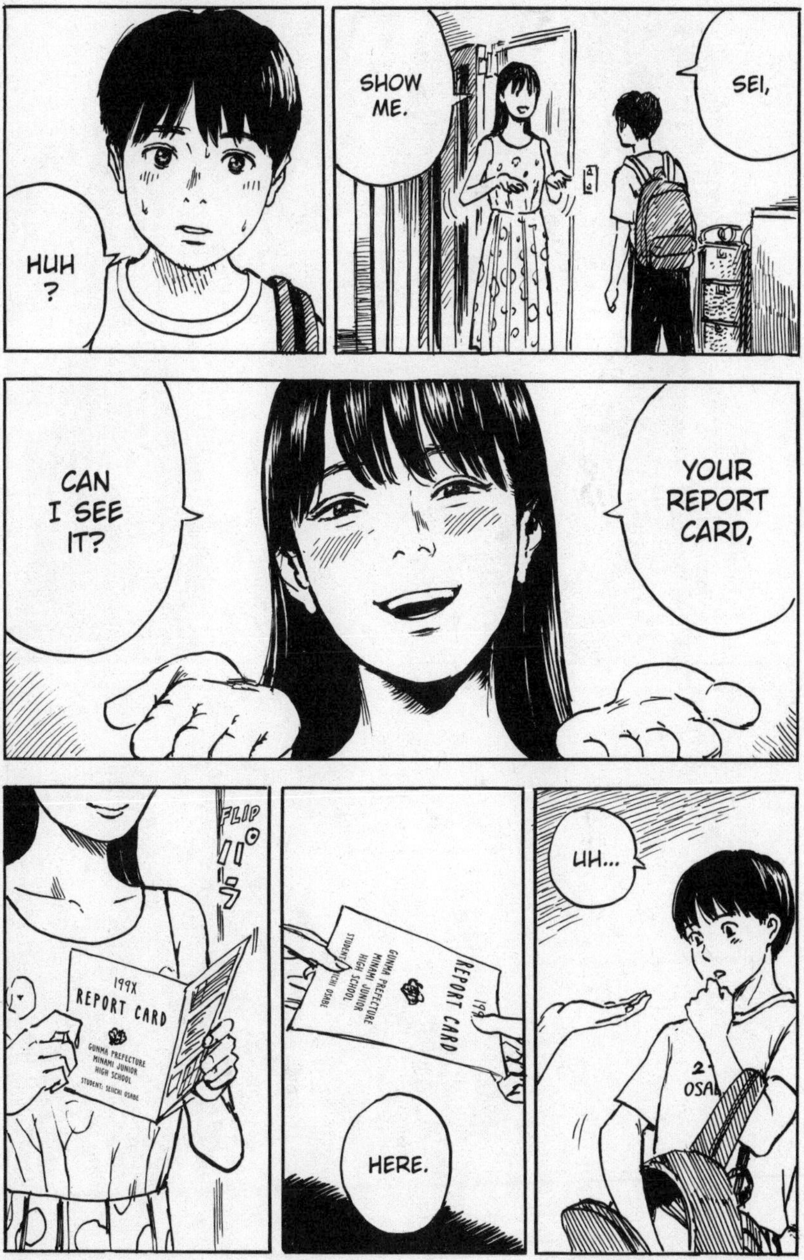
SEI,
SHOW ME.
HUH ?
YOUR REPORT CARD,
CAN I SEE IT?
UH...
HERE.
FLIP
パラ
199X
REPORT CARD
GUNMA PREFECTURE
MINAMI JUNIOR
HIGH SCHOOL
STUDENT: SEIICHI OSABE

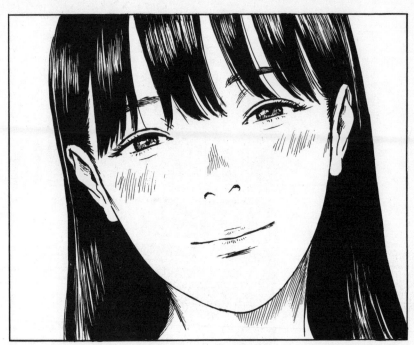

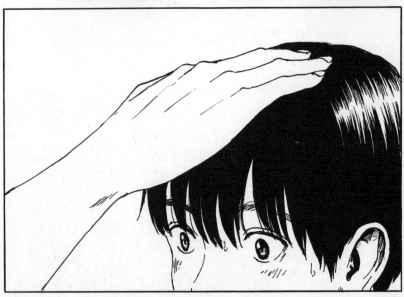

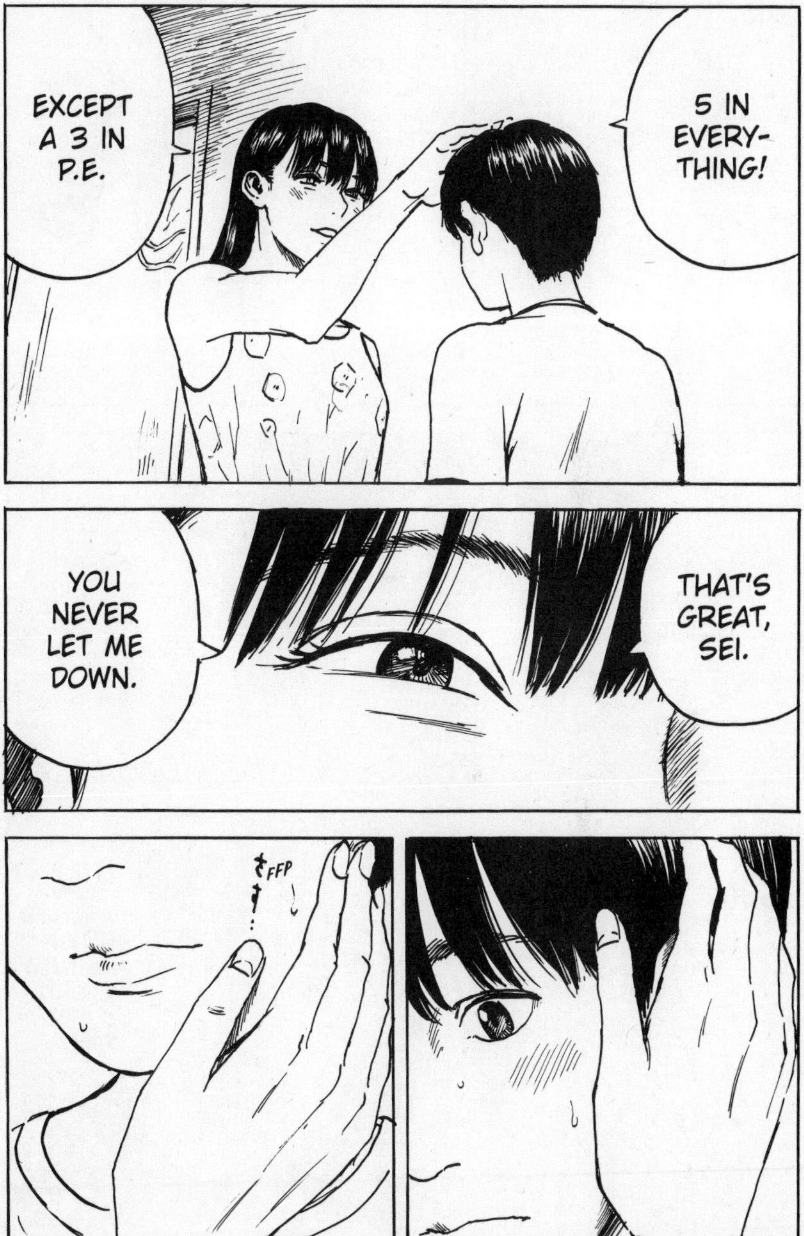
5 IN EVERYTHING!
EXCEPT A 3 IN P.E.
THAT'S GREAT, SEI.
YOU NEVER LET ME DOWN.
FFP

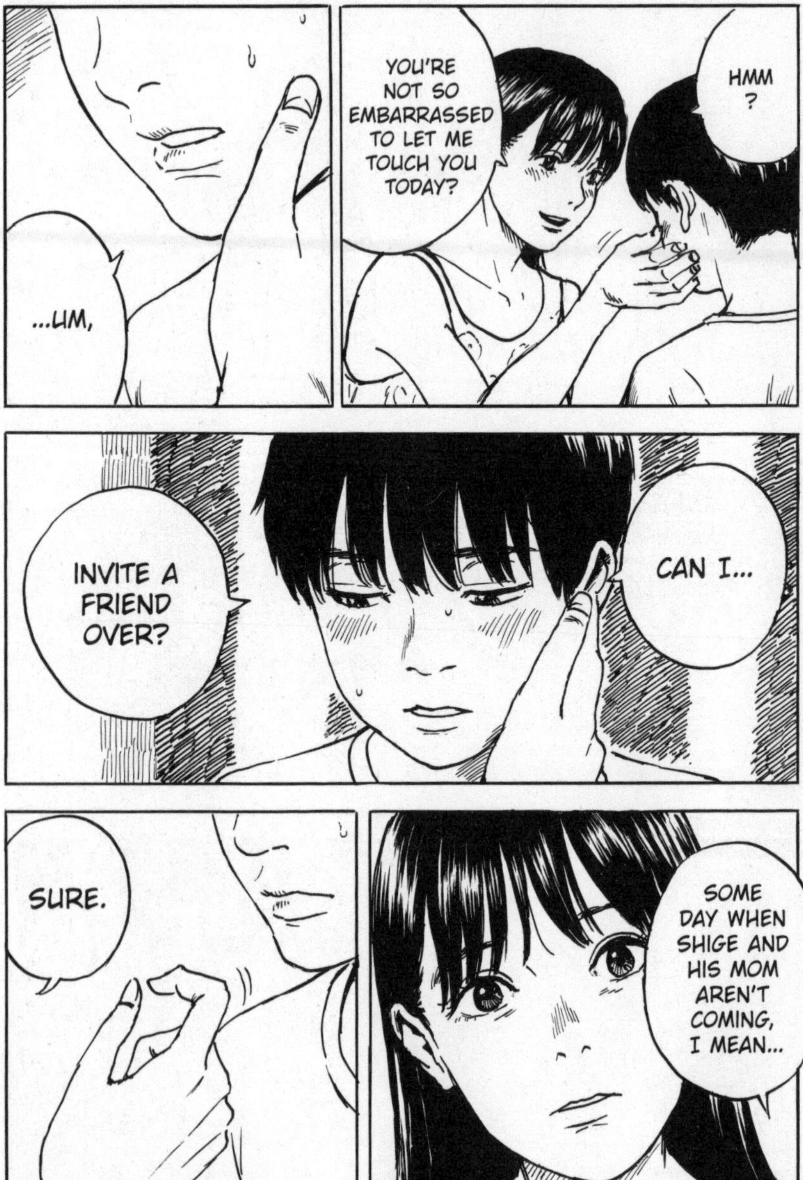
HMM ?
YOU'RE NOT SO EMBARRASSED TO LET ME TOUCH YOU TODAY?
...UM,
CAN I...
INVITE A FRIEND OVER?
SOME DAY WHEN SHIGE AND HIS MOM AREN'T COMING, I MEAN...
SURE.

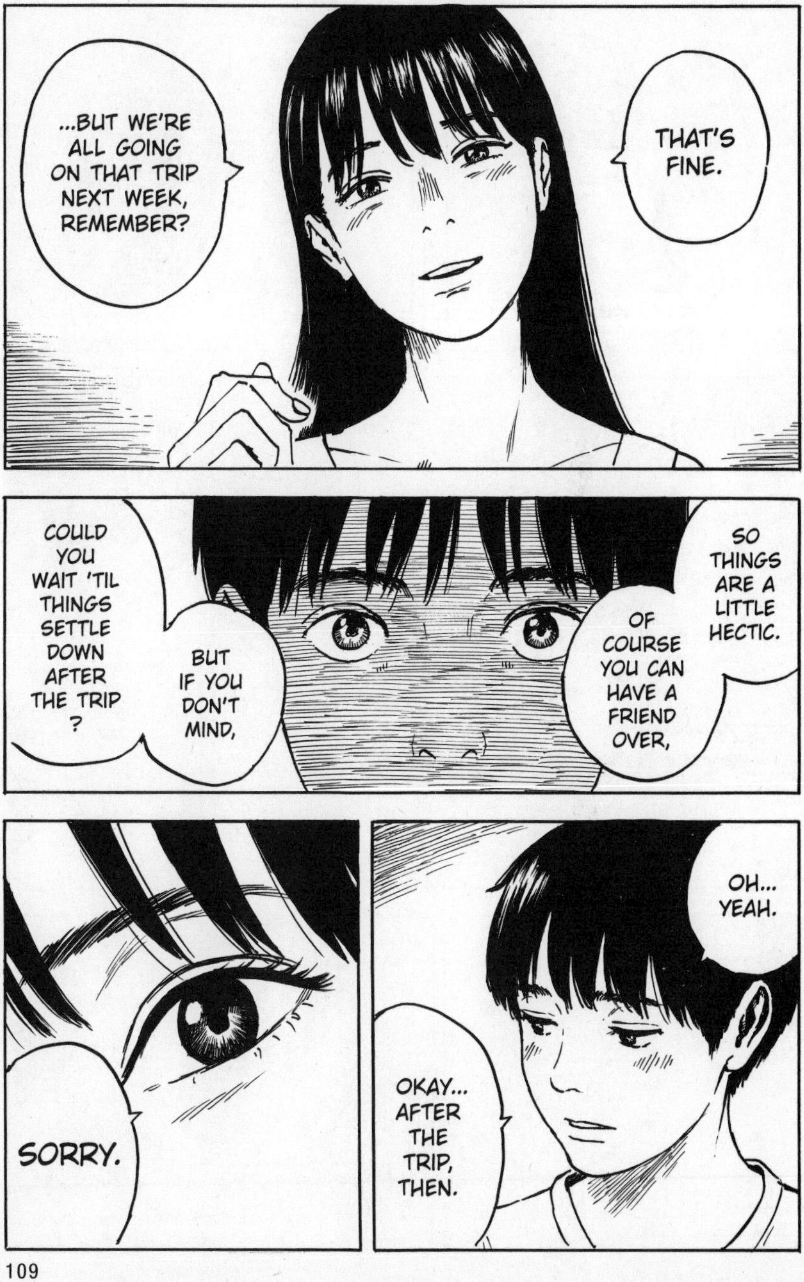
THAT'S FINE.
...BUT WE'RE ALL GOING ON THAT TRIP NEXT WEEK, REMEMBER?
SO THINGS ARE A LITTLE HECTIC.
OF COURSE YOU CAN HAVE A FRIEND OVER,
BUT IF YOU DON'T MIND,
COULD YOU WAIT 'TIL THINGS SETTLE DOWN AFTER THE TRIP ?
OH... YEAH.
OKAY... AFTER THE TRIP, THEN.
SORRY.

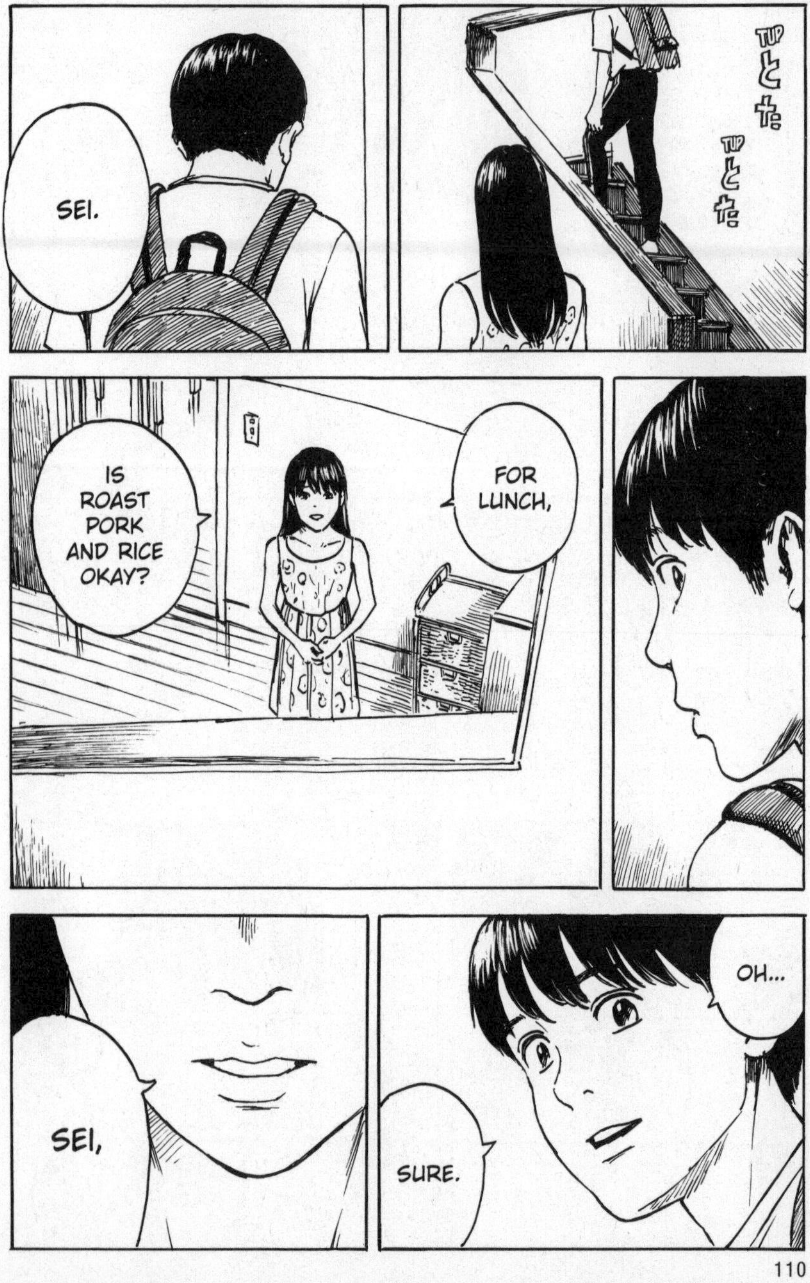
TUP
とた
TUP
とた
SEI.
FOR LUNCH,
IS ROAST PORK AND RICE OKAY?
OH...
SURE.
SEI,

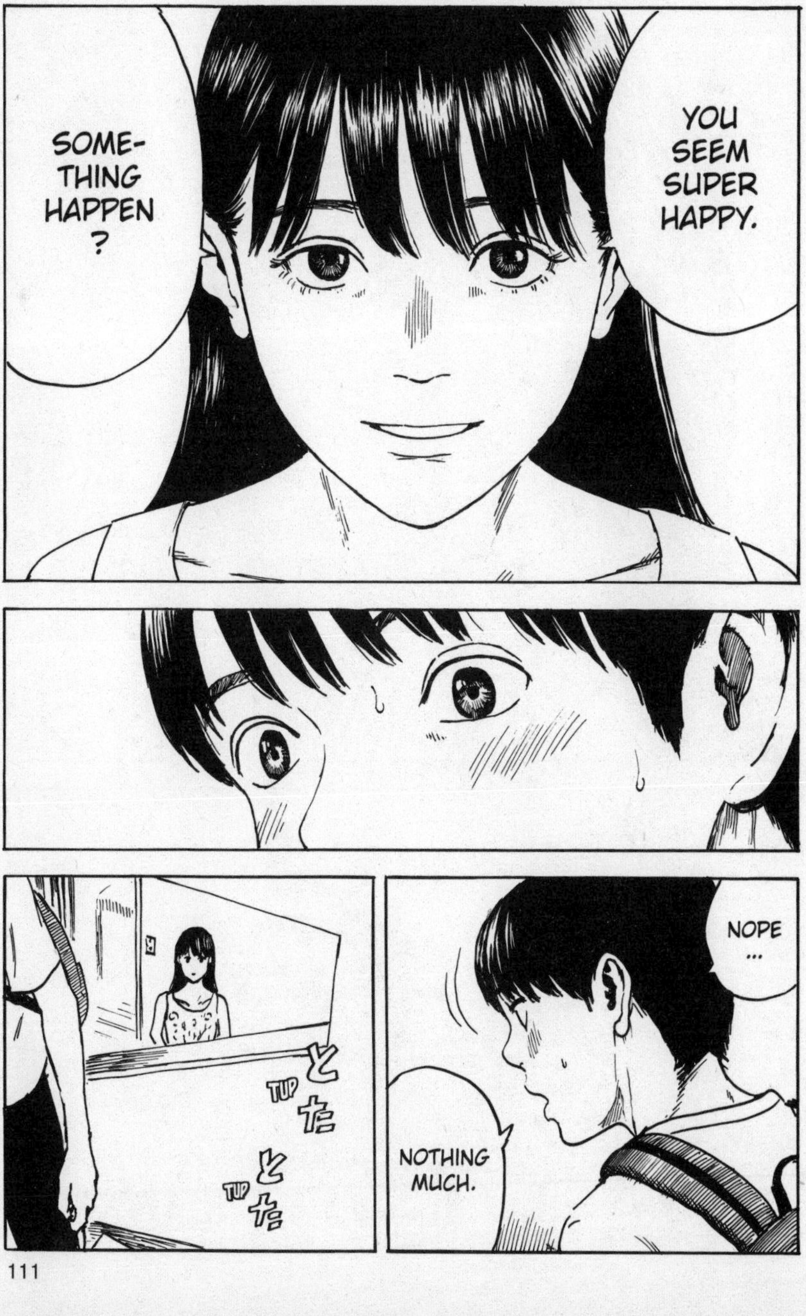
YOU SEEM SUPER HAPPY.
SOME-THING HAPPEN ?
NOPE ...
NOTHING MUCH.
TUP とた
TUP とた

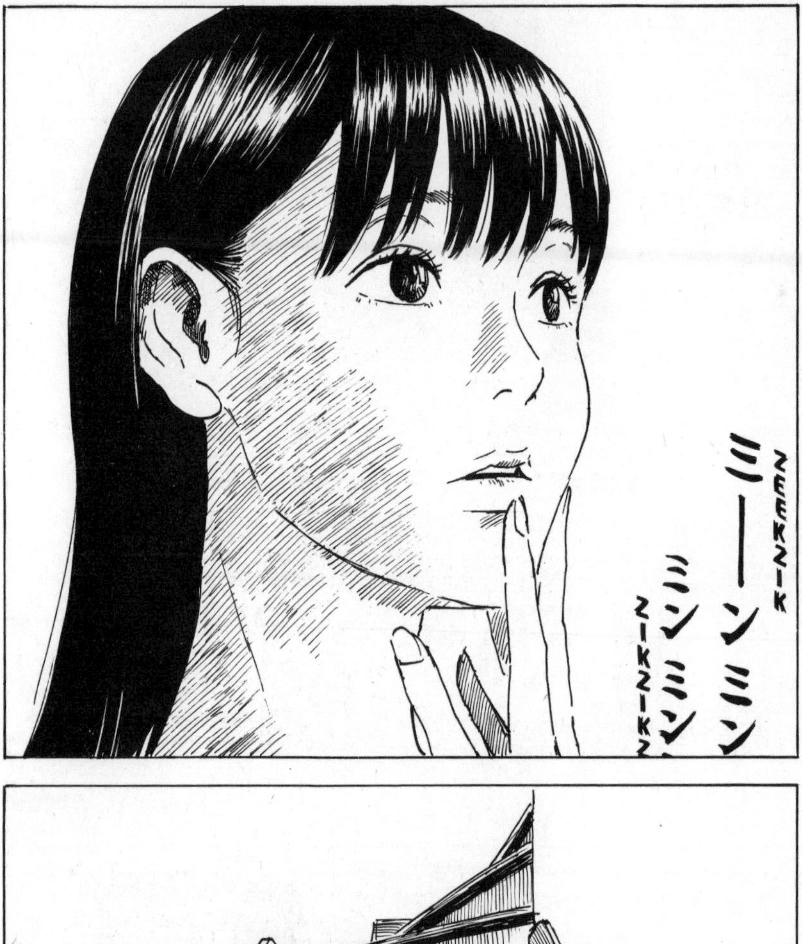
ZEEKZIK
ミーンミン
ミンミンミ
ZIKZIKZ

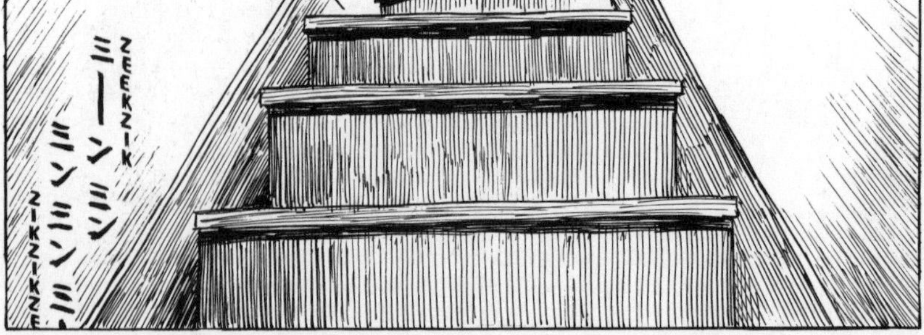
ZEEKZIK
ミーンミン
ミンミンミ
ZIKZIKZE

CHAPTER 4 Perfect Weather

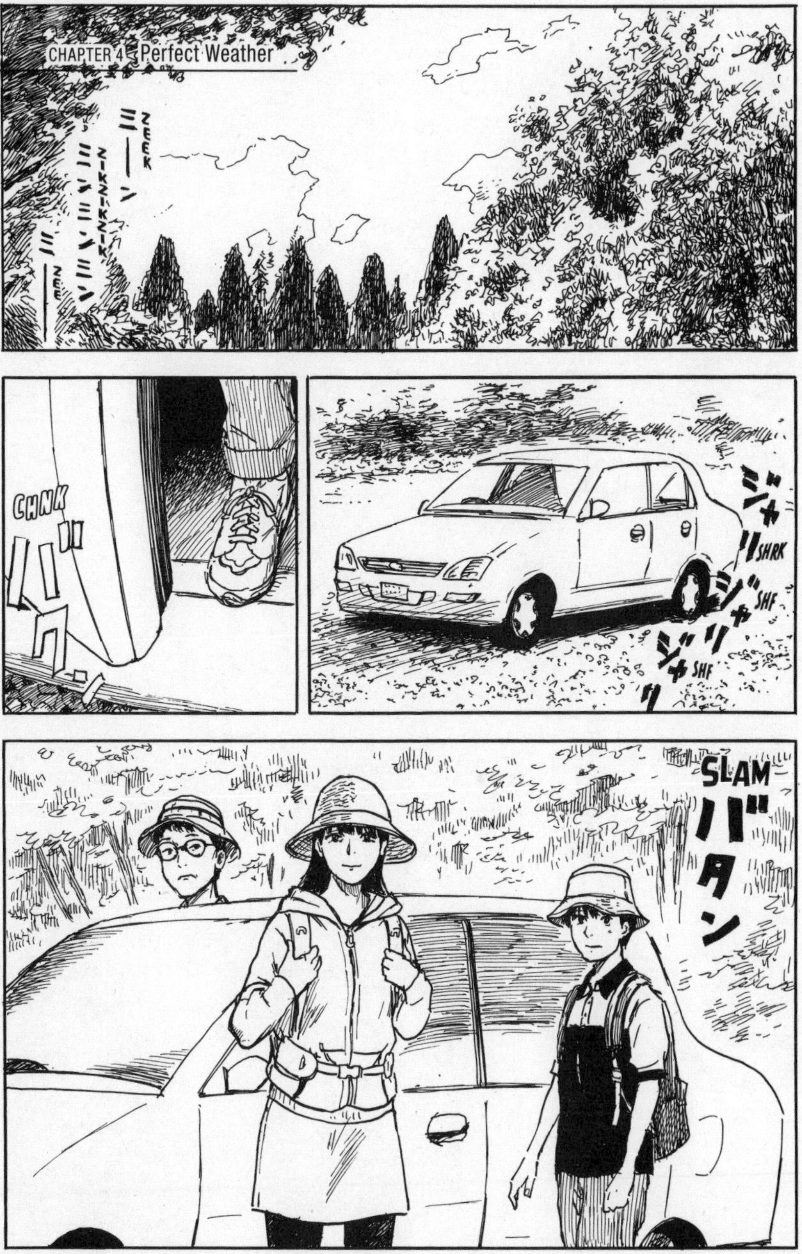
ミーン
ZEEK
ミンミンミン
ZIKZIKZIK
ミー
ZEE
ジャリ
SHRK
ジャリ
SHF
ジャリ
SHF
CHNK
SLAM
バタン

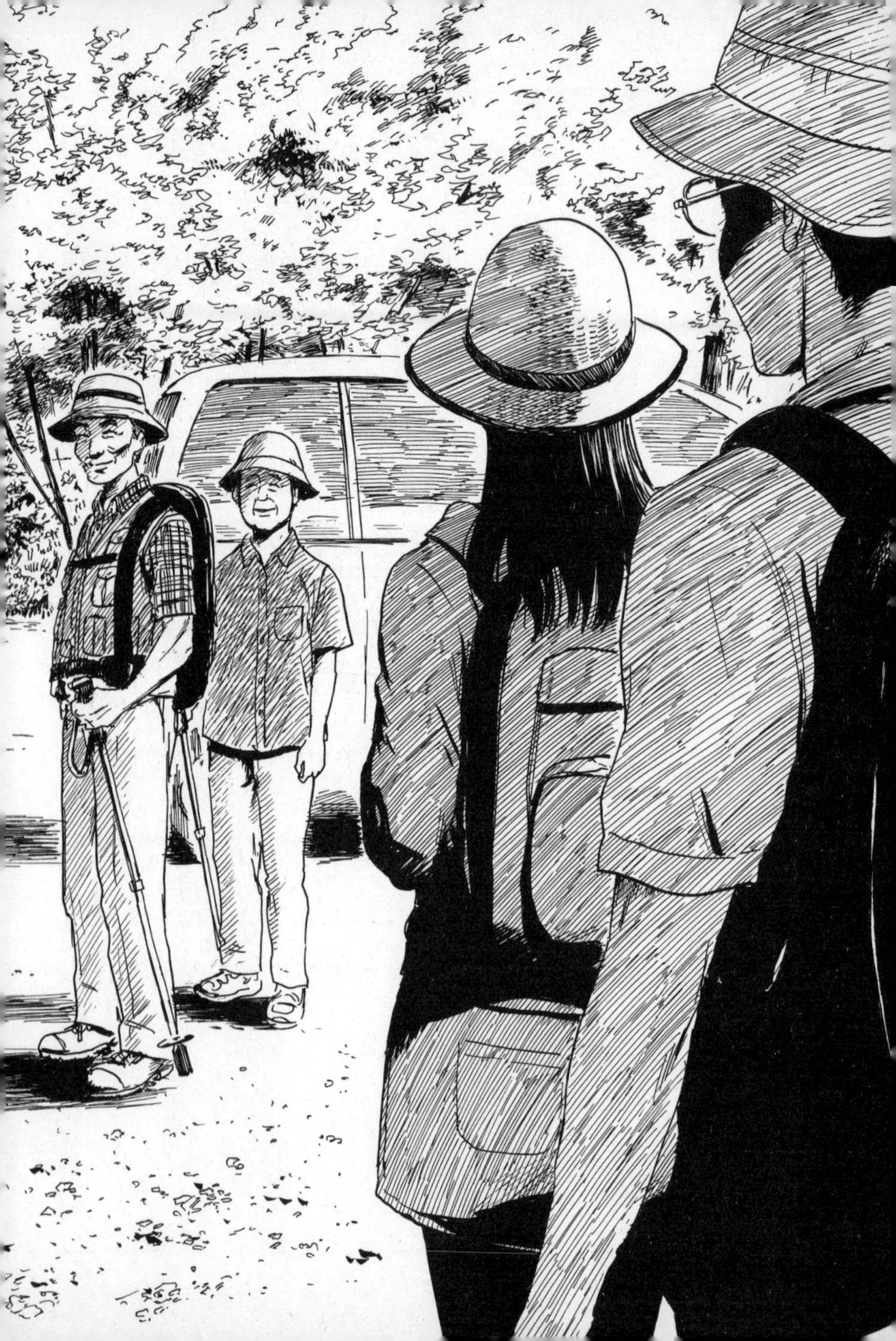

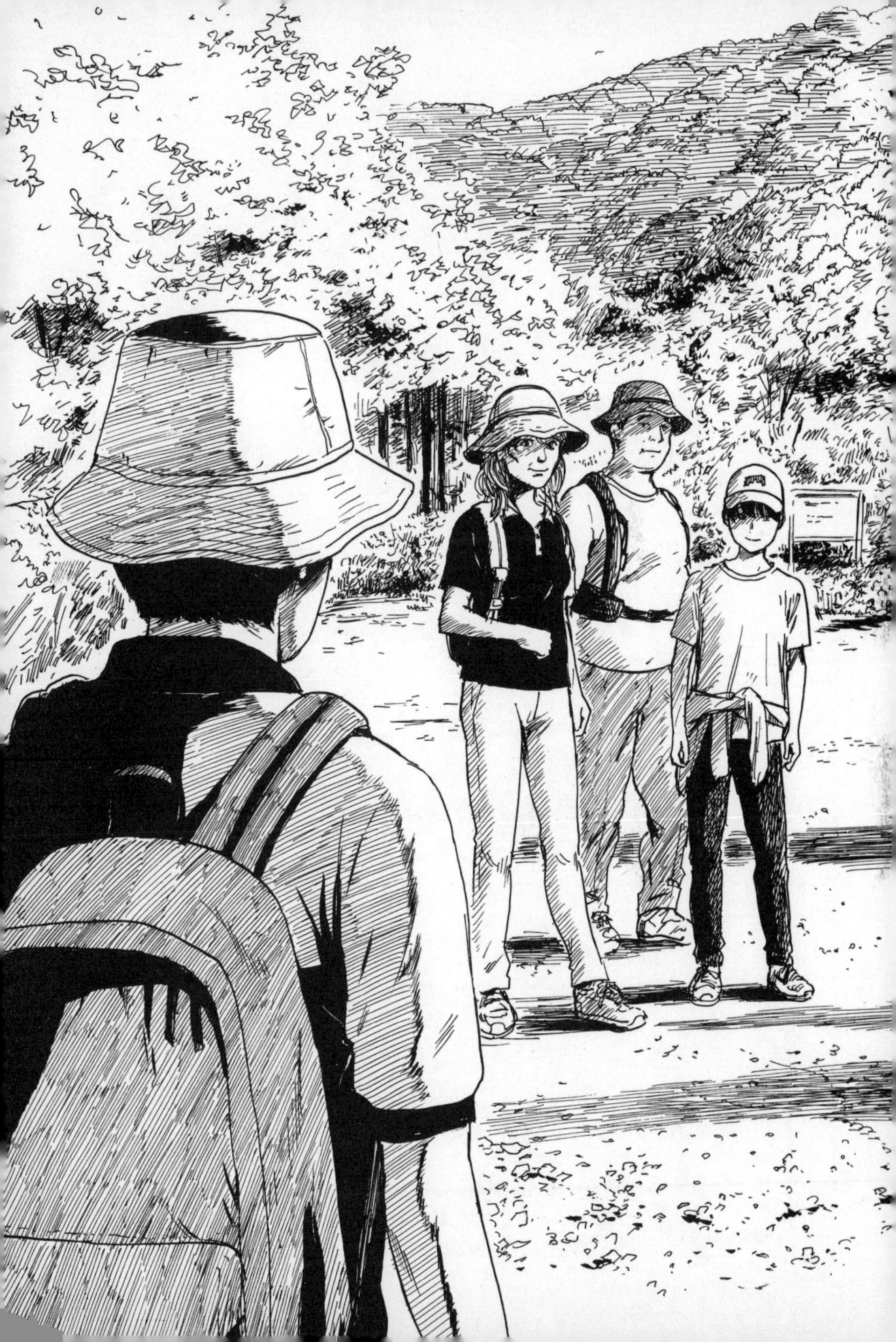

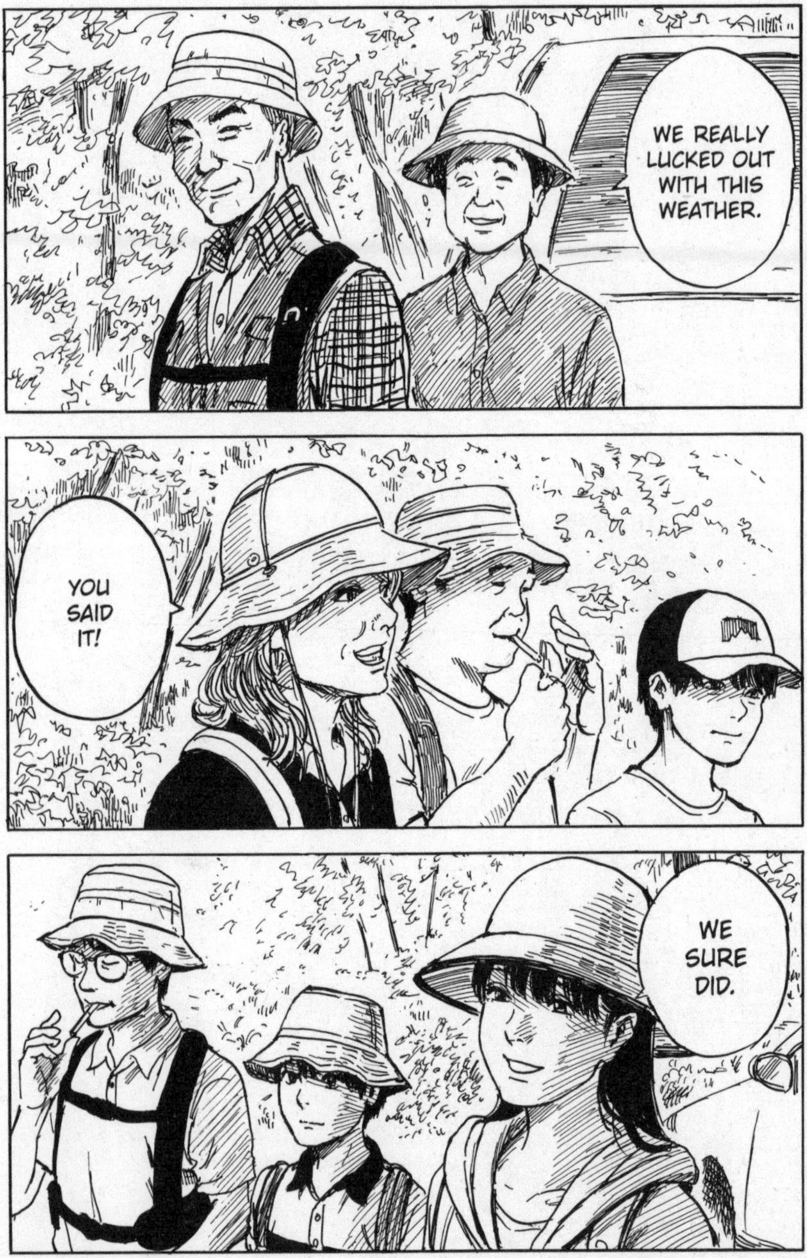
WE REALLY LUCKED OUT WITH THIS WEATHER.
YOU SAID IT!
WE SURE DID.

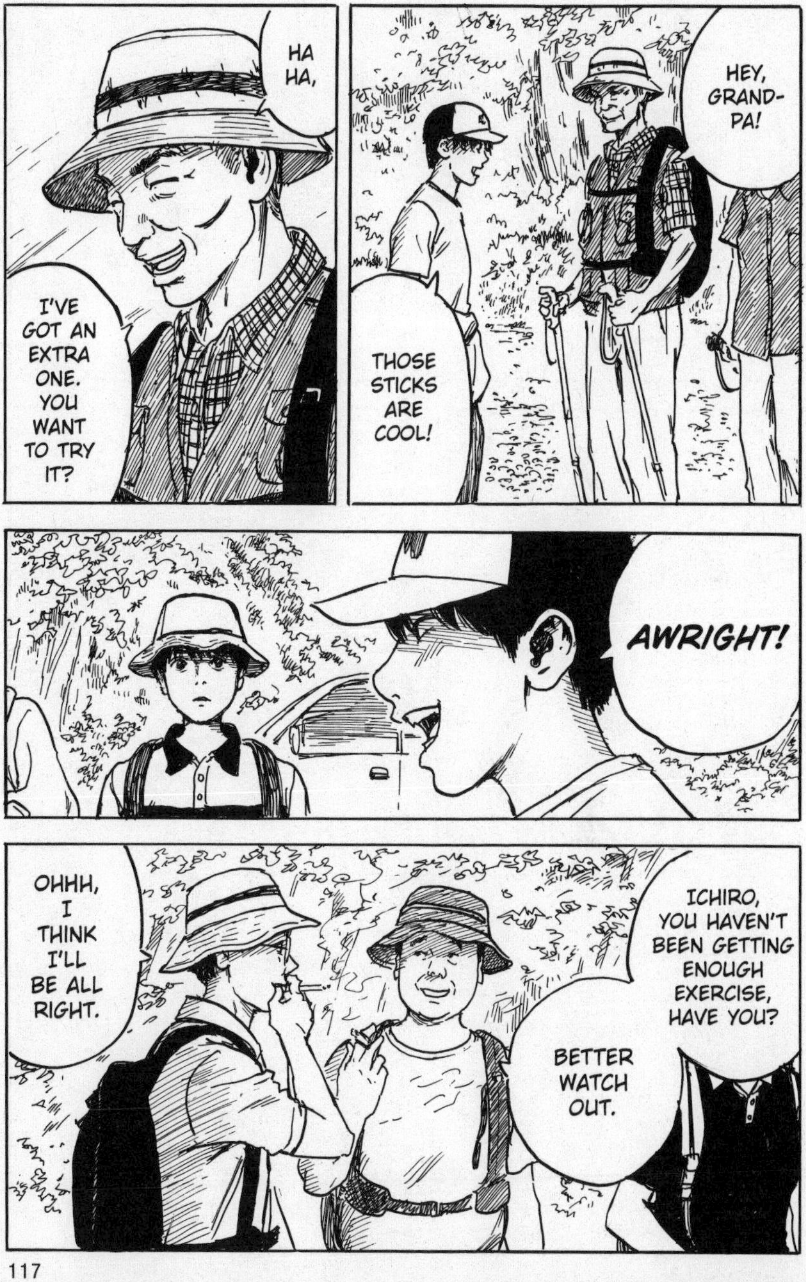
HEY, GRANDPA!
THOSE STICKS ARE COOL!
HA HA,
I'VE GOT AN EXTRA ONE. YOU WANT TO TRY IT?
AWRIGHT!
ICHIRO, YOU HAVEN'T BEEN GETTING ENOUGH EXERCISE, HAVE YOU?
BETTER WATCH OUT.
OHHH, I THINK I'LL BE ALL RIGHT.

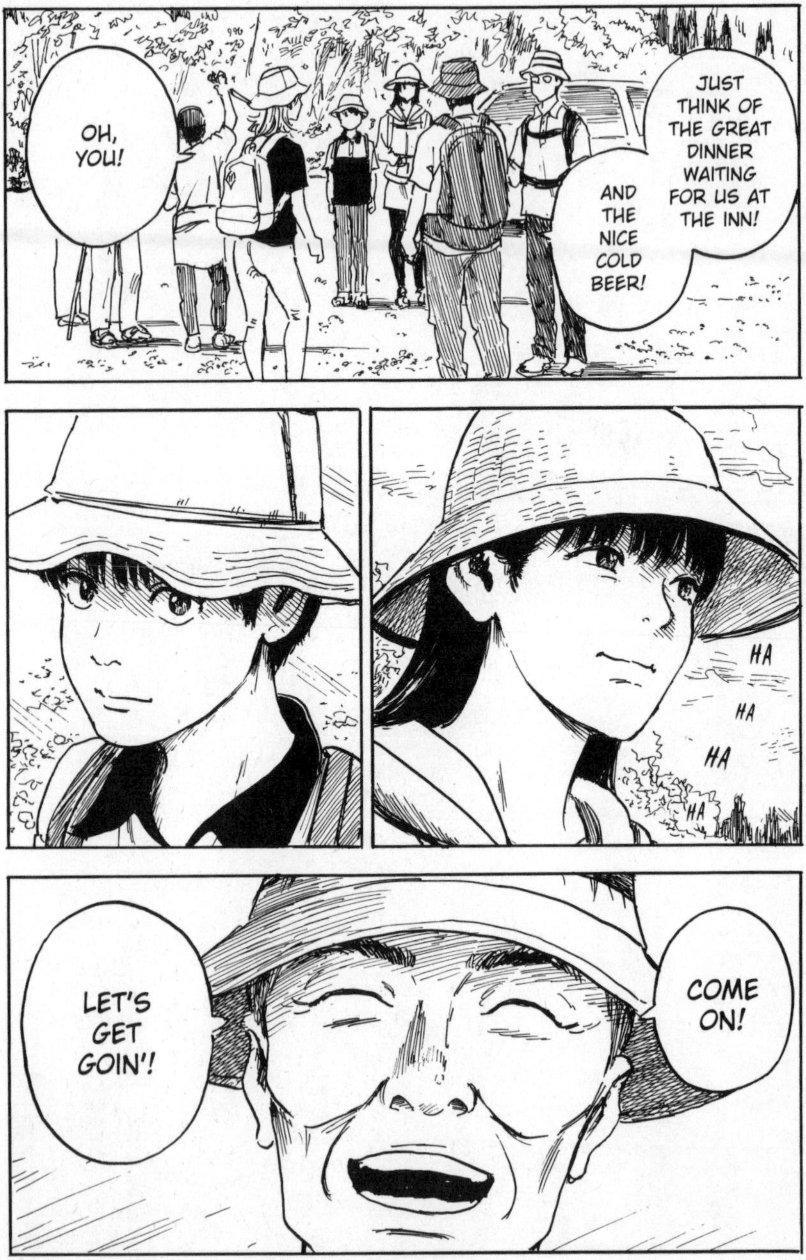
JUST THINK OF THE GREAT DINNER WAITING FOR US AT THE INN!
AND THE NICE COLD BEER!
OH, YOU!
HA HA HA HA
COME ON!
LET'S GET GOIN'!

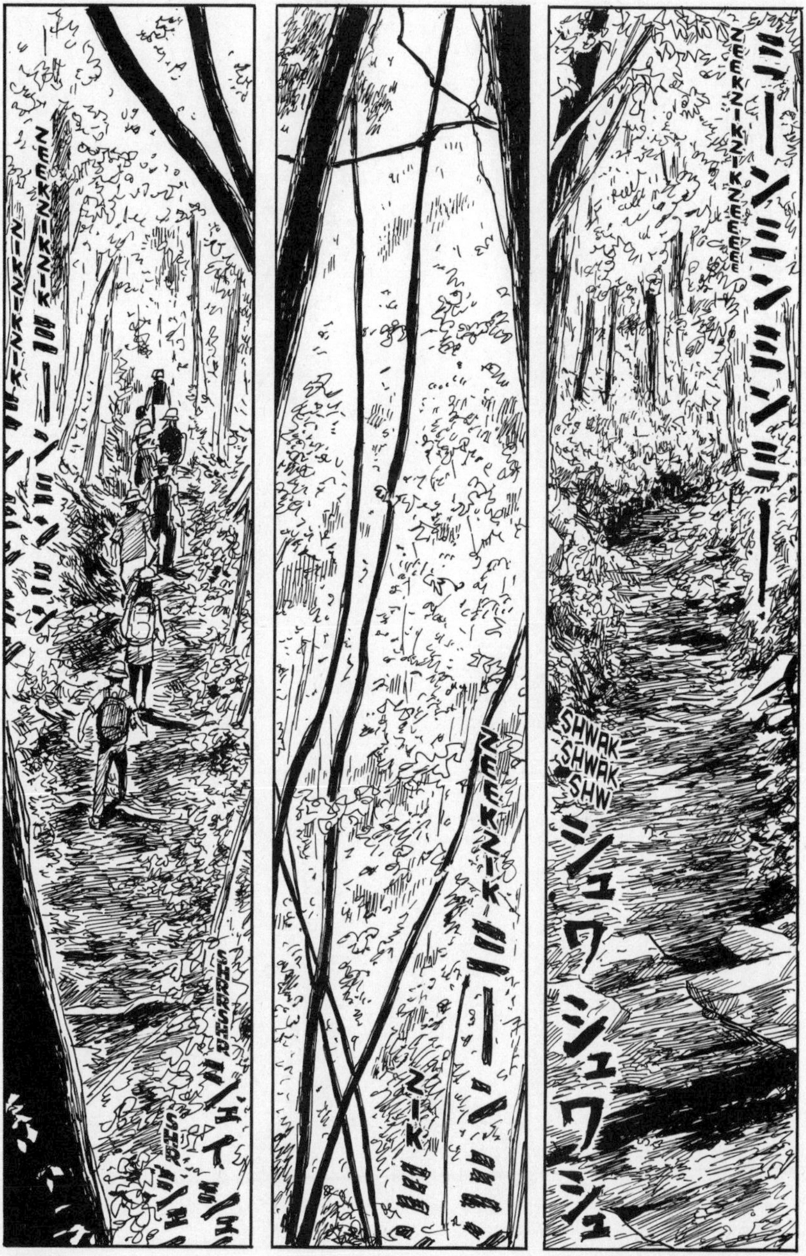
ミーンミンミンミー!
ZEEKZIKZIKZEEEEE
SHWAK SHWAK SHW
シュワシュワシュ
ZEEKZIK
ミーンミンミ
ZIK
ZEEKZIKZIK
ミーンミンミンミ
ZIKZIKZIK
SHRRSHR
SHR

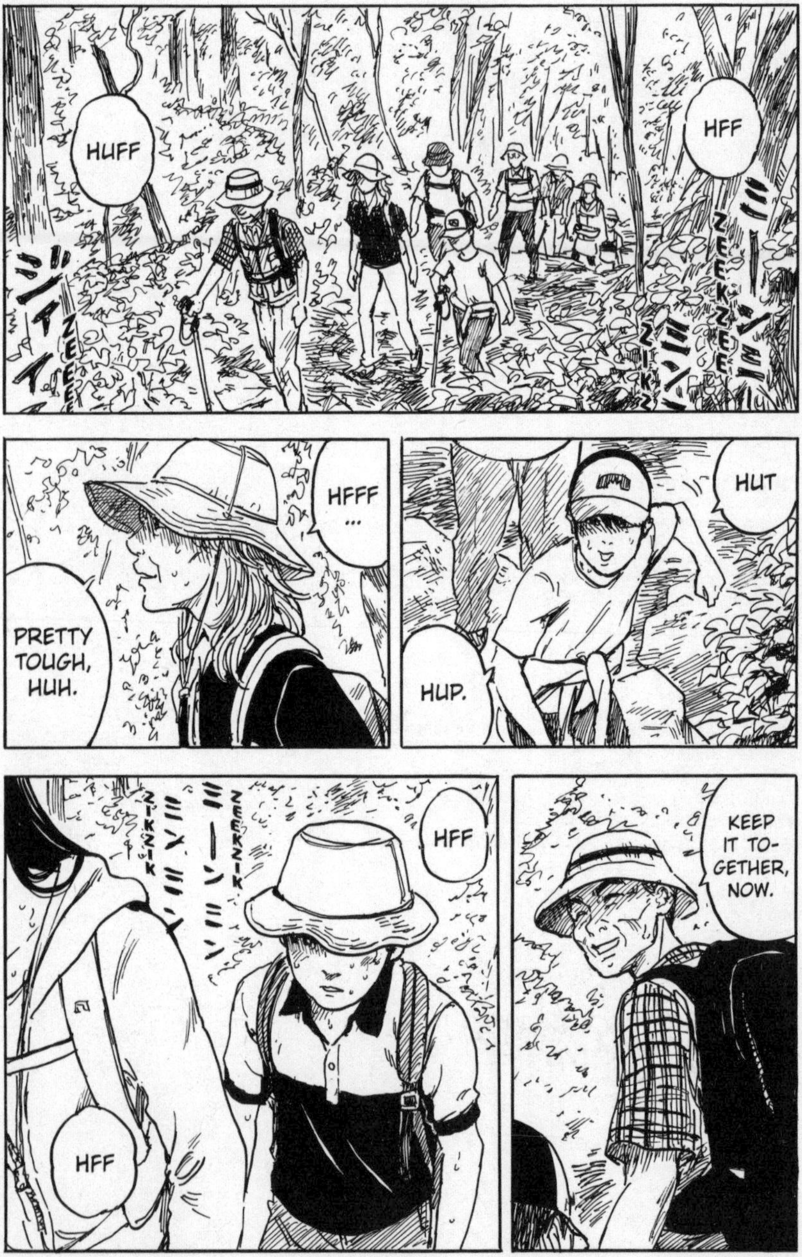
HFF
ZEEKZEE
ZIKZIK
HUFF
ZEEEE
HUT
HUP.
HFFF ...
PRETTY TOUGH, HUH.
KEEP IT TO-GETHER, NOW.
HFF
ZEEKZIK
ZIKZIK
HFF

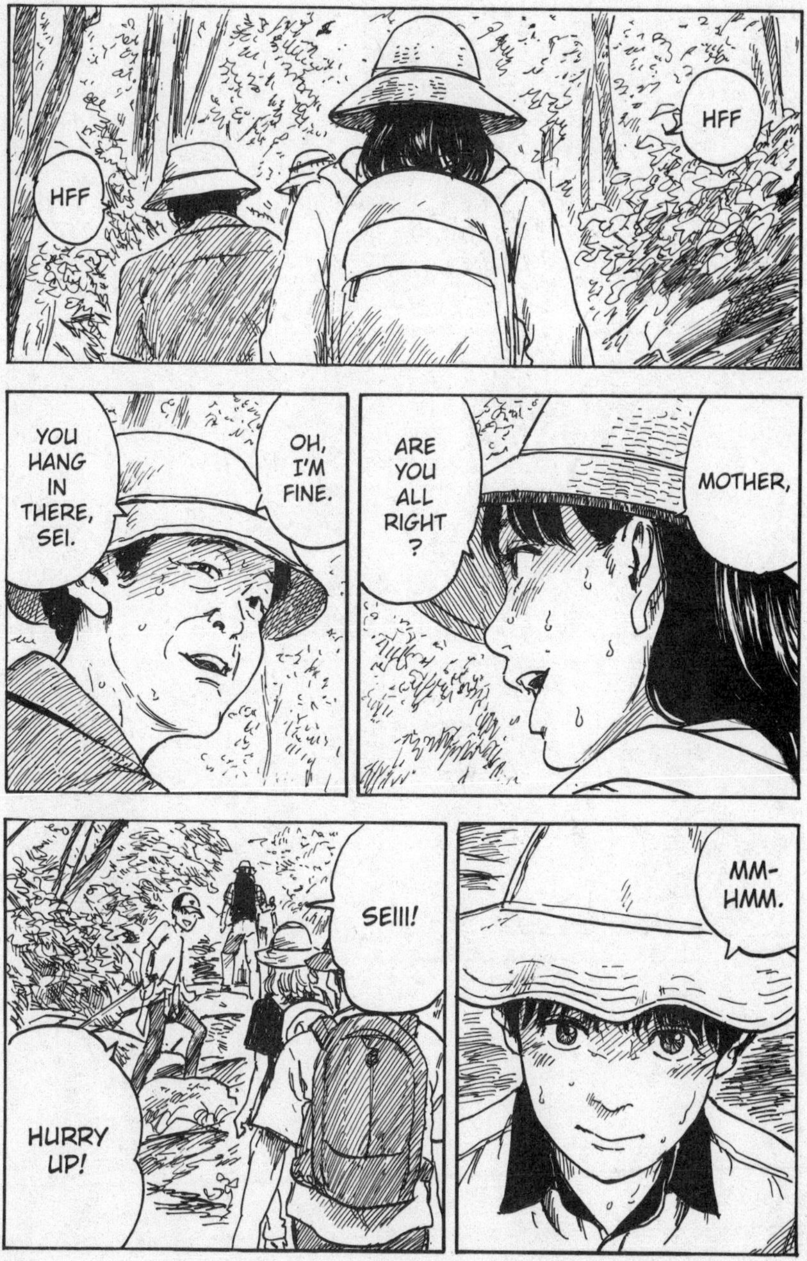
HFF
HFF
MOTHER,
ARE YOU ALL RIGHT?
OH, I'M FINE.
YOU HANG IN THERE, SEI.
MM-HMM.
SEIII!
HURRY UP!

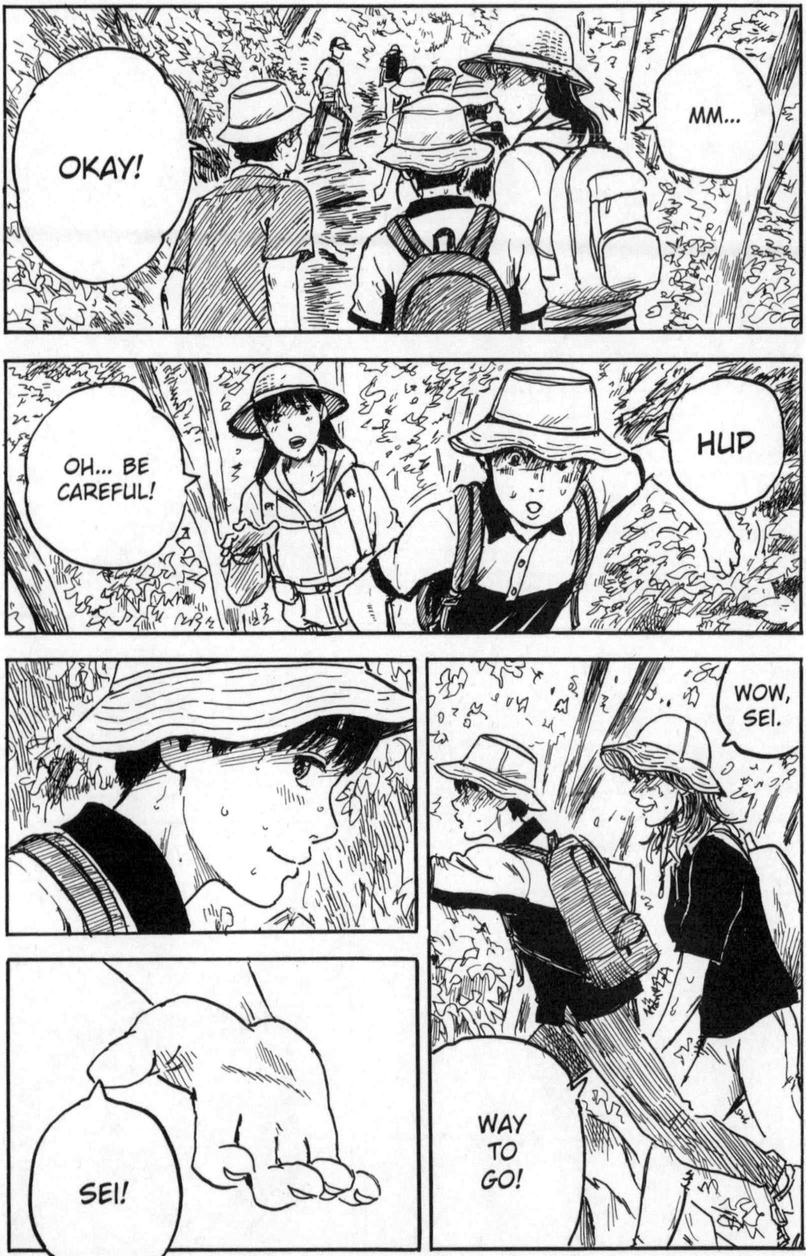
MM...
OKAY!
HUP
OH... BE CAREFUL!
WOW, SEI.
WAY TO GO!
SEI!

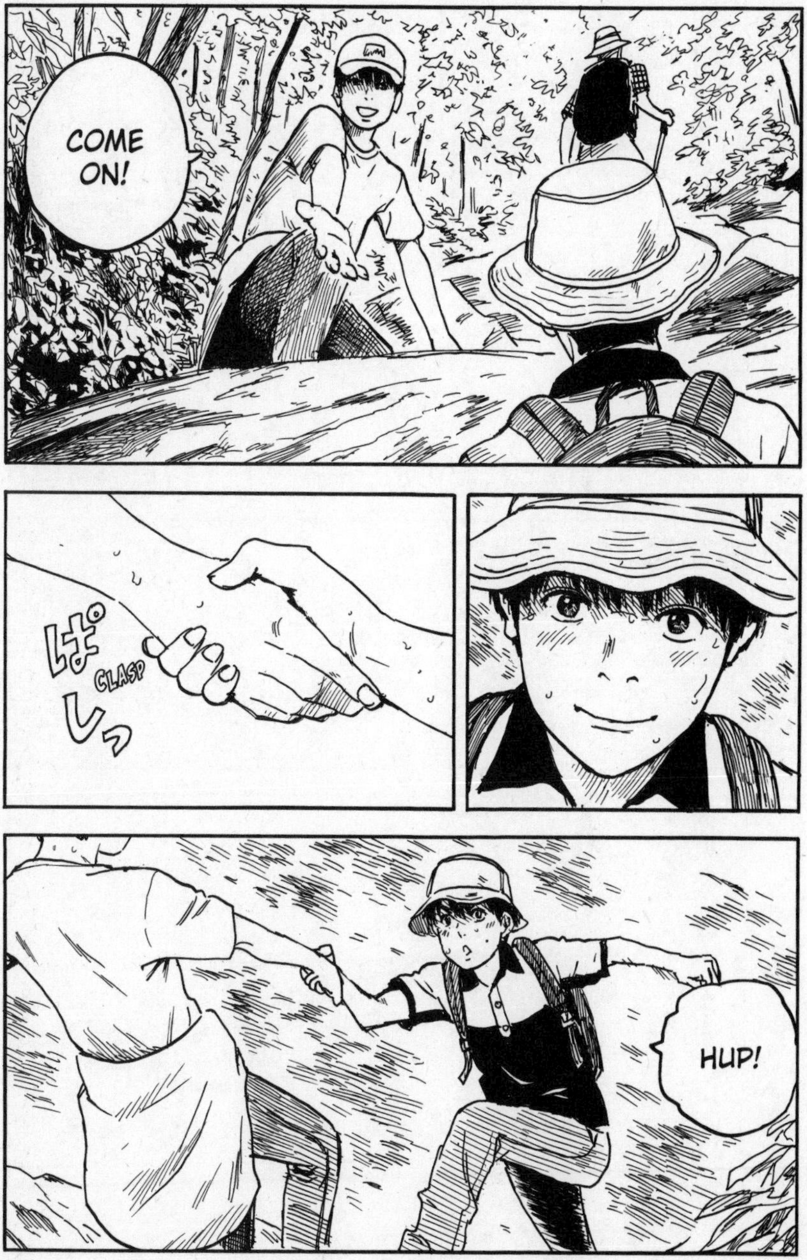
COME ON!
ぱしっ
CLASP
HUP!

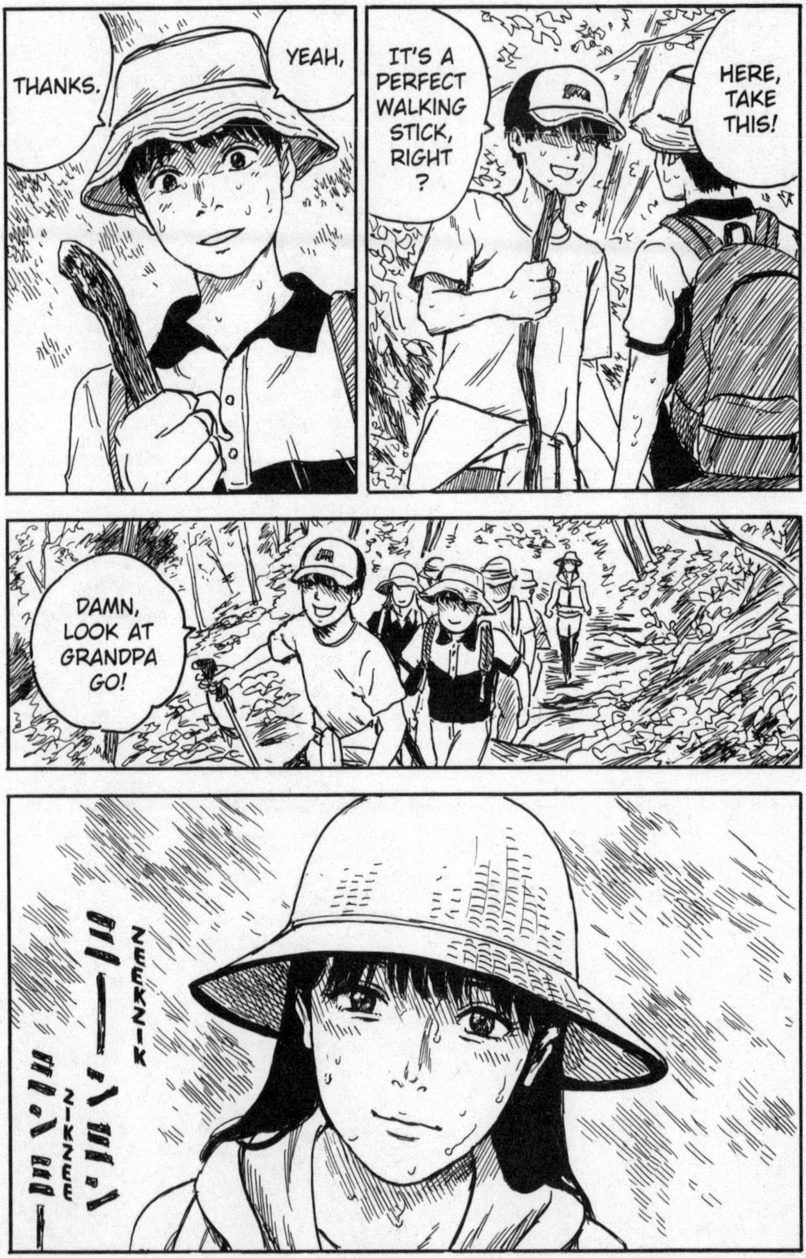
HERE, TAKE THIS!
IT'S A PERFECT WALKING STICK, RIGHT?
YEAH,
THANKS.
DAMN, LOOK AT GRANDPA GO!
ZEEKZIK
ZIKZEE

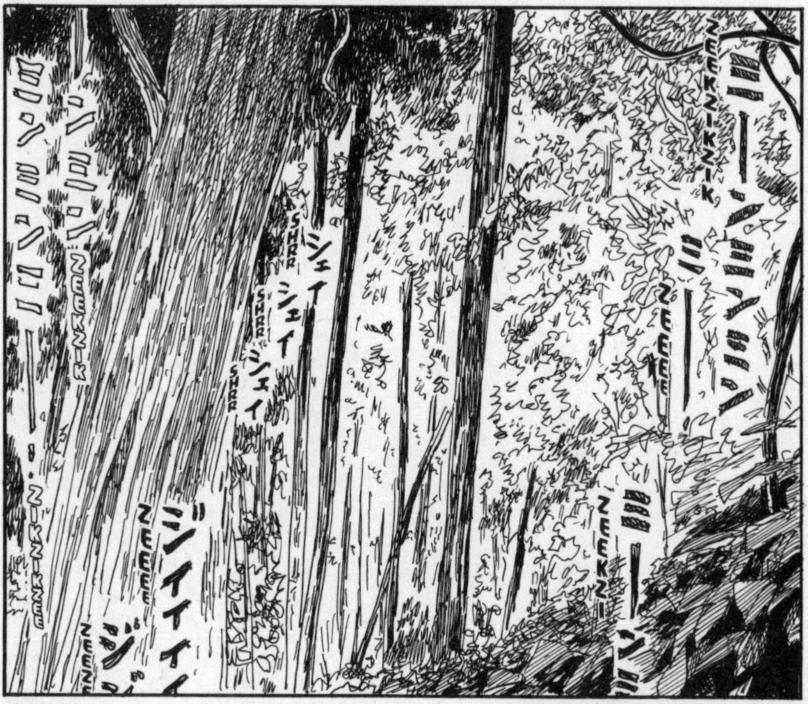
ZEEKZIKZIK
ZEEEE
ZEEKZI
シェイ
SHRR
シェイ
SHRR
シェイ
SHRR
ZEEKZIK
ZIKZIKZEE
ジイイイイ
ZEEEEE

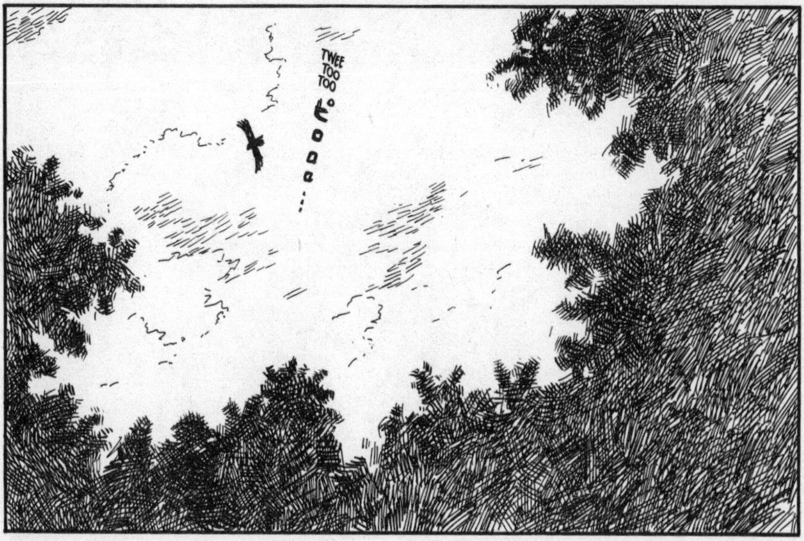
TWEE TOO TOO

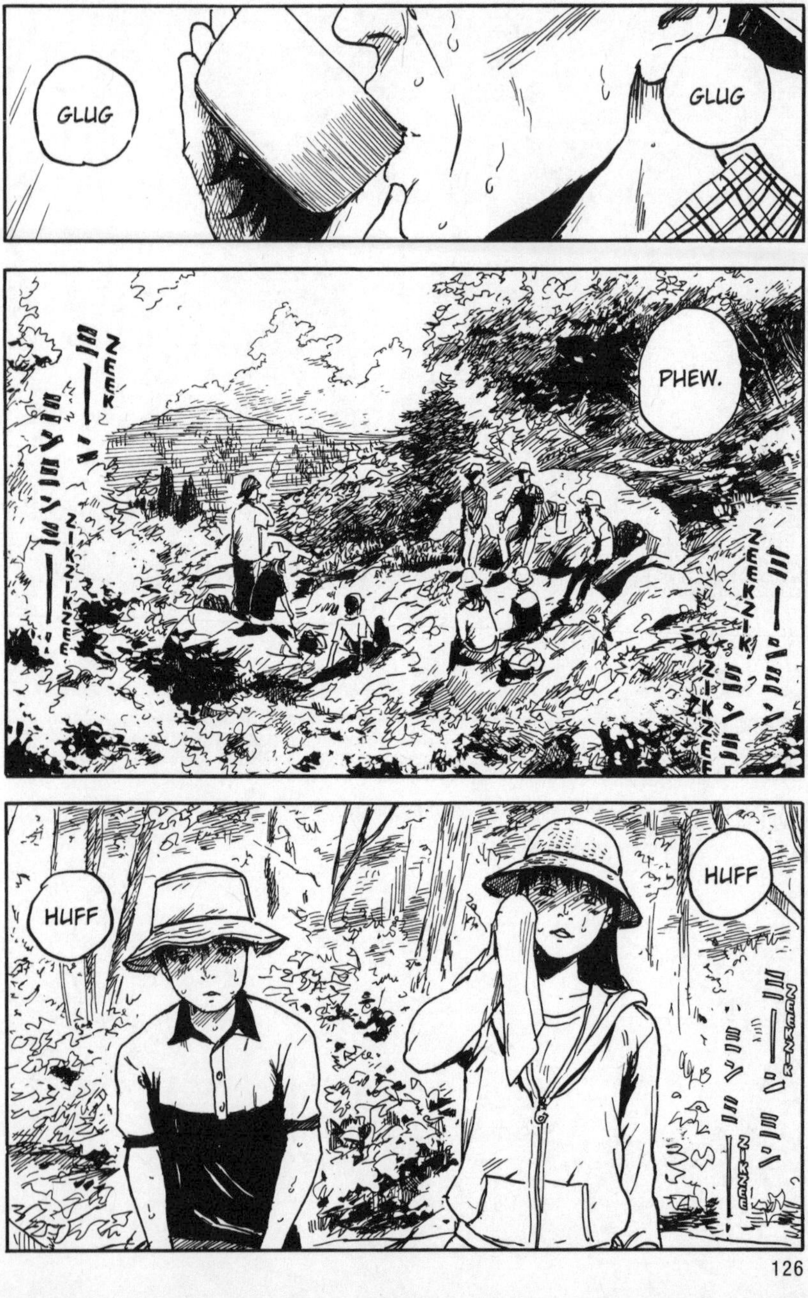
GLUG
GLUG
PHEW.
ZEEKZIK
ZIKZEE
ZEEK
ZIKZIKZEE
HUFF
HUFF
ZEEKZIK
ZIKZEE

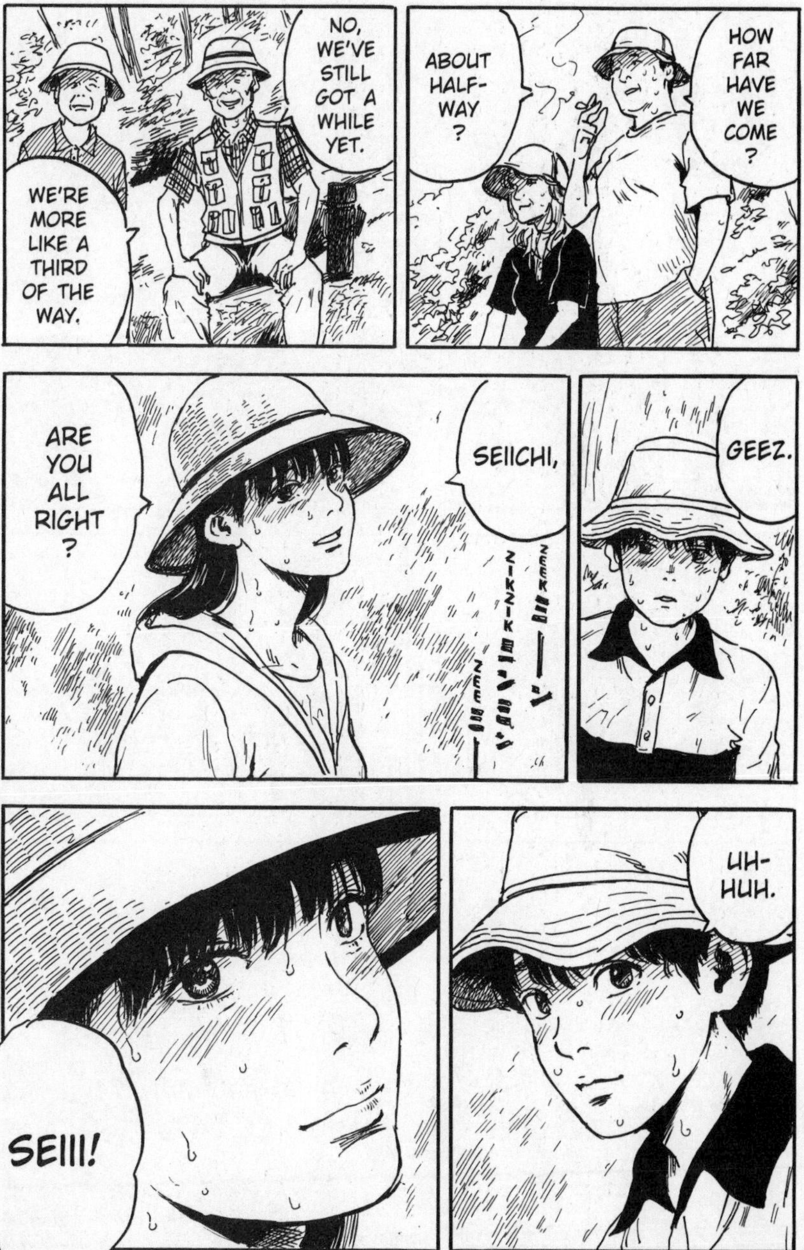
HOW FAR HAVE WE COME?
ABOUT HALF-WAY?
NO, WE'VE STILL GOT A WHILE YET.
WE'RE MORE LIKE A THIRD OF THE WAY.
GEEZ.
SEIICHI,
ZEEK
ZIKZIK
ZEE
ARE YOU ALL RIGHT?
UH-HUH.
SEIII!

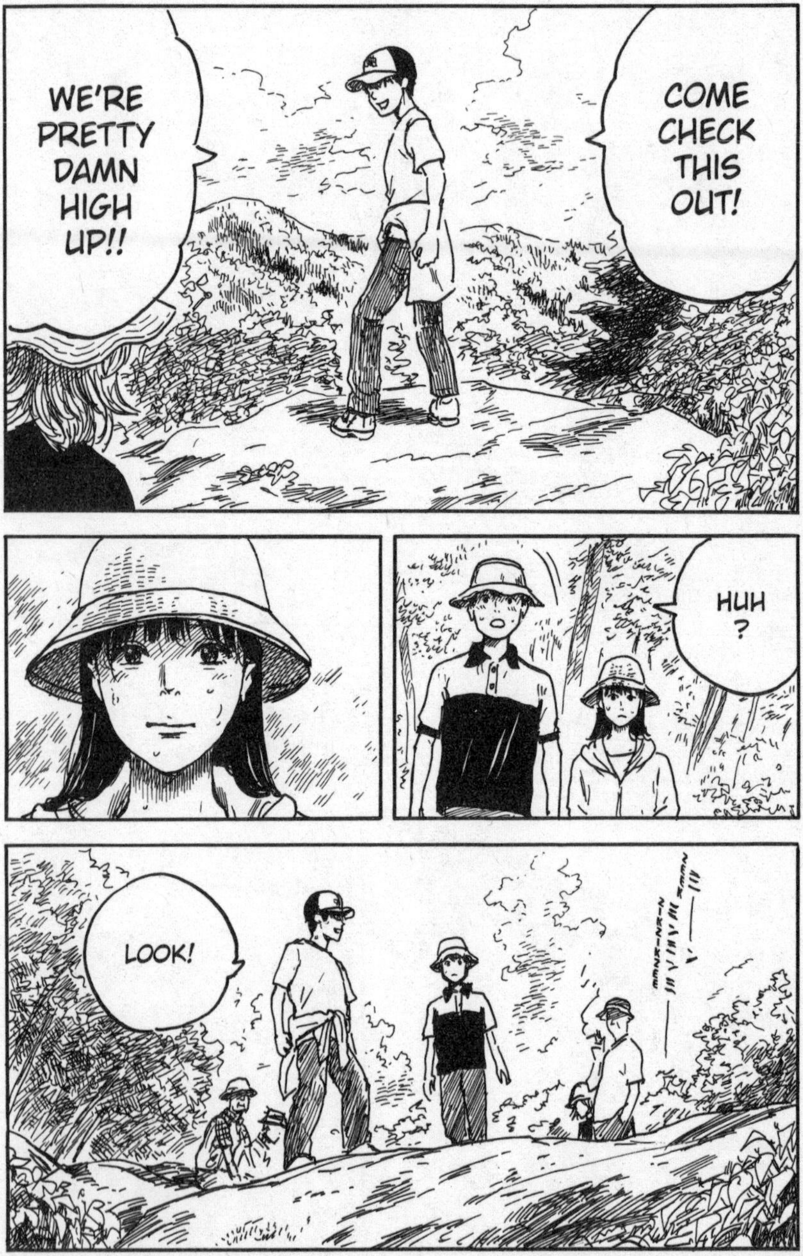
COME CHECK THIS OUT!
WE'RE PRETTY DAMN HIGH UP!!
HUH?
LOOK!

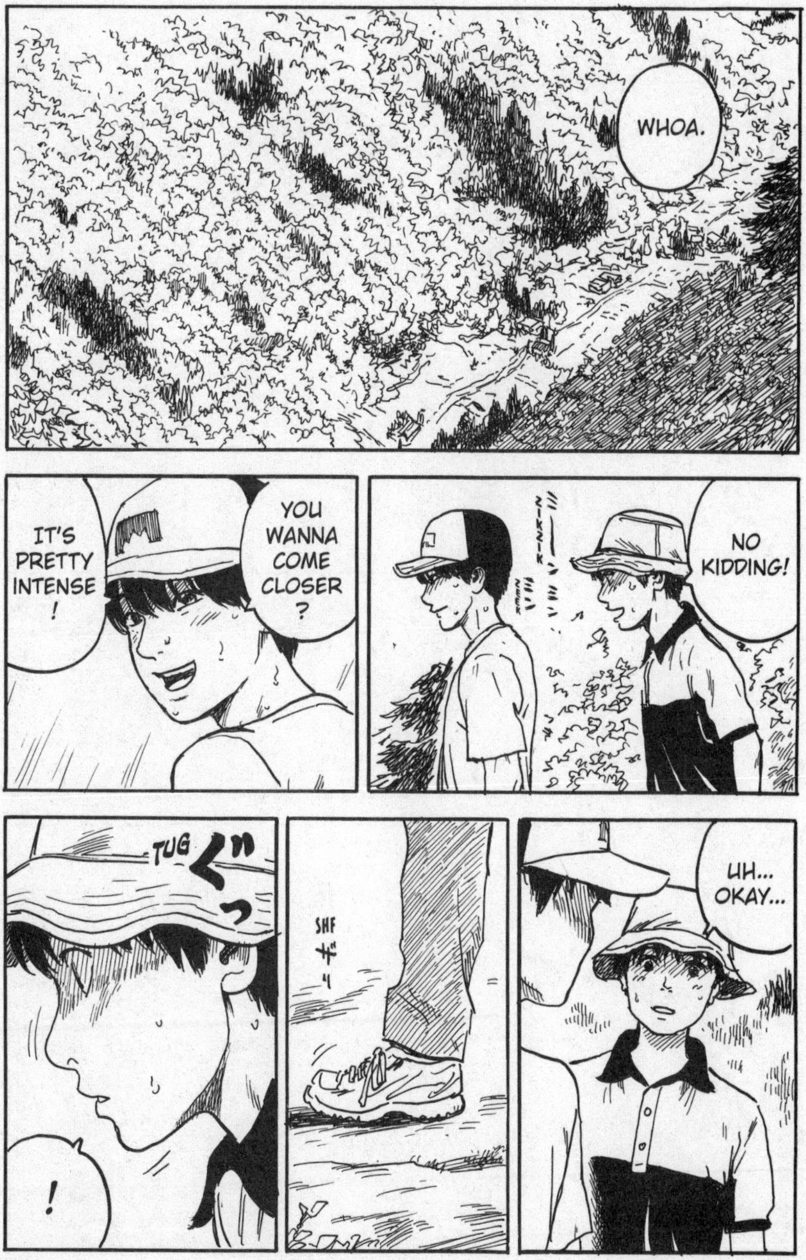
WHOA.
NO KIDDING!
ZIKZIK
YOU WANNA COME CLOSER?
IT'S PRETTY INTENSE!
UH... OKAY...
SHF
TUG
!

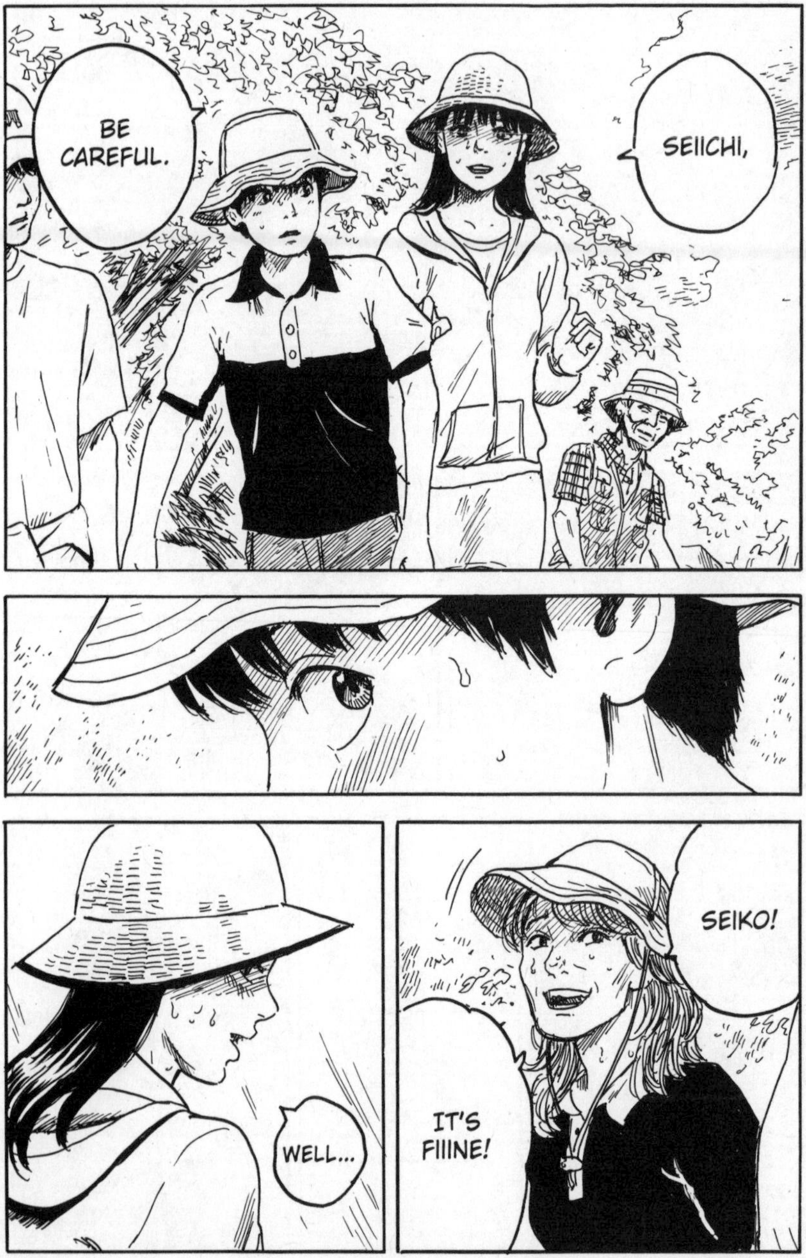
SEIICHI,
BE CAREFUL.
SEIKO!
IT'S FIIINE!
WELL...

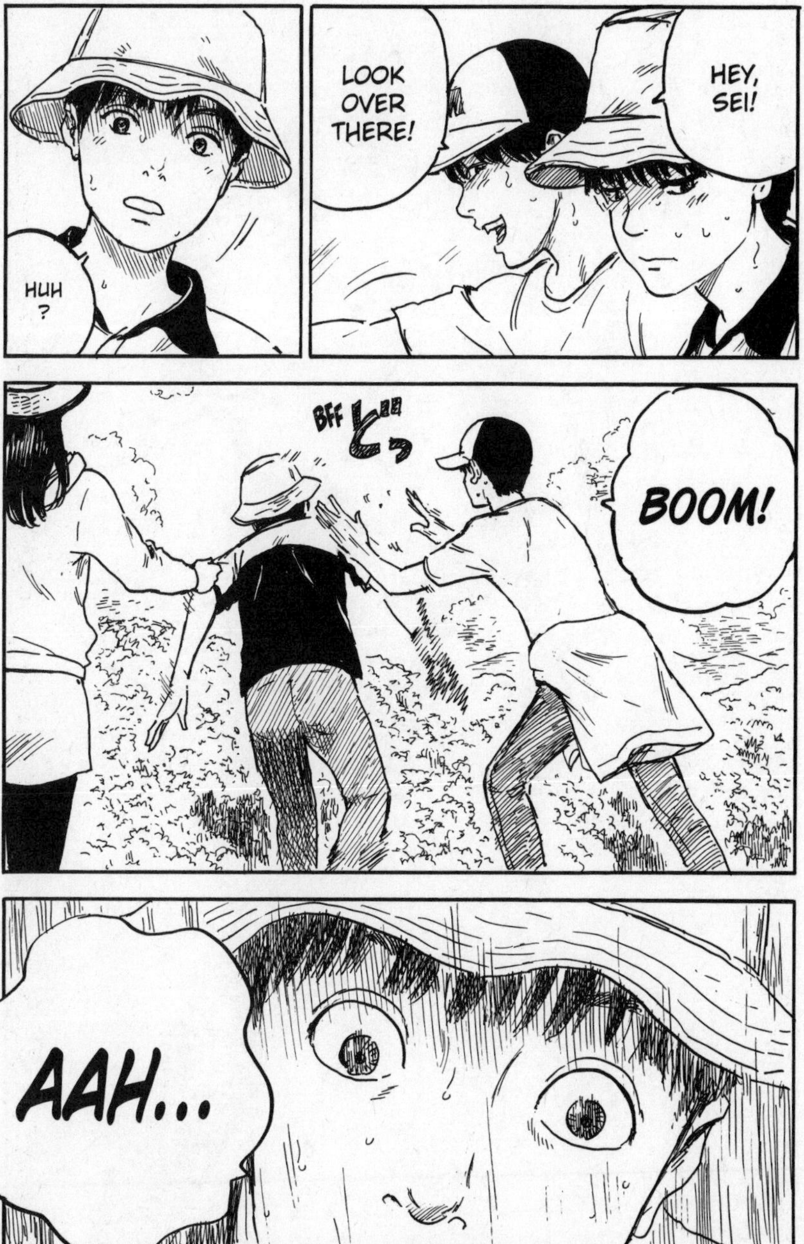
HEY, SEI!
LOOK OVER THERE!
HUH ?
BOOM!
BFF どっ
AAH...

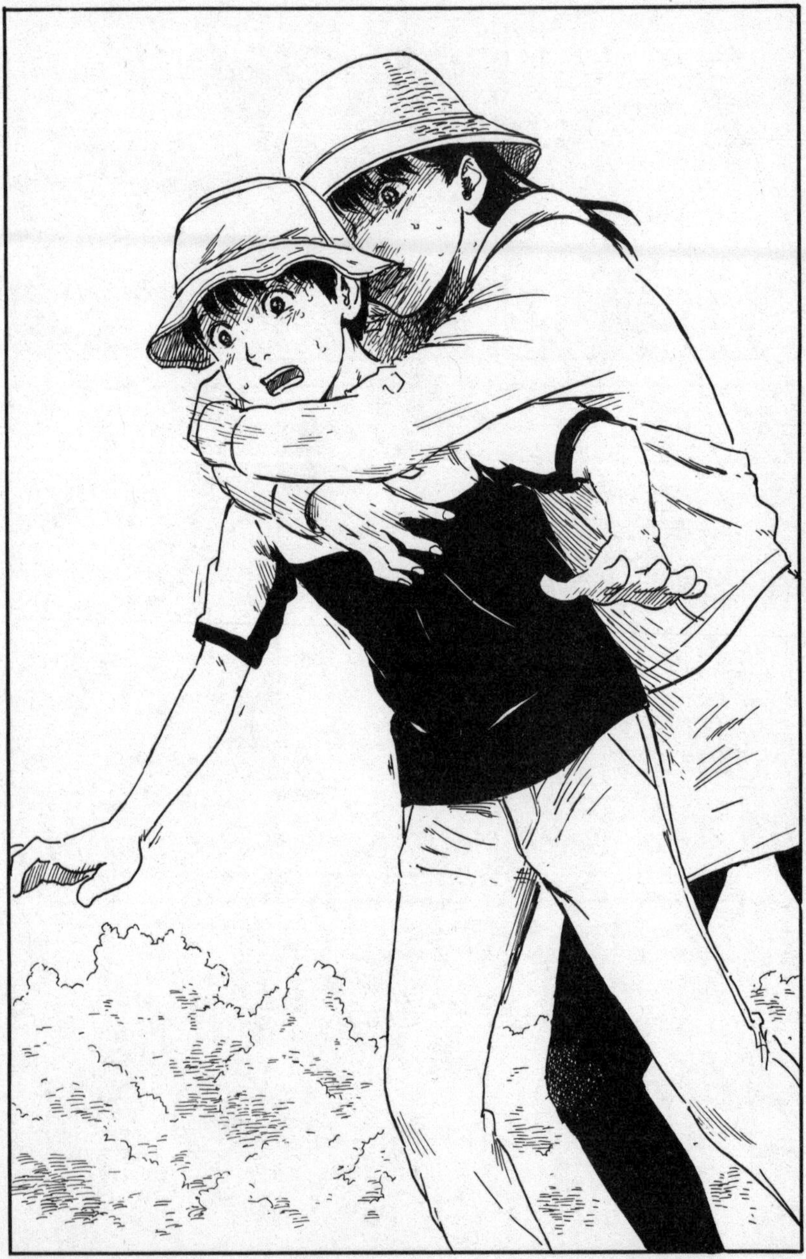

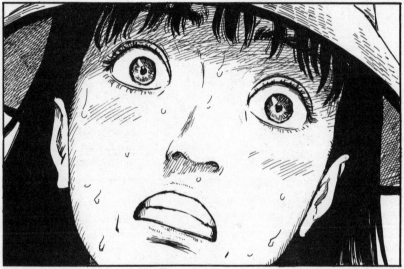

AH HA
HA HA
HA HA!

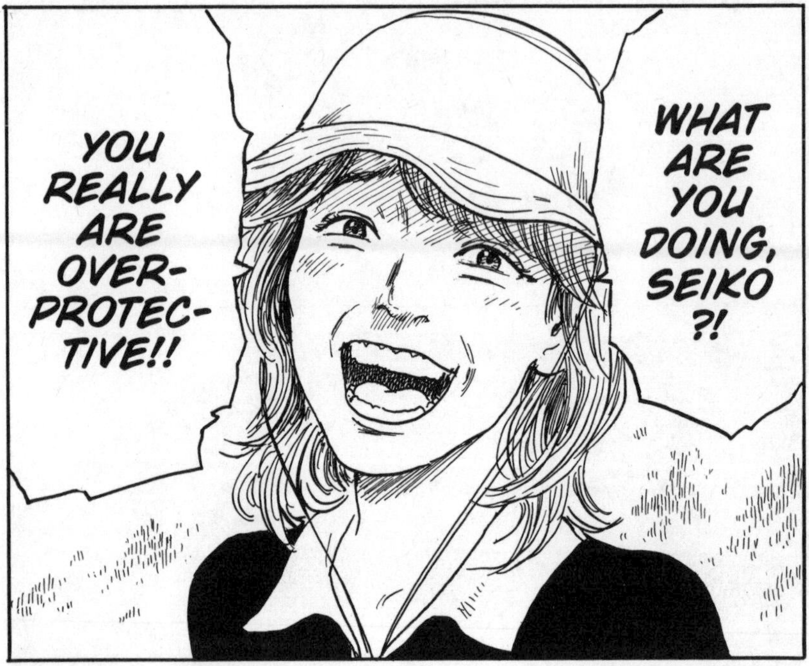
WHAT ARE YOU DOING, SEIKO?!
YOU REALLY ARE OVERPROTECTIVE!!

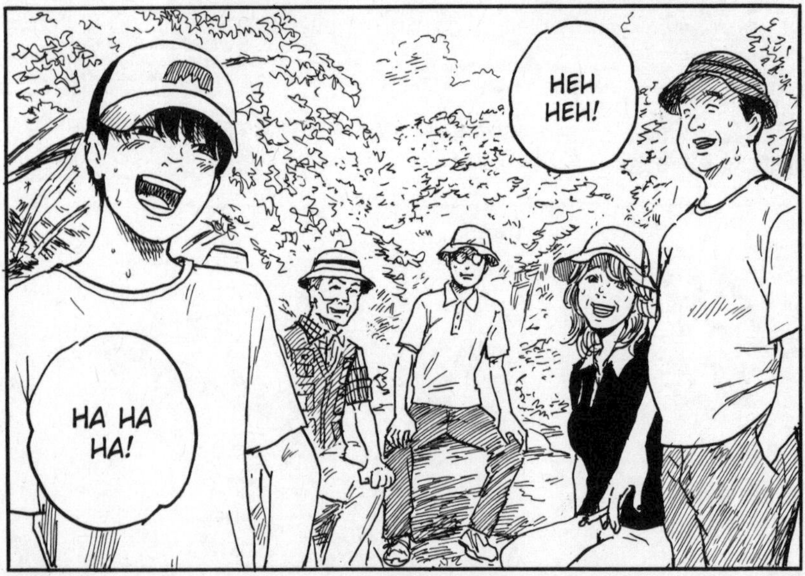
HEH HEH!
HA HA HA!

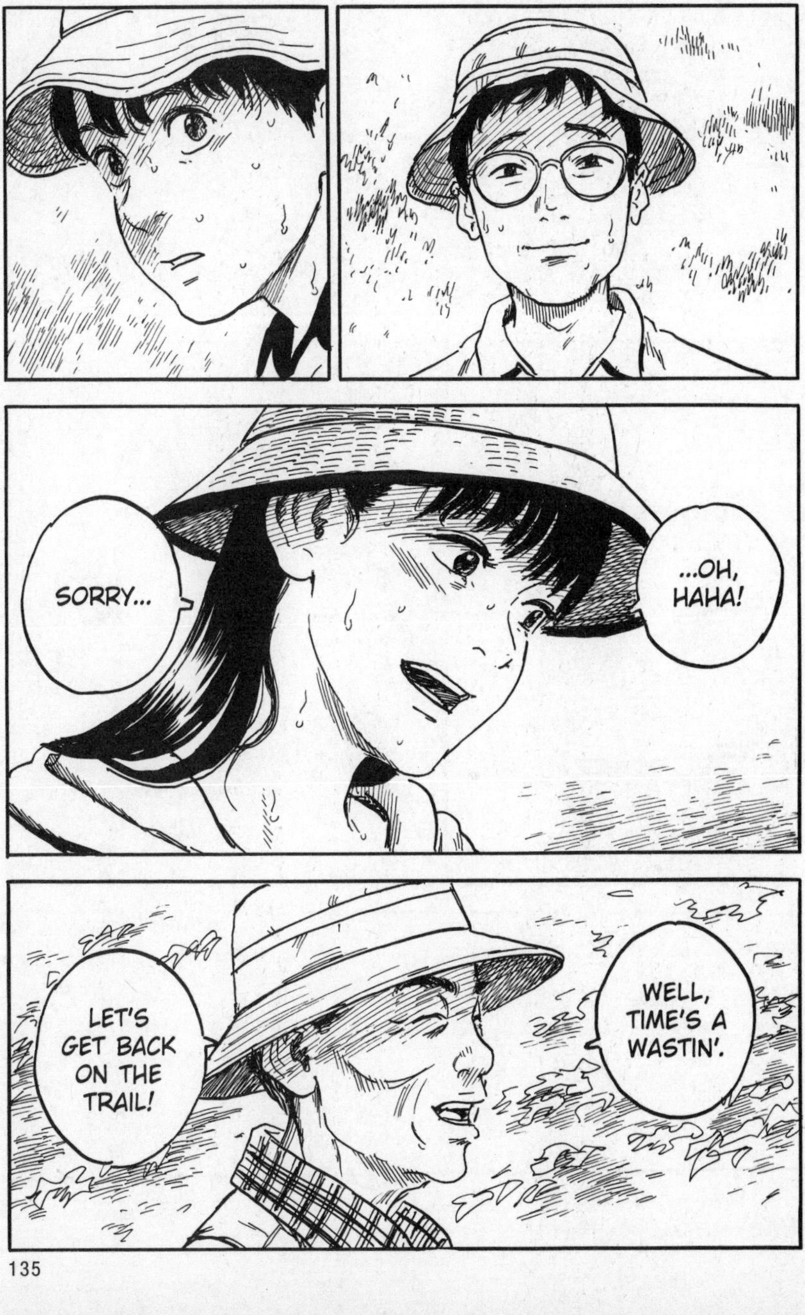
...OH, HAHA!
SORRY...
WELL, TIME'S A WASTIN'.
LET'S GET BACK ON THE TRAIL!

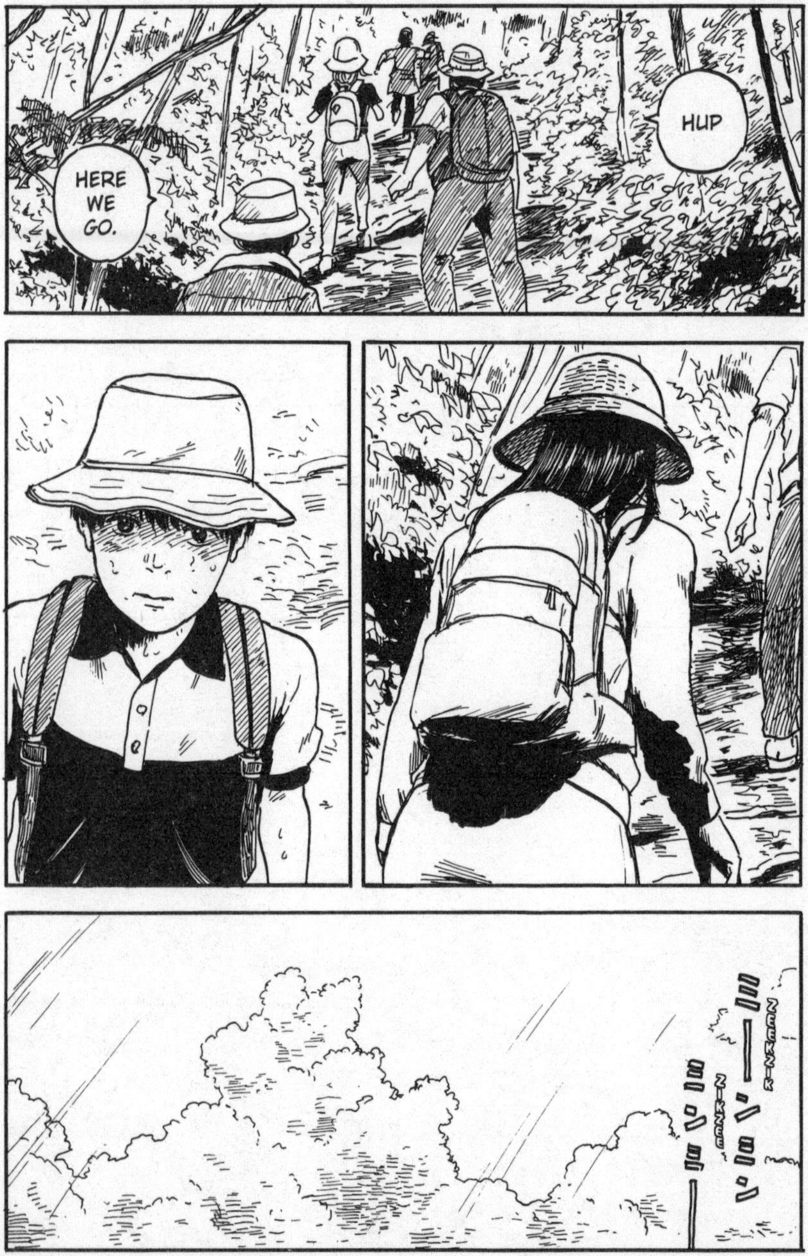
HUP
HERE WE GO.
ZEEKZIK
ZIKZEE

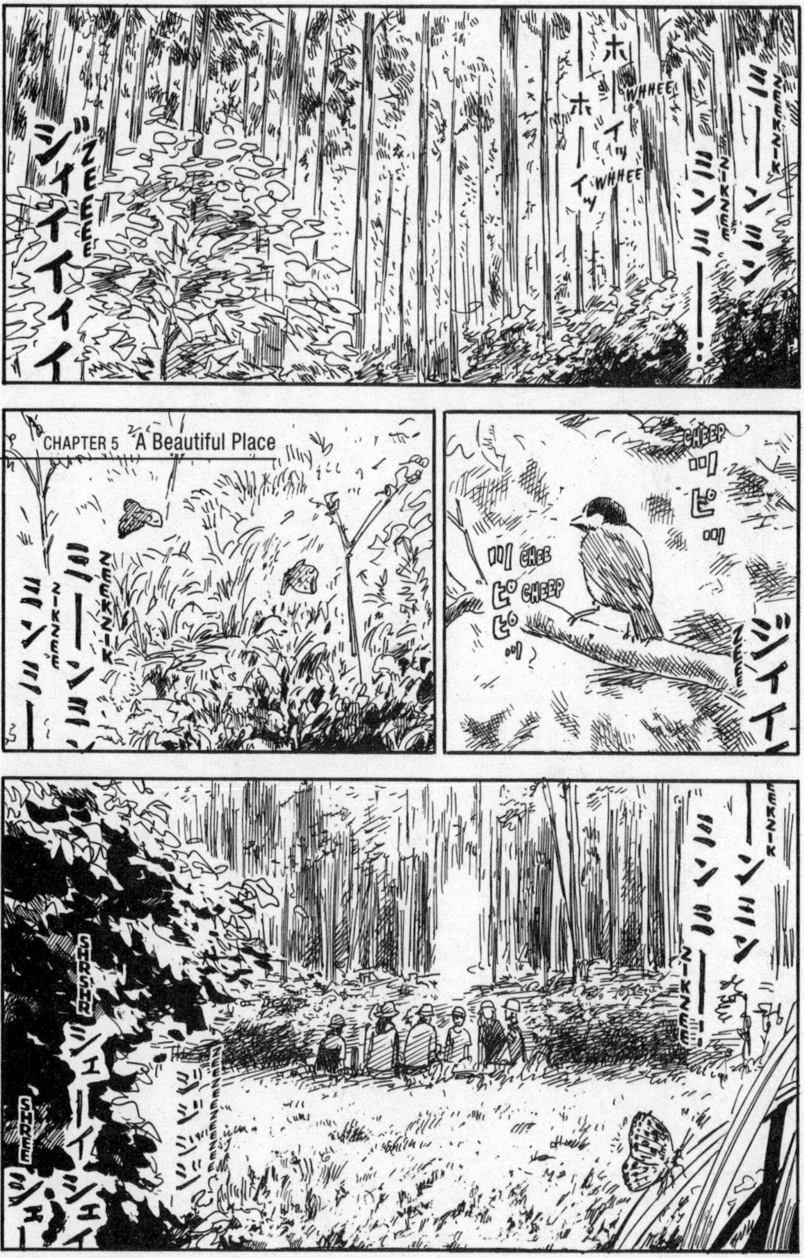
ミーンミンミンミー!!
ZEEKZIK ZIKZEE
ホーイッ ホーイッ
WHHEE WHHEE
ジィイイイ
ZEEEE
ピッピッ
CHEEP
ジイイ
ピッピピッ
CHEE CHEEP
CHAPTER 5 A Beautiful Place
ミーンミンミー
ZEEKZIK ZIKZEE
ーンミンミンミー!!
ZEEKZIK ZIKZEE
ジジジジジ
ZEEZEEZEE
シェーイシェイシェー
SHRSHR SHREE

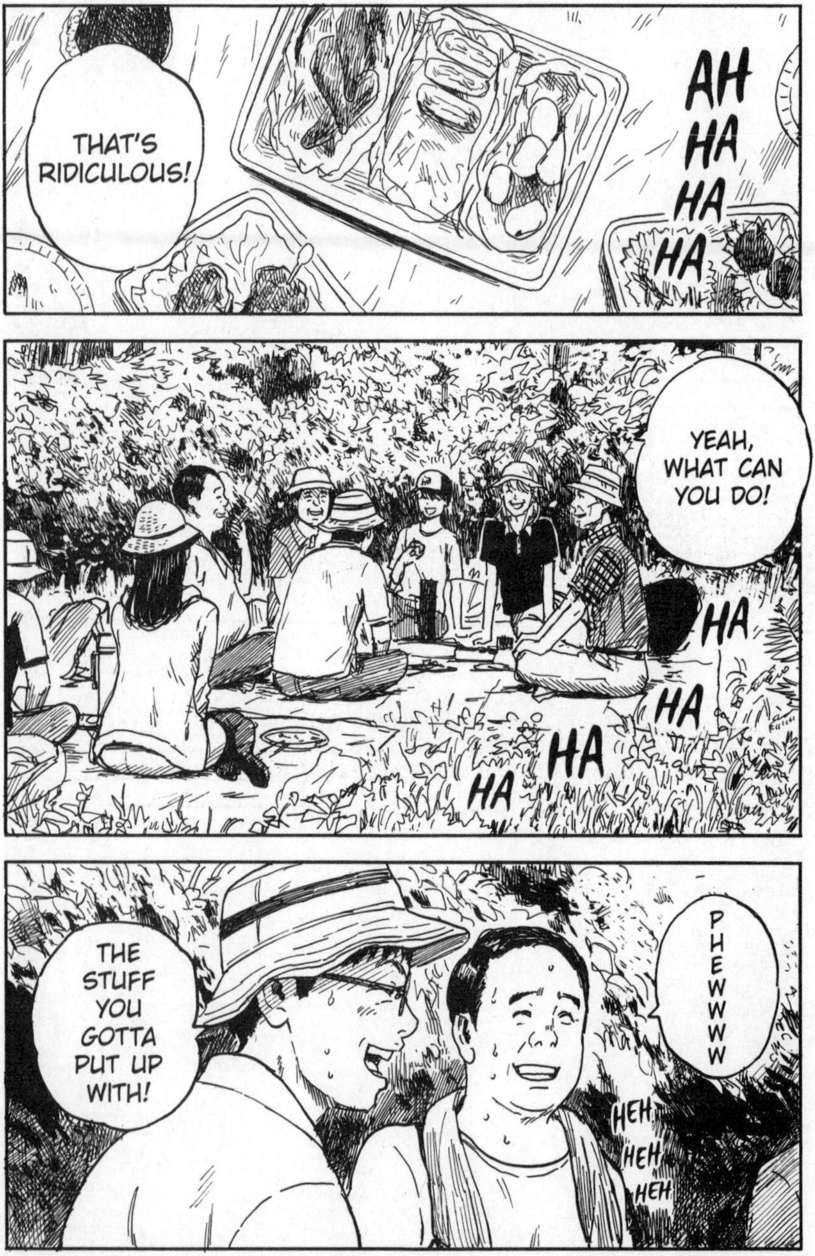
AH HA HA HA
THAT'S RIDICULOUS!
YEAH, WHAT CAN YOU DO!
HA HA HA HA
PHEWWWW
HEH HEH HEH
THE STUFF YOU GOTTA PUT UP WITH!

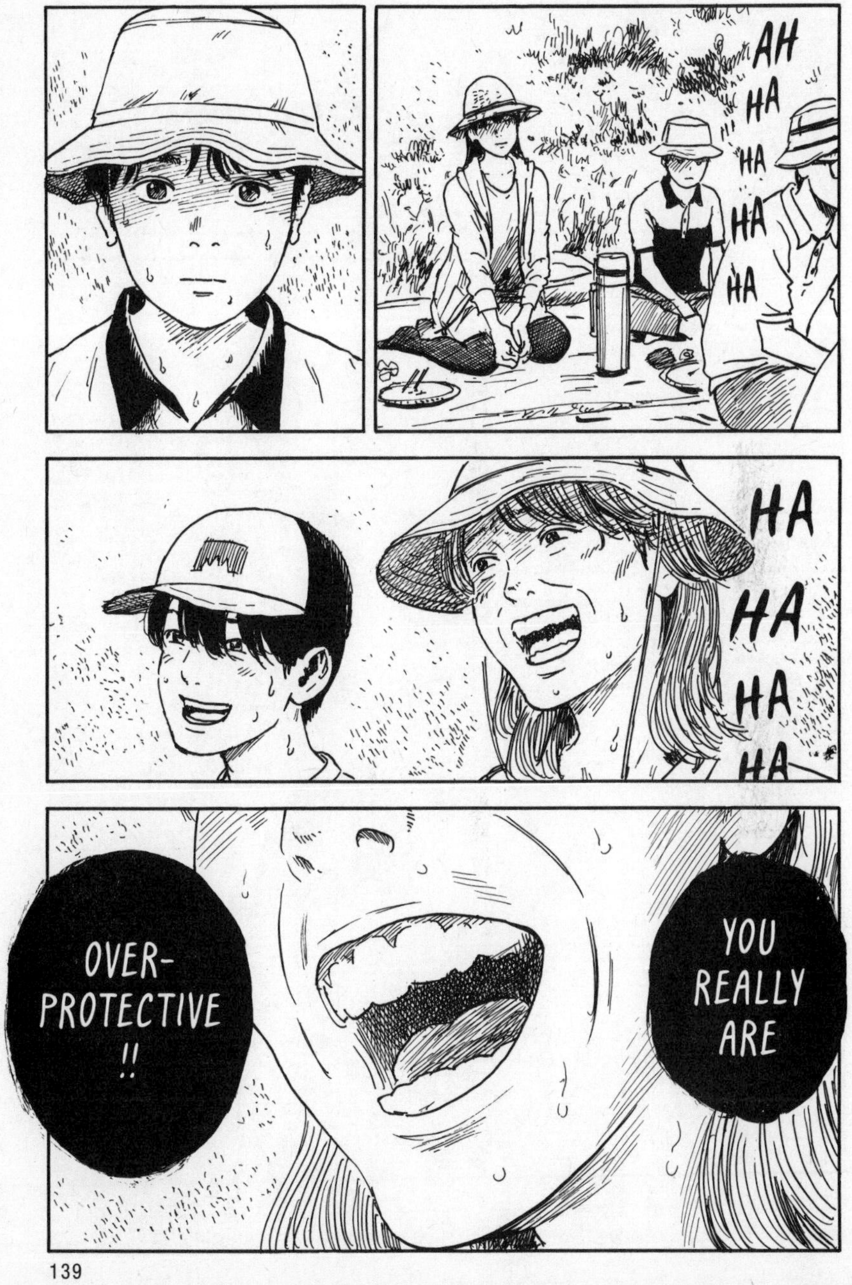
AH HA HA HA HA
HA HA HA HA
YOU REALLY ARE
OVER-PROTECTIVE !!

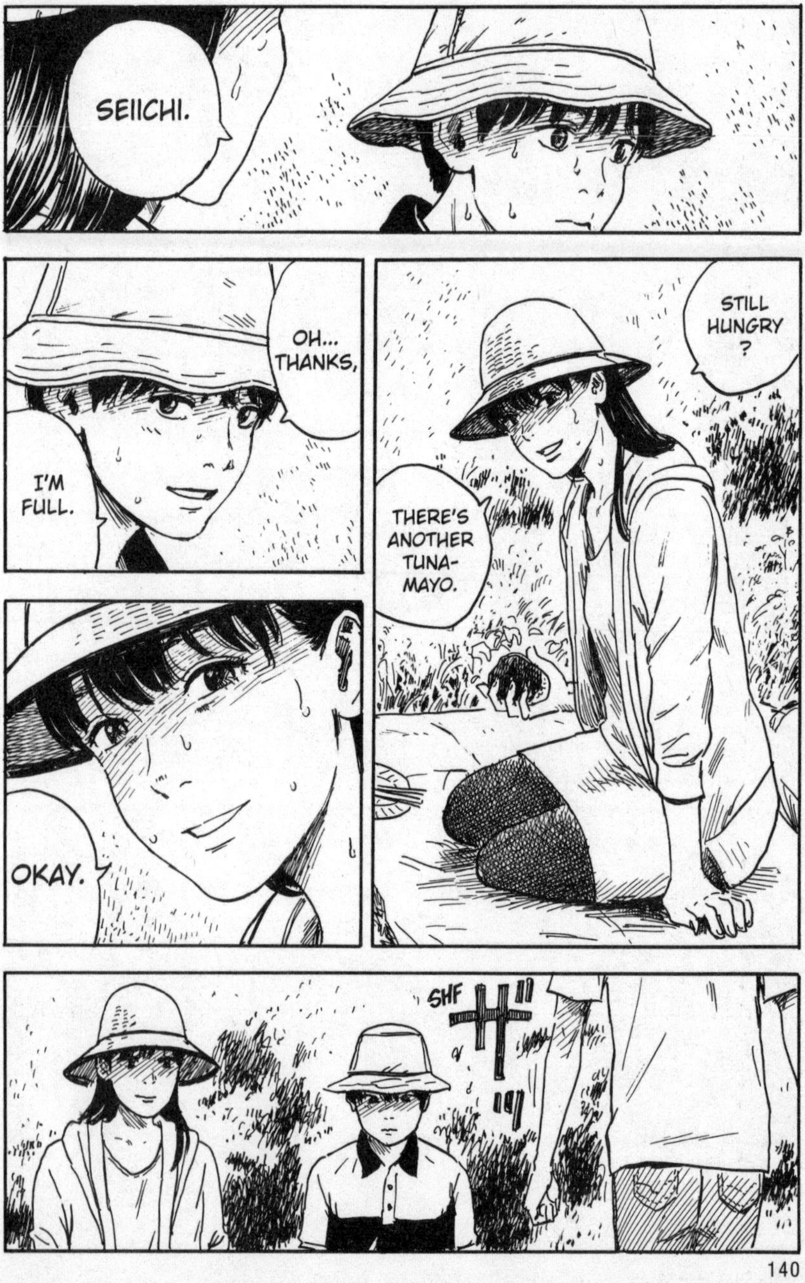
SEIICHI.
STILL HUNGRY ?
THERE'S ANOTHER TUNA-MAYO.
OH... THANKS,
I'M FULL.
OKAY.
SHF

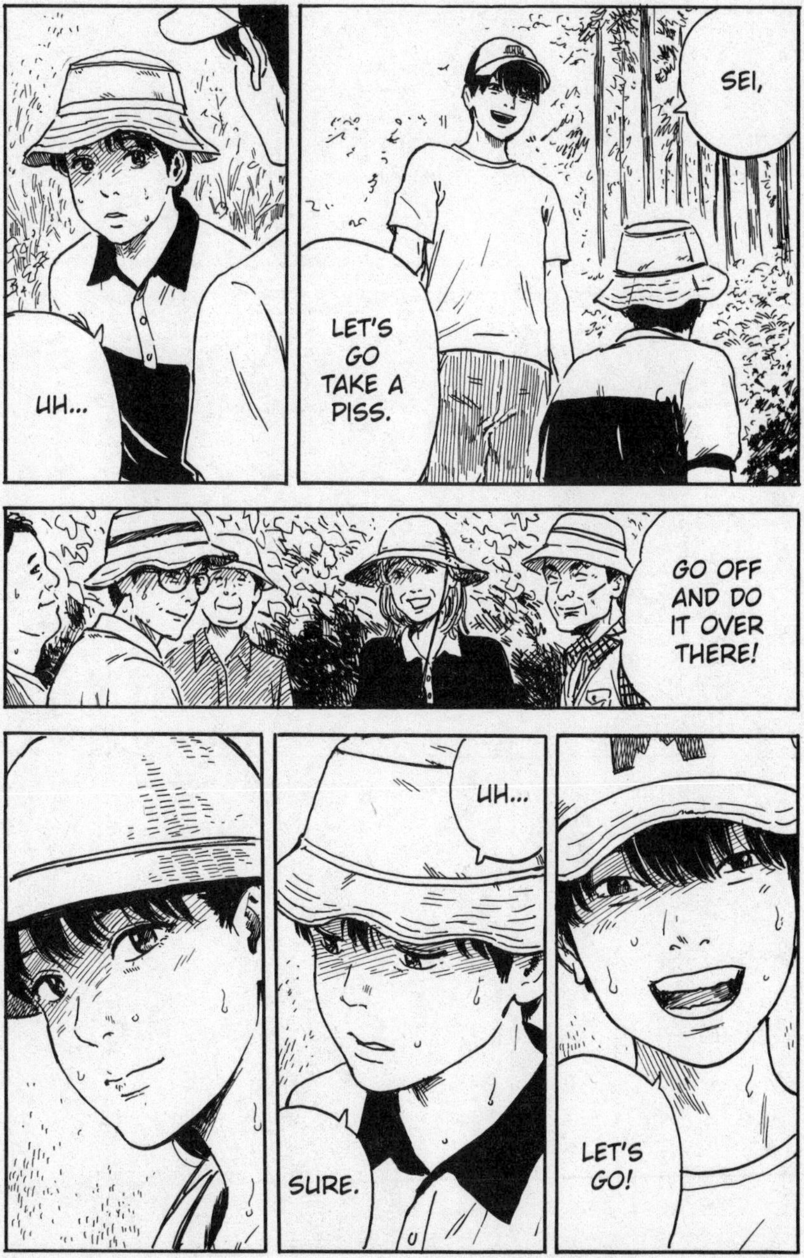
SEI,
LET'S GO TAKE A PISS.
UH...
GO OFF AND DO IT OVER THERE!
LET'S GO!
UH...
SURE.

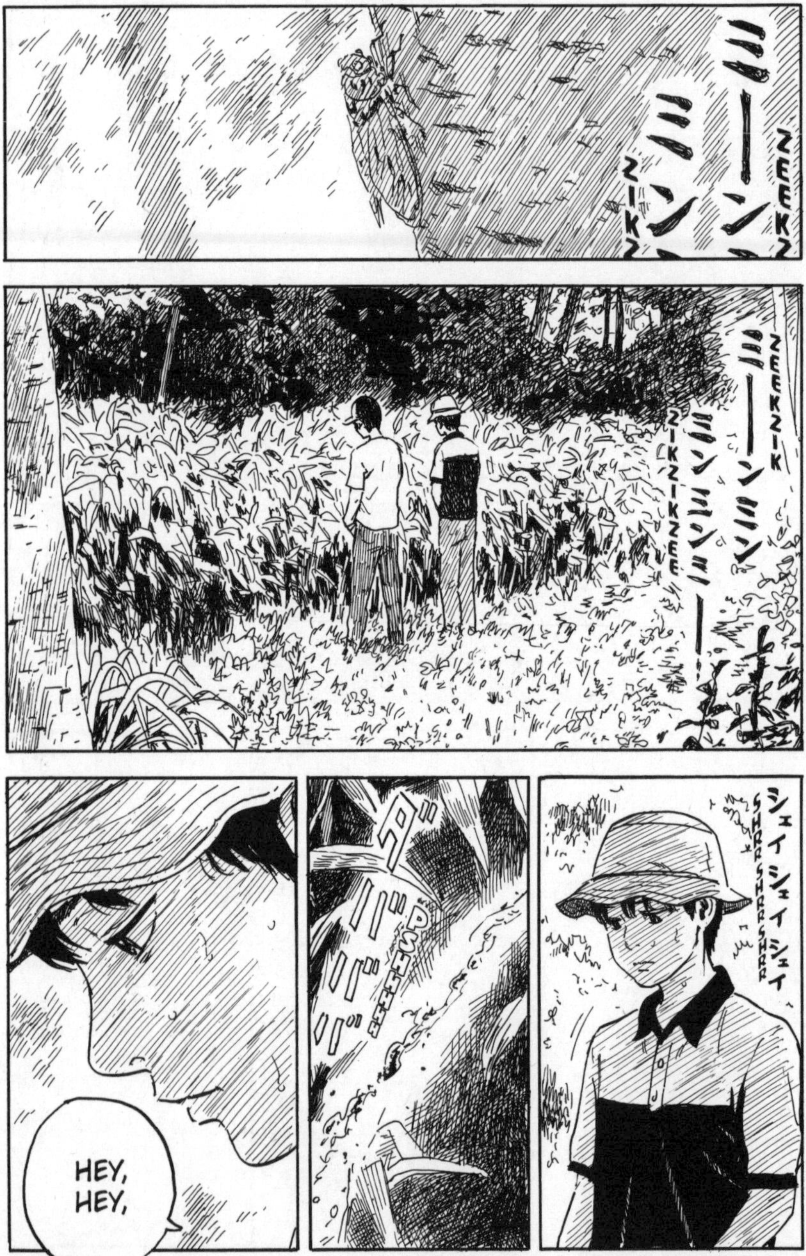
ミーンミン
ZEEKZ ZIKZ
ミーンミンミン ミンミンミー…!
ZEEKZIK ZIKZIKZEE
シェイシェイシェイシェイ
SHRRSHRRSHRR
ダバババ
PSHHHHH
HEY, HEY,

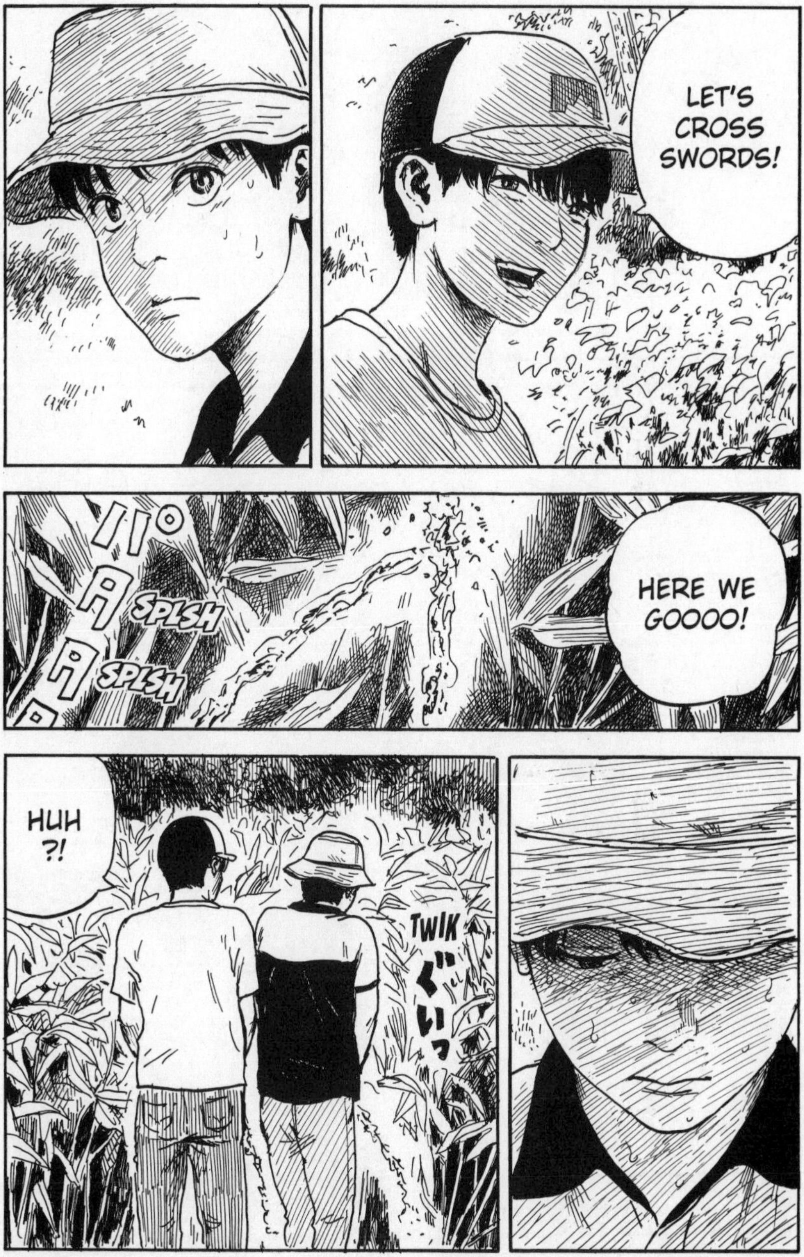
LET'S CROSS SWORDS!
HERE WE GOOOO!
SPLSH
SPLSH
TWIK
HUH ?!

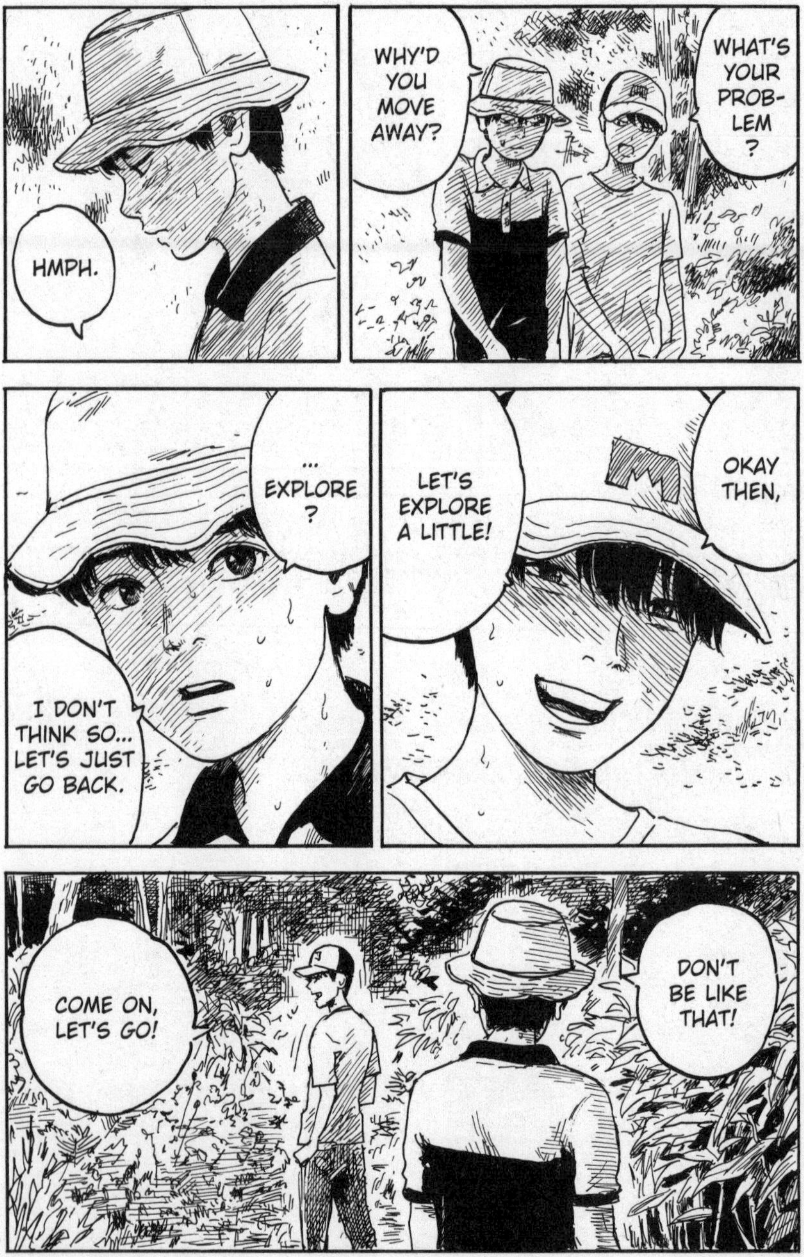
WHAT'S YOUR PROB-LEM ?
WHY'D YOU MOVE AWAY?
HMPH.
OKAY THEN,
LET'S EXPLORE A LITTLE!
... EXPLORE ?
I DON'T THINK SO... LET'S JUST GO BACK.
DON'T BE LIKE THAT!
COME ON, LET'S GO!

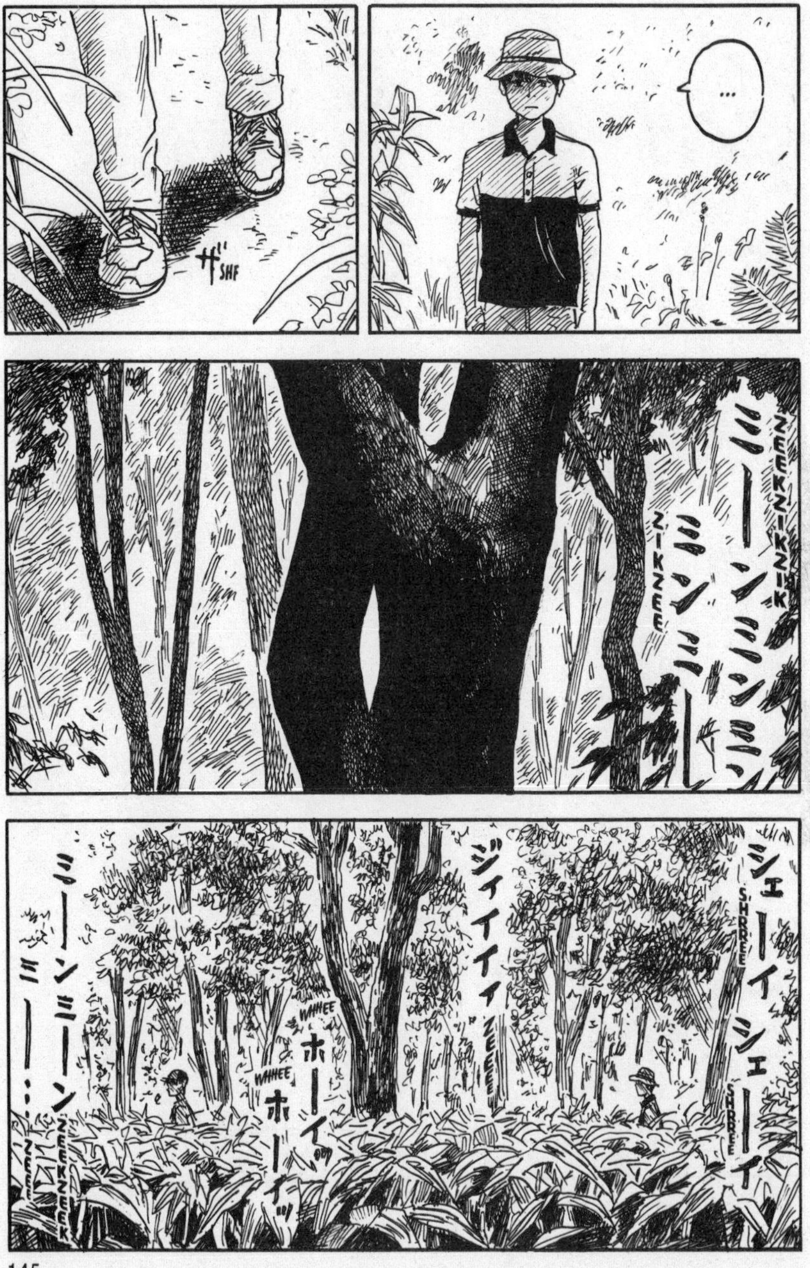
…
ザッ
SHF
ミーンミンミンミッ
ZEEKZIKZIK
ミンミンミーー
ZIKZEE
シェーイ
SHREE
シェーイ
SHREE
ジイイイ
ZEEEE
ホーイ
WHHEE
ホーイ
WHHEE
ミーンミーン
ZEEKZEEK
ミーー…
ZEEE

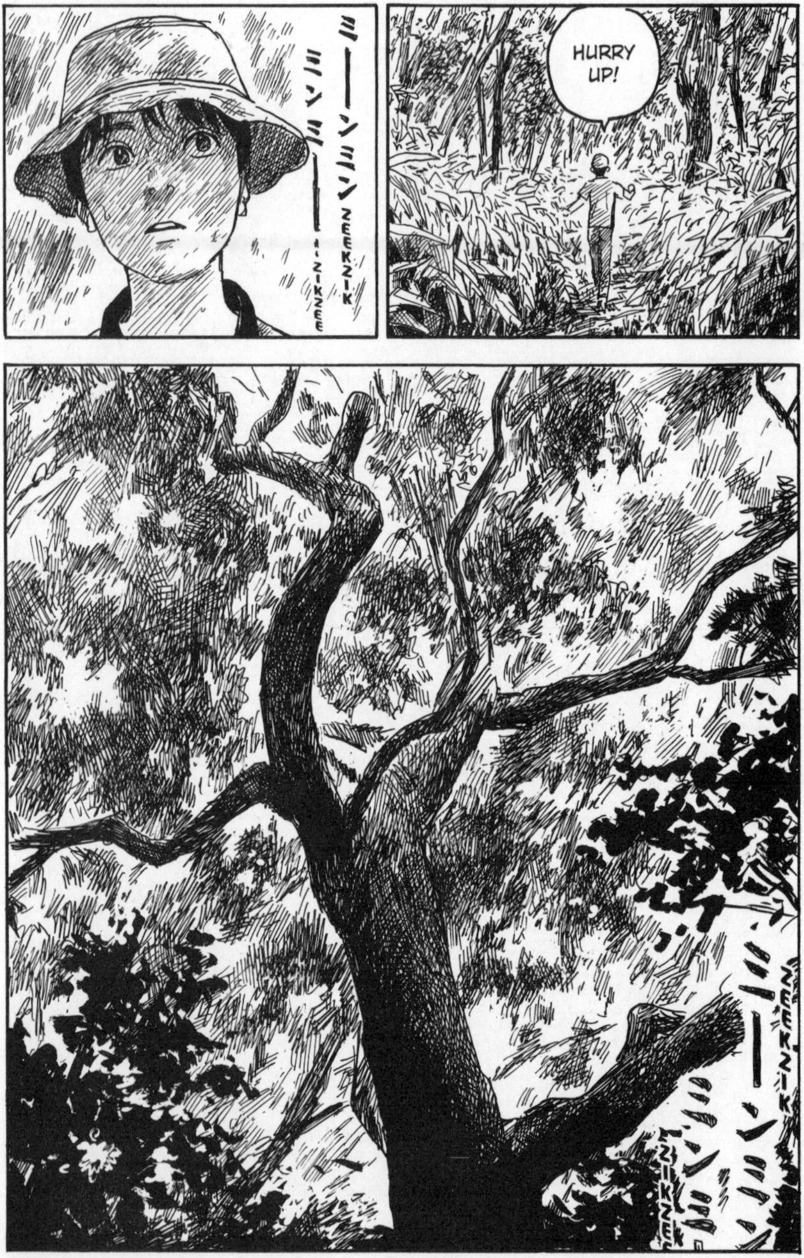
HURRY UP!
ミーーンミンミン
ZEEKZIK
ミンミーー
ZIKZEE
ミーーンミンミン
ZEEKZIK
ZIKZEE

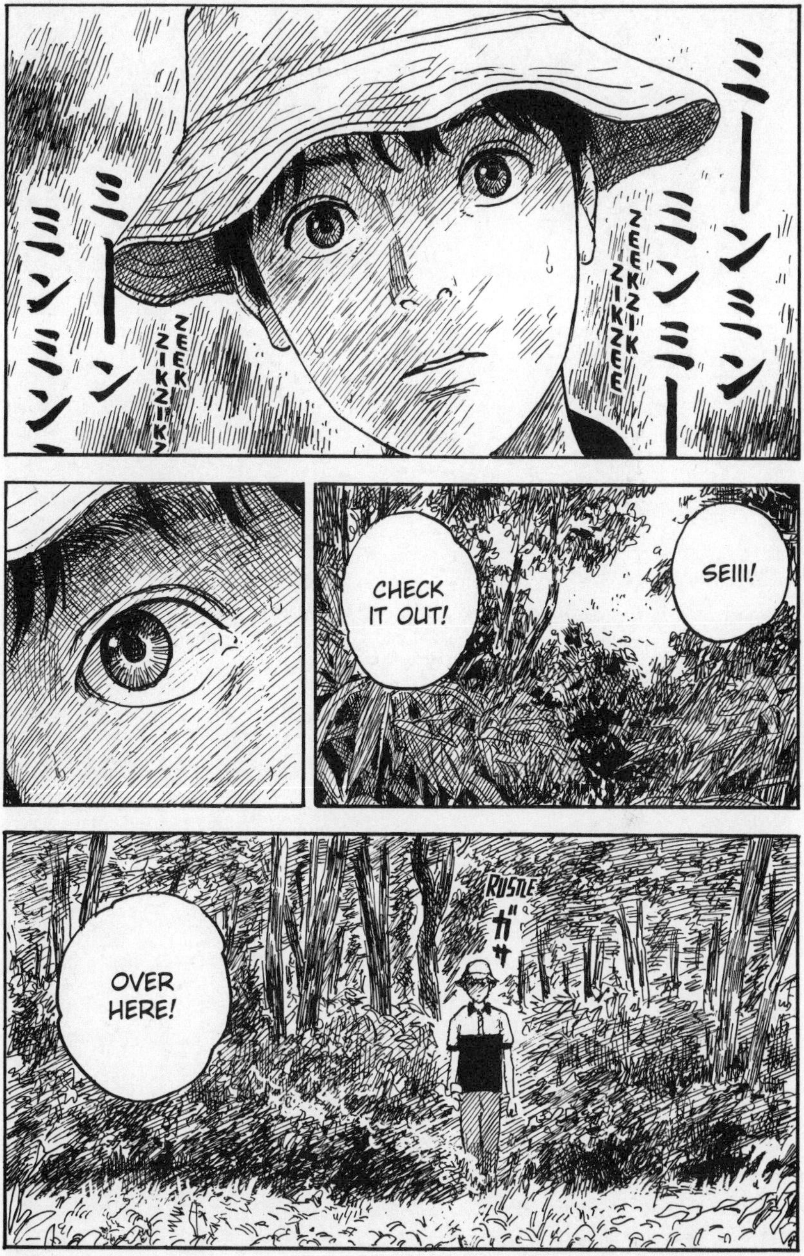

ミーンミンミンミー
ZEEKZIK ZIKZEE
ミーンミンミン
ZEEK ZIKZIKZ
SEIII!
CHECK IT OUT!
RUSTLE
ガサ
OVER HERE!

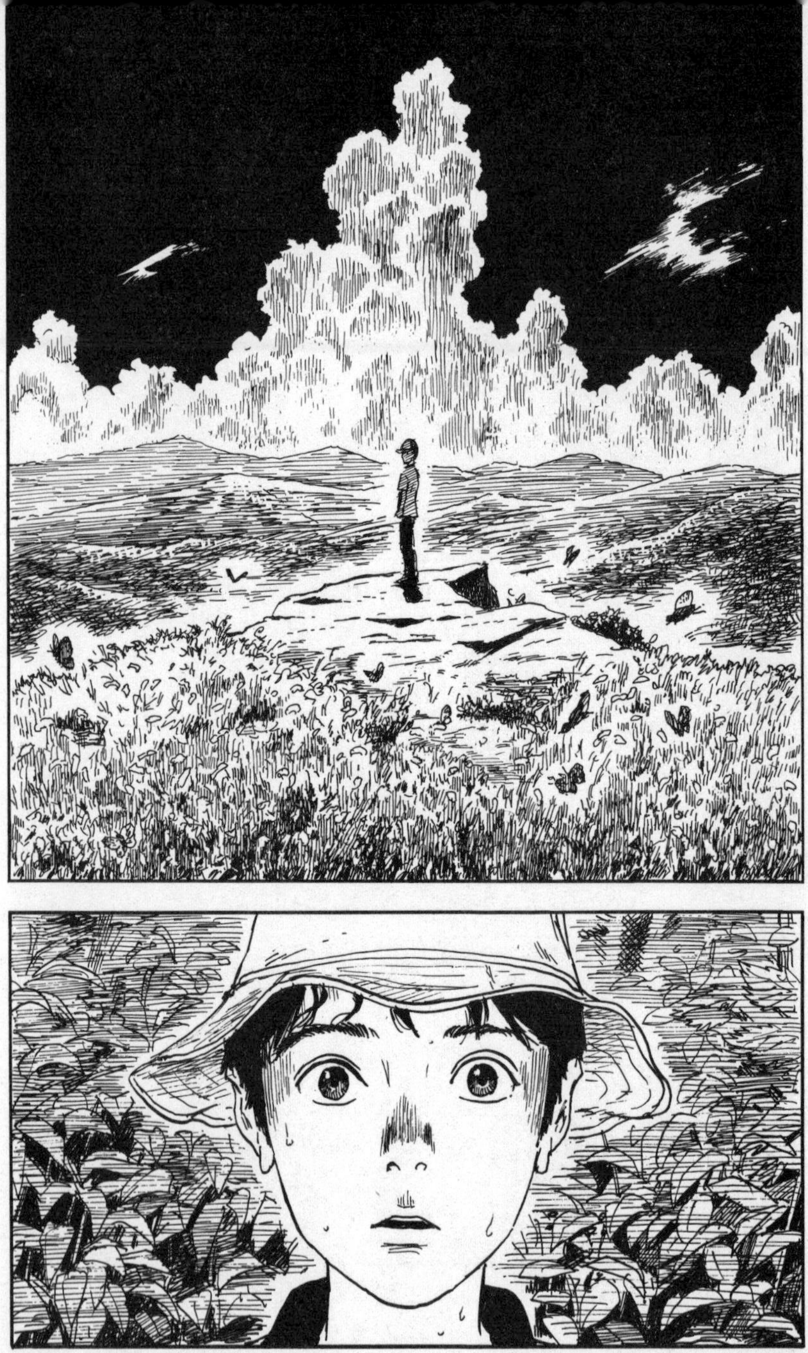

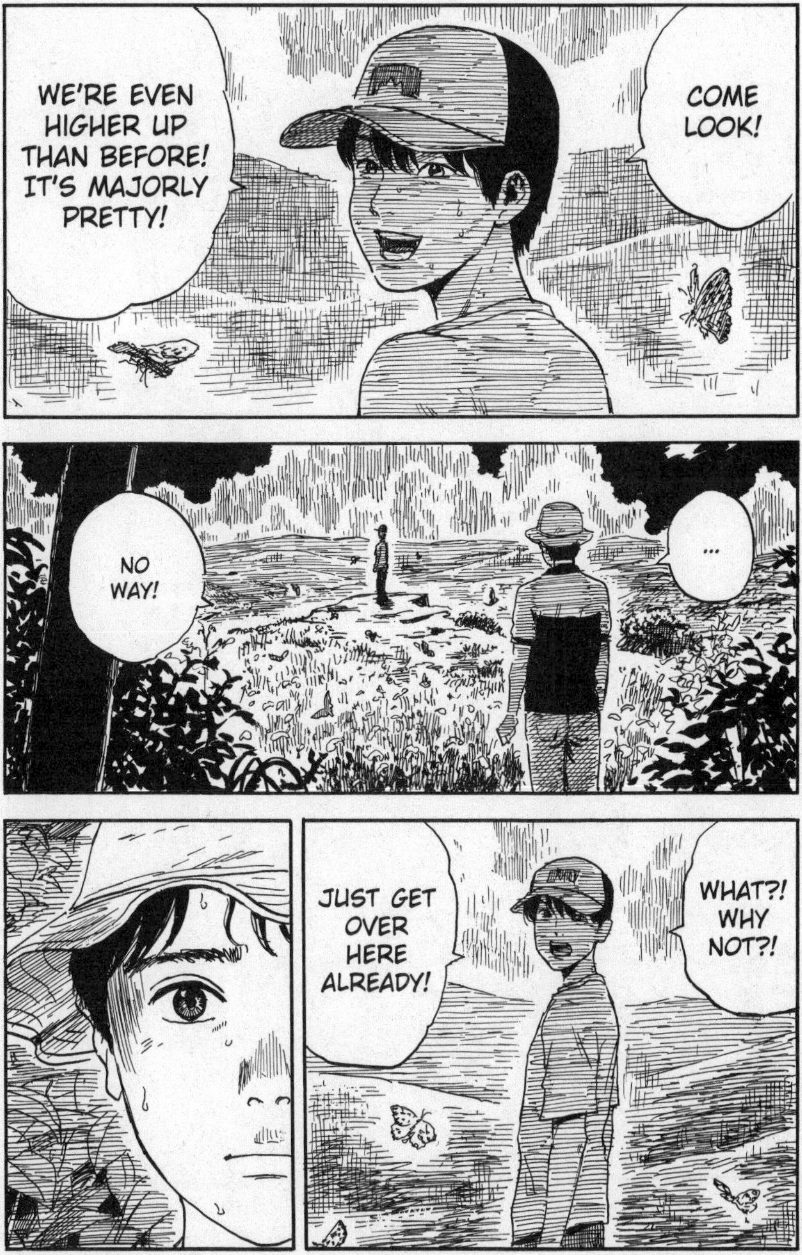
COME LOOK!
WE'RE EVEN HIGHER UP THAN BEFORE! IT'S MAJORLY PRETTY!
...
NO WAY!
WHAT?! WHY NOT?!
JUST GET OVER HERE ALREADY!

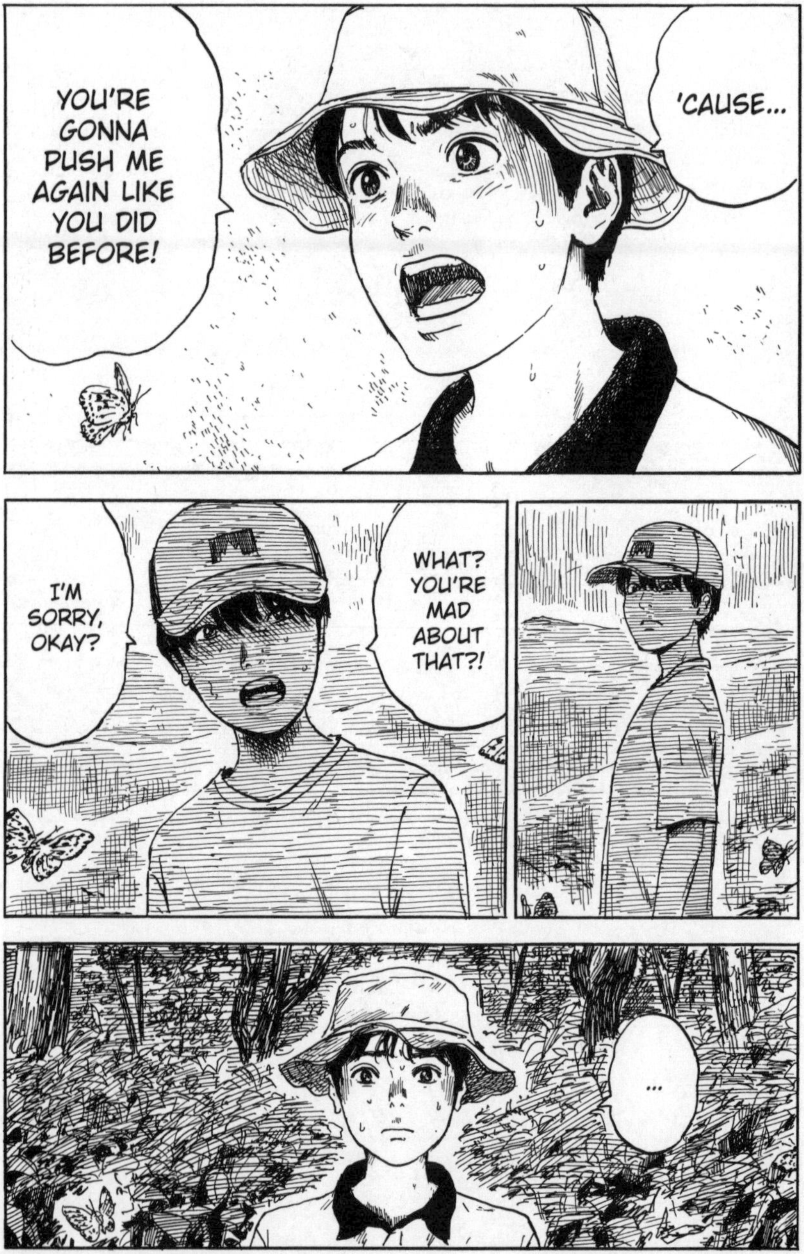
'CAUSE...
YOU'RE GONNA PUSH ME AGAIN LIKE YOU DID BEFORE!
WHAT? YOU'RE MAD ABOUT THAT?!
I'M SORRY, OKAY?
...

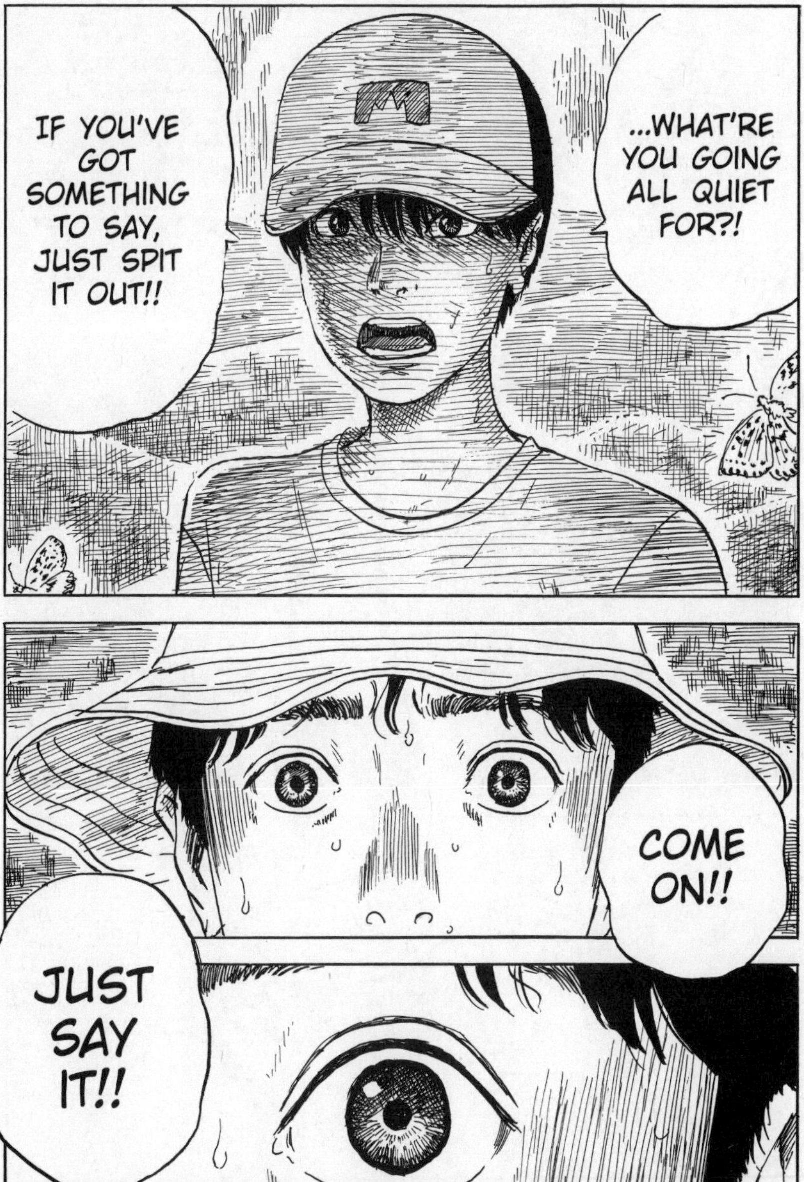
...WHAT'RE YOU GOING ALL QUIET FOR?!
IF YOU'VE GOT SOMETHING TO SAY, JUST SPIT IT OUT!!
COME ON!!
JUST SAY IT!!

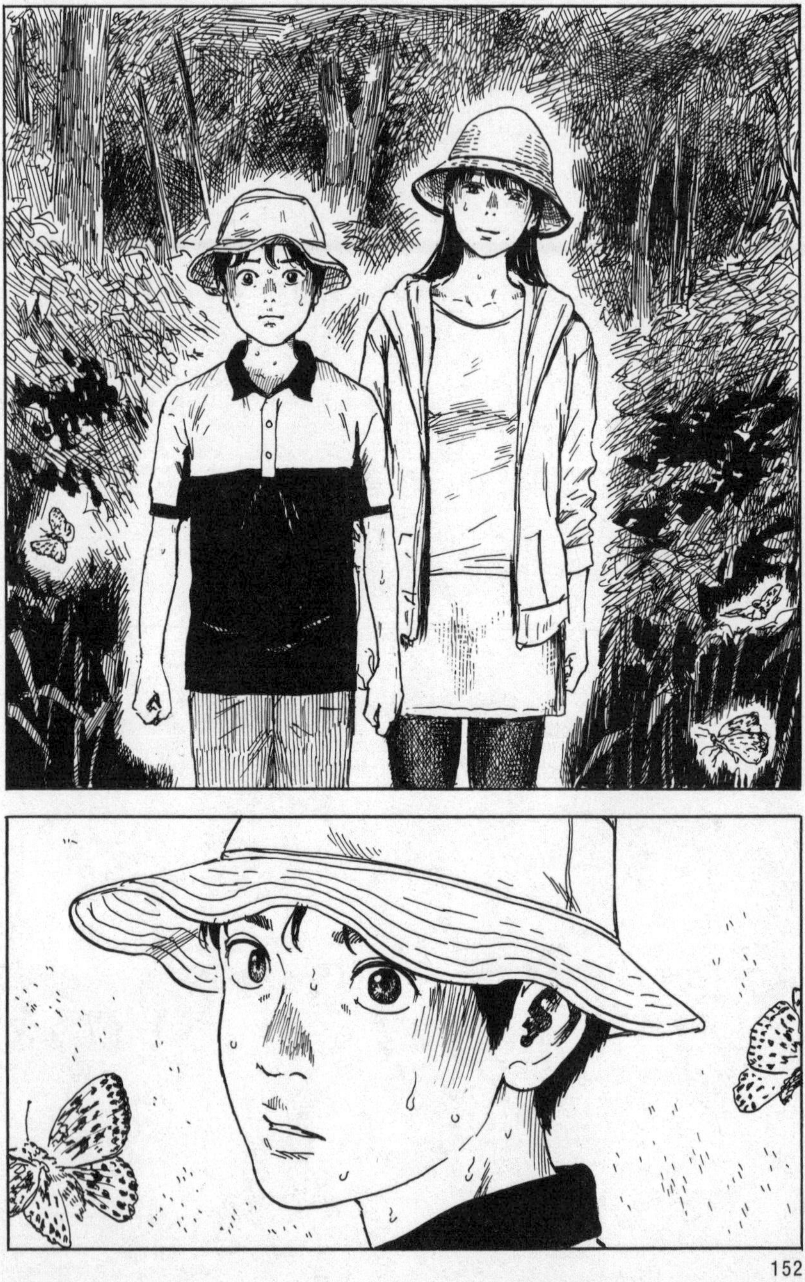

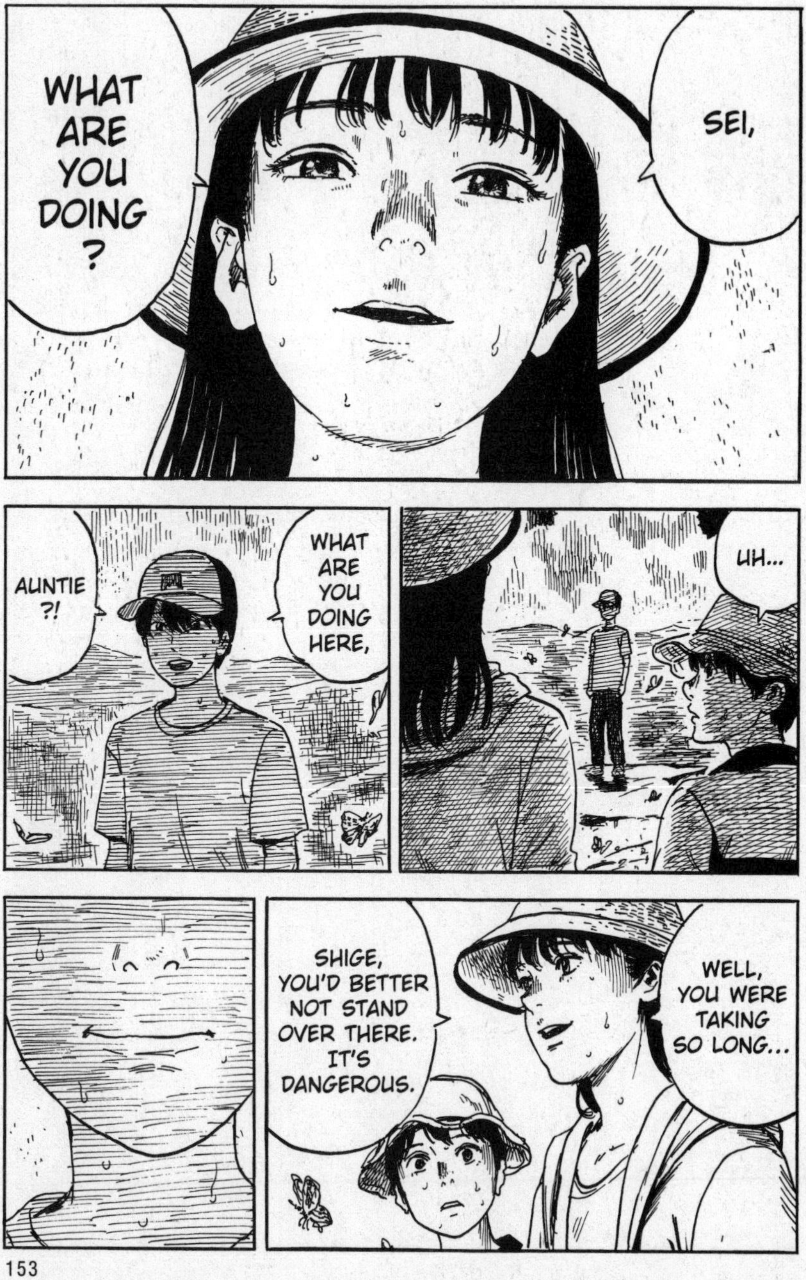
SEI,
WHAT ARE YOU DOING?
UH...
WHAT ARE YOU DOING HERE,
AUNTIE?!
WELL, YOU WERE TAKING SO LONG...
SHIGE, YOU'D BETTER NOT STAND OVER THERE. IT'S DANGEROUS.

WOOOOO
SHIGE!
STOP IT, THAT'S DANGER-OUS!
WHAT'RE YOU TALKIN' ABOUT ?!
MOM WAS RIGHT, YOU'RE SO OVER-PROTECTIVE!

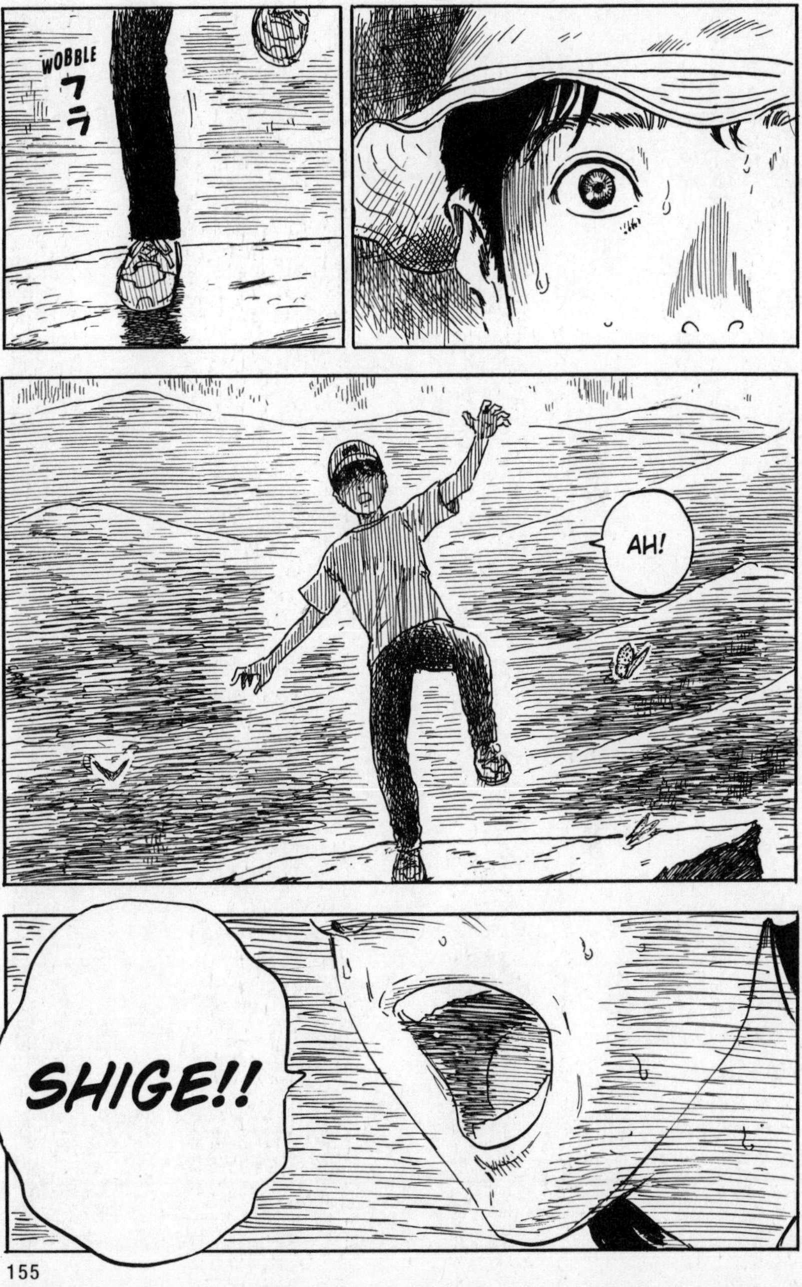
WOBBLE
フラ
AH!
SHIGE!!

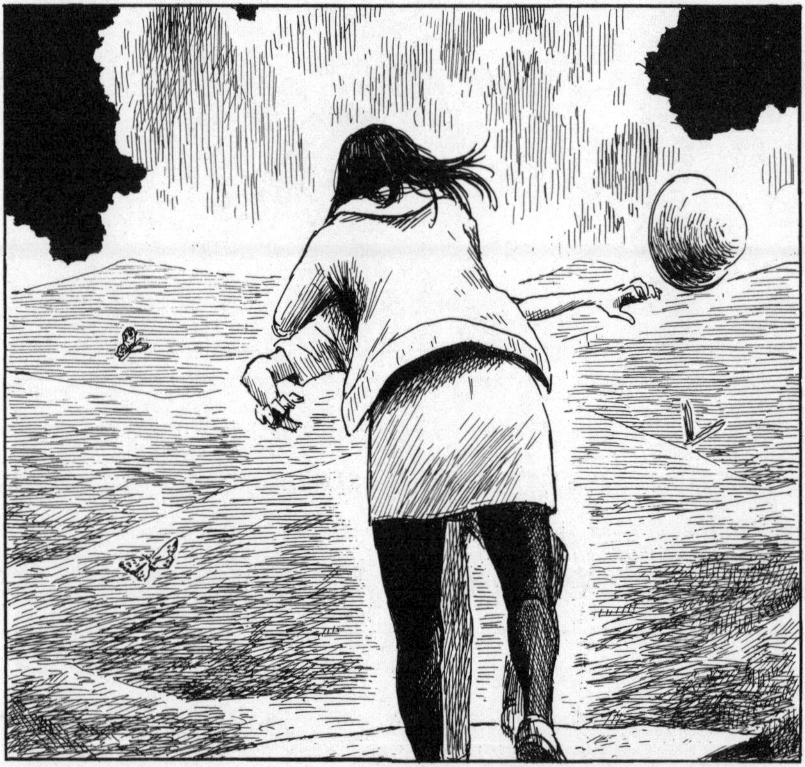
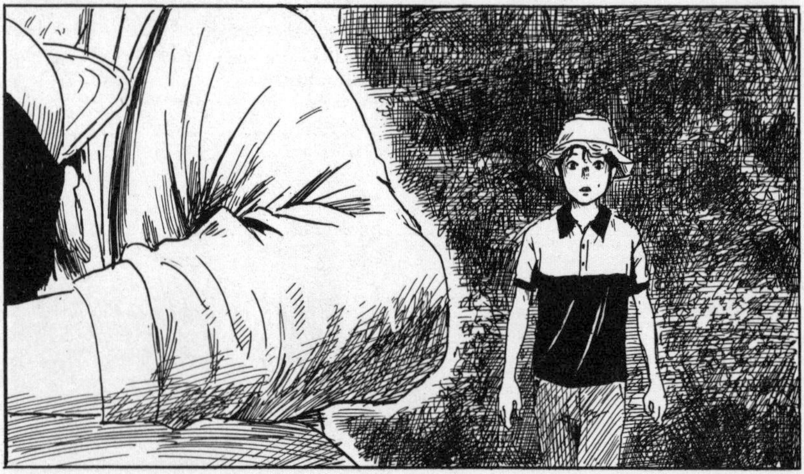

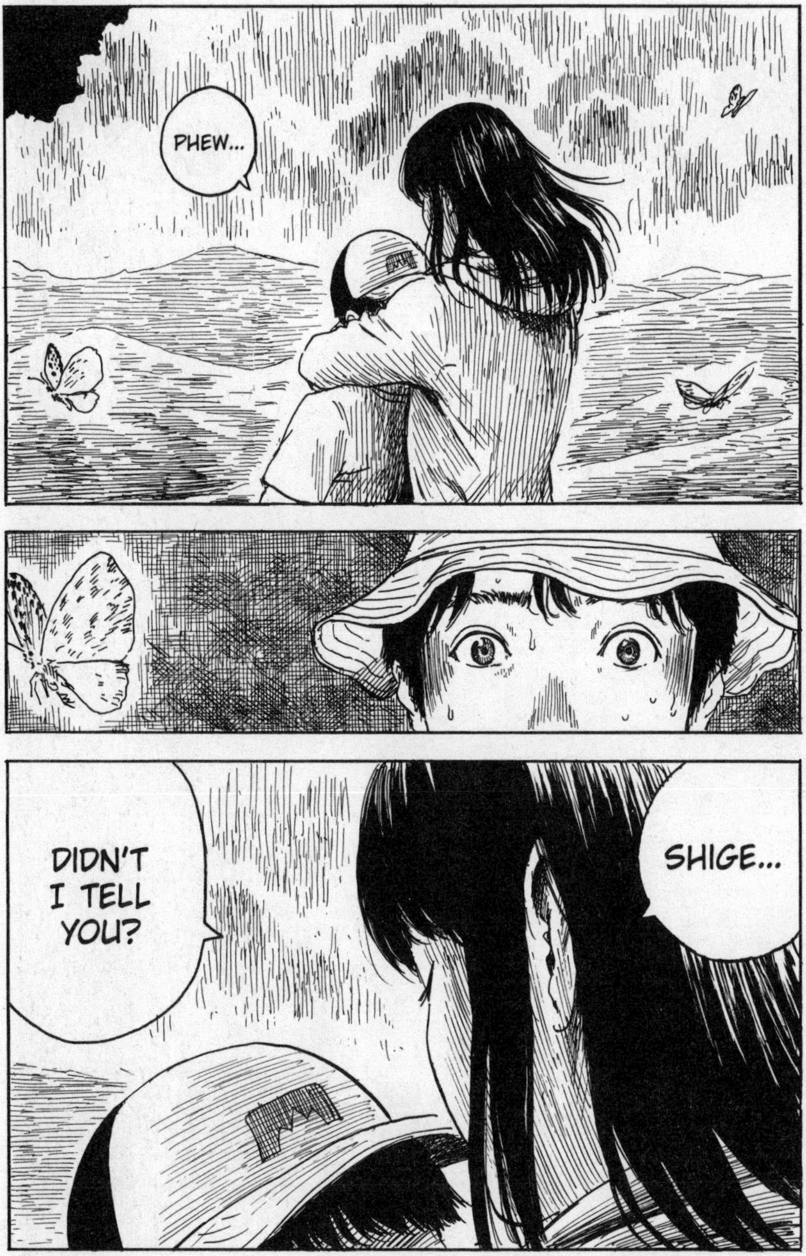
PHEW...
SHIGE...
DIDN'T I TELL YOU?

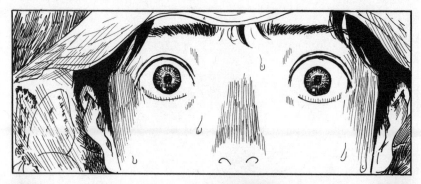

I SAID I WAS FINE...

...OH, SHUT UP!

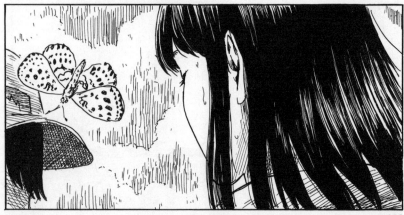

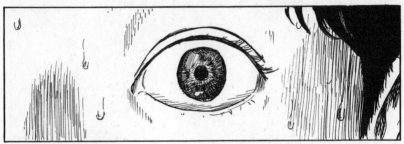

AUNTIE?

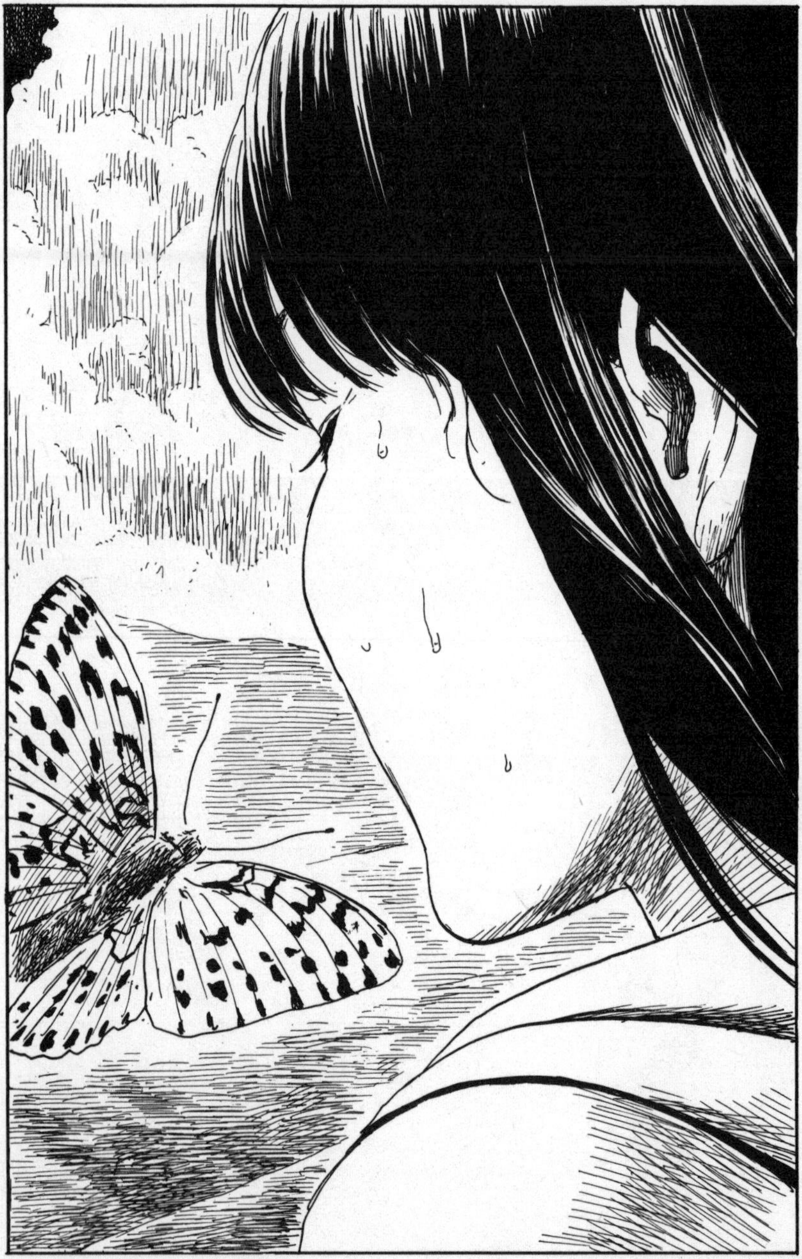

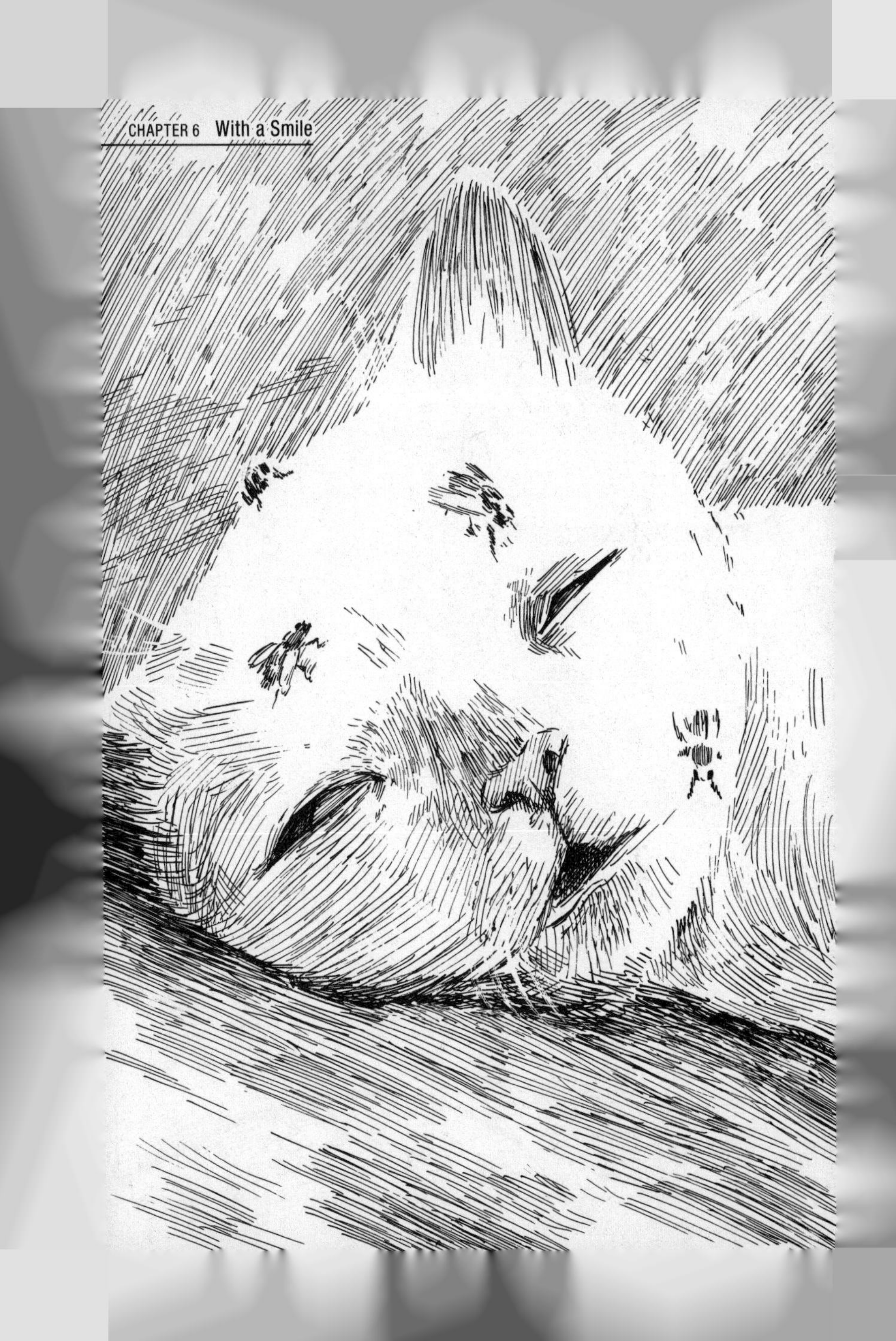
CHAPTER 6 With a Smile

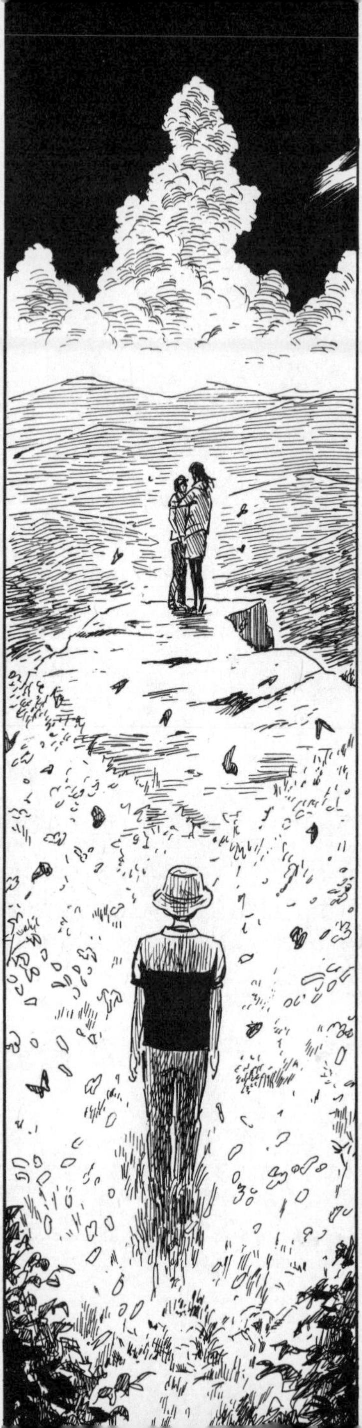
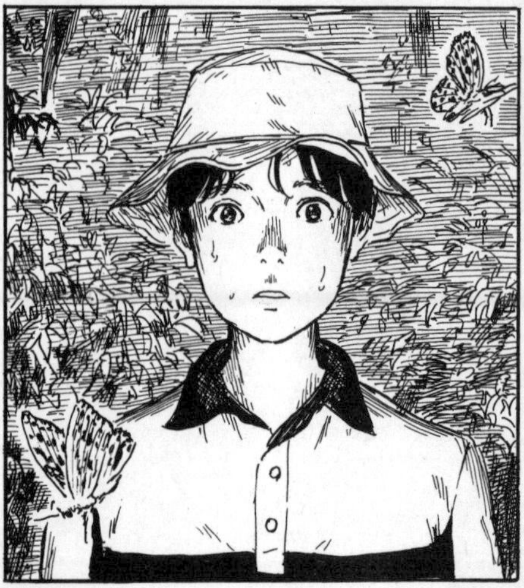
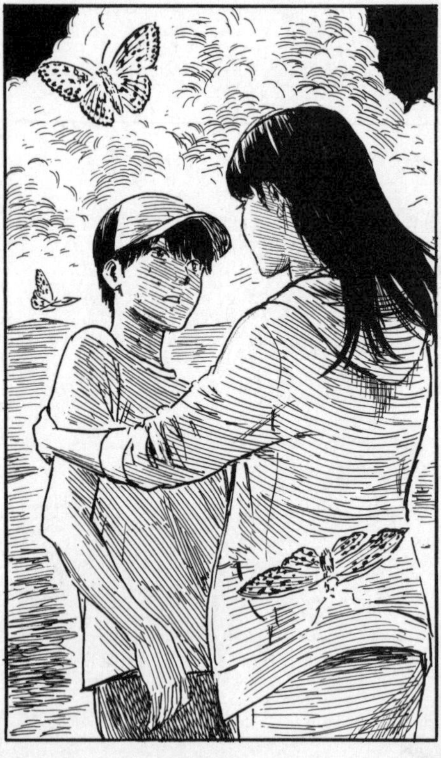

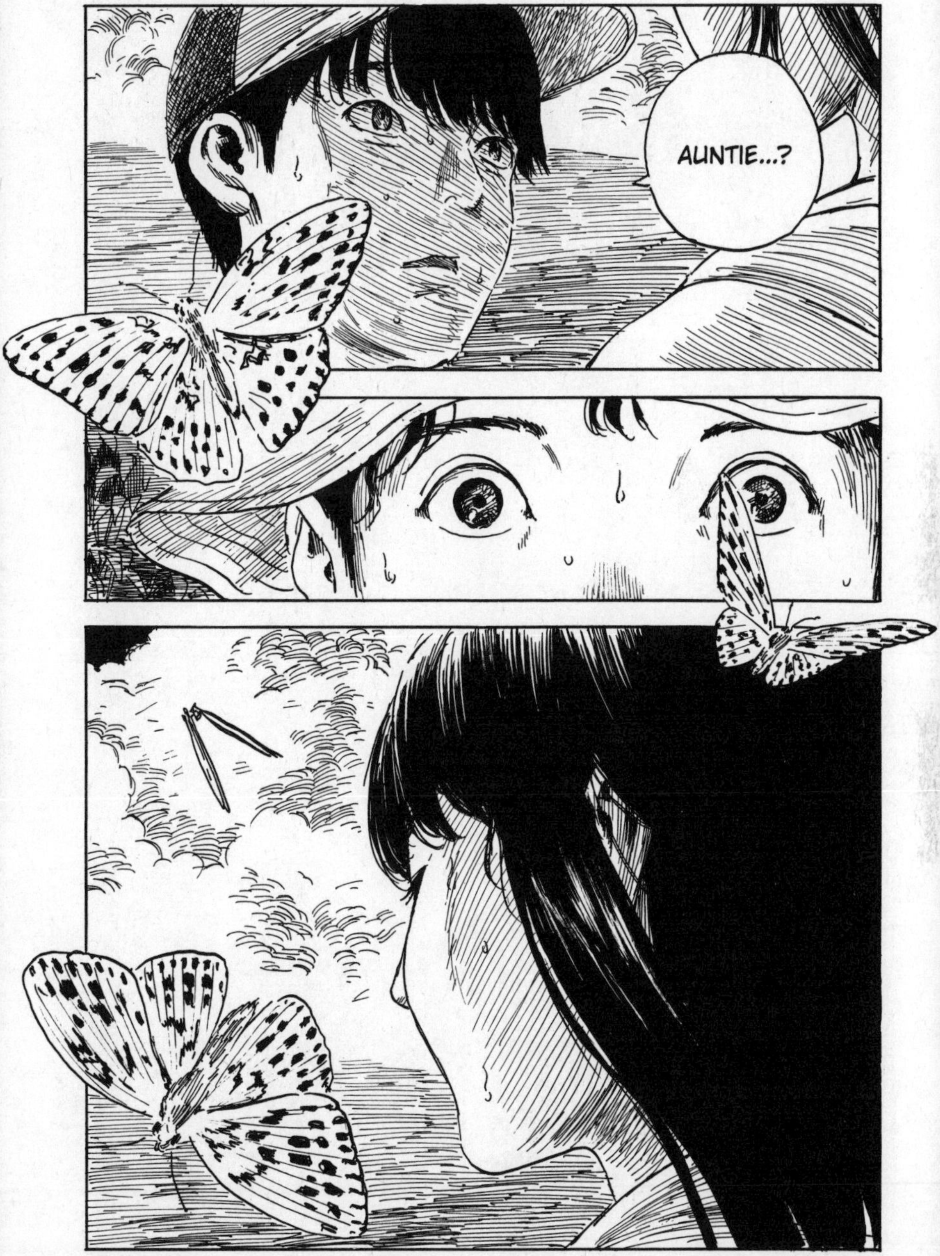
AUNTIE...?

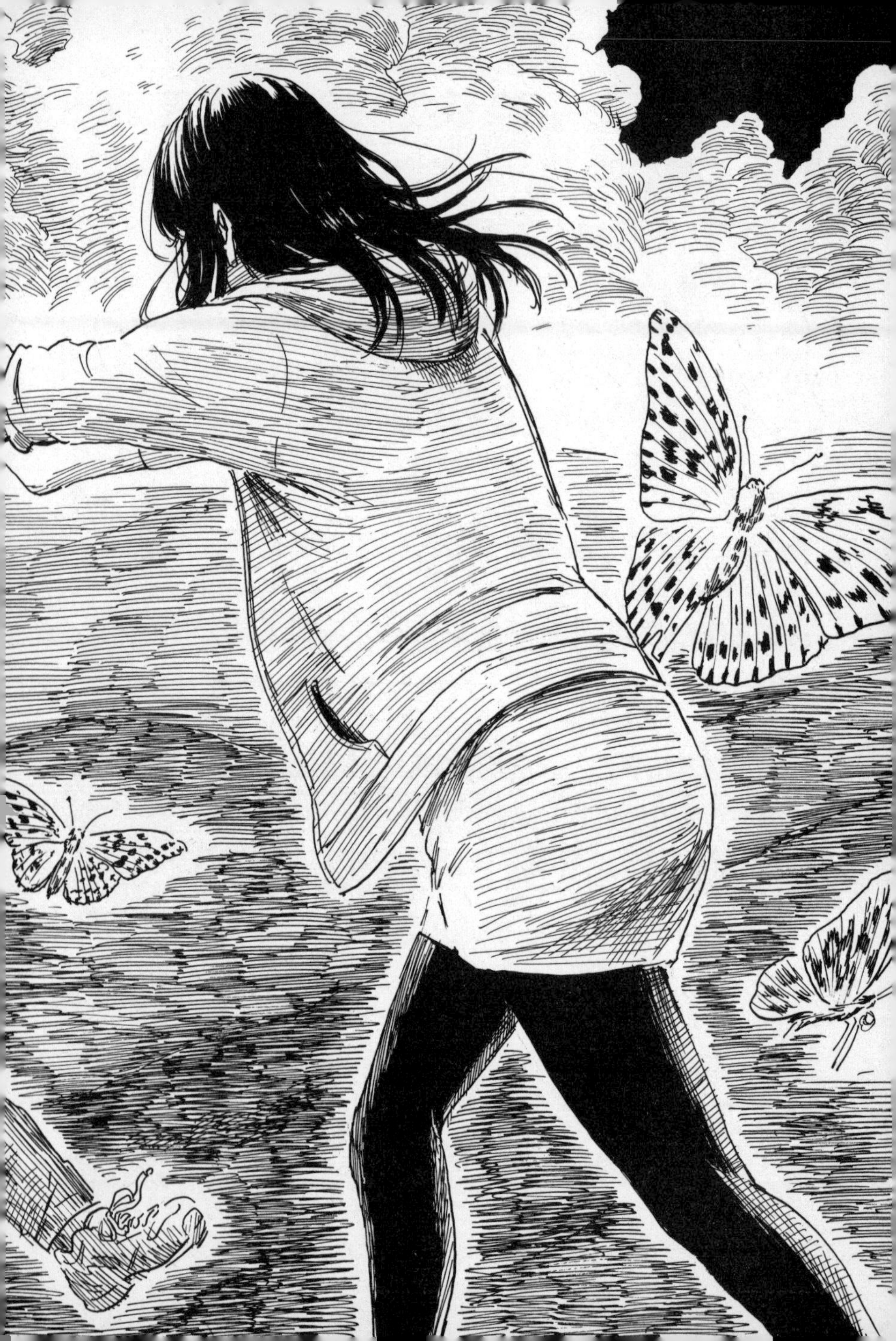

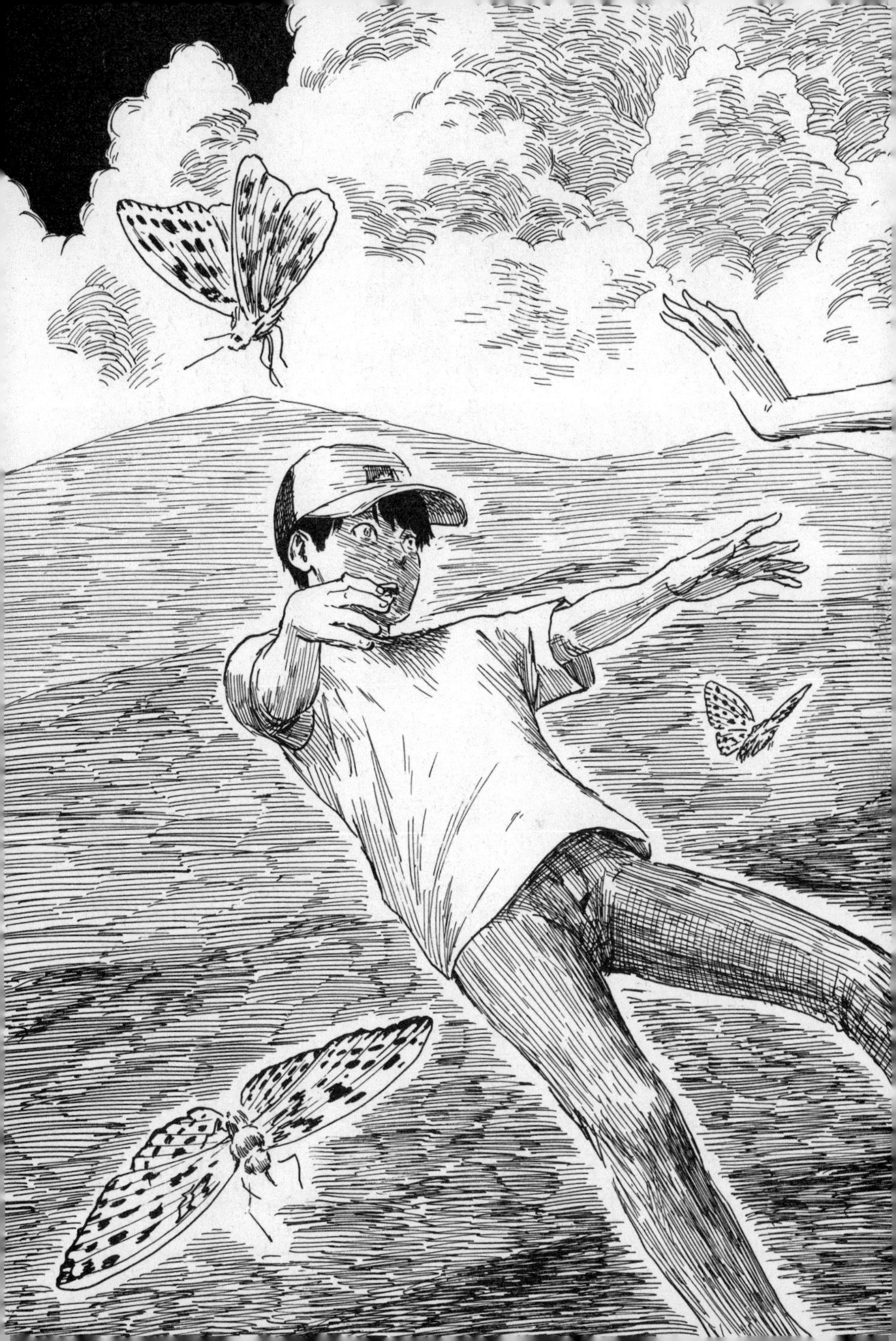

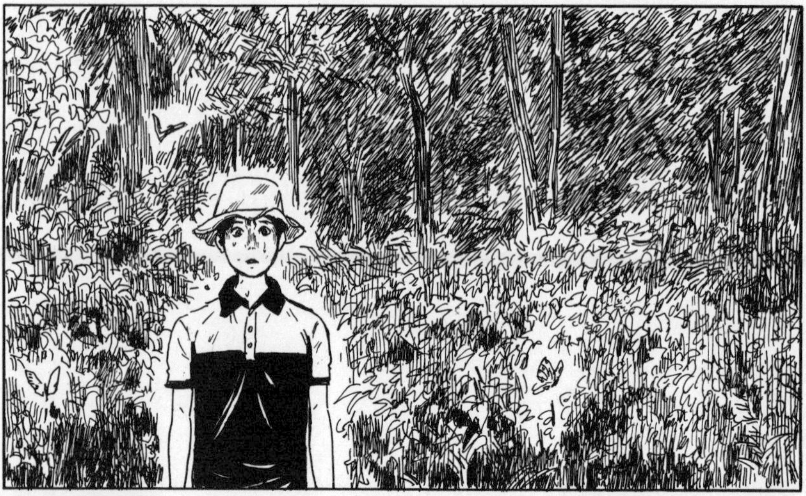
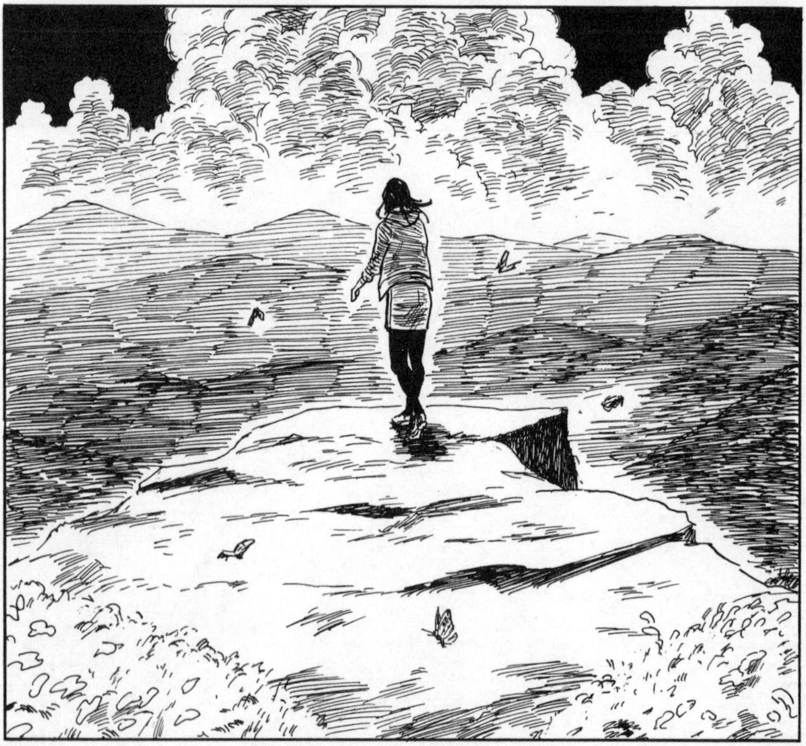

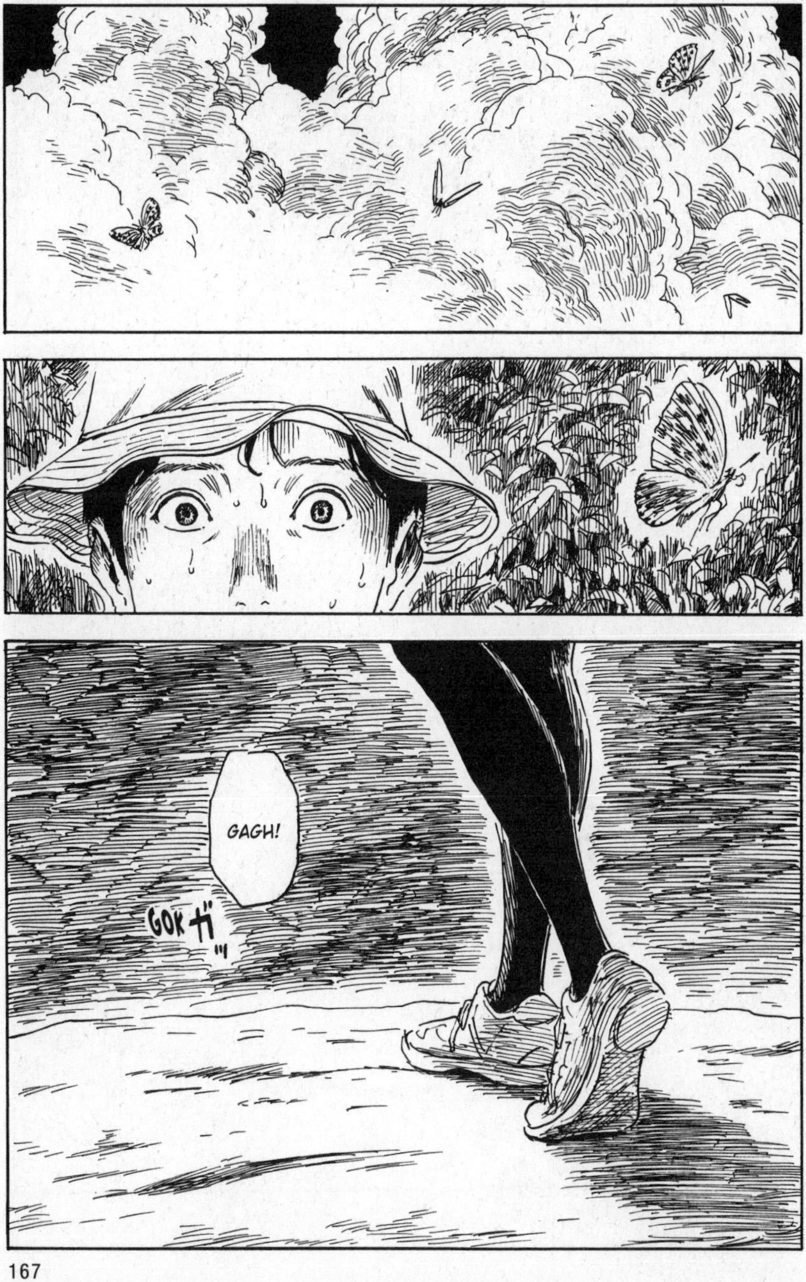
GAGH!
GOK ガ

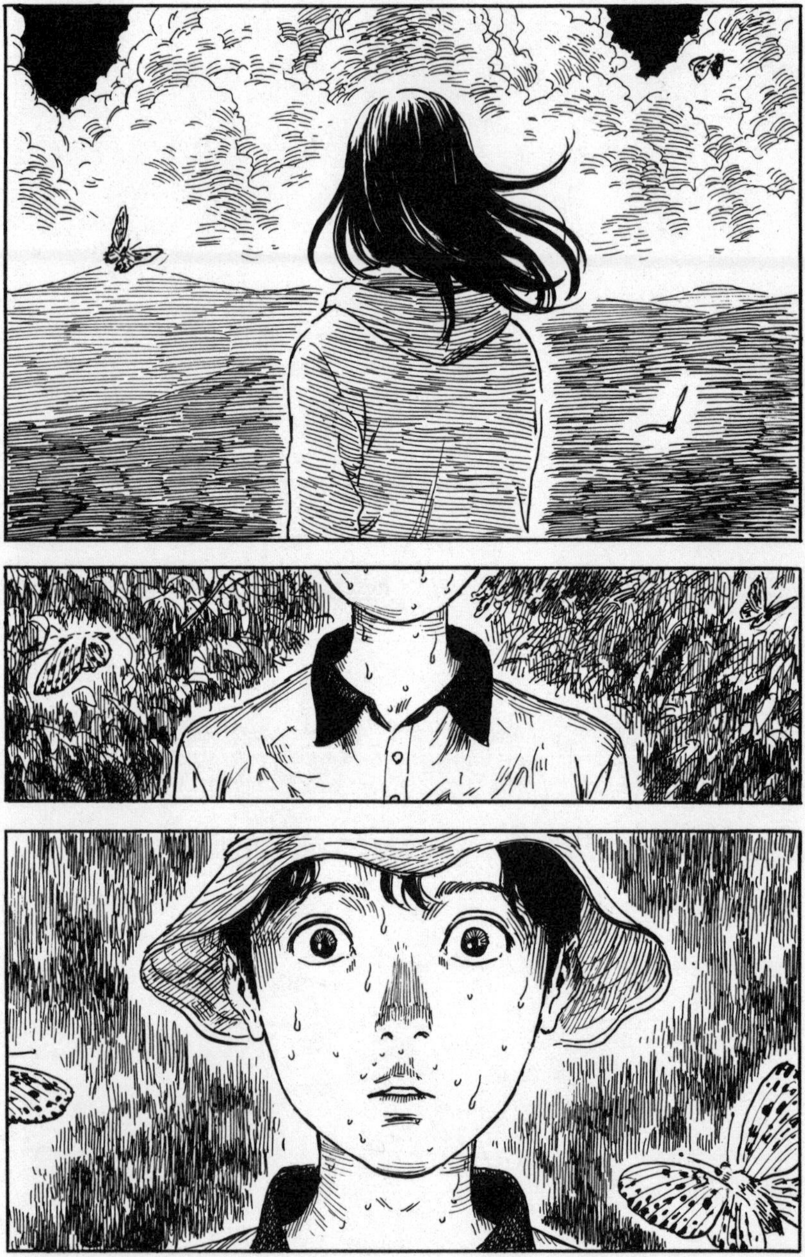

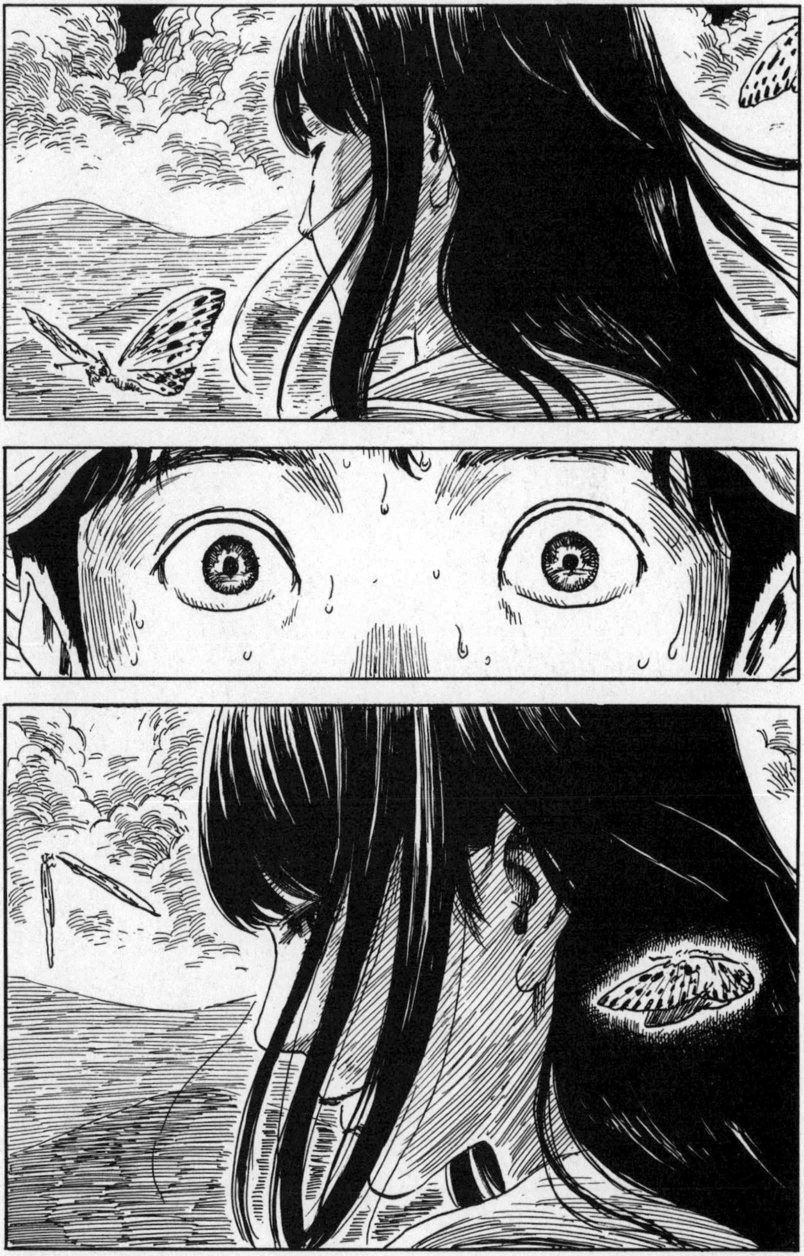

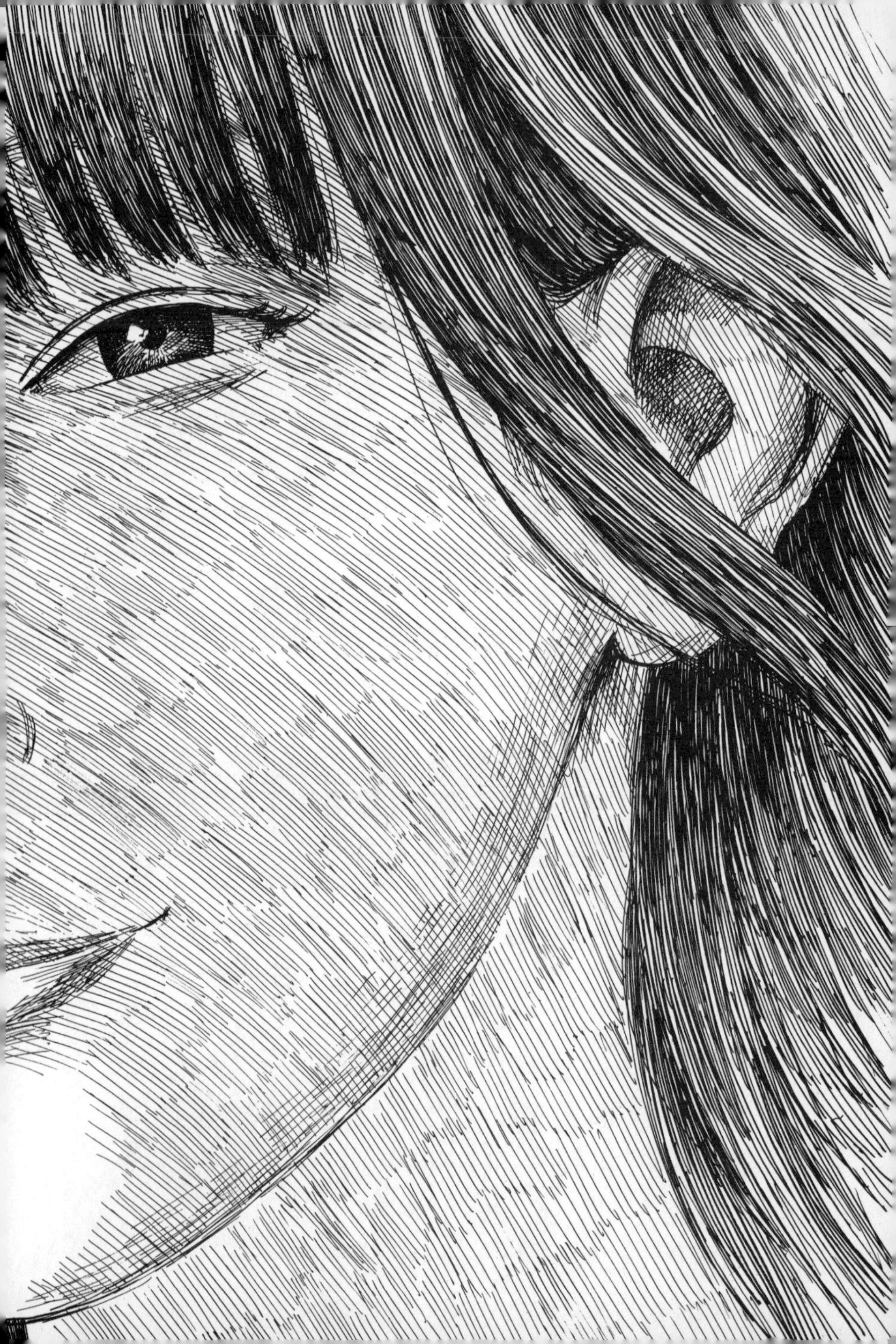

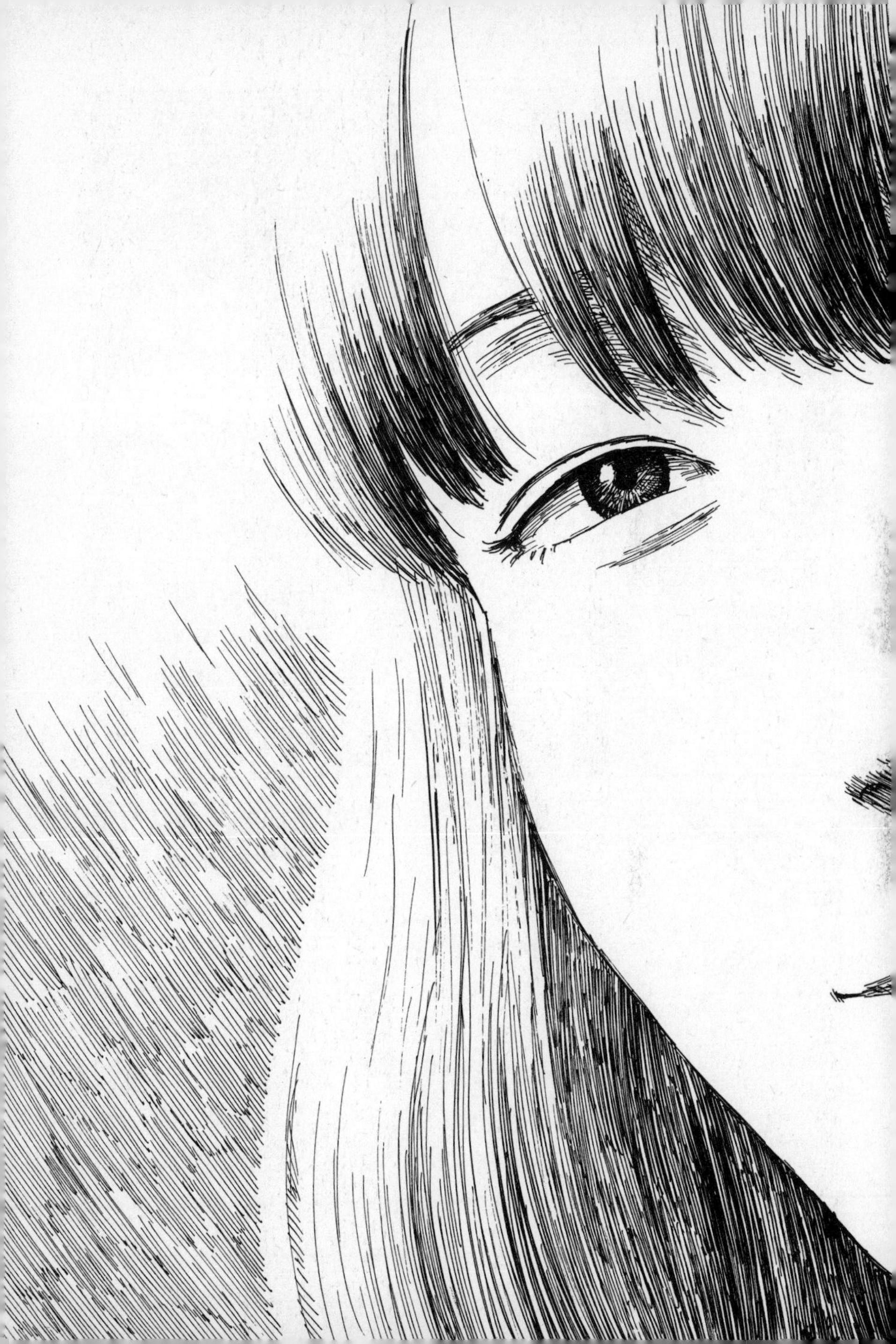

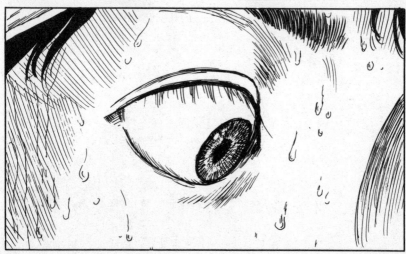

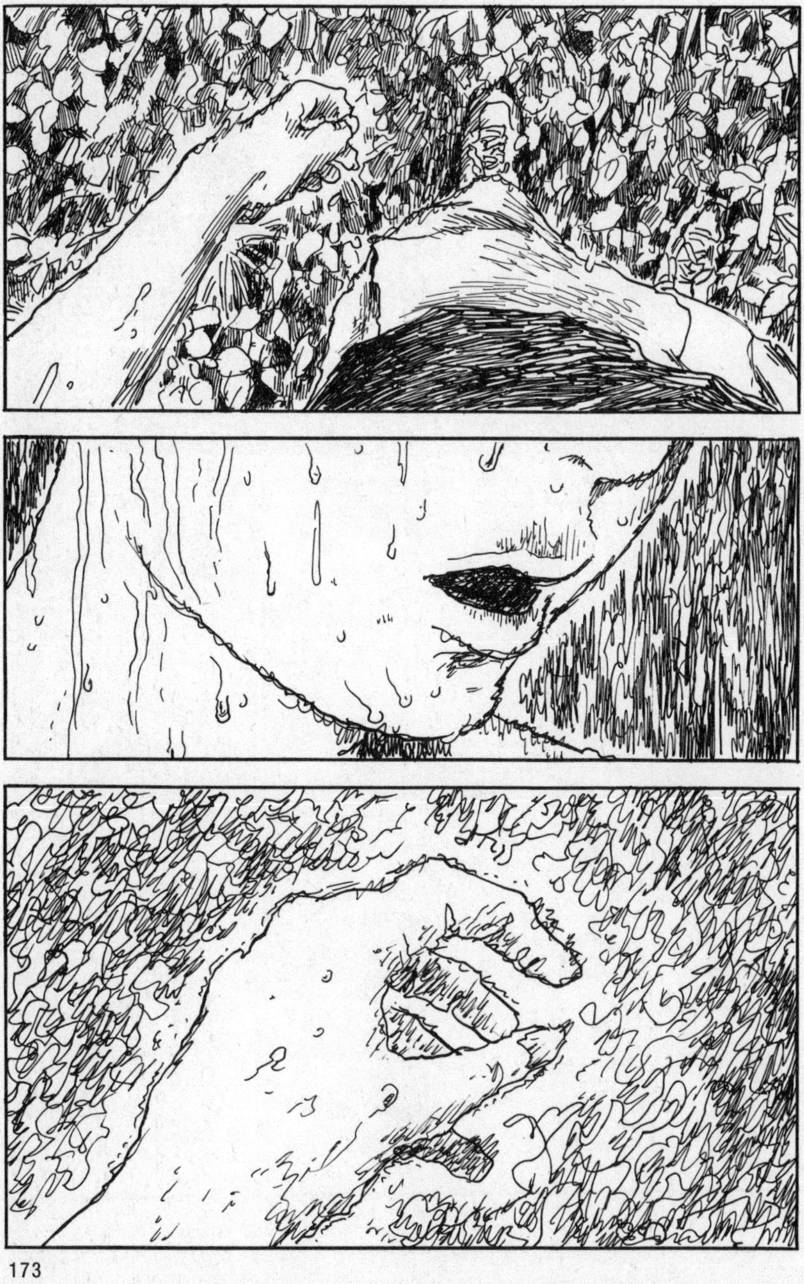

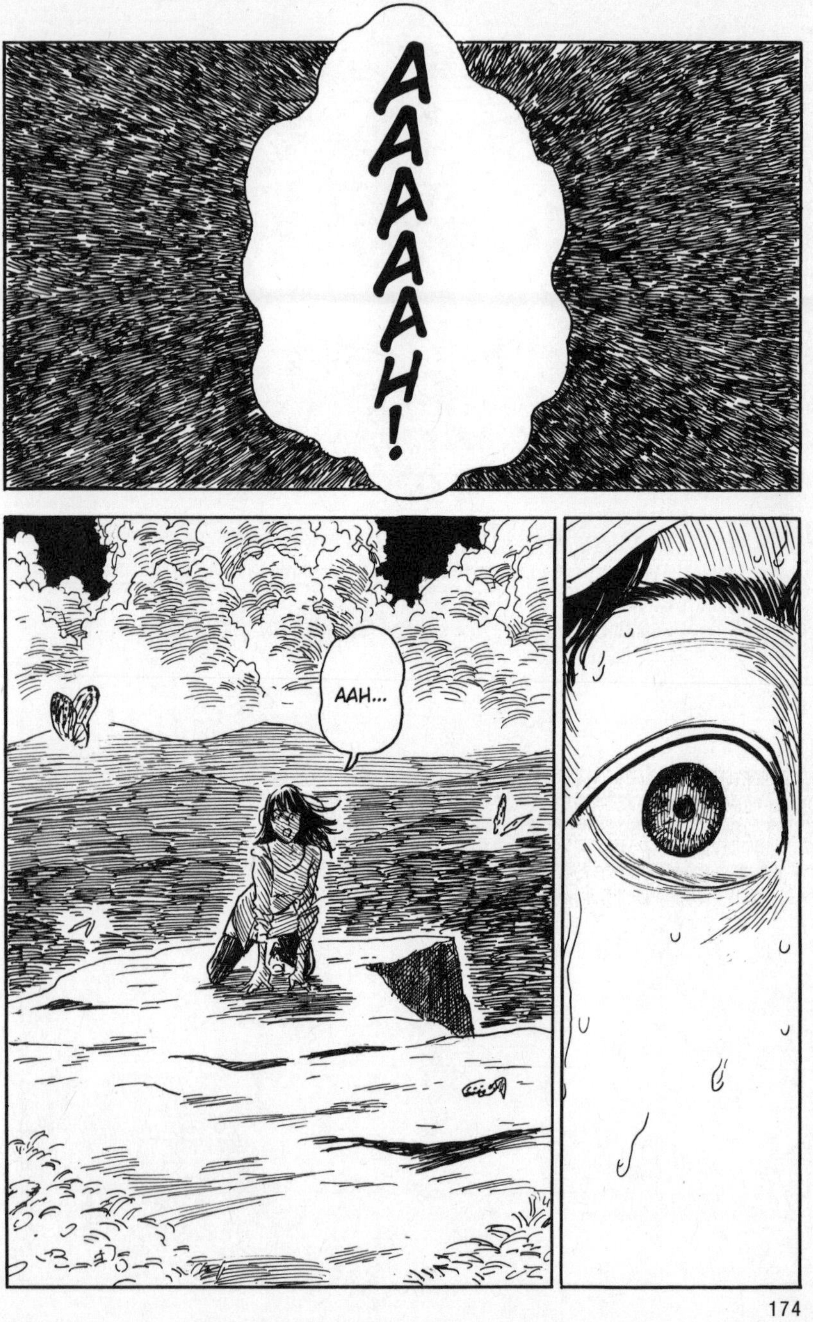
AAAAAH!
AAH...

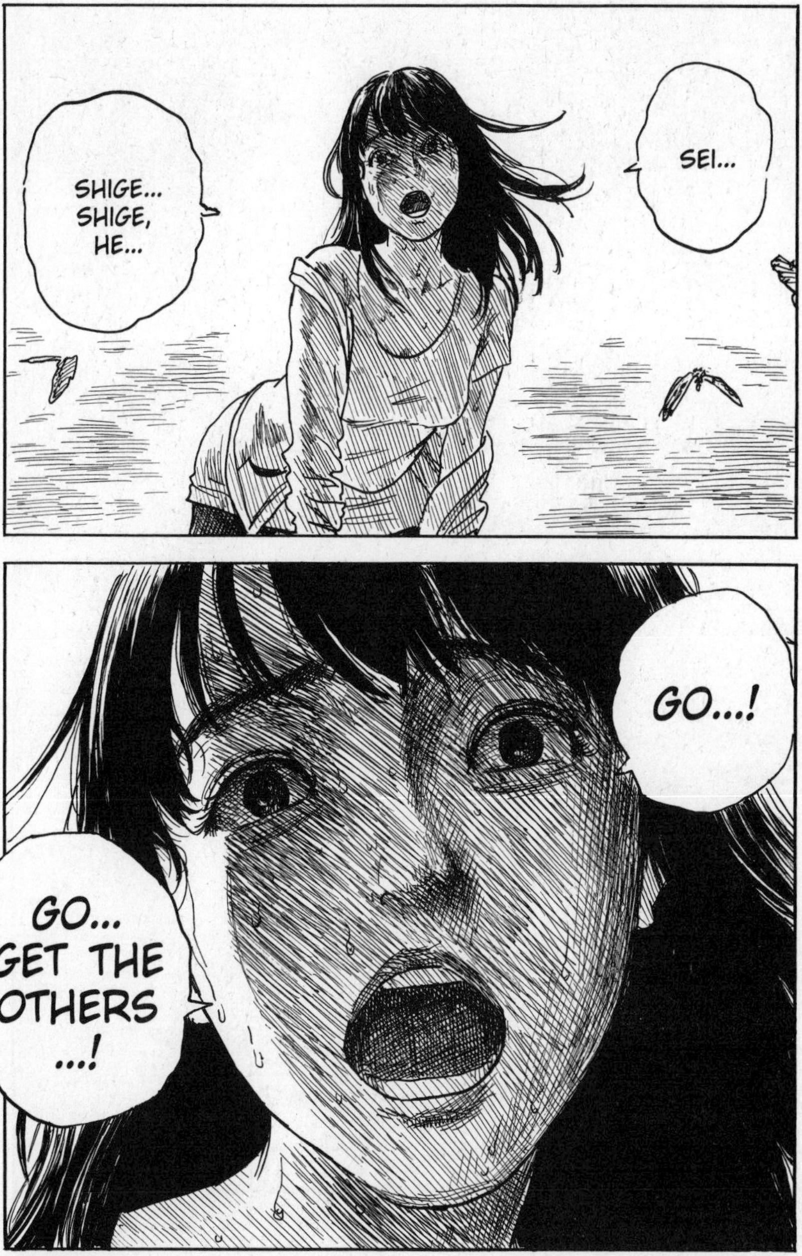
SEI...
SHIGE... SHIGE, HE...
GO...!
GO... GET THE OTHERS ...!

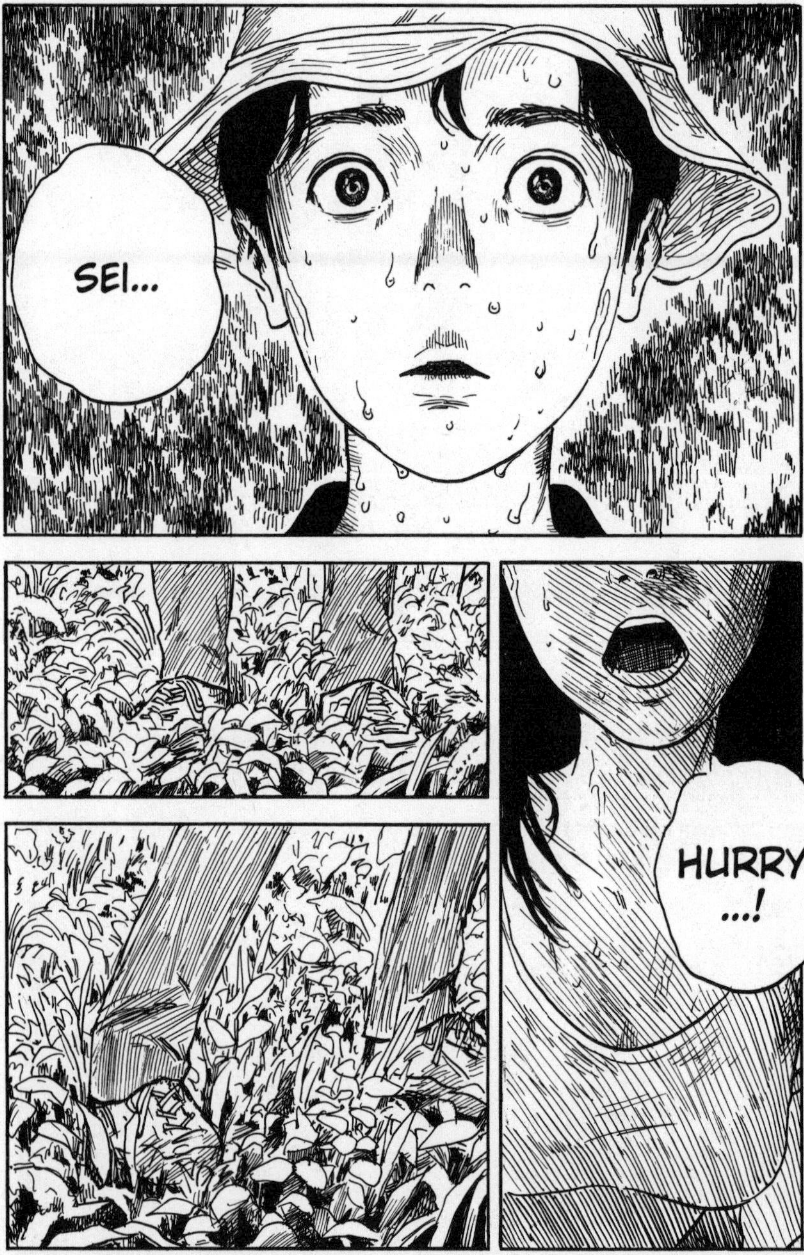
SEI...
HURRY ...!

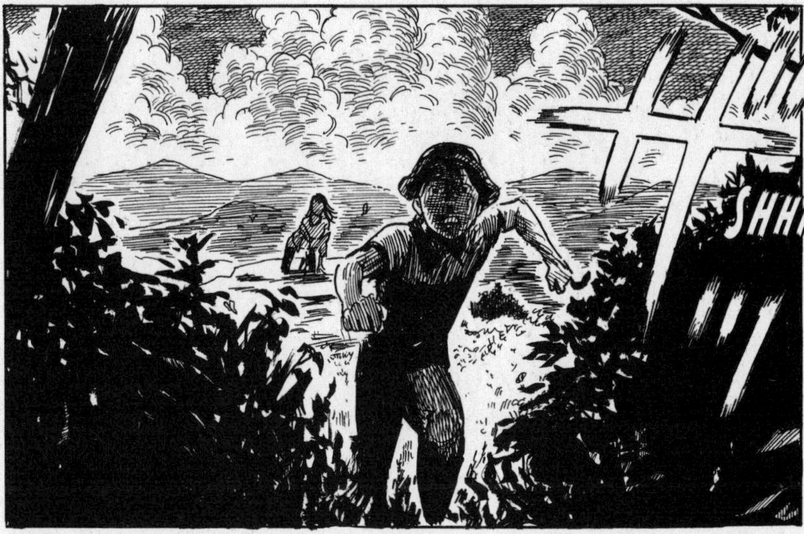
SHHF

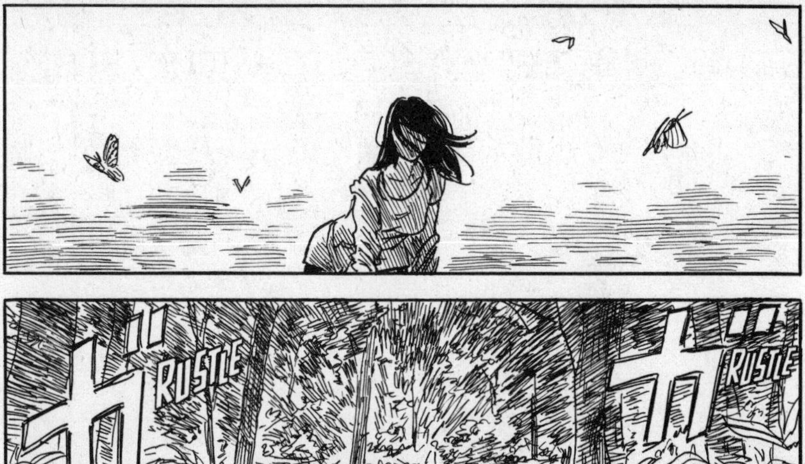

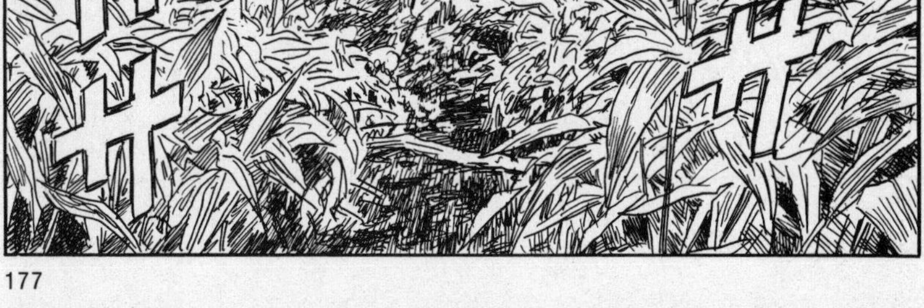
RUSTLE
RUSTLE

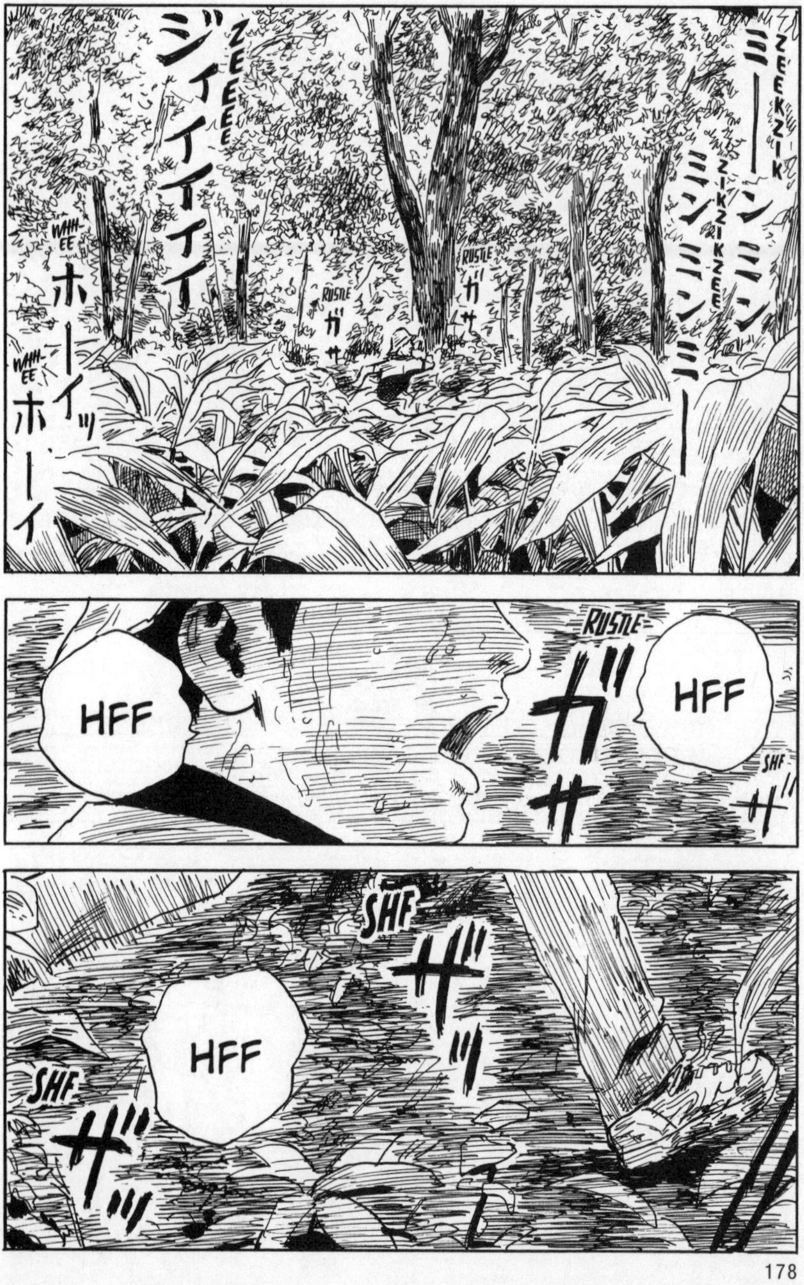
ZEEKZIK
ミーーンミンミン
ZIKZIKZEE
ミンミンミー
RUSTLE
ガサ
RUSTLE
ガサ
ZEEEEE
ジイイイイ
WHH-EE
ホーイッ
WHH-EE
ホーイ
SHF
ザ
HFF
RUSTLE
ガサ
HFF
SHF
ザッ
HFF
SHF
ザッ

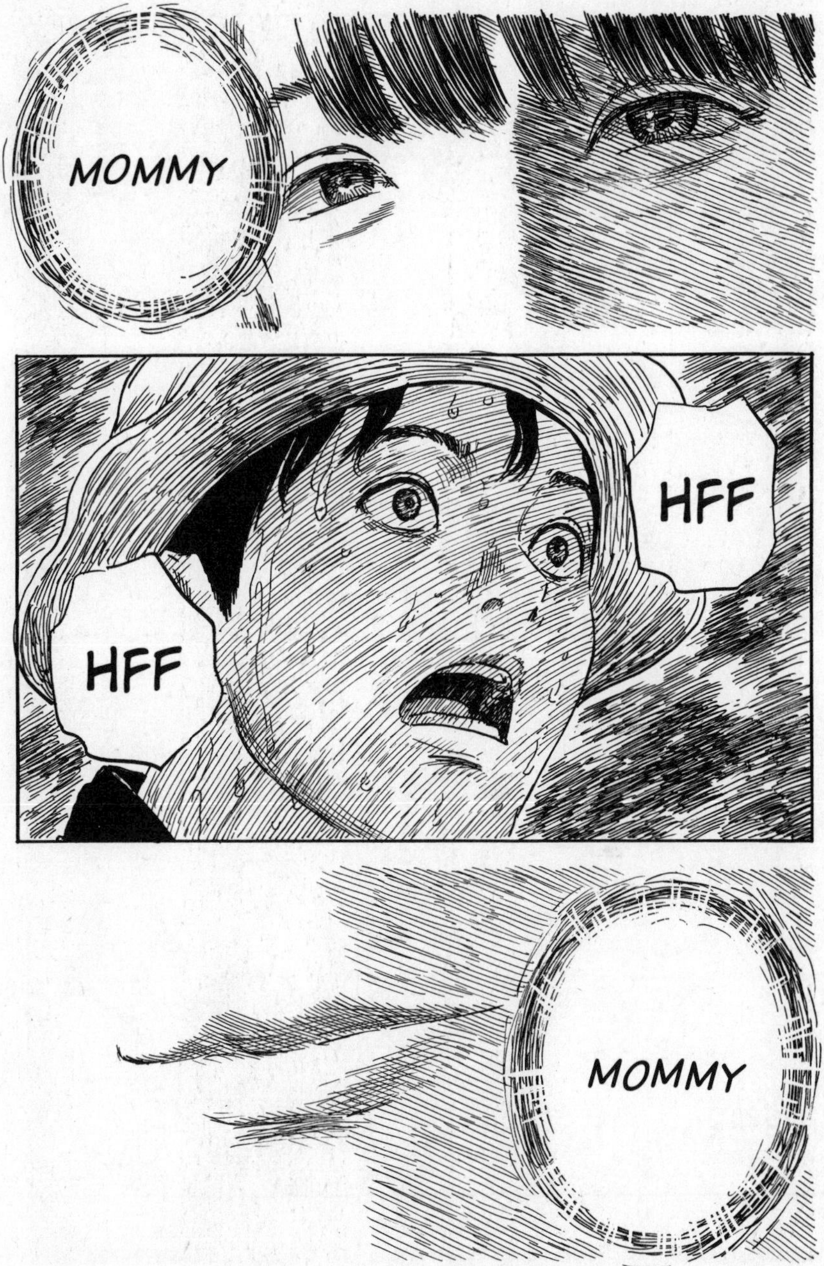
MOMMY
HFF
HFF
MOMMY

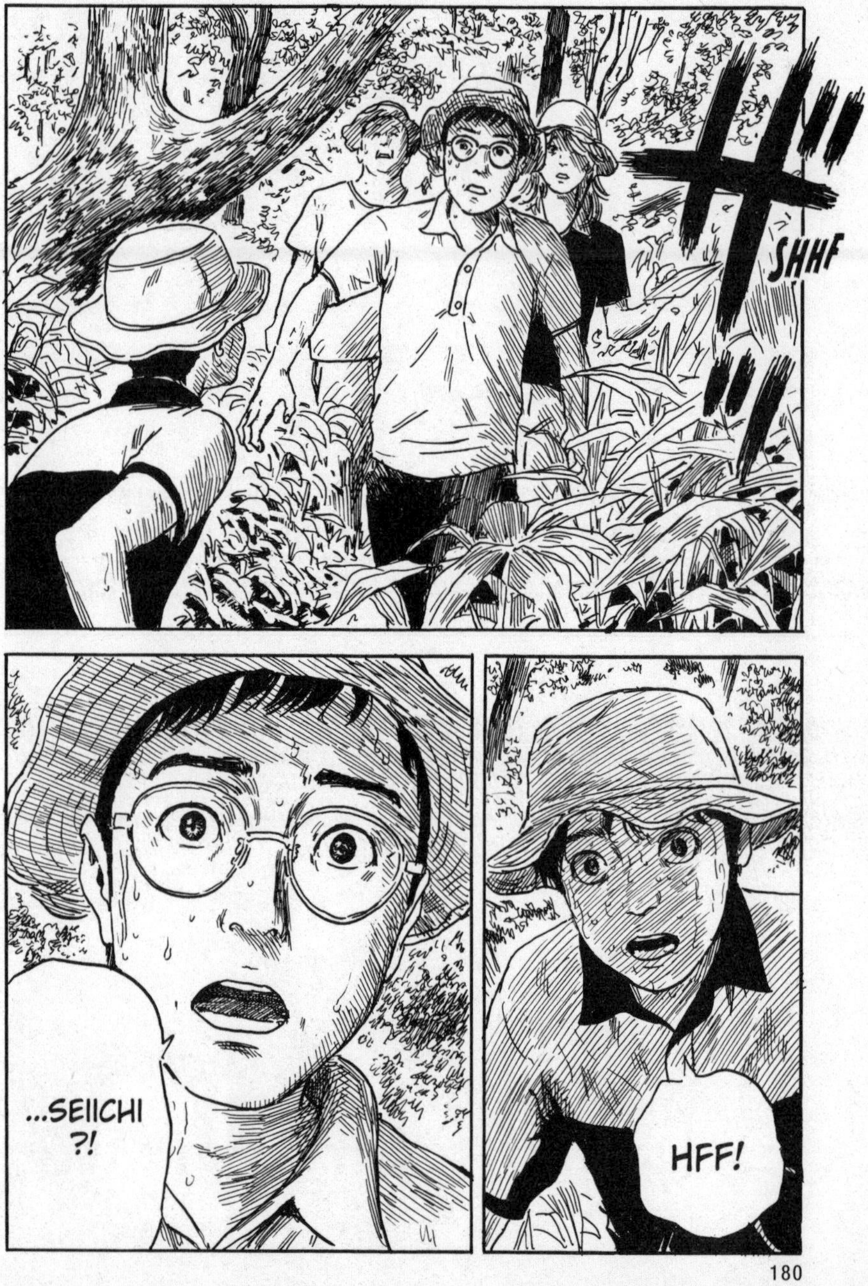
SHHF
HFF!
...SEIICHI ?!

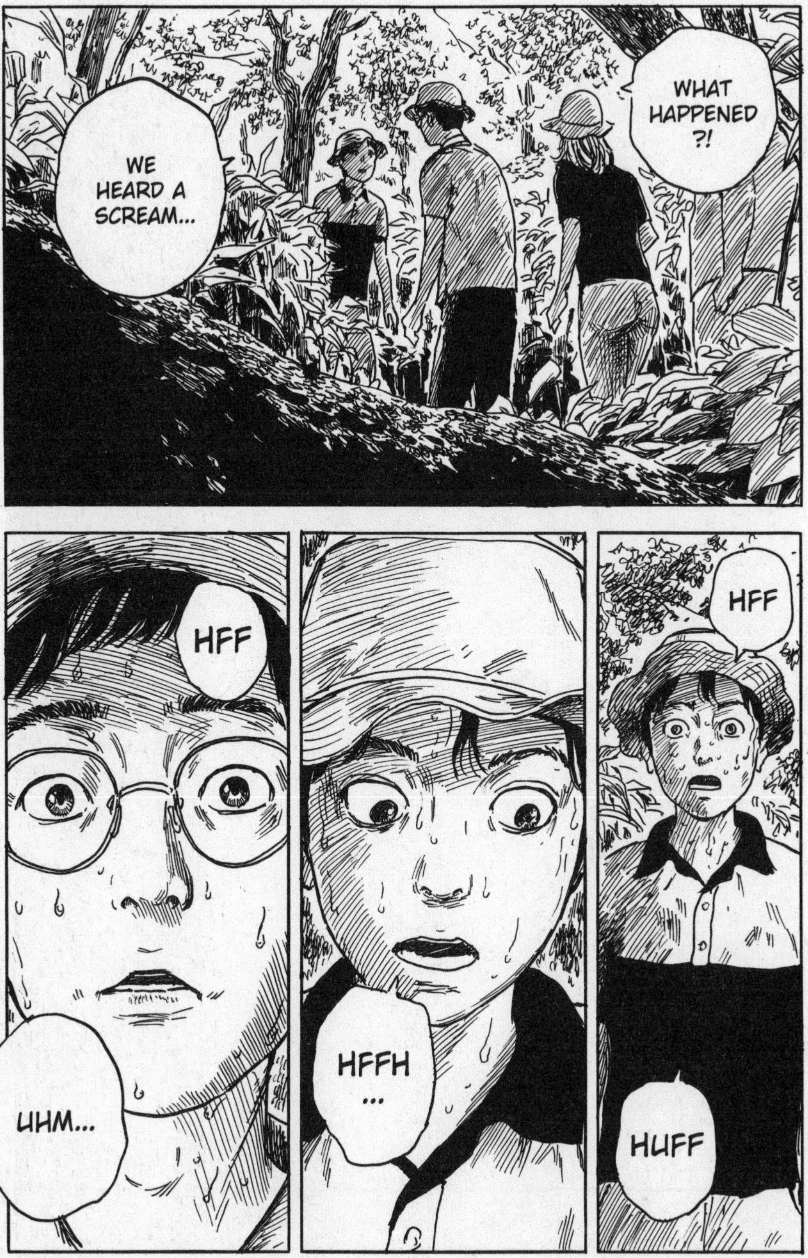
WHAT HAPPENED ?!
WE HEARD A SCREAM...
HFF
HUFF
HFFH ...
HFF
UHM...

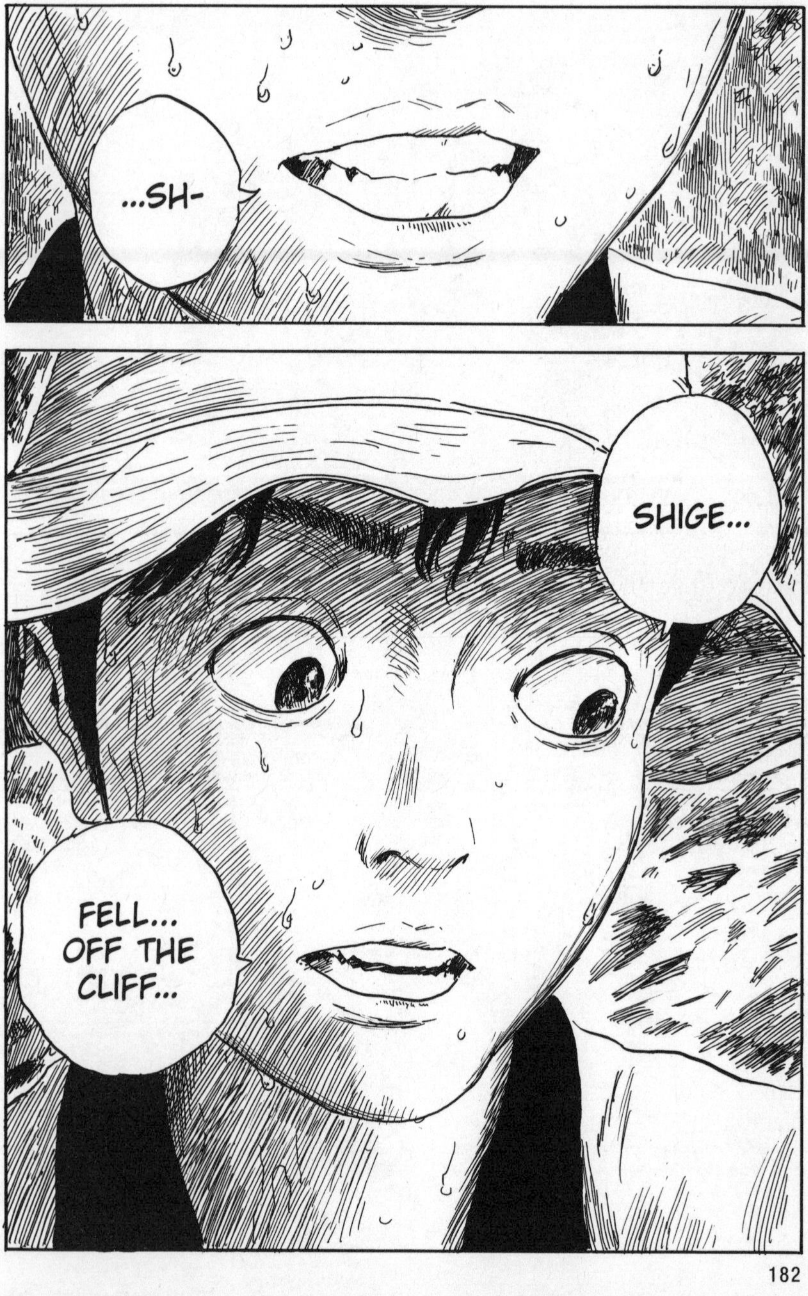
...SH-
SHIGE...
FELL... OFF THE CLIFF...

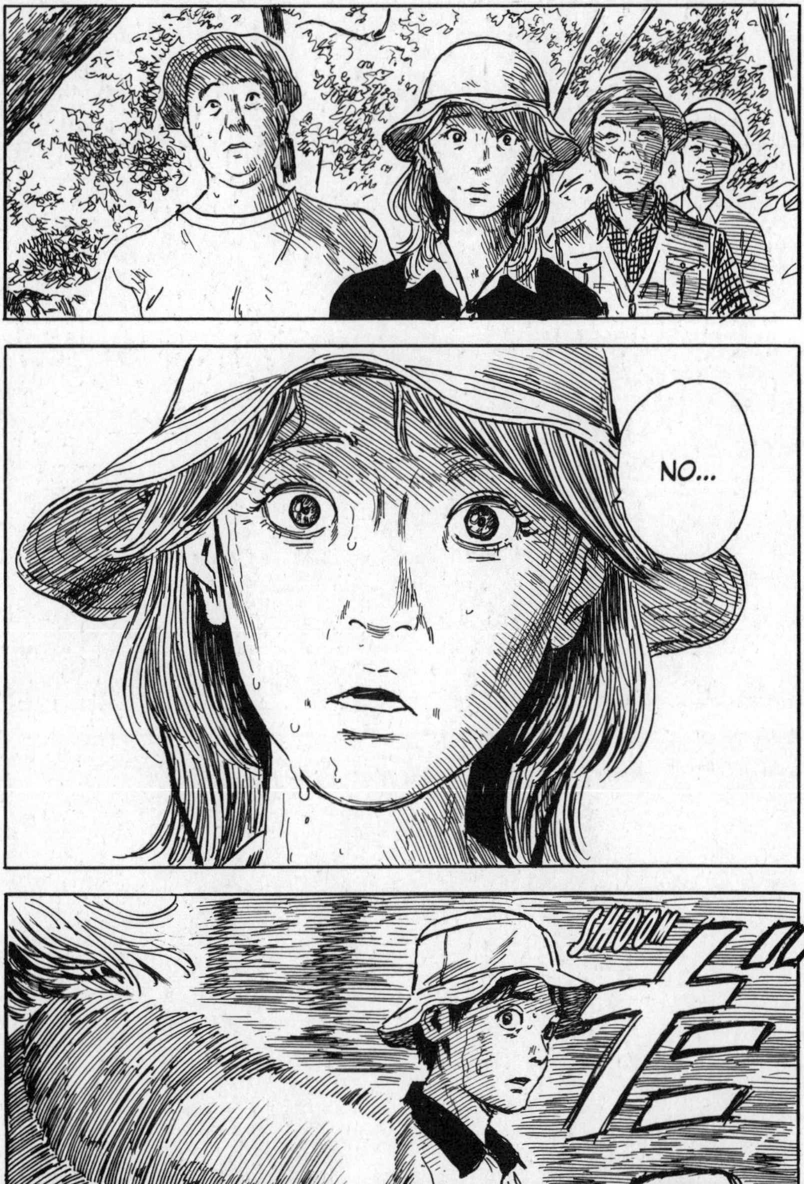
NO...
SHOOM

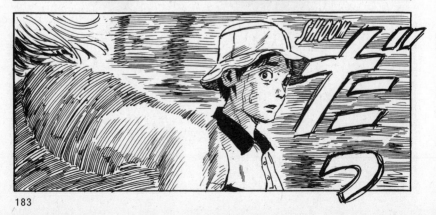

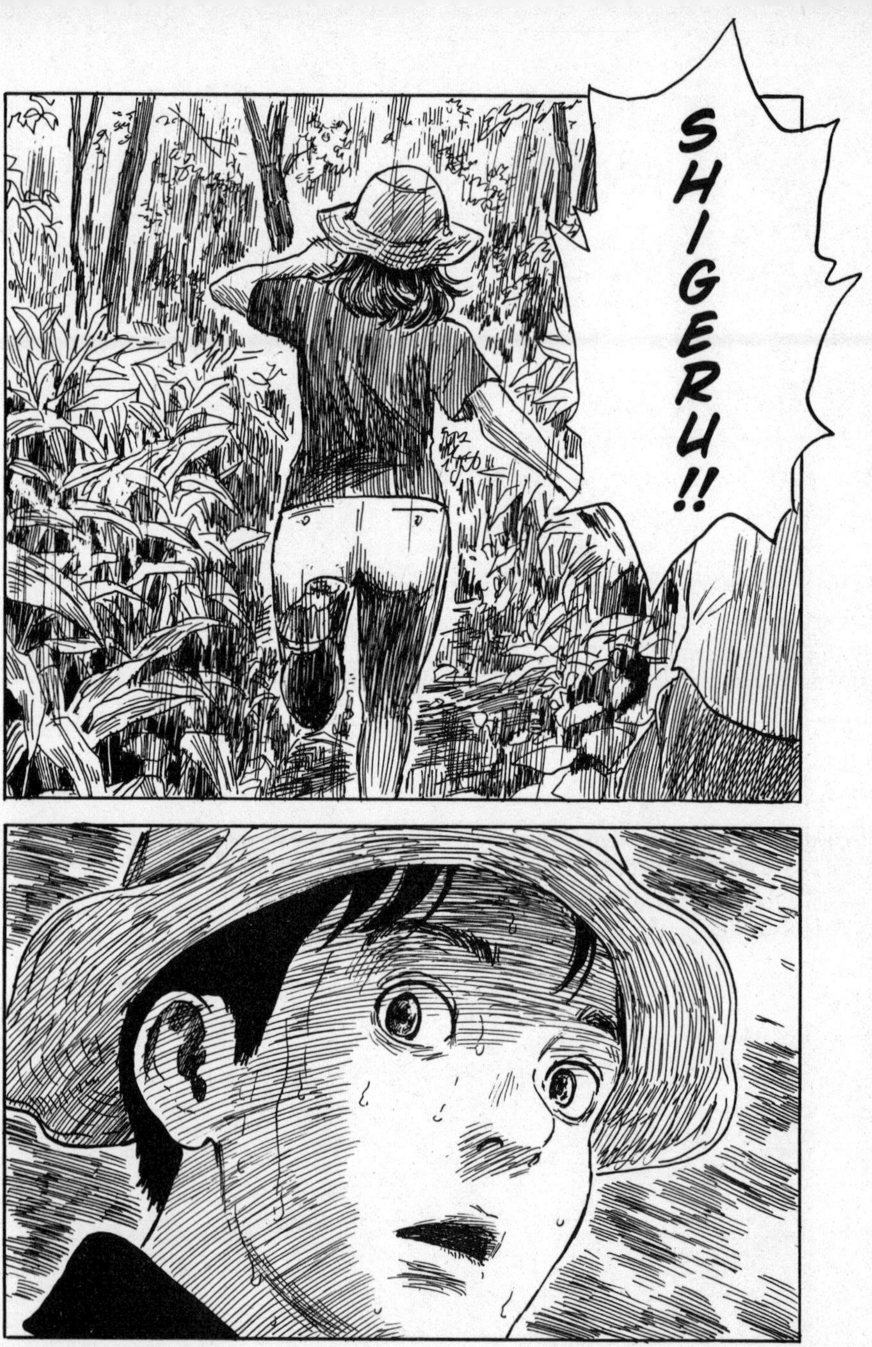
SHIGERU!!

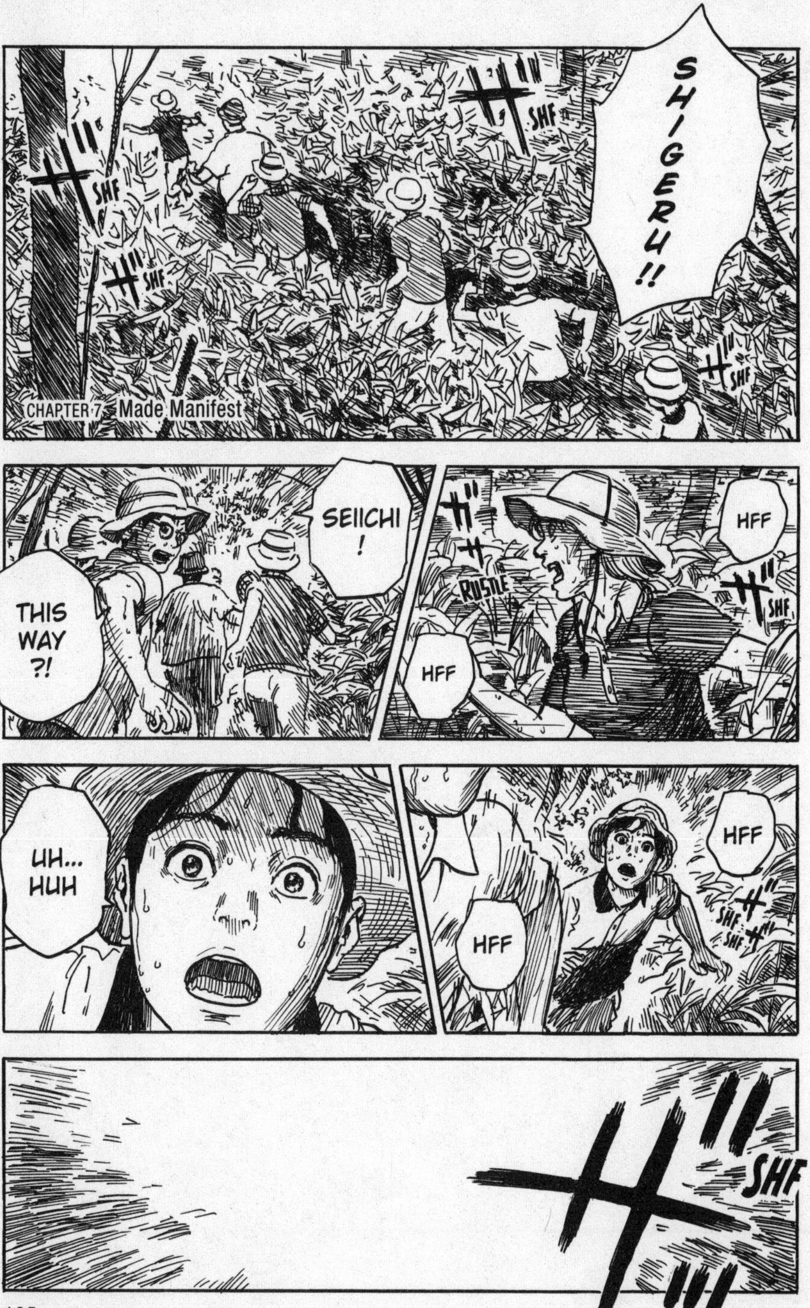
SHIGERU!!
SHF
SHF
SHF
SHF
CHAPTER 7 Made Manifest
HFF
SHF
RUSTLE
HFF
SEIICHI!
THIS WAY?!
HFF
SHF
SHF
HFF
UH... HUH
SHF

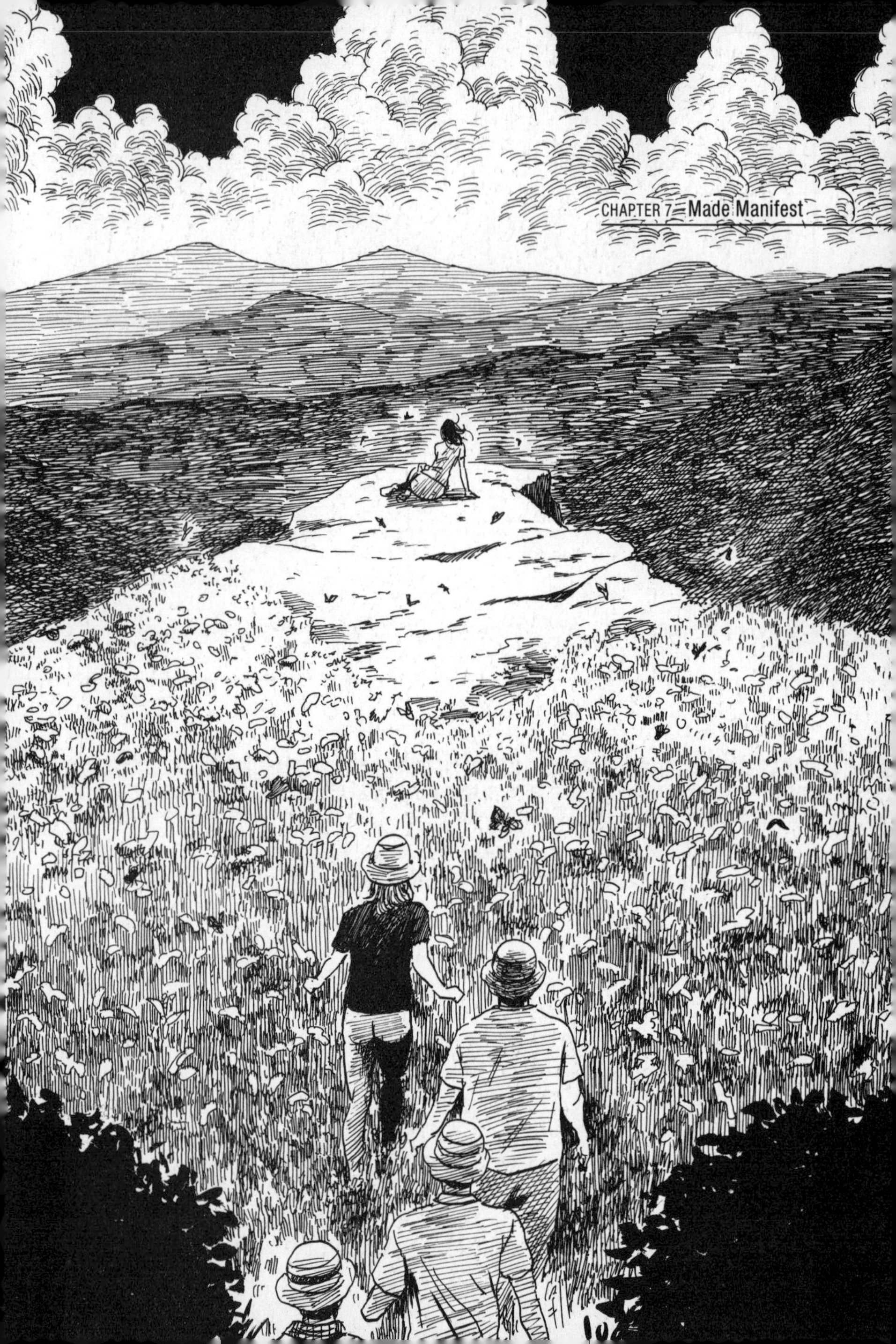
CHAPTER 7 — Made Manifest

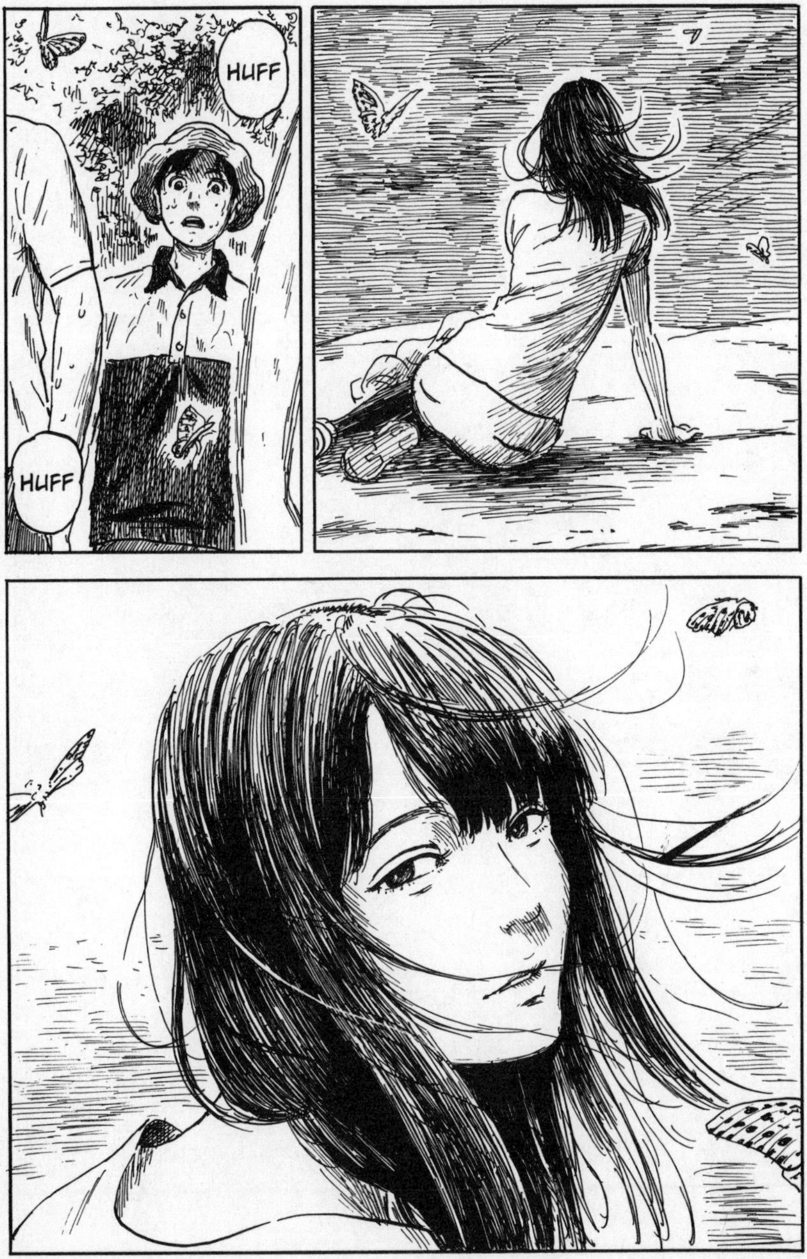
HUFF
HUFF

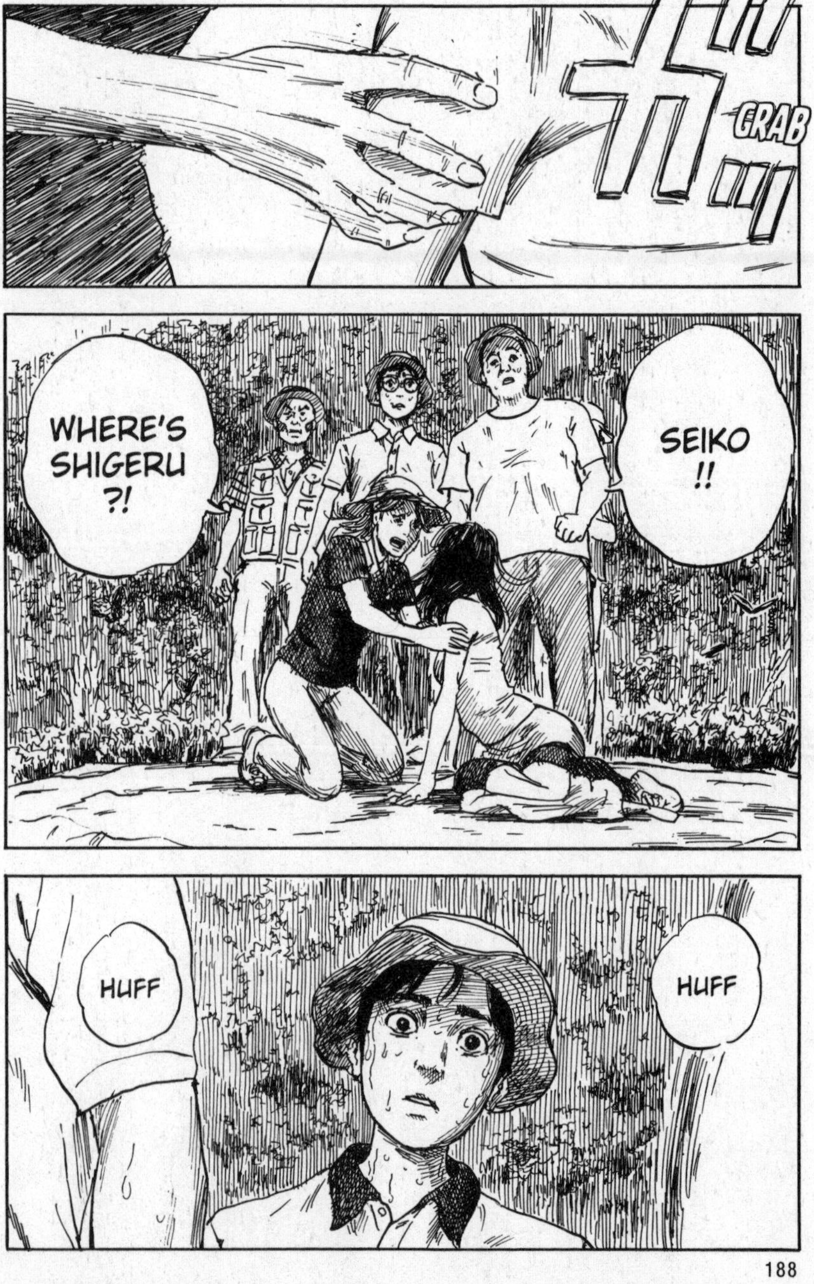
ガッ
GRAB
SEIKO !!
WHERE'S SHIGERU ?!
HUFF
HUFF

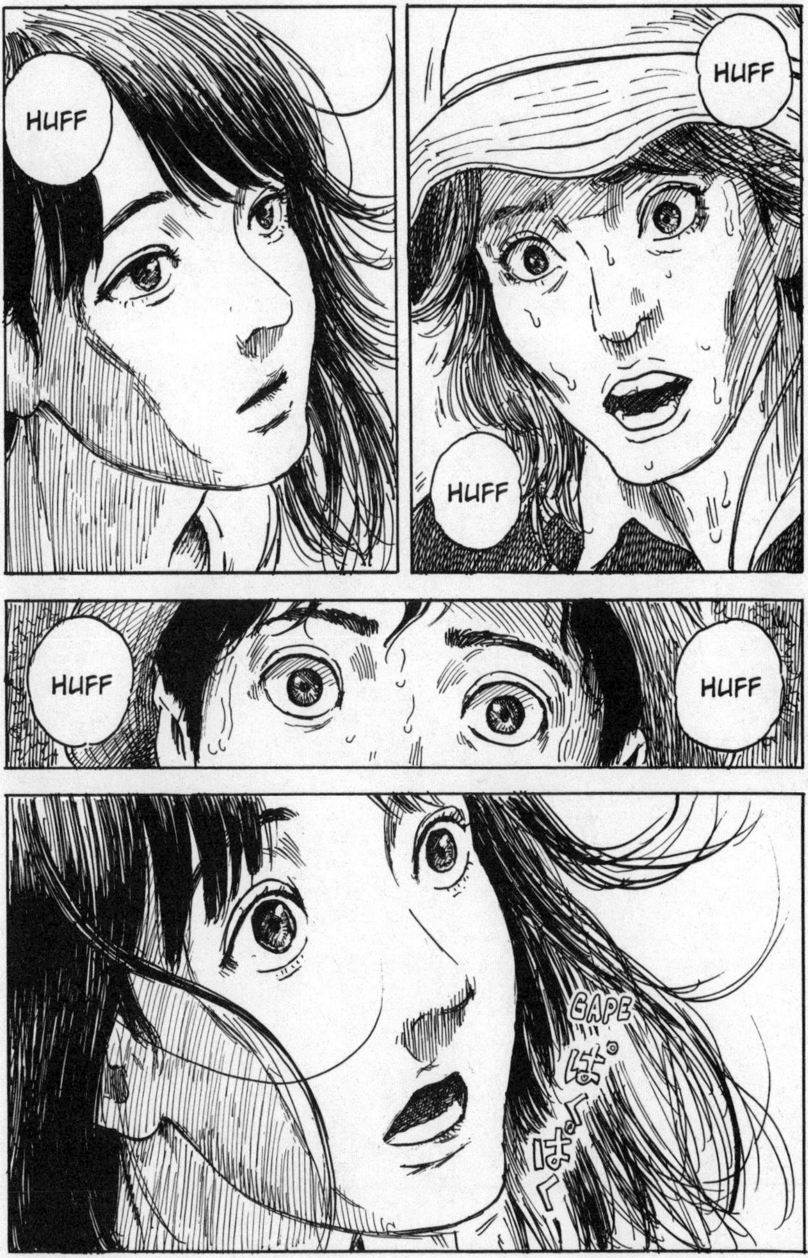
HUFF
HUFF
HUFF
HUFF
HUFF
GAPE
ぱくぱく

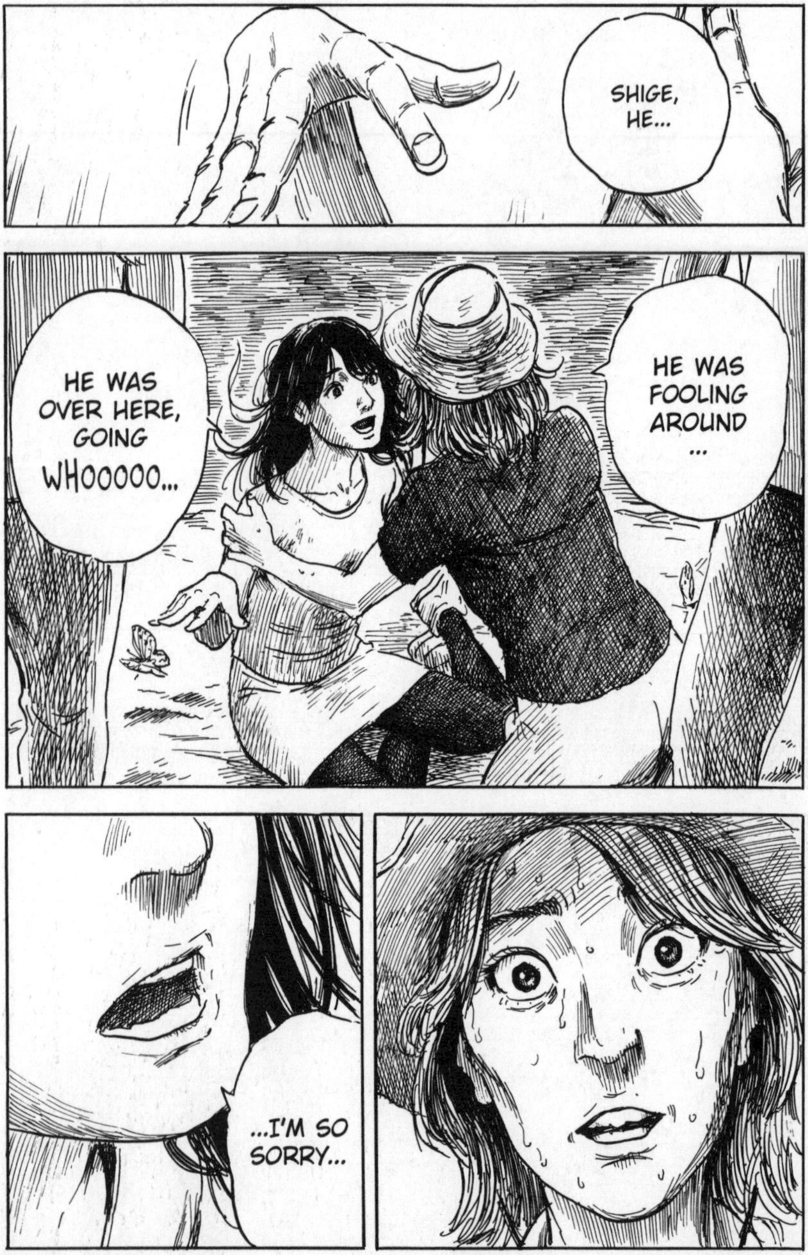
SHIGE, HE...
HE WAS FOOLING AROUND ...
HE WAS OVER HERE, GOING WHOOOOO...
...I'M SO SORRY...

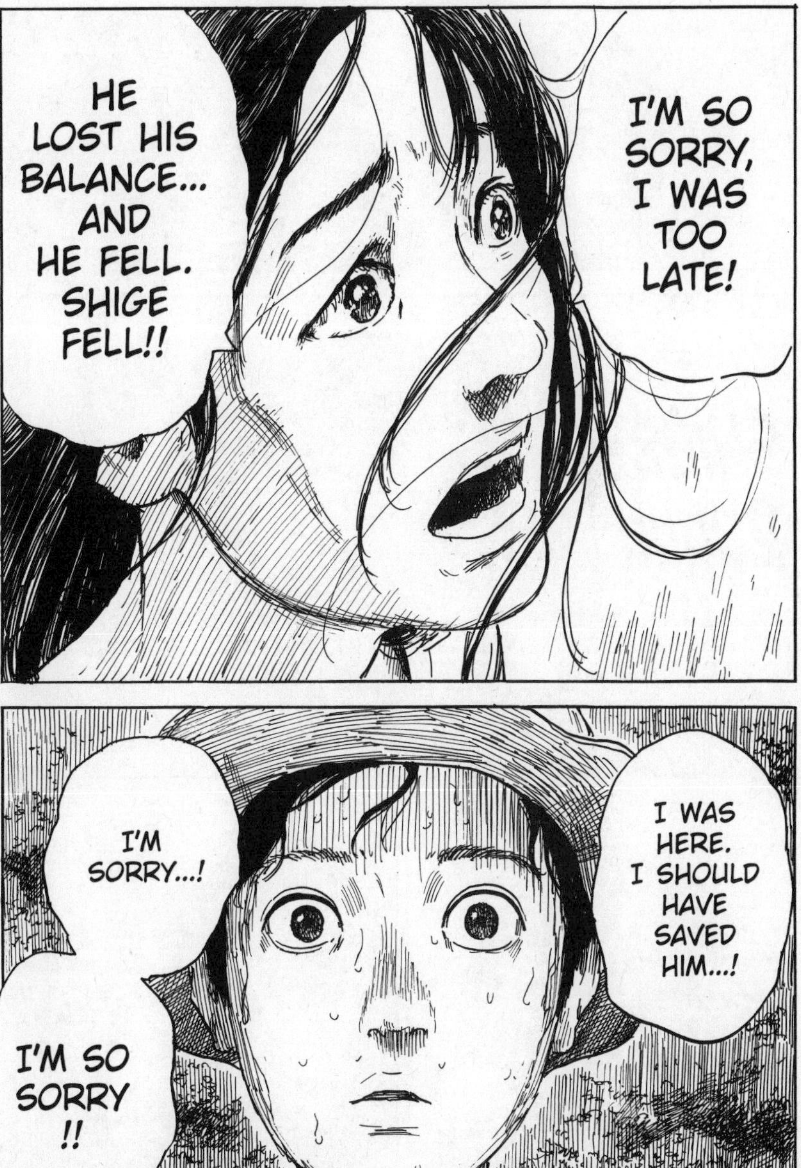
I'M SO SORRY, I WAS TOO LATE!
HE LOST HIS BALANCE... AND HE FELL. SHIGE FELL!!
I WAS HERE. I SHOULD HAVE SAVED HIM...!
I'M SORRY...!
I'M SO SORRY !!

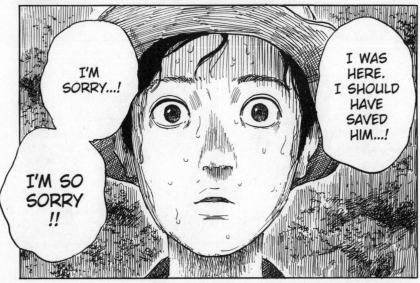

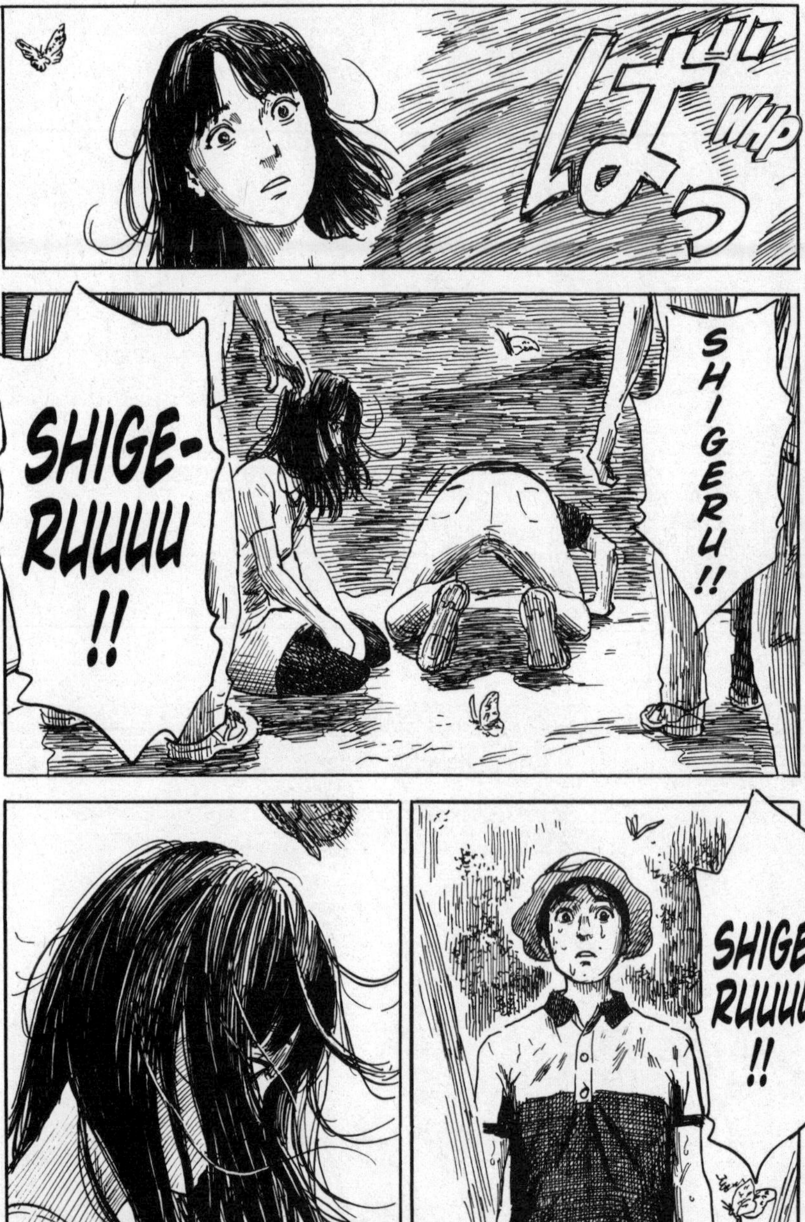
ばっ
WHP
SHIGERU!!
SHIGE-RUUUU!!
SHIGE-RUUUU!!

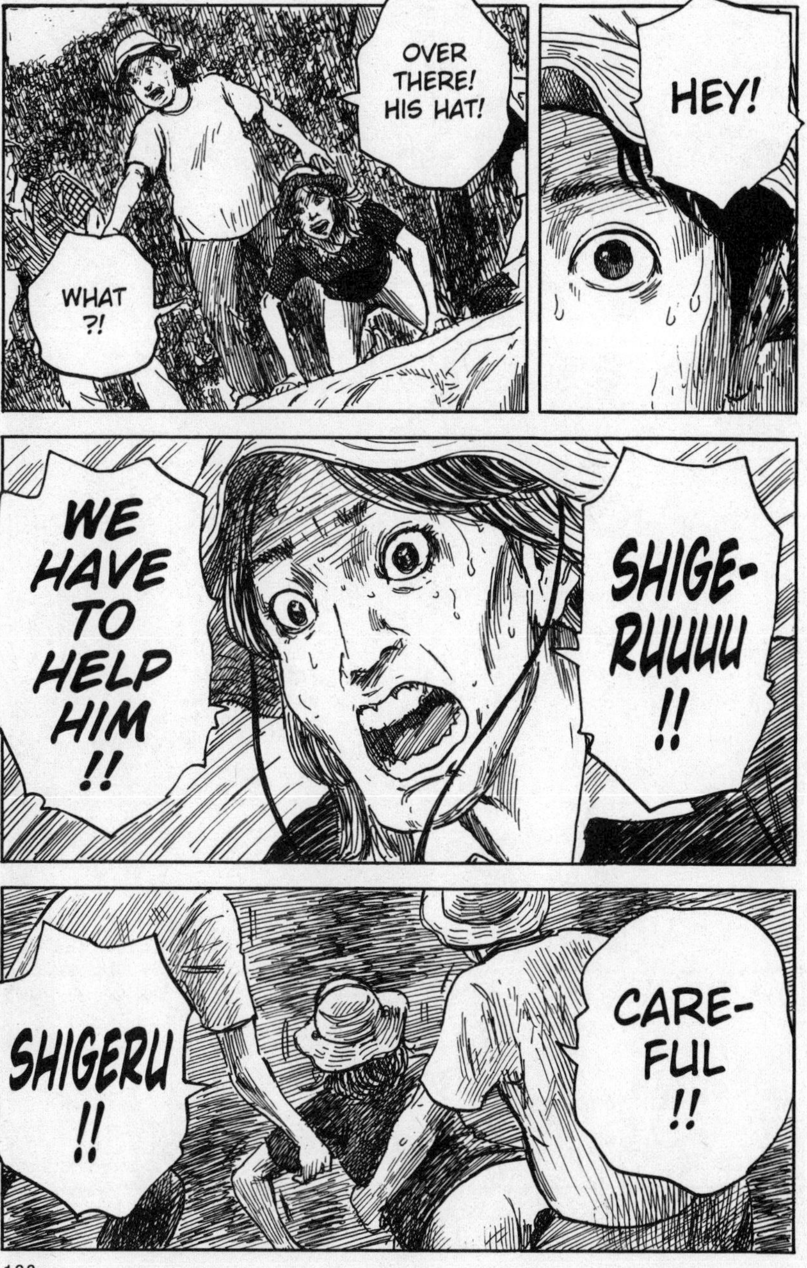
HEY!
OVER THERE! HIS HAT!
WHAT?!
SHIGE-RUUUU!!
WE HAVE TO HELP HIM!!
CARE-FUL!!
SHIGERU!!

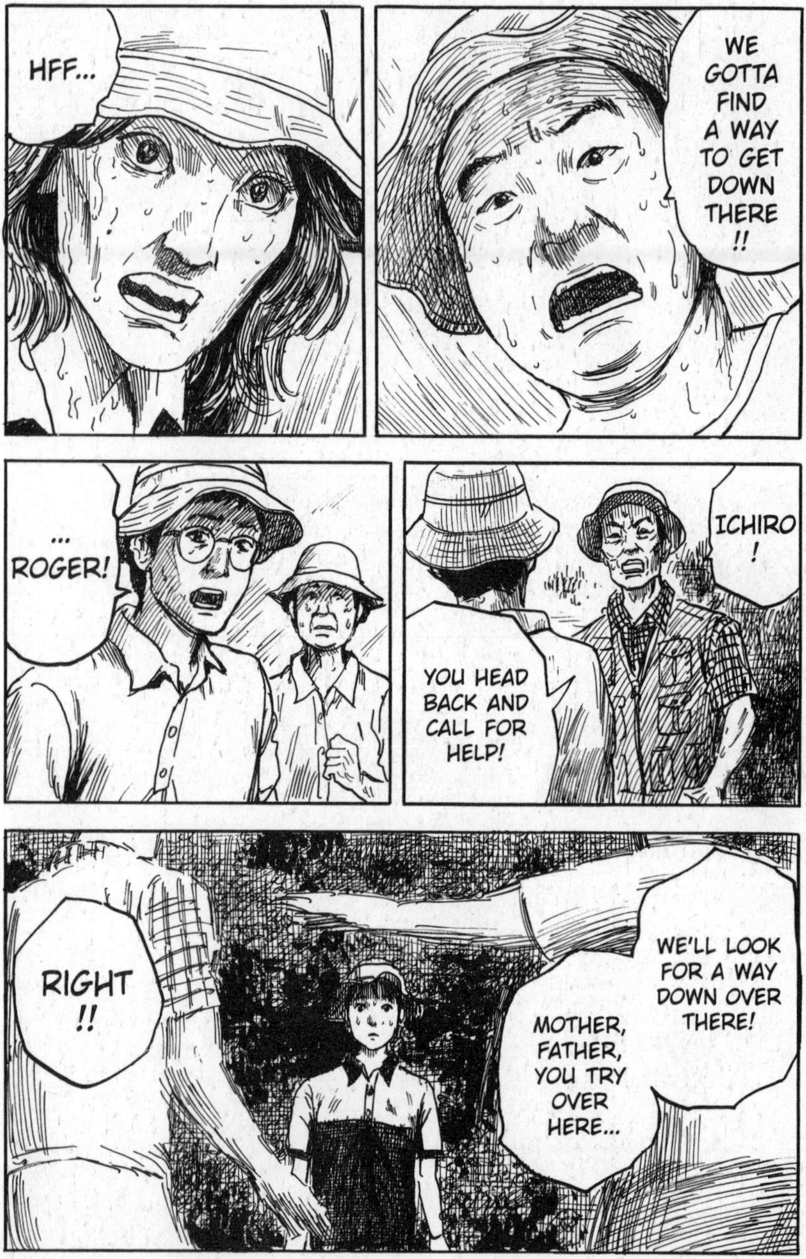
WE GOTTA FIND A WAY TO GET DOWN THERE!!
HFF...
ICHIRO!
YOU HEAD BACK AND CALL FOR HELP!
... ROGER!
WE'LL LOOK FOR A WAY DOWN OVER THERE!
MOTHER, FATHER, YOU TRY OVER HERE...
RIGHT!!

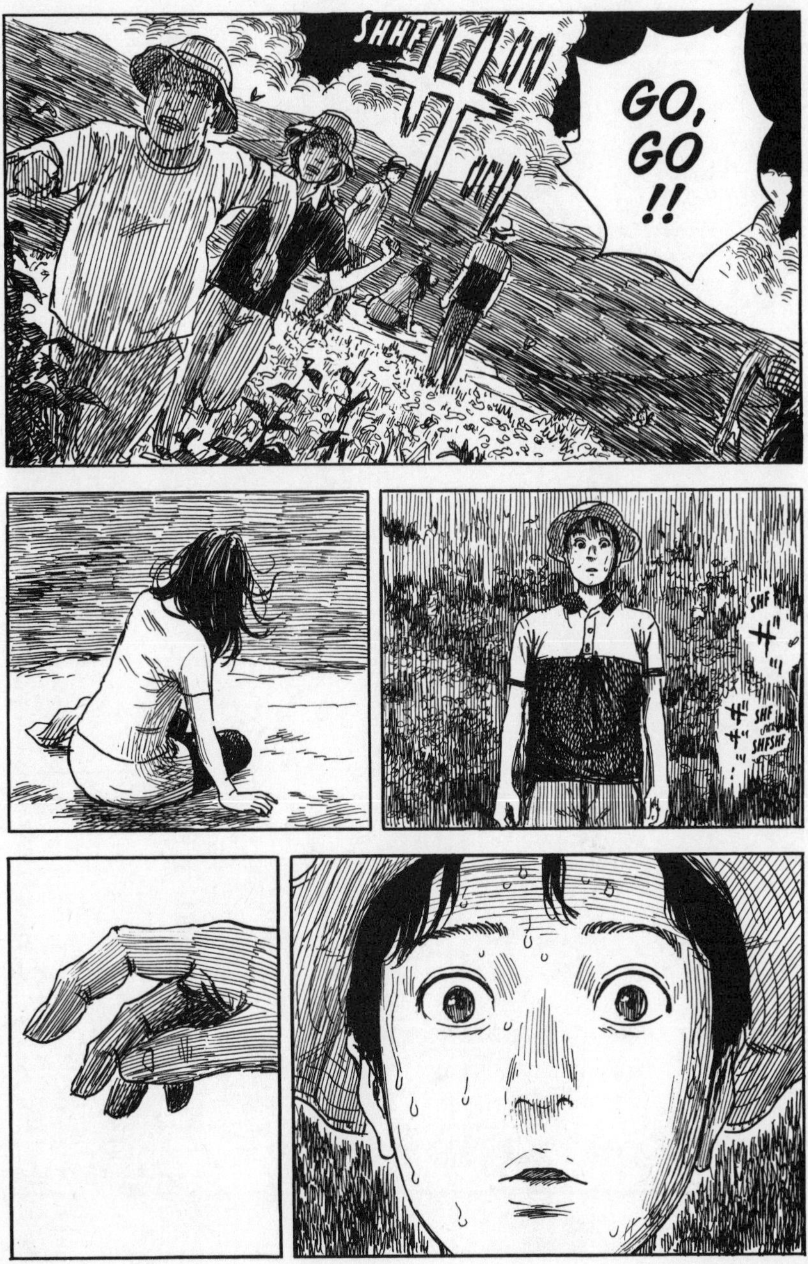
GO, GO!!
SHHF
SHF
SHF
SHFSHF

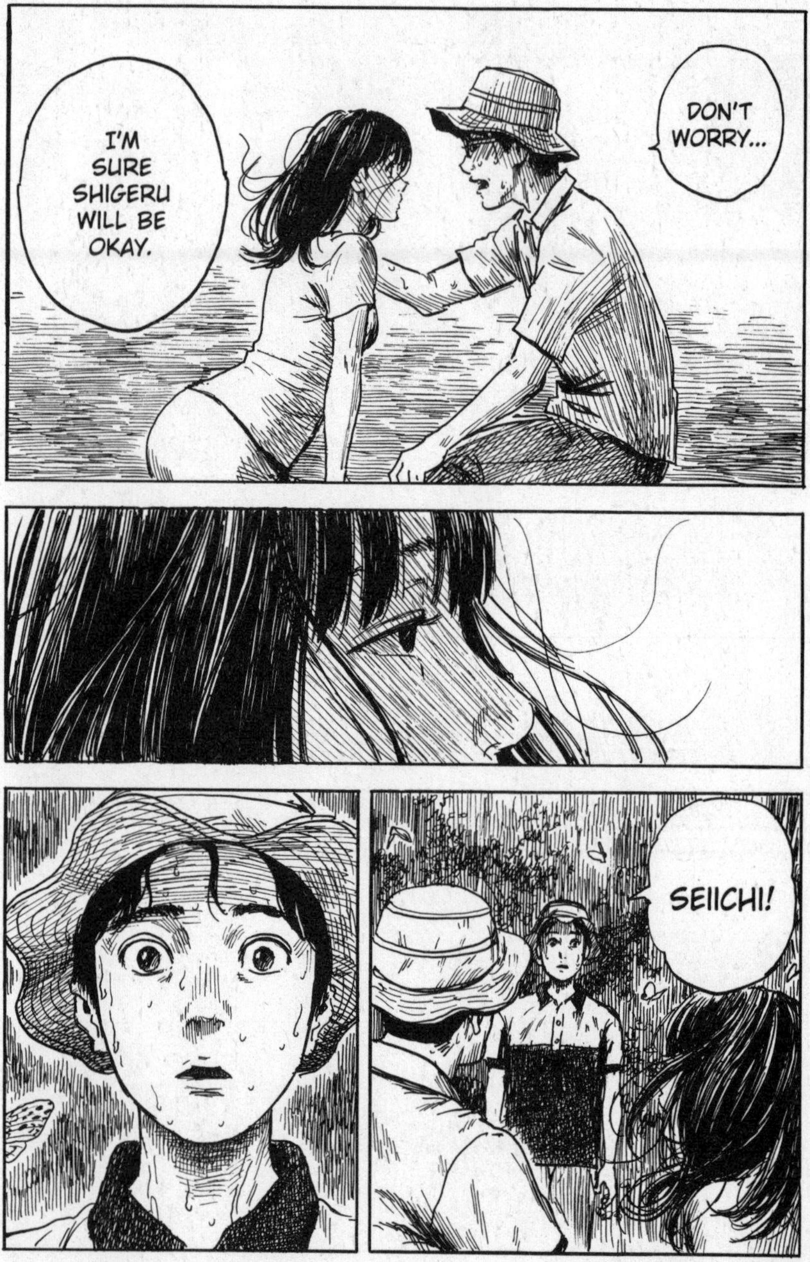
DON'T WORRY...
I'M SURE SHIGERU WILL BE OKAY.
SEIICHI!

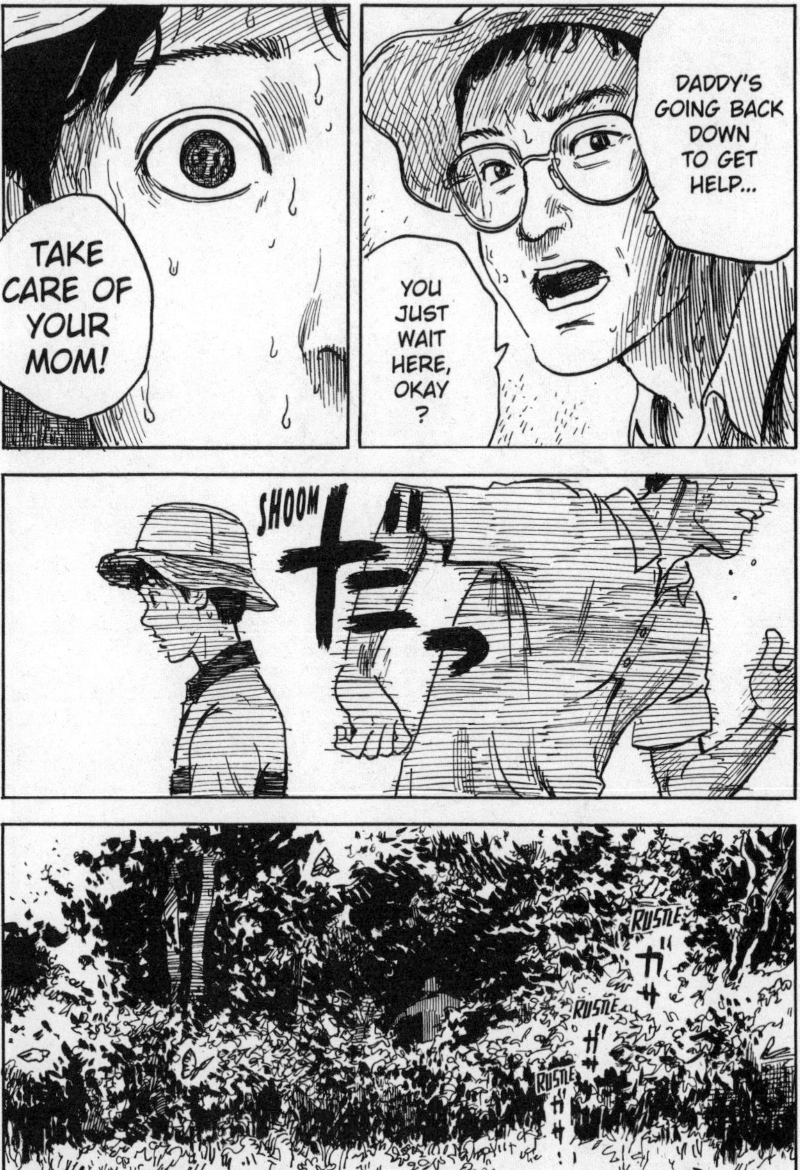
DADDY'S GOING BACK DOWN TO GET HELP...
YOU JUST WAIT HERE, OKAY?
TAKE CARE OF YOUR MOM!
SHOOM
RUSTLE
RUSTLE
RUSTLE

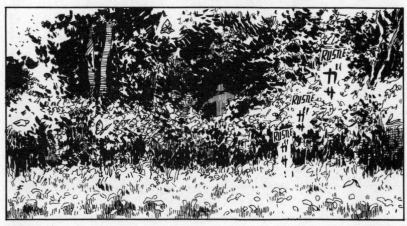

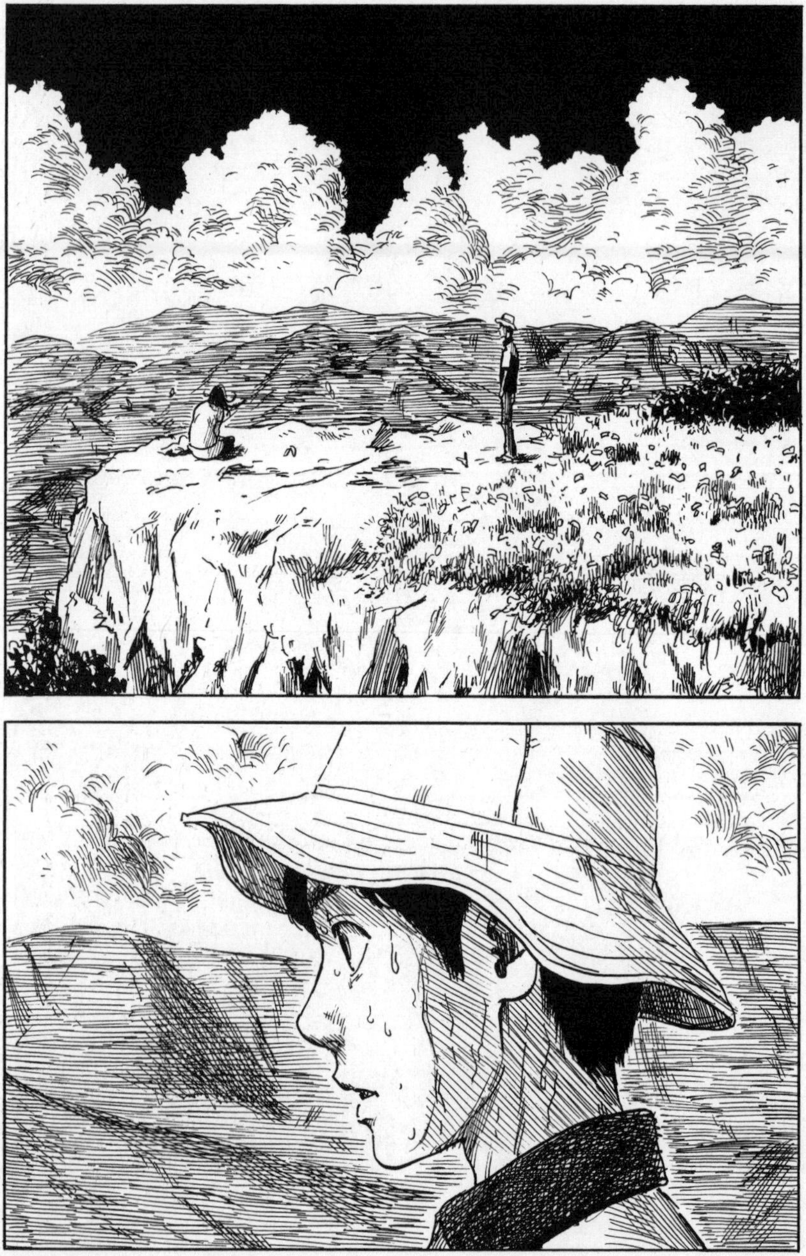

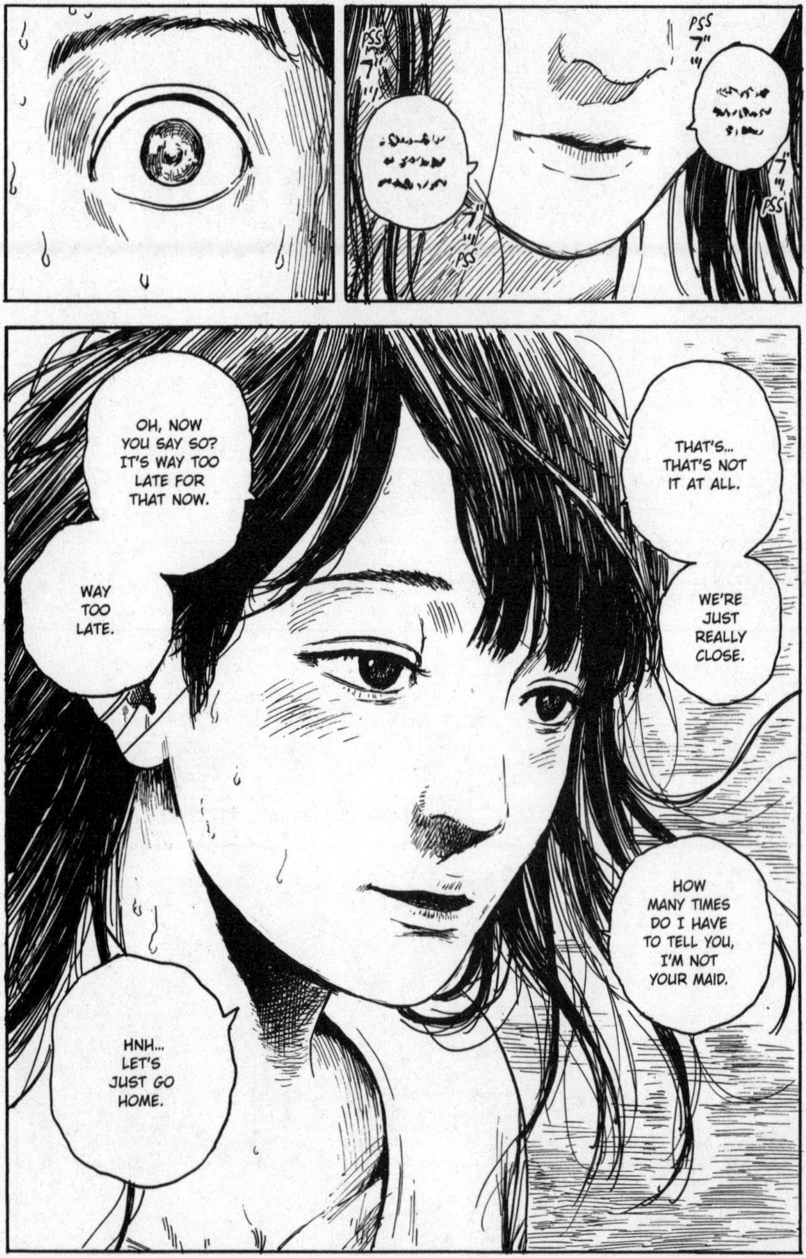
PSS
PSS
PSS
PSS
THAT'S... THAT'S NOT IT AT ALL.
WE'RE JUST REALLY CLOSE.
OH, NOW YOU SAY SO? IT'S WAY TOO LATE FOR THAT NOW.
WAY TOO LATE.
HOW MANY TIMES DO I HAVE TO TELL YOU, I'M NOT YOUR MAID.
HNH... LET'S JUST GO HOME.

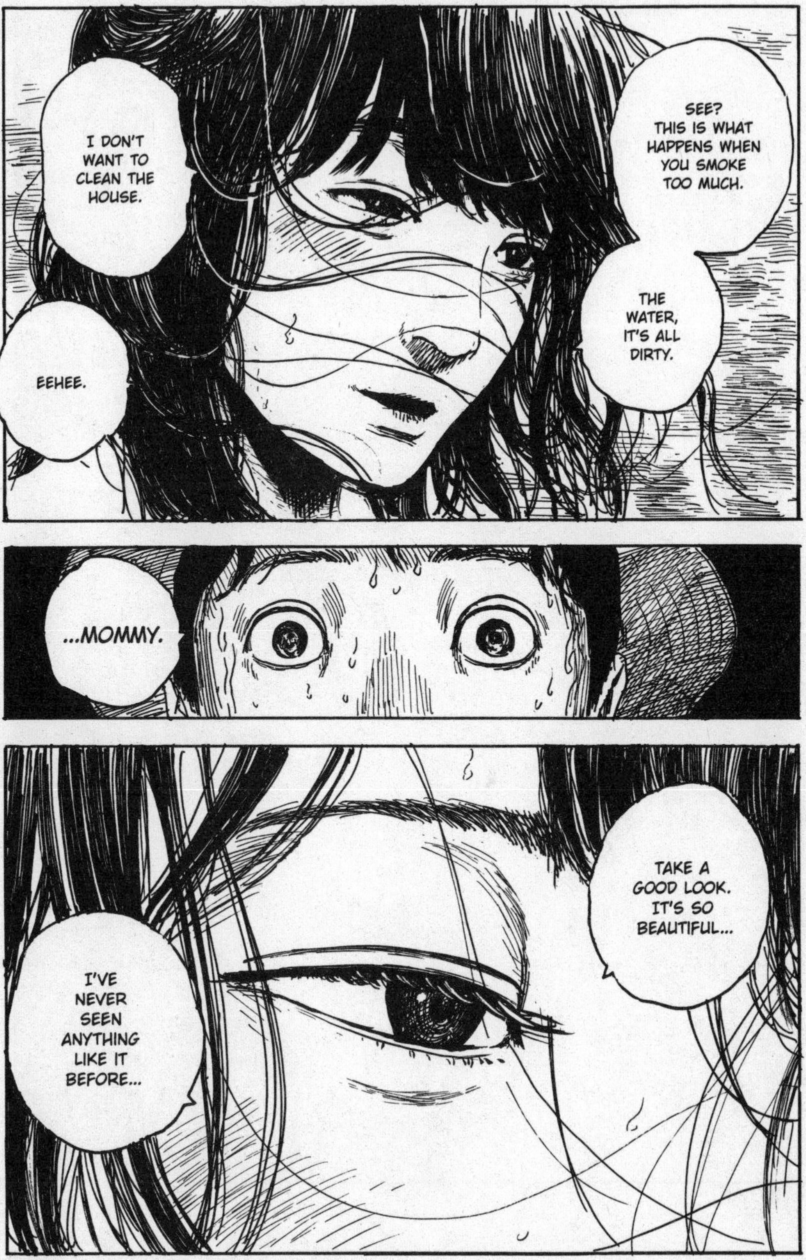
SEE? THIS IS WHAT HAPPENS WHEN YOU SMOKE TOO MUCH.
THE WATER, IT'S ALL DIRTY.
I DON'T WANT TO CLEAN THE HOUSE.
EEHEE.
...MOMMY.
TAKE A GOOD LOOK. IT'S SO BEAUTIFUL...
I'VE NEVER SEEN ANYTHING LIKE IT BEFORE...

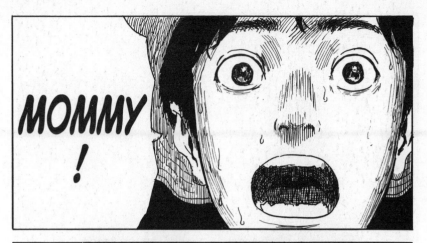

MOMMY
!

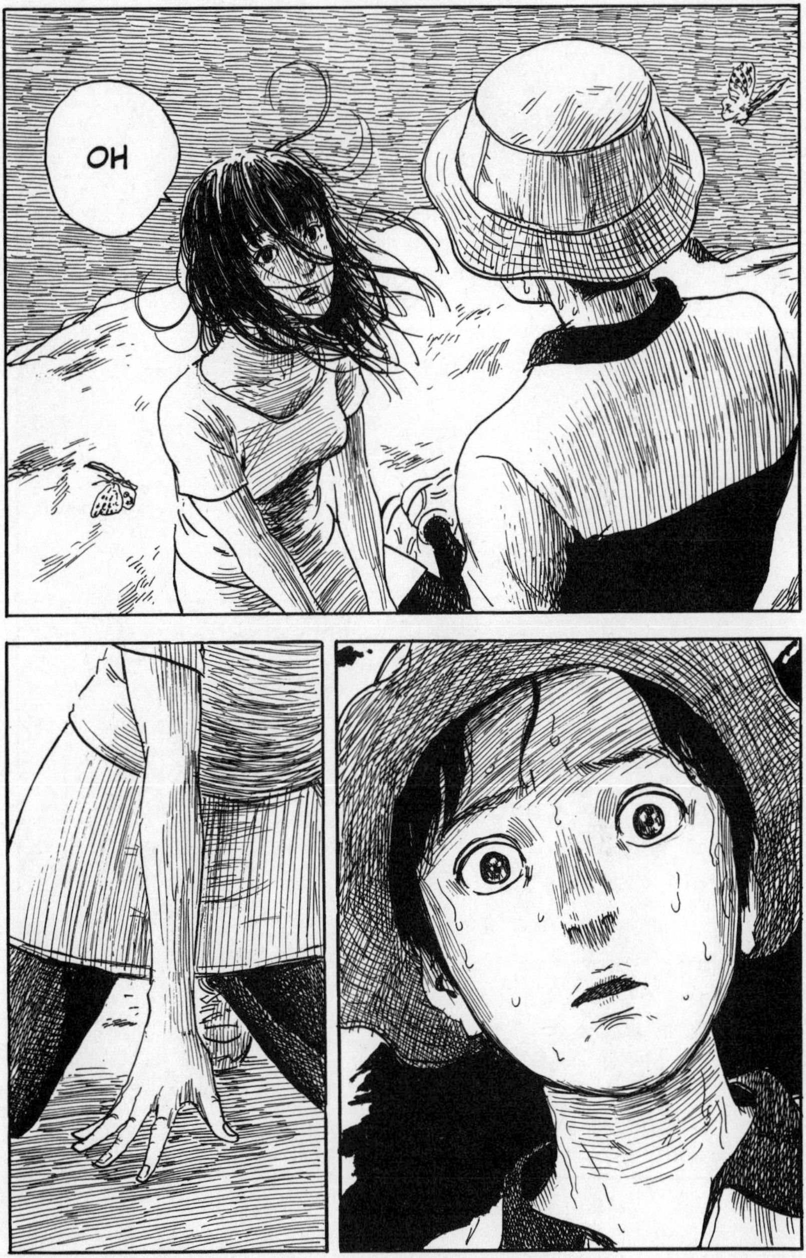
OH

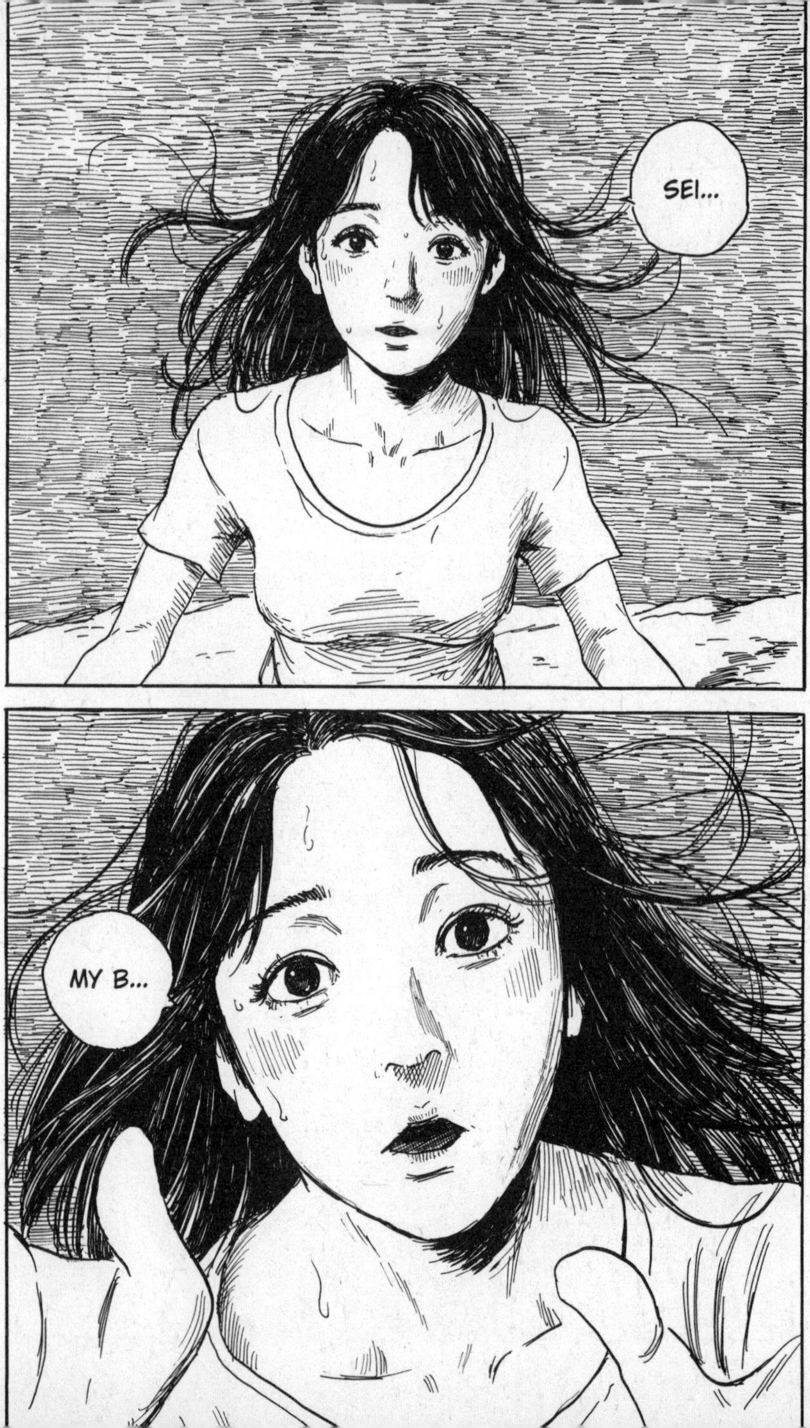
SEI...
MY B...

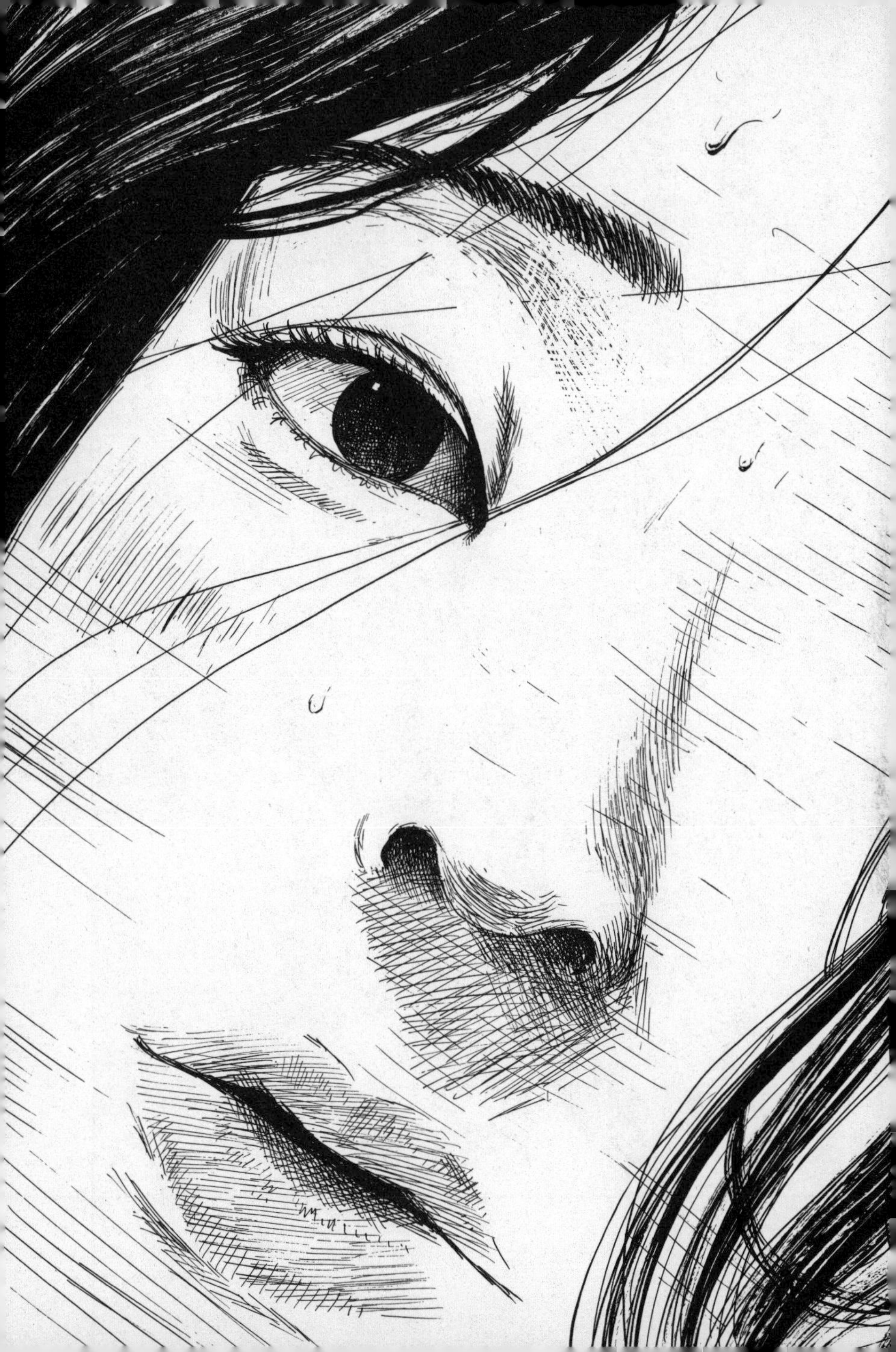

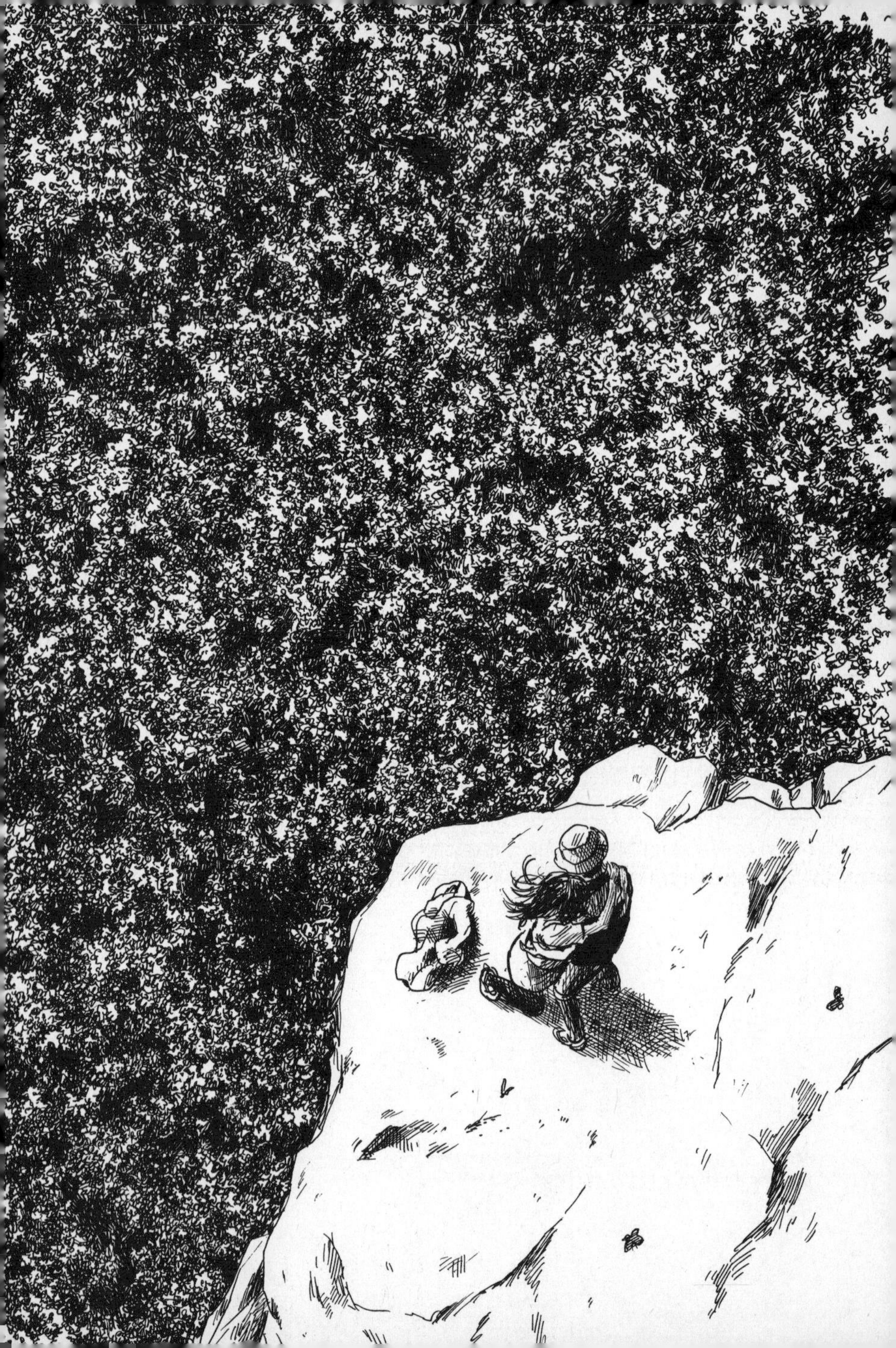

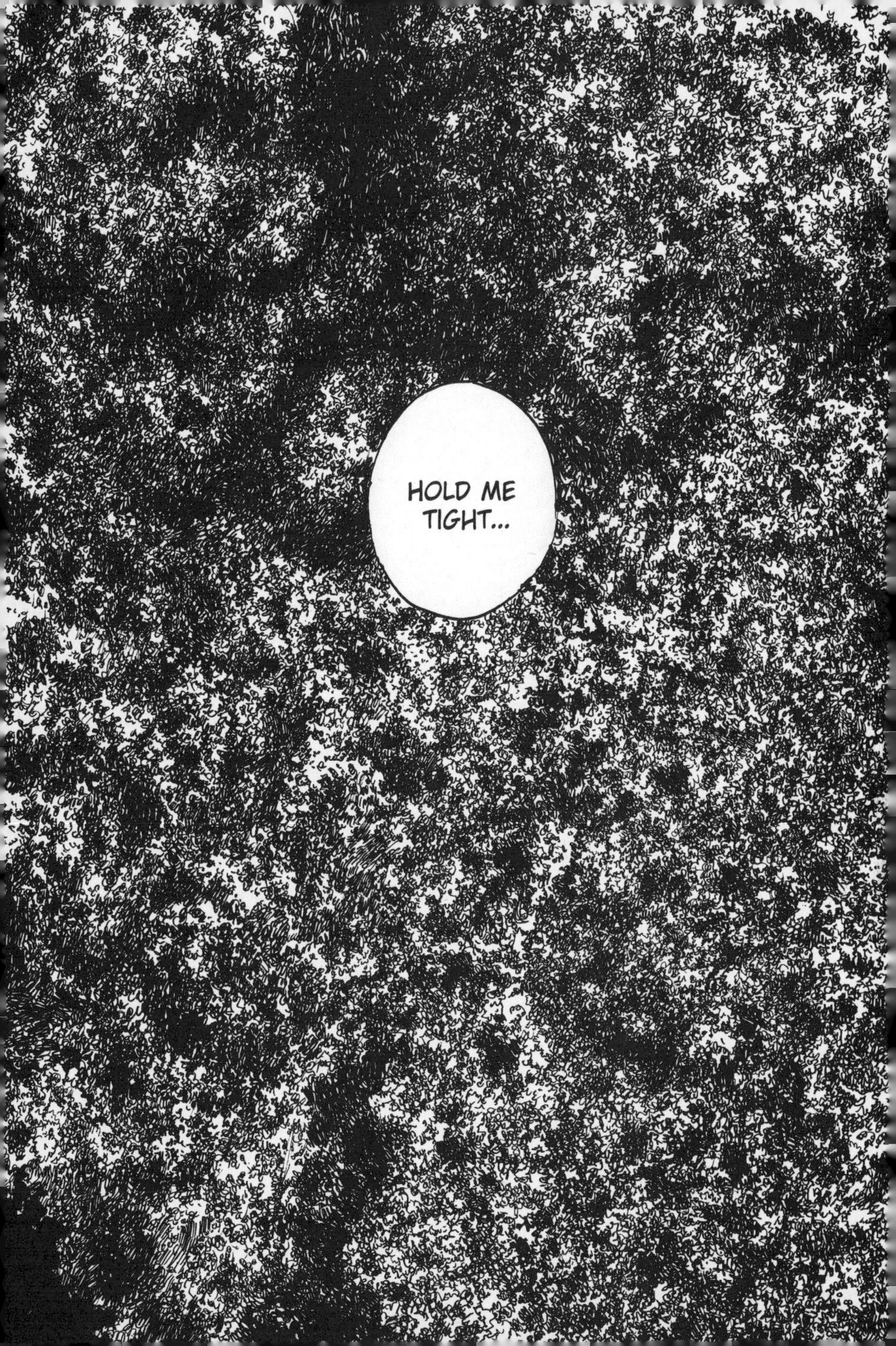
HOLD ME TIGHT...

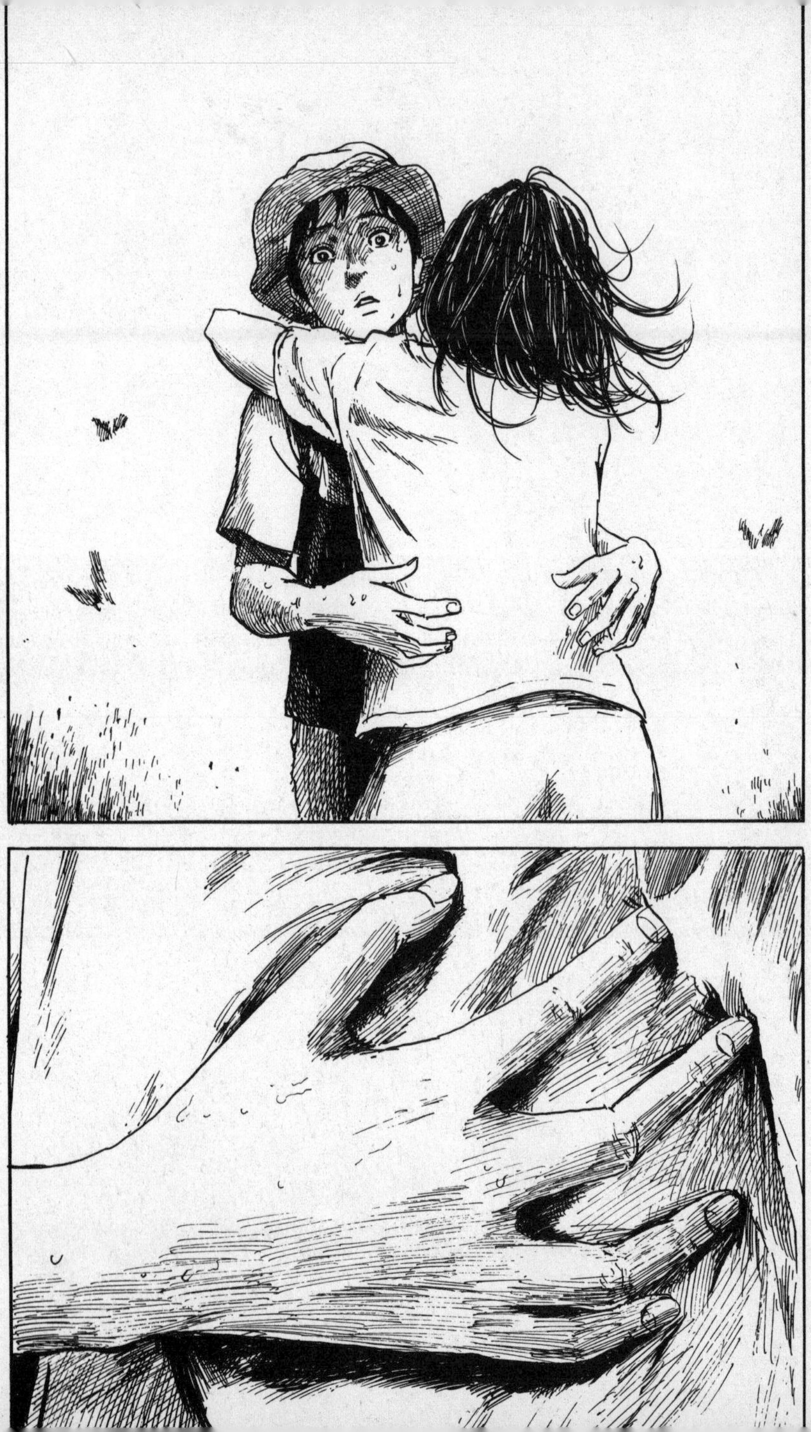

Blood on the Tracks VOLUME 1 • END

Photo Album

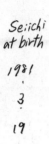 Seiichi
at birth

1981
.
3
.
19

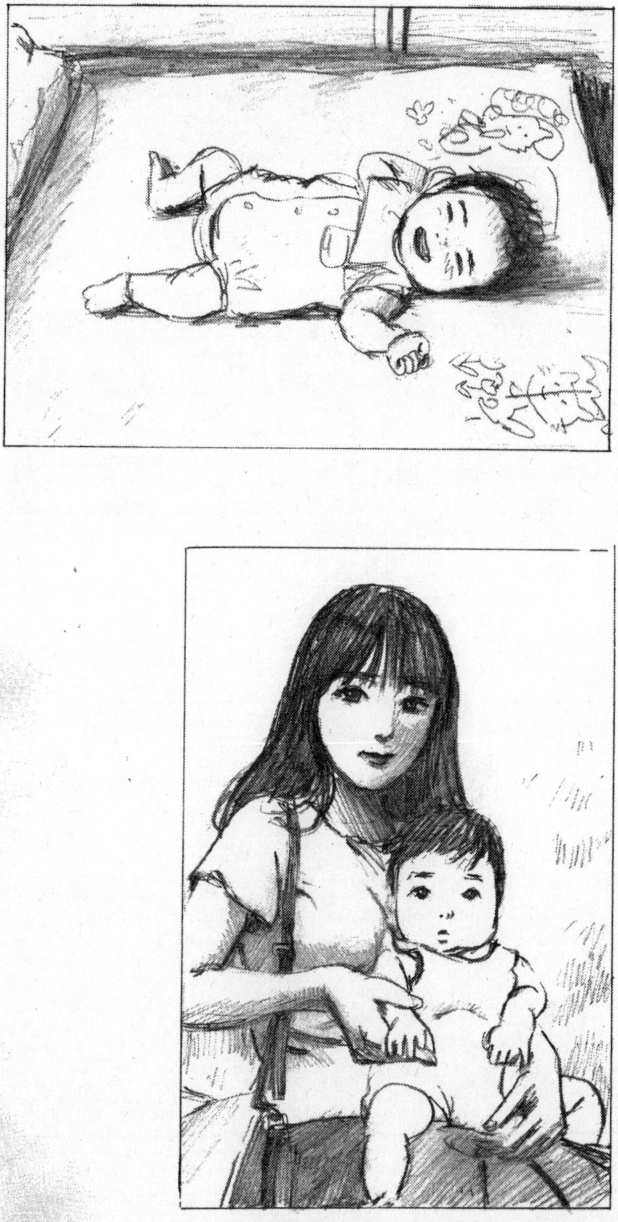

With
daddy

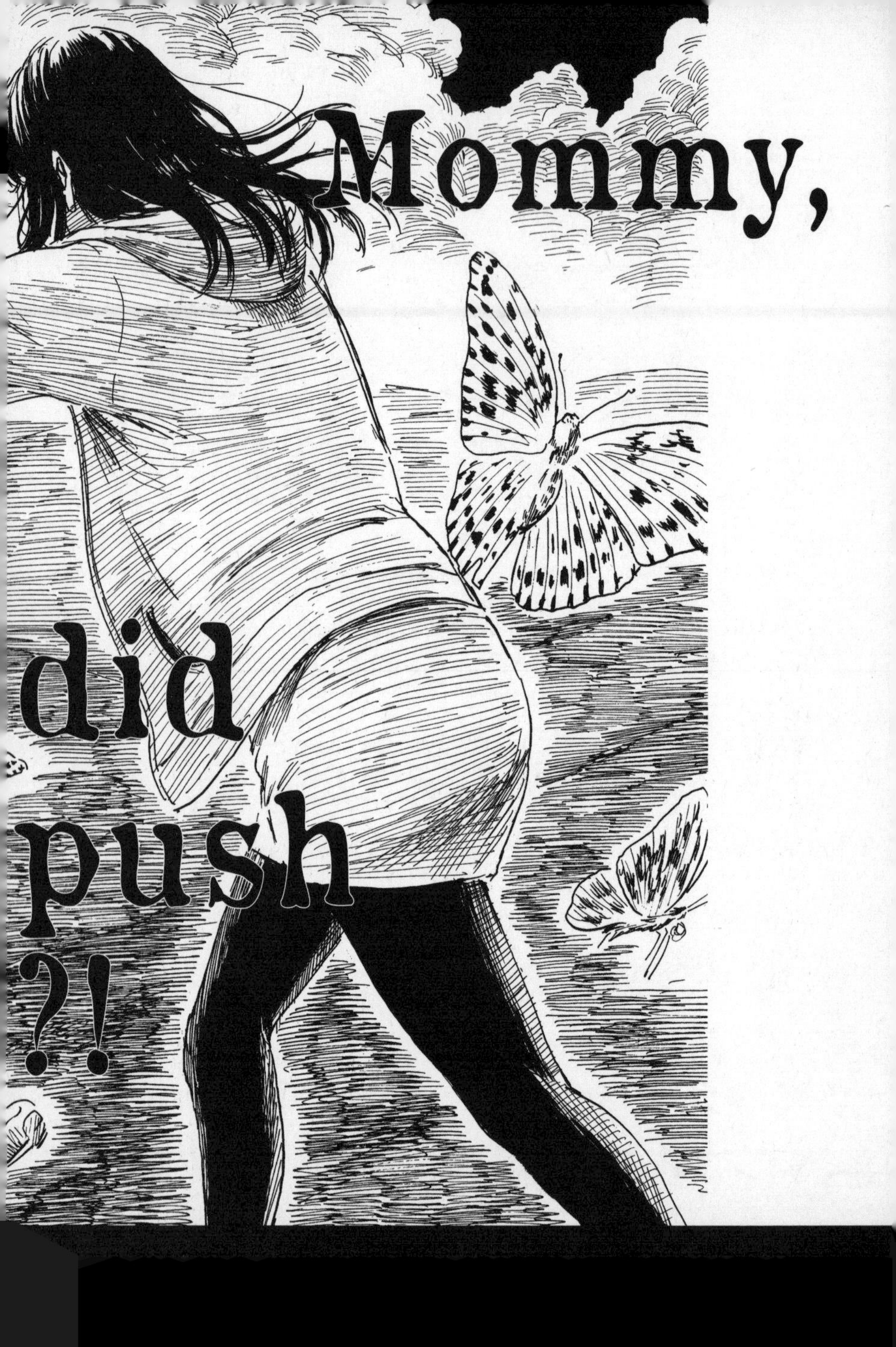

Mommy,
did push
?!

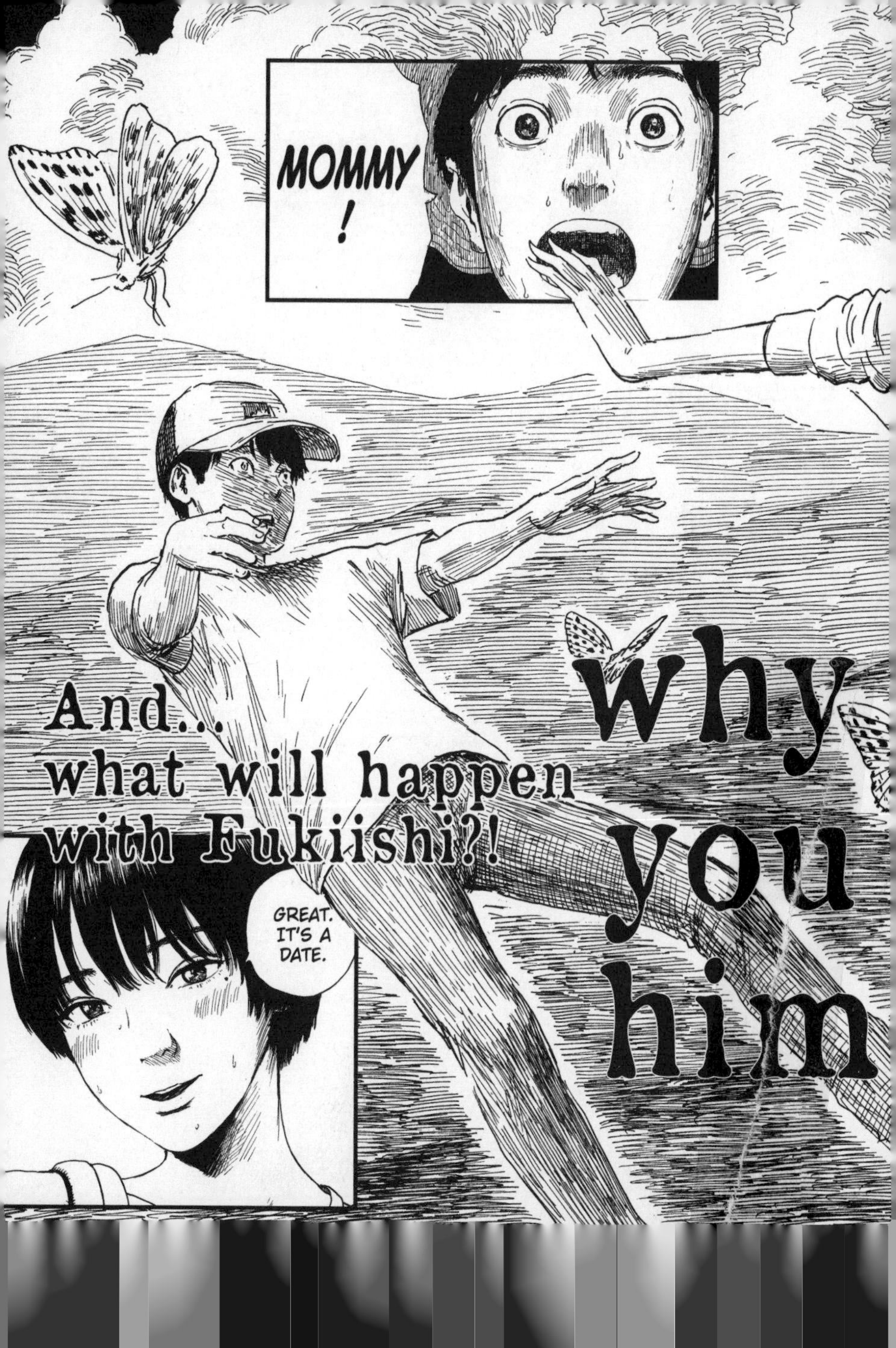
MOMMY!
why
you
him
And...
what will happen
with Fukiishi?!
GREAT. IT'S A DATE.

Blood on the Tracks 1

A Vertical Comics Edition

Editor: Daniel Joseph
Translation: Daniel Komen
Production: Risa Cho
          Evan Hayden

CHI NO WADACHI 1
by Shuzo OSHIMI

© 2017 Shuzo OSHIMI
All rights reserved.
Original Japanese edition published by SHOGAKUKAN.
English translation rights in the United States of America and Canada
arranged with SHOGAKUKAN through Tuttle-Mori Agency, Inc.

Translation provided by Vertical Comics, 2020
Published by Vertical Comics, an imprint of Kodansha USA Publishing, LLC., New York

Originally published in Japanese as *Chi no Wadachi 1* by Shogakukan, 2017
Chi no Wadachi serialized in *Big Comic Superior*, Shogakukan, 2017-

This is a work of fiction.

ISBN: 978-1-949980-13-4

Manufactured in the United States of America

First Edition

Kodansha USA Publishing, LLC.
451 Park Avenue South
7th Floor
New York, NY 10016
www.vertical-comics.com

Vertical books are distributed through Penguin-Random House Publisher Services.